A SHORT REFERENCE GRAMMAR OF IRAQI ARABIC

Wallace M. Erwin

Georgetown University Press
Washington, D.C.

Georgetown University Press, Washington, D.C.

Printed in the United States of America

10 9 8 7 6 5 4 3 2 1 2004

This book is printed on acid-free paper meeting
the requirements of the American National Standard
for Permanence in Paper for Printed Library Materials.

The research reported herein was performed pursuant to a contract with the United States Office of Education, Department of Health, Education, and Welfare.

Library of Congress Cataloging-in-Publication Data

Erwin, Wallace M.
A short reference grammar of Iraqi Arabic / Wallace M. Erwin
p. cm. — (Georgetown classics in Arabic language and linguistics)
Originally published: Washington, D.C. : Georgetown University Press, 1963, in series: Arabic series / Georgetown University, Institute of Languages and Linguistics ; no. 4.
ISBN 1-58901-010-8 (pbk. : alk. paper)
1. Arabic language—Dialects—Iraq. 2. Arabic language—Grammar. I. Title. II. Series.

PJ6823.E7 2004
492.7'7'09567—dc22

2003049538

30

Georgetown Classics in Arabic Language and Linguistics

Karin C. Ryding and Margaret Nydell, series editors

For some time, Georgetown University Press has been interested in making available seminal publications in Arabic language and linguistics that have gone out of print. Some of the most meticulous and creative scholarship of the last century was devoted to the analysis of Arabic language and to producing detailed reference works and textbooks of the highest quality. Although some of the material is dated in terms of theoretical approaches, the content and methodology of the books considered for the reprint series is still valid and, in some cases, unsurpassed.

With global awareness now refocused on the Arab world, and with renewed interest in Arab culture, society, and political life, it is essential to provide easy access to classic reference materials, such as dictionaries and reference grammars, and to language teaching materials. The components of this series have been chosen for their quality of research and scholarship, and have been updated with new bibliographies and introductions to provide readers with resources for further study.

Georgetown University Press hereby hopes to serve the growing national and international need for reference works on Arabic language and culture, as well as provide access to quality textbooks and audiovisual resources for teaching Arabic language in its written and spoken forms.

Books in the Georgetown Classics in Arabic Language and Linguistics series

Arabic Language Handbook
Mary Catherine Bateson

A Basic Course in Iraqi Arabic with Audio MP3 Files
Wallace M. Erwin

A Basic Course in Moroccan Arabic
Richard S. Harrell with Mohammed Abu-Talib and William S. Carroll

A Dictionary of Iraqi Arabic: English–Arabic, Arabic–English
B. E. Clarity, Karl Stowasser, Ronald G. Wolfe, D. R. Woodhead, and Wayne Beene, Editors

A Short Reference Grammar of Iraqi Arabic
Wallace M. Erwin

A Short Reference Grammar of Moroccan Arabic with Audio CD
Richard S. Harrell

To B.S.E., who helped every step of the way.

Contents

Arabic Research at Georgetown University

In the thirty-five years since the original publication of Wallace M. Erwin's *A Basic Course in Iraqi Arabic*, the world of research in Arabic theoretical linguistics has expanded but the production of professional quality textbooks in colloquial Arabic has remained limited. Despite the passage of years, the Richard Slade Harrell Arabic Series has consistently been in demand from Georgetown University Press because of the quality of research that went into its composition, the solid theoretical foundations for its methodology, and the comprehensive coverage of regional Arabic speech communities.

The Arabic Department at Georgetown University (now Department of Arabic Language, Literature and Linguistics) recognizes the need to sustain the tradition of research and publication in Arabic dialects and has continued dialectology field research and textbook production, most notably with Margaret (Omar) Nydell's Syrian Arabic Video Course, a three-year research project funded by Center for the Advancement of Language Learning from 1991 to 1994.

Currently, Dr. Nydell is leading a four-year dialectology research project aimed at producing "conversion" courses to assist learners of Modern Standard Arabic in converting their knowledge and skills of written Arabic to proficiency in selected Arabic dialects. This project is part of a proposal prepared by the National Capital Language Resource Center under the directorship of Dr. James E. Alatis and Dr. Anna Chamot. The first Arabic dialect tackled under this research project was Iraqi, and the Iraqi conversion short course was field tested successfully in the summer of 2003. In developing the materials for the conversion course, the most authoritative English sources of information were the two seminal texts produced by Wallace Erwin and published by Georgetown University Press in the 1960s, and which the Press is reissuing this year, *A Basic Course in Iraqi Arabic* and *A Short Reference Grammar of Iraqi Arabic*.

We pay tribute to the tradition initiated and led by Richard Harrell, the founder of this series and of the original Arabic Research Program at Georgetown University. Harrell's scholarship and creative energy set a standard in the field and yielded an unprecedented and as yet unsurpassed series of, as he put it, "practical tools for the increasing number of Americans whose lives bring them into contact with the Arab world."

For more information about the Department of Arabic Language, Literature and Linguistics at Georgetown University, its course offerings, its degree programs, and its research agenda, see www.georgetown.edu/departments/arabic.

Karin C. Ryding
Sultan Qaboos bin Said Professor of Arabic

The History of the Arabic Research Program
Institute of Languages and Linguistics
Georgetown University

The Arabic Research Program was established in June 1960 as a contract between Georgetown University and the United States Office of Education under the provisions of the Language Development Program of the National Defense Educaton Act.

The first two years of the research program, 1960–1962 (contract number SAE-8706), were developed to the production of six books, a reference grammar, and a conversational English–Arabic dictionary in the cultivated spoken forms of Moroccan, Syrian, and Iraqi Arabic. The second two years of the research program, 1962–1964 (contract number OE-2-14-029), called for the further production of Arabic-English dictionaries in each of the three varieties of Arabic mentioned above, as well as comprehensive basic courses in the Moroccan and Iraqi varities.

The eleven books of this series, of which the present volume is one, are designed to serve as practical tools for the increasing number of Americans whose lives bring them into contact with the Arab world. The dictionaries, the reference grammars, and the basic courses are oriented toward the educated American who is a layman in linguistic matters. Although it is hoped that the scientific linguist and the specialist in Arabic dialectology will find these books both of interest and of use, matters of purely scientific and theoretical importance have not been directly treated as such, and specialized scientific terminology has been avoided as much as possible.

As is usual, the authors or editors of the individual books bear final scholarly responsibility for the contents, but there has been a large amount of informal cooperation in our work. Criticism, consultation, and discussion have gone on constantly among the senior professional members of the staff. The contribution of more junior research assistants, both Arab and American, is also not to be underestimated. Their painstaking assembling and ordering of raw data, often in manners requiring considerable creative intelligence, has been the necessary prerequisite for further progress.

Staff work has been especially important in the preparation of the dictionaries. Although the contributing staff members are named on the title page of the individual dictionaries, special mention must be made of Mr. Karl Stowasser's work. His lexicographical experience, acquired in his work on the English version of Professor Wehr's *Arabisches Wörterbuch für die Schriftsprache der Gegenwart* (Hans Wehr, *A Dictionary of Modern Written Arabic,* ed. J. Milton Cowan [Ithaca, N.Y.: Cornell University Press, 1961]), along with his thorough knowledge of Arabic, has been critically important for all our lexicographical work, covering the entire range from typography to substantive entries in the dictionaries.

In most cases the books prepared by the Arabic Research Program are the first of their kind in English, and in some cases the first in any language. The preparation of them has been a rewarding experience. It is hoped that the public use of them will be equally so. The undersigned, on behalf of the entire staff, would like to ask the same indulgence of the reader as Samuel Johnson requested in his first English dictionary: To remember that although much has been left out, much has been included.

Richard S. Harrell
Associate Professor of Linguistics
Georgetown University
Director,
Arabic Research Program

Foreword
to the Georgetown Classics Edition

This Iraqi reference grammar, published in 1963, is still the definitive study of the language. Dr. Wallace Erwin wrote this reference grammar, accompanied by a basic course in Iraqi Arabic and dictionaries of the dialect, and it stands as a major contribution to Arabic dialectology.

This reference grammar is clear and thorough, and presents a useful overview of the Iraqi dialect. There are not many books that deal with Iraqi as a whole. In the 1950s some Iraqi materials were produced by oil companies and at the Jesuit college in Baghdad, but Iraqi has been less studied than most dialects. The Defense Language Institute (DLI) in Monterey, California, has developed much training material in the dialect that is military-oriented but very useful. Other titles include *Introduzione ai Dialetti Arabi* by Oliver Duran (Milan: Centro Studi Camito-Semitici), 1995; and *From MSA to the Iraqi Dialect* by Margaret Nydell (Arlington, VA: DLS Press), 1991.

The subjects discussed in this book include communal dialects, the use of auxiliary particles, the "analytical genitive" word /maal/, verb morphology, and broken plurals. In the past thirty years there have been monographs, articles, and dissertations dealing with certain features of Iraqi, and these are readily available to specialists. However, far more research is needed, and perhaps the current political prominence of Iraq will lead to this result.

It is gratifying to have this important and timely book once again in print and widely available.

Margaret Nydell

This reference grammar is a research text in the descriptive structural linguistics tradition, and is still the best English reference guide to the spoken language of Iraq. It is a good example of scholarship whose methodology is dated but still utterly sound. The organization is clear and thorough, and the examples and grammatical descriptions are well-conceived and designed so that they can be read and understood by learners and linguists alike.

Wallace Erwin's contributions to Arabic linguistics and language teaching during the 1960s, 1970s, and 1980s formed a body of impeccable scholarship that was foundational to the field of teaching Arabic as a foreign language, and to Arabic descriptive structural linguistics. In addition to his two volumes on Iraqi Arabic, he was one of the founding authors of the original audio-lingual–based Elementary Modern Standard Arabic series published by the University of Michigan in 1968, which had a profound impact on the field of Arabic language teaching—generations of Arabists have an indelible memory of the "big orange book."

As a scholar, teacher, and administrator, Wallace Erwin embodied the highest professional standards. As chair of the Arabic Department at Georgetown University from 1964 to 1981, he pioneered the development of the Arabic curriculum and teaching methodology at Georgetown to the point where it led most other American universities in size, quality, and effectiveness at the undergraduate and graduate levels. He served on the executive board of the American Association of Teachers of Arabic and was elected its president in 1972.

Fortunately, I was able to have Wallace Erwin as a professor of Arabic linguistics (Classical Arabic Structure and Arabic Dialectology) and as the mentor of my dissertation, but my most lasting impression of Dr. Erwin was the result of being his teaching assistant for two years in basic and intermediate Arabic. His methodology style was gifted, energetic, demanding, systematic, and yet deeply humanistic, and it made lasting impressions on his students and on this apprentice teacher. He was able to combine an aura of control and authority with an artful use of humor and easy-goingness. He was, quite simply, the best.

Now that Wally is retired, we hope that seeing these books reissued will give him cause to celebrate and to know how much his contributions have been appreciated.

Karin C. Ryding
Sultan Qaboos bin Said Professor of Arabic

Preface

This book presents an outline of the phonology, morphology, and syntax of colloquial Iraqi Arabic as spoken by educated Muslims in Baghdad. Although it is designed to serve primarily as a reference work for students engaged in acquiring a practical command of the language, I hope that it will also prove useful to others whose interest lie in the field of linguistics or general Arabic studies.

In the past very little has been written on the Arabic dialects of Iraq in general, and even less on those of Baghdad in particular. A list of works published before 1961 may be found in Haim Blanc's article, "Iraqi Arabic Studies" in *Arabic Dialect Studies,* edited by Harvy Sobelman (Washington, D.C.; Center for Applied Linguistics of the Modern Language Association and The Middle East Institute, 1962; an earlier version of the article appeared in the *Middle East Journal* 13:449–53 (1959)). Several works of more recent date may be mentioned here. First, there are two books in Arabic, both written by Sheikh Jalal Al-Hanafi, and published with the assistance of the Iraqi Ministry of Education: *Proverbs of Baghdad,* Vol. 1 (Baghdad, 1962), the first of two volumes containing a collection of colloquial Baghdad proverbs with explanations and comments in Classical Arabic; and *Dictionary of the Baghdadi Dialect,* Vol. 1 (Baghdad, 1963), the first of several volumes containing colloquial words and phrases with definitions and comments in Classical Arabic. Another recent work, written in German is Nisar Malaika's *Grundzüge der Grammatik des arabischen Dialektes von Bagdad* (Wiesbaden: Otto Harrassowitz, 1963), a description of the colloquial Arabic of Baghdad, including sections on phonology, morphology, and syntax. Lastly, a monograph by Haim Blanc entitled *Communal Dialects in Baghdad* is scheduled for publication in 1964 by the Center for Middle Eastern Studies of Harvard University.

My task in the preparation of this book has been lightened by the cooperation of many people, both here and in Baghdad, and to all of them I express my heartfelt gratitude. In particular I wish to thank my Iraqi associates Mr. Faisal Al-Khalaf, Mr. Majid Damah, Mr. Munir Malaika, and Mr. Husain Mustafa, and also those who participated for briefer periods. With their fine knowledge of both Arabic and English, these gentlemen have given invaluable assistance, and I am most grateful to them all. My thanks go also to Dr. Haim Blanc for permission to read the manuscript of his forthcoming monograph and for a number of helpful comments; to Miss. Alexandra Selim for an onerous typing job well done; and to Georgetown University for serving as an academic home during the course of our work. Finally, I acknowledge with deep appreciation my indebtedness to the authors of the National Defense Education Act and to its administrators in the Office of Education of the Department of Health, Education, and Welfare, for the contract which made the work possible.

W. M. E.
Washington, D.C.
December 1963

PART ONE
PHONOLOGY

1. SOUNDS

The sounds of Iraqi are presented below in tabular form and described individually thereafter.

CONSONANTS

			Bilabial	Labio-dental	Interdental	Dental	Palatal	Velar	Postvelar	Pharyngeal	Glottal
	Stops	Voiceless	*p*			*t*		*k*	*q*		ʔ
		Voiced	*b*			*d*		*g*			
	Spirants	Voiceless		*f*	*θ*	*s*	*š*	*x*		*ḥ*	*h*
		Voiced			*δ*	*z*		*ġ*		*ε*	
	Affricates	Voiceless					*č*				
		Voiced					*j*				
	Nasals		*m*			*n*					
	Semivowels		*w*				*y*				
	Lateral					*l*					
	Flap					*r*					
EMPHATICS	Stops	Voiceless	*ṗ*			*ṭ*					
		Voiced	*ḅ*								
	Spirants	Voiceless				*ṣ*					
		Voiced		*f̣*	*δ̣*	*ẓ*					
	Nasal		*ṃ*								
	Lateral					*ḷ*					

VOWELS

Short	Front	Central	Back
High	*i*		*u*
Mid			*o*
Low		*a*	
Long			
High	*ii*		*uu*
Mid	*ee*		*oo*
Low		*aa*	

1.1 CONSONANTS

Consonant sounds may be voiceless or voiced. A voiceless sound is one in which there is no vibration of the vocal cords, for example the final s sound in the English word bus. A voiced sound is one in which there is simultaneous vibration of the vocal cords, for example the final z sound in the English word buzz. In Iraqi, as in English, there are several pairs of consonants which are produced in exactly the same way except that one is voiceless and the other voiced, for example *s* and *z*, *t* and *d*, and *k* and *g*.

1.1.1 Stops

A stop is a sound in which the breath-stream is momentarily halted by a complete closure at some point along the vocal tract.

A. *p* Voiceless bilabial stop

Similar to English p as in pale, apiece, leap. The closure is formed by the two lips, which come together briefly and then separate.

parda	'curtain'
puuši	'veil'
piip	'drum' (container)

B. *b* Voiced bilabial stop

The voiced counterpart of *p*. Similar to English b as in bake, cabin, rib.

beet	'house'
zibid	'butter'
kitab	'he wrote'

C. *t* Voiceless dental stop

Similar to English *t* as in take, attack, bat, except that in the production of the Iraqi sound the tip of the tongue touches the upper gum at the point where the teeth emerge, also touching the rear surface of the teeth, whereas in the English sound the point of tongue contact is somewhat farther back on the gum ridge.

tiin	'figs'
kutub	'books'
naamat	'she slept'

D. *d* Voiced dental stop

The voiced counterpart of *t*. Similar to English d as in desk, adapt, fed, except that the point of tongue contact is the same as that described for Iraqi *t* (see C above).

daris	'lesson'
qadam	'foot'
baarid	'cold'

E. *k* Voiceless velar stop

Similar to the English k sound as in kick, baking, deck. The back part of the tongue touches the back part of the roof of the mouth in the area of the soft palate (velum).

kaamil	'complete'
mukaan	'place'
tirak	'he left'

F. *g* Voiced velar stop

The voiced counterpart of *k*. Similar to English g as in get, ago, big.

gaal	'he said'
liga	'he found'
foog	'above'

G. *q* Voiceless postvelar stop

There is no similar English sound. The extreme back part of the tongue forms a closure by momentarily touching the extreme rear of the soft palate in the area of the uvula.

qaamuus	'dictionary'
muqaabala	'interview'
saayiq	'driver'

H. *ʔ* Glottal stop

The glottal stop does not exist as a distinctive speech sound in English, but it is nevertheless frequently produced by all English-speakers, sometimes as a variant of another sound (as in button or bottle with the glottal stop instead of the t sound), and often in the exclamations uh-oh or ah-ah, with the glottal stop between the vowel sounds. In Iraqi the glottal stop is a distinctive speech sound. It is produced by the action of the vocal cords, which close together completely, thus momentarily blocking the breath stream at the glottis, and then separate. It is, by its nature, voiceless.

ʔaani	'I'
siʔal	'he asked'
wuzaraaʔ	'ministers' (of government)

1.1.2 Spirants

A spirant is a sound in which the breath-stream is not completely halted, as in stops, but is caused to pass with audible friction through a narrow opening produced by constriction somewhere along the vocal tract.

A. *f* Voiceless labio-dental spirant [1]

Similar to English f as in fan, affair, belief. The lower lip lightly touches the upper teeth, and the breath passes with some friction through the imperfect closure thus formed.

faat	'he passed by'
kaafi	'enough'
seef	'sword'

B. *θ* Voiceless interdental spirant

Similar to the English th sound as in thank, ether, breath. The tongue tip protrudes slightly between the upper and lower teeth, touching both, and the breath passes with friction through and around the partial obstruction thus formed.

θoob	'shirt'
miθil	'like'
θaaliθ	'third'

C. *δ* Voiced interdental spirant

The voiced counterpart of *θ*. Similar to the English th sound as in than, either, breathe.

δaak	'that'
haaδa	'this'
fuulaaδ	'steel'

D. *s* Voiceless dental spirant

Similar to English s as in seen, basin, hiss. The tip of the tongue approaches the point where the upper teeth emerge from the gum and there forms a narrow, groove-like channel running in a rear-front direction. The breath passes through this channel and strikes the rear surface of the upper teeth, producing clearly audible friction.

[1] The corresponding voiced labio-dental spirant *v*, as in English van, is sometimes heard in a few borrowed words, for example *viiza* 'visa'.

sana	'year'
nisa	'he forgot'
fluus	'money'

E. *z* Voiced dental spirant

The voiced counterpart of *s*. Similar to English z as in zeal, lazy, fizz.

zeen	'good'
wazin	'weight'
meez	'table'

F. *š* Voiceless palatal spirant

Similar to the English sh sound as in sheep, bishop, dish, but with less lip-rounding. The upper surface of the front part of the tongue approaches the roof of the mouth in the area just behind the gum-ridge, and there forms a narrow, slit-like opening through which the breath passes with friction.

šii	'thing'
miša	'he walked'
leeš	'why'

G. *x* Voiceless velar spirant

This sound does not exist as a distinctive speech sound in English, but it is sometimes produced by English-speakers in exclamations such as the one commonly written "Ugh!". In German it occurs as the "back ch sound", as in doch or Bach. The back part of the tongue approaches the roof of the mouth in the region of the soft palate, close enough to form a narrow opening, but not touching, and the breath passes through with friction.

xaamis	'fifth'
duxuul	'entrance'
laax	'other'

H. *ġ* Voiced velar spirant

The voiced counterpart of *x*. This sound does not exist as a distinctive speech sound in English, but it is sometimes produced by English-speakers in exclamations, for example in "Ugh!" when voicing continues throughout.

ġeem	'clouds'
luġa	'language'
faariġ	'empty'

I. *ɀ* Voiceless pharyngeal spirant

There is no similar sound in English. The walls of the pharynx contract to form a narrower passage than that afforded by their normal position, and the breath passes fairly forcefully through this narrowed passage, creating a friction-noise different in quality and greater in degree than that heard in either Iraqi or English *h*.

ɀaal	'situation'
waaɀid	'one'
raaɀ	'he went'

J. *ɛ* Voiced pharyngeal spirant

This sound is classified as the voiced counterpart of *ɀ*, but it differs from *ɀ* not only in voice but also in certain other characteristics. There is no similar sound in English. The walls of the pharynx contract to form a narrow, constricted passage as in *ɀ*, and there is simultaneous vibration of the vocal cords; but the breath passes through the constricted pharynx with less force than in *ɀ* and with far less audible friction. Moreover, when the *ɛ* is in final position, the release of the constriction occurs slightly after the vocal cords have stopped vibrating, and then occurs abruptly and with some aspiration. The result is that a final *ɛ* tends to sound somewhat like *ɛ* followed by the glottal stop *ʔ*.

ɛizam	'he invited'
zaɛal	'anger'
ʔabiiɛ	'I sell'

K. *h* Voiceless glottal spirant

This sound is similar to English h as in home, ahead. (In English the h sound occurs only before a vowel, but the Iraqi *h* may occur before a vowel, before a consonant, or at the end of a word.) The breath passes through the glottis, the opening between the vocal cords, as it does for all Iraqi sounds, but in the case of *h* there is no closure or constriction elsewhere in the vocal tract and thus a slight glottal friction, or breathing noise, is audible. The tongue and lips simultaneously assume the position of the following vowel, or retain that of the preceding vowel. Although *h* is classified as a voiceless sound, it may be somewhat voiced when it occurs between vowels or adjacent to a voiced consonant.

hadaf	'target'
šaahid	'witness'
ʔahlan	'welcome'
kirah	'he disliked'

1.1.3 Affricates

An affricate is a sound which begins like a stop, with a complete closure, and ends like a spirant, with an incomplete closure. There are two in Iraqi, one voiceless and one voiced.

A. *č* Voiceless palatal affricate

Similar to the English ch sound as in cheese, achieve, rich. It begins somewhat like the voiceless stop *t* and ends somewhat like the voiceless spirant *š*. The front part of the tongue touches the roof of the mouth in the area of the ridge just behind the upper teeth (and thus slightly behind the point of contact for *t*), forming a momentary closure. Then, instead of making the abrupt release characteristic of *t* and other stops, the tongue moves away from its contact slowly enough so that the released breath passes through the still narrow opening with the friction noise characteristic of *š*. The transition between the *t*-like element and the *š*-like element is very rapid, and the total effect for Iraqi-speakers or English-speakers is that of a single sound.

čaay	'tea'
biča	'he cried'
čaakuuč	'hammer'

B. *j* Voiced palatal affricate

The voiced counterpart of *č*, similar to English j as in jail, pajamas, hedge. It begins somewhat like the voiced stop *d* and ends somewhat like the voiced spirant which occurs as the second consonant sound in the English word measure.

jaahil	'child'
sijin	'jail'
zooj	'pair'

1.1.4 Nasals

A nasal is a sound in which the breath-stream passes through the nose. There are two nasals in Iraqi; both are voiced.

A. *m* Bilabial nasal

Similar to the English m as in meat, timid, seem. The lips close, blocking the oral passage, and the breath-stream passes through the nose.

meez	'table'
simač	'fish'
lizam	'he held'

B. *n* Dental nasal

Similar to the English n as in neat, diner, ten. The tip of the tongue touches the upper gum at the point where the teeth emerge, blocking the oral passage, and the breath-stream passes through the nose.

naas	'people'
šinu	'what'
been	'between'

1.1.5 Semivowels

A semivowel is a sound which is phonetically similar to some vowel but functions in a given language like a consonant. There are two in Iraqi; both are voiced.

A. *w* High back rounded semivowel

Similar to English w as in well, away. It is phonetically similar to the high back rounded vowel *u* (1.2.1 B). The back part of the tongue is high, and the lips are rounded. (For *w* at the end of a syllable, see 2.1.)

ween	'where'
wulid	'boys'
zawaaj	'marriage'

B. *y* Voiced high front unrounded semivowel

Similar to English y as in yell, beyond. It is phonetically similar to the high front unrounded vowel *i* (1.2.1 A). The front part of the tongue is high, and the lips are unrounded. (For *y* at the end of a syllable, see 2.1.)

yaabis	'dry'
zaayir	'visitor'
bayaan	'proclamation'

1.1.6 Lateral

A lateral is a sound in which there is an obstruction at some point along the center line of the vocal tract and the breath-stream passes out along the sides. The Iraqi lateral is voiced.

l Lateral

This sound is less similar to the usual American English l than is its emphatic counterpart *ḷ* (see 1.1.8). Some speakers use, in the first syllable of the word million, an l sound which is different from the one they use in mill; for such speakers the former may be compared to the Iraqi *l*. The tip of the tongue touches the upper gums at the point where the teeth emerge (thus slightly farther forward than in English), and the air escapes on both sides. The rest of the tongue is relaxed and relatively level, whereas in the usual English l (and in Iraqi *ḷ*) the central part is depressed and the back part relatively raised.

laazim	'necessary'
mila	'he filled'
šaal	'he picked up'

1.1.7 Flap

A flap is an extra-short stop made by a quick tap of a mobile articulator such as the tongue against an opposing surface.

r Flap

This sound is *not* similar to the r of American English. It is, however, quite similar to the flap sound of t or d in the usual normal-speed American pronunciation of such words as city, Betty, cataract, body, caddy, modify. The tip of the tongue makes one brief tap against the ridge just behind the upper teeth. The *r* is generally voiced, but may be voiceless when it is at the beginning of a word and followed by an unvoiced consonant, or when final in the utterance.

raas	'head'
baarid	'cold'
zaar	'he visited'

1.1.8 Emphatics

Among the consonants described above are nine (*p*, *b*, *t*, *f*, *δ*, *s*, *z*, *m*, *l*) which have counterparts distinguished from them by the feature of emphasis: *p̣*, *ḅ*, *ṭ*, *f̣*, *δ̣*, *ṣ*, *ẓ*, *ṃ*, *ḷ*. Such consonants are called respectively plain and emphatic.[1] In Iraqi, plain-emphatic pairs are found only among those consonants whose basic articulation involves the lips or the front part of the tongue. In the articulation of plain members of such pairs, the central and back parts of the tongue are relatively relaxed and form a continuous, evenly sloping, and somewhat convex upper surface. The corresponding emphatic consonants, on the other hand, are characterized by the following features in addition to the basic lip or tongue-tip activity: (1) The central part of the tongue is slightly depressed and the back part raised, so that the upper surface of the tongue is concave; (2) the tongue as a whole is tense and somewhat retracted; and (3) there is some constriction of the pharynx walls. In addition to

---

[1] The terms "emphatic" and "emphasis" are traditional labels and should not be taken literally to mean that consonants thus described are articulated more loudly or forcefully than others. The terms "velarized" and "velarization" are also used to describe these consonants.

these general characteristics, the labial[1] emphatics *p̣, ḅ, f̣, ṃ* may have some labialization when a vowel (especially *a*) follows; that is, they are released with an increased rounding of the lips which gives the impression of a slight *w* sound before the vowel. Finally, emphasis in a consonant affects the quality of neighboring vowels in characteristic ways, described in 1.2 below. The emphatic consonants are described individually below in the order in which they appear on the chart.

A. *p̣* Voiceless bilabial stop, emphatic

The emphatic counterpart of *p*. The lips come together, as in *p*, but there is little or no aspiration. Before a vowel, the central part of the tongue is depressed and the back part relatively raised. There is some labialization.

p̣aṃp̣	'pump'
ḷaṃp̣a	'lamp'
ʔawrup̣p̣a	'Europe'

B. *ḅ* Voiced bilabial stop, emphatic

The emphatic counterpart of *b*. The lips come together as in *b*, but the central part of the tongue is depressed and the back part is relatively raised. Before a vowel there is some labialization.

ḅang	'bank'
ḅagg	'gnats'
ḅaaḅa	'daddy'
ṭooḅa	'ball'

C. *ṭ* Voiceless dental stop, emphatic

The emphatic counterpart of *t*. The front part of the tongue touches the gum ridge just behind the upper teeth, making contact over a slightly larger area than in *t*. The central part of the tongue is depressed and the back part is relatively raised. There is little or no aspiration.

ṭeer	'bird'
xaṭar	'danger'
qaaṭ	'suit'

D. *f̣* Voiceless labio-dental spirant, emphatic

The emphatic counterpart of *f*. The upper lip and lower teeth touch, and air passes through with friction, as in *f*. The central part of the tongue is depressed

[1] Here and elsewhere the term "labial" refers to both bilabial and labio-dental sounds.

and the back part is relatively raised. Before a vowel there is some labialization.

f̣akk	'he opened'
ġurf̣a	'room'
ṣaf̣f̣	'class'

E. *δ̣* Voiced interdental spirant, emphatic

The emphatic counterpart of *δ*. The tip of the tongue protrudes between the teeth, and the breath passes through this partial obstruction. The central part of the tongue is depressed and the back part relatively raised.

δ̣oog	'tasting'
ʒaaδ̣ir	'present'
mariiδ̣	'sick'

F. *ṣ* Voiceless dental spirant, emphatic

The emphatic counterpart of *s*. The front part of the tongue approaches a point on the upper gum ridge a little farther back than for *s*, and there forms a narrow channel through which the breath passes with audible friction. The central part of the tongue is depressed and the back part is relatively raised.

ṣeef	'summer'
wuṣal	'he arrived'
rigiṣ	'dancing'

G. *ẓ* Voiced dental spirant, emphatic

The emphatic counterpart of *z*. The tip of the tongue approaches the upper gum ridge near the teeth and there forms a groove through which the breath passes with friction, and the vocal cords simultaneously vibrate, as in *z*. The central part of the tongue is depressed, and the back part is relatively raised.

jaẓẓ	'it creaked'

H. *ṃ* Bilabial nasal, emphatic

The emphatic counterpart of *m*. The lips close, blocking the oral passage; and the breath-stream passes through the nose, as in *m*. The central part of the tongue is depressed and the back part relatively raised. Before a vowel there is some labialization.

ṃaaṃa	'mommy'
ṃaay	'water'
huṃṃa	'they'

I. *ḷ* Lateral, emphatic

The emphatic counterpart of *l*. It is similar to the usual American English l, especially the final l in such words as in mill, feel, or bell. The tip of the tongue touches the upper gum ridge slightly farther back than in *l*. The central part of the tongue is depressed and the back part relatively raised. As in *l*, the air passes out at the sides, and there is simultaneous vibration of the vocal cords.

ḷaṭiif	'nice'
gaḷub	'heart'
xaaḷ	'maternal uncle'
šuġuḷ	'work'

On the basis of their importance as distinctive sounds, the emphatic consonants are divided into two groups: (1) The primary emphatics, *ṭ*, *ṣ*, *δ̣*, play a major role in the phonological structure of the language. The distinction between one of these and its plain counterpart is equivalent in importance to that between, say *d* and *t*: an inadvertent substitution of emphatic for plain or vice versa results in a different word or in unintelligible nonsense. The primary emphatics occur in almost any environment (that is, next to or near any other sounds), including most of the environments in which their plain counterparts also may occur; if a primary emphatic occurs in a given root (4.1.1) it generally occurs in all words of that root; many pairs of words are distinguished only by the difference between a primary and its plain counterpart, for example:

tiin	'figs'	*ṭiin*	'clay'
seef	'sword'	*ṣeef*	'summer'
δaaƐ	'he broadcast'	*δ̣aaƐ*	'he got lost'

(2) The secondary emphatics, *p̣*, *ḅ*, *f̣*, *ṃ*, *ẓ*, *ḷ*, have a less independent status as distinctive sounds. Only a few pairs of words are distinguished solely by the difference between a secondary emphatic and its plain counterpart (and most of these pairs involve *l* and *ḷ*), for example:

baaba	'his door'	*ḅaaḅa*	'daddy'
xaali	'empty'	*xaaḷi*	'my uncle'
gal-la	'he told him'	*gaḷḷa*	'he fried'

In most cases a secondary emphatic and its plain counterpart play a complementary role, the occurrence of the one or the other being automatically determined by the environment and thus having no effect on meaning. For example, next to another emphatic, a secondary emphatic rather than its plain counterpart may be expected:

xuṭḅa	'engagement'
wuṣḷa	'piece'

The four labial emphatics *p̣*, *ḅ*, *f̣*, *ṃ* also usually occur, instead of their plain counterparts, when the other, or nearest, consonants in the word are emphatics, velars, or *r*, or a combination of these:

ḅaṣiiṭ	'easy'
ṭooḅa	'ball'
ḅarra	'outside'
ṃarra	'time'
f̣akk	'he opened'
ð̣arḅa	'a hit, a blow'
ġurf̣a	'room'
rugḅa	'neck'
rikaḅ	'he rode'

(Elsewhere in this book, a labial emphatic will be marked by the subscript dot only when confusion with another word might otherwise result, or when it occurs in an unusual environment.)

The emphatic *ḷ* and its plain counterpart *l* are somewhat less automatically restricted by their environment than are the four labial plain-emphatic pairs. For example, the emphatic *ḷ* occurs, for no reason involving environment, in the word *ʔaḷḷa* 'God', and the related *baḷḷa* 'please' and *waḷḷa* 'really, certainly'; the plain *l* occasionally occurs in what are described below as typical *ḷ* environments; and sometimes the two sounds vary freely in a given word. By and large, however, when the emphatic *ḷ* does occur, it is in one of the following environments: next to another emphatic as shown above; preceding another emphatic though separated from it by a short vowel; following *g*, *x*, or *ġ*; or following a labial when the latter is preceded by *g*, *x* *ġ*, or an emphatic, or *r*:

ḷaṭiif	'nice, pleasant'
ʔaθgaḷ	'heavier'
xaaḷ	'uncle'
šuġuḷ	'work'
ṭaḅuḷ	'drum'
gaṃuḷ	'lice'
raṃuḷ	'sand'

Following an emphatic and separated from it by a short vowel, both *ḷ* and *l* occur, some speakers more commonly using one and some the other, with no distinction in meaning:

wuṣaḷ, wuṣal	'he arrived'
čaṭaḷ, čaṭal	'fork'

The emphatic *ẓ* is less common. Where it does occur, it is generally in a syllable beginning with *j*, or in a word in which nearby consonants are a combination of emphatic, labial, velar, and *r*:

jaẓẓ	'it creaked'
jiẓdaan	'wallet'
jiẓṃa	'boot'
ẓuṃaṭ	'he bragged'

or in a word where it occurs as a result of the assimilation of the emphatic *ṣ* to a following voiced consonant (2.5):

ʔaṣdiqaaʔ[1]	(pronounced *ʔaẓdiqaaʔ*)	'friends'
ṣġayyir	(pronounced *ẓġayyir*)	'little'

1.2 VOWELS

Iraqi has nine vowels, four short and five long. Short vowels are shorter in actual time of duration than long vowels, and may also differ from them in quality. All vowels in Iraqi have a much wider range of variation than vowels in English. Within this range, the precise phonetic quality of a given vowel depends upon its position in the word and the nature of the adjacent consonants (the environment). In the descriptions which follow, such differing qualities of a vowel are termed variants. Only the major variants are described below, and the statements on their environments are meant to be illustrative, not exhaustive.

1.2.1 Short

A. *i* Short high front unrounded vowel

There are four major variants.

(1) A sound similar in quality to the i in machine but shorter in duration. This variant occurs when the vowel is final or followed by *y*: [2]

---

[1] The transcription here and in similar cases does not reflect assimilation when doing so would change a root consonant (see 4.1.1).

[2] Some speakers use a vowel sound of this quality before a single consonant other than *y* in certain words, notably in verbal nouns of Classes VII through X (6.1.1.7 to 6.1.1.10), for example *šti̲raak* 'subscription', and a few other words, for example *šari̲ka* 'company'. Other speakers use in such words the variants described below.

beeti	'my house'
dazz-li	'he sent to me'
Ɛiraaqi	'Iraqi'
tarbiya	'education'

(2) A sound between the vowels of tick and took, similar to the vowel of just in the usual pronunciation of just a minute (i.e., not the vowel of just in a just man). This variant occurs principally when the vowel is next to an emphatic, or between *r* and a labial or a velar:

ṣidfa	'incident'
ṣiṭṭaƐaš	'sixteen'
ṣinaaƐa	'industry'
ʔaδ̣inn	'I suppose'
ʔiδ̣baara	'dossier, file'
ṭilaƐ	'he went out'
biṭ-ṭiyyaara	'on the airplane'
rikaḅ	'he rode'
rigṣa	'dance'
faariġ	'empty'

(3) A sound between the vowels of bit and bet. This variant occurs principally when the vowel is before *ʒ* or *Ɛ*, or between one of these and *r*:

siʒab	'he withdrew'
ʔiʒna	'we'
liƐba	'game'
ʔiƐlaan	'announcement'
ʒirag	'he burned'
Ɛiraf	'he knew'

(4) A sound similar to the vowel of bit. This variant occurs in environments other than those described above:

jibin	'cheese'
zibil	'garbage'

sitra	'jacket'
šikil	'manner, way'
štira	'he bought'
minnak	'from you'
yikšif	'it fades'
bis-suug	'in the market'
l-iktaab	'the book'

B. *u* Short high back rounded vowel

There are three major variants.

(1) A sound similar in quality to the vowel of boot but shorter in duration. This variant occurs when the vowel is final or followed by *w*, or when it is in an unstressed open syllable not next to an emphatic:

ʒilu	'sweet, pretty'
šuufu	'look P'
naamu	'sleep P'
duwa	'medicine'
suʔaal	'question'
mudiir	'director'

(2) A sound between the vowels of bull and ball, but shorter in duration. This variant occurs when the vowel is next to *ʒ*, *ɛ*, or an emphatic, or when it is next to *r* and other neighboring consonants include two of the following: an emphatic, a labial, a velar:

ṣubuʒ	'morning'
muḍʒik	'funny'
ṭubar	'meat cleaver'
ʒubb	'love'
ɛumra	'his age'
ʔawrup̣p̣a	'Europe'
xurbat	'she broke down'
ġurfa	'room'

(3) A sound similar to the vowel of book, but with slightly more lip rounding. This variant occurs in most environments other than those described above:

beetkum	'your P house'
bunni	'brown'
xubuz	'bread'
kullhum	'all of them'
muslim	'Moslem'
nukta	'joke'
yaakul	'he eats'
yiskun	'he lives'
gul-li	'tell me'
gumit	'I got up'

C. *o* Short mid back rounded vowel

This sound is similar to the first part of the vowel in boat (i.e., without the final off-glide toward the vowel of boot); or, to use another comparison, it is similar in quality to the Iraqi long vowel *oo*, but shorter in length. It occurs in only a few words.

raadyo	'radio'
pyaano	'piano'
ṃaayo	'bathing suit'

D. *a* Short low central vowel

There are three major variants.

(1) A sound similar to the first vowel of father but shorter in duration. This variant occurs when the vowel is next to *ʒ* or *Ɛ*, or final in the sequence *-aaha*:

maʒall	'place'
looʒa	'board'
šaƐar	'hair'
saaƐa	'hour'
waraaha	'behind her'

(2) A sound ranging between the vowels of father and fought. This variant occurs when the vowel is next to an emphatic. When it is final after an emphatic it is closer to the a of father:

ṣaff	'class'
faṣil	'season'
gaṣṣ	'he cut'
ð̣ann	'he thought'
ḥið̣ar	'he attended'
marað̣	'illness'
ṭabiib	'doctor'
muṭar	'rain'
šaṭṭ	'river'
furṣa	'opportunity'
beeð̣a	'egg'
ṣooṭa	'his voice'

(3) A sound ranging between the vowels of bet and bat. This variant occurs in most environments other than those described above:

beeta	'his house'
salla	'basket'
šakk	'doubt'
qiima	'cost'
namla	'ant'
hiyya	'she'
wannas	'he entertained'
gal-la	'he told him'
čaanat	'she was'

1.2.2 Long

A. *ii* Long high front unrounded vowel

A sound similar to the i in machine:

ti̱i̱n	'figs'
θigi̱i̱l	'heavy'
jari̱i̱da	'newspaper'
yilgi̱i̱	'he finds him'

When an emphatic precedes or follows, there may be an audible transition from emphatic to vowel or from vowel to emphatic in the form of a short glide with somewhat the quality of the vowel in but. This glide is most noticeable when the emphatic is final, as in the first three examples following:

rixi̱i̱ṣ	'cheap'
mari̱i̱δ	'sick'
baṣi̱i̱ṭ	'easy'
ṭi̱i̱n	'clay'
ṣi̱i̱ni	'Chinese'
Ɛaδi̱i̱m	'splendid'

B. *ee* Long mid front unrounded vowel

There are two major variants.

(1) A sound ranging from the vowel of fez (slightly prolonged) to the *first element* in the vowel of phase (that is, without the latter's final offglide toward the vowel of ease). This variant occurs when the vowel follows a back consonant (*k, g, q, ʔ, x, ġ, z̧, Ɛ, h,*) or an emphatic:

štike̱e̱t	'I complained'
dagge̱e̱t	'I knocked'
buqe̱e̱na	'we stayed'
xe̱e̱r	'good'
ġe̱e̱r	'other than'
gaz̧z̧e̱e̱t	'I coughed'
Ɛe̱e̱n	'eye'
ṣe̱e̱f	'summer'
muδe̱e̱t	'I signed'
nṭe̱e̱na	'we gave'

(2) A diphthong sound consisting of two elements, the first like the vowel of eat (but very short), and the second like the vowel of let. This variant occurs after non-back, non-emphatic consonants:

beet	'house'
teel	'wire'
θneen	'two'
deen	'debt'
leel	'night'
meez	'table'
čeela	'a measure'
ɛalee	'on him'

In both variants, if the vowel is next to an emphatic: the same kind of transition may occur as that described in A above:

ṣeef	'summer'
beeδ̣	'eggs'

C. *aa* Long low central vowel.[1]

There are two major variants.

(1) A sound ranging from the vowel of had to that of hod, but longer than either in duration. This variant occurs when the vowel is not next to an emphatic:

baab	'door'
θaani	'second'
jaab	'he brought'
ɀaawal	'he tried'
δaak	'that'
siyaasa	'policy'
šaaf	'he saw'

[1] This is the only long vowel which sometimes occurs in final unstressed position, though only in a few words, for example *ʔiδaa* 'if'. In such words the *aa* may be somewhat shorter in length than elsewhere, but retains the characteristic quality of *aa* as opposed to that of short *a*. See also 3.2.

Ɛaadatan	'usually'
ġaali	'expensive'
faas	'axe'
kaafi	'enough'
laazim	'necessary'
maalak	'yours'
naar	'fire'
ṗaaṙiis	'Paris'

(2) A sound ranging from the vowel of <u>hod</u> to that of <u>haul</u>, but longer than either in duration and without the lip-rounding of the latter. This variant occurs when the vowel is next to an emphatic:

ṣaar	'he became'
ṣaaniƐ	'servant-boy'
ġaaṣ	'he dived'
ḍaabuṭ	'officer'
ḍaag	'he tasted'
ṭaar	'he flew'
ṭaaliƐ	'having gone out'
qaaṭ	'suit'
xaaḷi	'my uncle'
ḅaaḅa	'daddy'

D. *uu* Long high back rounded vowel

There are two major variants.

(1) A sound similar to the vowel of <u>choose</u>, except that the lips maintain the same rounded position throughout and do not, as in the English vowel, become more rounded at the end than at the start. This variant occurs when the vowel is not next to an emphatic:

truuζ	'she goes'
duuda	'worm'
šuuf	'look'

muu	'not'
yzuuruu	'they visit him'

(2) A sound between the vowel of choose and the *first element* of the vowel of chose (that is, without the latter's final offglide toward the vowel of ooze). This variant occurs when the vowel is next to an emphatic:

ṣuuf	'wool'
yġuuṣ	'he dives'
ʔaḍuug	'I taste'
ṭuul	'length'
nxuuṭ	'we stir'

E. *oo* Long mid back rounded vowel

There are two major variants.

(1) A sound similar to the *first element* in the vowel of chose (that is, without the final offglide toward the vowel of ooze). This variant occurs when the vowel is not next to an emphatic:

θoob	'shirt'
xooš	'good'
dooxa	'dizziness'
šaafoo	'they saw him'
moot	'death'
yoom	'day'

(2) A sound similar to the vowel of ball. This variant occurs when the vowel is next to an emphatic:

ṣoob	'river bank'
ḍoog	'tasting'
ṭoob	'cannon'

2. SOUNDS IN COMBINATION

2.1   DIPHTHONGS

Diphthongs in Iraqi are sequences of a short or long vowel and a semivowel (*w* or *y*) in the same syllable. There are four common diphthongs:

A.   *aw*

Similar to the vowel sound in English <u>how</u>, but shorter and with a more marked <u>oo</u>-like element (as in <u>boot</u>) at the end:

ʔ<u>aw</u>saɛ	'wider'
q<u>aw</u>s	'arch'
šaaf<u>aw</u>	'they saw'

When final or before a consonant, the same sound is represented in some words by *aww* (see 2.2.2):

j<u>aww</u>	'atmosphere, air'
z<u>aww</u>lat	'she transferred'

B.   *aaw*

Like *aw* but held longer before the final <u>oo</u>-like element:

z<u>aaw</u>lat	'she tried'
tɛ<u>aaw</u>naw	'they cooperated'

C.   *ay*

Between the vowel sounds in English <u>rate</u> and <u>right</u>, but shorter and with a marked <u>ee</u>-like element (as in <u>feet</u>) at the end:

j<u>ay</u>š	'army'
b<u>ay</u>ti	'domestic'
ʔ<u>ay</u>	'which'

When final or before a consonant, the same sound is represented in some words by *ayy* (see 2.2.2):

f<u>ayy</u>	'shade'
m<u>ayy</u>ta	'dead F'

D. *aay*

Like the long vowel *aa* followed quickly by an ee-like element (as in feet):

ġaayta	'his purpose'
haay	'this F'

Two other diphthongs occur much less commonly:

E. *iw*

Like the vowel in English bit followed quickly by the vowel of boot:

stiwṭaan	'settling down'

F. *eew*

Like the Iraqi long *ee* followed quickly by the vowel of English boot:

meewtak	'your M fruit'
ʒleew	'sweet, good-looking'

2.2 DOUBLE CONSONANTS

Any Iraqi consonant may occur double. In English, double consonant sounds occur only in transitions from one word or compound-element to another, for example in hot time or pen-knife; in Iraqi, double consonant sounds also frequently occur within a single word. When a stop consonant (1.1.1) is doubled, the closure is maintained slightly longer before release than for the corresponding single consonant:

sitta	'six'
baddal	'he changed'
rukkaab	'passengers'

Similarly, when an affricate (1.1.3) is doubled, the closure is maintained slightly longer before release than for the corresponding single consonant. The result, for *čč*, is like the English sequence t ch in rat cheese; for *jj*, like d j in red jam:

siččiina	'knife'
sajjal	'he registered'

When a spirant (1.1.2), nasal (1.1.4), or lateral (1.1.6) is doubled, the continuous sound is prolonged slightly longer than for the corresponding single consonant:

hassa	'now'
sammeet	'I named'
ṭallaɛ	'he took out'

When the spirant *ε* (1.1.2 J) is doubled, the sound is prolonged slightly longer than for a single *ε*, as described above, and is then released abruptly and with some aspiration. A double *εε* thus tends to sound somewhat like a prolonged *ε* followed by the glottal stop *ʔ*:

naεεas	'he was sleepy'

A doubled semivowel (1.1.5) between two vowels shows the following characteristics: The sequences *-uww-*, *-oww*, and *-iyy-* sound like *-uuw-*, *-oow-*, and *-iiy-* respectively:

huwwa	'he'
suwwaaq	'drivers'
raadyowwaat	'radios'
hiyya	'she'
šamsiyyatha	'her umbrella'

The sequence *-aww-* sounds like the diphthong *aw* followed by the consonant *w*; the sequence *-ayy-* like the diphthong *ay* followed by the consonant *y*:

sawwa	'he did'
εalayya	'on me'

2.2.1 Initial

Not all double consonants occur initially. Most of those which do are the result of a combination of certain one-consonant prefixes and stems which happen to begin with the same consonant.[1]

b-baġdaad	'in Baghdad'
t-taariix	'the date'
ttifqaw	'they agreed'
θ-θaani	'the second'
j-jaamiε	'the mosque'
ddaxxal	'he interfered'
δδakkárit	'I remembered'
r-raʔiis	'the president'
z-zibid	'the butter'

[1] See 2.4 for optional helping vowel.

š-šifit	'what did you see'
ṣ-ṣeef	'the summer'
ḍ-ḍaabuṭ	'the officer'
ṭ-ṭeer	'the bird'
l-luġa	'the language'
mmaššiṭ	'having combed'
nnisa	'it was forgotten'
w-wuṣal	'and he arrived'
yyabbis	'he dries' (tr)
č-čaakuuč	'the hammer'

2.2.2 Medial

Between two vowels any double consonant can occur. A few examples follow:

tra??as	'he became chairman'
dabbar	'he arranged'
sajjal	'he registered'
hassa	'now'
baṭṭa	'duck'
šaġġaḷ	'he employed'
laffeet	'I wrapped'
salla	'basket'
damma	'his blood'
jawwa	'under'
ɛalayya	'on me'
qaþþaṭ	'it became full'
raggi	'watermelon'
baččaaha	'he made her cry'

Before another consonant, a double consonant becomes single in pronunciation:

dabbrat	'she arranged'	is pronounced	"*dabrat*"
salltak	'your basket'	is pronounced	"*saltak*"

In this book the spelling with a double letter is retained in such cases, however, in order to show the relationship between such words as the following:

dabbar	'he arranged'
dabbrat	'she arranged'
salla	'basket'
salltak	'your basket'

2.2.3 Final

As far as the sound itself is concerned, a final double consonant is the same as the corresponding single consonant; for example, the final consonant sound of *maẓall* 'place' is the same as the final consonant sound of *siẓal* 'he pulled'. The difference lies in the stress (3): a word ending in a double consonant has stress on the last syllable: *maẓáll* ; a word ending in a single consonant (unless the latter is preceded by a long vowel) has stress elsewhere: *síẓal*. Some other examples follow:

ʔaẓibb	'I like'
mistiɛidd	'prepared'
ʔaṣarr	'he insisted'
yiṭrašš	'he grows deaf'
tindall	'you know'

If a suffix beginning with a vowel is added to a word with a final double consonant, the latter becomes a medial double consonant between two vowels (2.2.2 above) and is pronounced double:

maẓall	'place'
maẓallaat	'places'
ʔaẓibb	'I like'
ʔaẓibba	'I like him'

If a suffix beginning with a consonant is added to a word with a final double consonant, the latter becomes a medial double consonant before another consonant (2.2.2 above) and is pronounced like a single consonant:

maẓallha	'her place'
ʔaẓibbhum	'I like them'

2.3 CONSONANT CLUSTERS

A consonant cluster is a group of two or more different consonants not separated by any vowels. In Iraqi, clusters of more than three different consonants do not occur. Clusters of three consonants occasionally occur, especially in a few combinations involving the end of one word and the beginning of another, for example *ʔalf marra* 'a thousand times'. (See 2.3.3 for final consonant clusters as in *ʔalf*.) However, every such combination may also be and more commonly is, pronounced with a vowel between the first and second consonant: *ʔalif marra*. The following remarks therefore are concerned with two-consonant clusters,[1] which are very common in initial and medial positions.

2.3.1 Initial

Most two-consonant clusters, though not all, may occur at the beginning of words.[2] The following list of examples is not exhaustive.

b-ġurufti	'in my room'	*qreena*	'we read'
tqarrir	'you M decide'	*lsaan*	'tongue'
θneen	'two'	*l-meez*	'the table'
druus	'lessons'	*mεallim*	'having taught'
rtikab	'he committed'	*nẓall*	'it was solved'
staεmal	'he used'	*hwaaya*	'a lot, much'
štira	'he bought'	*gbaaḷ*	'facing, in front of'
š-biik	'what's the matter with you?'	*člaab*	'dogs'
fluus	'money'		

A semivowel *w* or *y* as the first consonant of an initial cluster has a more vowel-like than consonant-like quality, similar to that of the vowels *uu* and *ii* respectively, but shorter in length.

wlaaya	'city'
yriid	'he wants'

---

[1] Including those spelled with a double consonant plus another consonant, as in *maẓallha* 'her place', as such a spelling represents the sounds *lh* (see 2.2.2).

[2] See 2.4 for optional helping vowel.

When a preceding word or prefix ends in a consonant the semivowel sound may be similar to that of *uu* and *ii* in both quality and length.

hal-wlaaya	'this city'
š-yriid	'what does he want'

2.3.2 Medial

The most common position of occurrence of a two-consonant cluster is between two vowels. The following list illustrates only a few of the many possible combinations.

niktib	'we write'
nismaƐ	'we hear'
ḍarba	'a blow'
Ɛašra	'ten'
balwa	'trouble'
kallfat	'it F cost'
dammna	'our blood'

2.3.3 Final

Final clusters are somewhat rare. For convenience of description they can be divided into two types.

A. Semivowel plus consonant

A few words end in a semivowel (*w* or *y*) plus another consonant:

kawn	'universe'
qaws	'curve, arch'
jayš[1]	'army'

B. Nasal, *l*, *r* plus consonant

Some words end in a final cluster of which the first consonant is one of the nasals *m* or *n*, or *l*, or *r*. Many of these, however, also have alternative pronunciations in which a vowel separates the two:

[1] Also occasionally *jeeš*.

pamp	'pump'
banj (*banij*)	'anesthetic'
hind	'India'; girl's name
bang	'bank'
ʔalf (*ʔalif*)	'thousand'
silk (*silik*)	'wire'
ḥarb (*ḥarub*)	'war'
ġarb	'west'
l-karx	section of Baghdad
šarq	'east'
ṣirf	'pure'

2.4 HELPING VOWEL

When the processes of affixation or syntax would otherwise result in a cluster of more than two consonants,[1] a short vowel *i* occurs between the first and second of three or between the second and third of four consonants. This feature is known as the helping vowel. Its occurrence under these circumstances is automatic and does not affect meaning. The three-consonant situation commonly arises when a prefix ending in a consonant is attached to a form beginning with two consonants or a double consonant, or when a word ending in a consonant is followed without pause by a form beginning with two consonants or a double consonant.

b-	'in, with'
fluusak	'your money'
b-ifluusak	'with your money'
š-	'what'
triid	'you want'
š-itriid	'what do you want'

[1] Clusters consisting of a double consonant and another consonant count as two consonants only; see 2.2.2.

w-	'and'
ttifqaw	'they agreed'
w-ittifqaw	'and they agreed'
l-	'to'
n-naas	'the people'
lin-naas	'to the people'
ktaabi	'my book'
triid iktaabi?	'Do you want my book?'
dazzeet	'I sent'
l-maktuub	'the letter'
dazzeet il-maktuub	'I sent the letter'
štireet	'I bought'
θ-θoob	'the shirt'
štireet iθ-θoob	'I bought the shirt'

The four-consonant situation arises when a word ending in a double consonant (or in two consonants, which is rare) is followed immediately by a form beginning with two consonants or a double consonant.

dazz	'he sent'
dazz il-maktuub	'he sent the letter'
dazz iθ-θoob	'he sent the shirt'
hind	girl's name
hind itriid	'Hind wants'

The four-consonant situation also arises when the preceding word in combinations like those above is one which otherwise ends in a single consonant but in precisely this situation (i.e., when followed by a vowel) loses its stem vowel and thus ends in two consonants.

šifit	'I saw'
l-waziir	'the minister'
šift il-waziir	'I saw the minister'
d-daris	'the lesson'
θ-θaaliθ	'the third'
d-dars iθ-θaaliθ	'the third lesson'

When a form beginning with two consonants or a double consonant is the first (or only) word in an utterance, the helping vowel is optional.

qmaaš	'cloth'
or *iqmaaš*	
ttifqaw	'they agreed'
or *ittifqaw*	
l-maktuub	'the letter'
or *il-maktub*	
b-baġdaad	'in Baghdad'
or *ib-baġdaad*	

This optional helping vowel will not hereafter be indicated.

2.5 ASSIMILATION

When two different consonants come together in a cluster, one may assimilate to - that is, become more like - the other. The assimilation may be complete, in which case one consonant becomes identical to the other and the result is a double consonant; or it may be partial, in which case one consonant becomes more like the other in one or more respects but not in all. The two common types of partial assimilation are assimilation as to voice and as to emphasis. These are illustrated in the first two sections below; the third section illustrates some special types of assimilation that apply to certain individual consonants.[1] The forms shown in parentheses below indicate the usual or possible pronunciation of the assimilated consonants. As a general rule in this book hereafter, however, assimilation is not indicated when it affects a root consonant (4.1.1).

[1] For assimilation of *t*, see also 5.1.1.5.

2.5.1 As to voice

A. The voiceless spirants *f, θ, š, ṣ,* may become voiced before a voiced stop, a voiced spirant other than *ε*, or the voiced affricate *j*.

ẓufḍat	(*ẓuuḍat*)[1]	'she memorized'
ʔaθgaḷ	(*ʔaδgaḷ*)	'heavier'
ʔasdaas	(*ʔazdaas*)	'sixths'
mašġuul	(*mažġuul*)[2]	'busy'
ʔašjaar	(*ažjaar*)[2]	'trees'
ʔaṣdiqaaʔ	(*ʔaẓdiqaaʔ*)	'friends'

B. The voiced spirants *δ, z, ġ, ḍ,* the voiced affricate *j*, and the voiced stops *b, d, g* may become voiceless before a voiceless stop other than *ʔ*, a voiceless spirant other than *ẓ* and *h*, or the voiceless affricate *č*.

maδkuur	(*maθkuur*)	'mentioned'
ẓijazti	(*ẓijasti*)	'you F reserved'
staġfar	(*staxfar*)	'he asked pardon'
l-ijsuur	(*l-ičsuur*)	'the bridges'
libsat	(*lipsat*)	'she wore'
ʔadfaε	(*ʔatfaε*)	'I pay'
ʔagṭaε	(*ʔakṭaε*)	'I cut'

2.5.2 As to emphasis

The non-emphatic consonants *t, s, δ, p, b, f, m, z, l* may become emphatic before or after an emphatic consonant; the influence of the latter may extend not only to an adjacent consonant but throughout a syllable or farther.

ṣtidam	(*ṣṭidam*)	'he collided'
waṣfa	(*waṣf̣a*)	'prescription'
ʔaṭlub	(*ʔaṭḷuḅ*)	'I request'

---

[1] The sound v (as in English vest) occurs in Iraqi only when *f* is assimilated, as here, and in a few foreign words, but not as an independent sound.

[2] The sound ž (the middle consonant sound in English vision) occurs in Iraqi only when *š* is assimilated, as here, but not as an independent sound.

maṭƐam	(*ṃaṭƐam*)	'restaurant'
ṣaabuṭ	(*ṣaaḅuṭ*)	'officer'
laṭiif	(*ḷaṭiif*)	'nice'

Most occurrences of the secondary emphatics (*p̣*, *ḅ*, *f̣*, *ṃ*, *ẓ*, *ḷ*,) are due to automatic assimilation of this kind. One of these, however, *ḷ*, is not always so automatically assimilated as the others, particularly when it follows an emphatic in the same syllable but is not adjacent to it; for example, in *čaṭal* 'fork', the *l* may remain non-emphatic. See also 1.1.8.

2.5.3 Individual cases

The consonants *l*, *n*, *j* show special features of assimilation.

A. *l* followed by *n* may become *n*:

baddalna	(*baddanna*)	'we changed'
maalna	(*maanna*)	'ours'
ʔilna	(*ʔinna*)	'to us'

B. *n* followed by *b* or *m* may become *m*:

yinbaaƐ	(*yimbaaƐ*)	'it is sold'
yinmurad	(*yimmurad*)	'it is crushed'

Followed by *r* it may become *r*:

yinraad	(*yirraad*)	'it is needed'
ma-nruuḥ	(*ma-rruuḥ*)	'we do not go'

C. *j* followed by a voiced stop may become *ž* (see 2.5.1, Footnote 2):

šii jdiid	(*šii ždiid*)	'something new'

Followed by a voiceless stop it may become *š* :

jtimƐaw	(*štimƐaw*)	'they assembled'

2.6 SHORT VOWELS i AND u

The short vowel sounds *i* and *u*, when not final in a word, have a special relationship to each other. In some words, these two vowels are in contrast; that is, the occurrence of the one or the other makes a difference in meaning, for example *jimal* 'camel' versus *jumal* 'sentences'. Such contrasts are few. There are other words, for example *sudus* 'sixth', in which *i* and *u* are in free variation; that is, some speakers say *sudus* and some *sidis* or the same speaker may use both forms at different times. This kind of variation does not affect meaning, and generally passes unnoticed.

In a great many words, however, non-final *i* and *u* are in <u>complementary dis-</u><u>tribution</u>; that is, *i* tends to occur only between or near certain consonants, and *u* only between or near certain others. The occurrence of the one or the other is thus determined by the <u>environment</u>, and does not affect meaning. This kind of distribution is particularly common in words of certain patterns (4.1.1.5); for example, in Class I active participles, which have the pattern FaaMiL/FaaMuL, the last vowel is *i* if between *b* and *s*, as in *laabis* 'wearing', but *u* if between *r* and *f*, as in *Ɛaaruf* 'knowing'. It is also consistently found where a stem vowel (4.1.3.1) is *i* or *u*, and in cases of stem variation where a stem vowel is changed from *a* to *i* or *u* or shifted from a sequence -CCvC to a sequence -CiCC- or -CuCC- (see 4.1.3.1 B,C). The environment which determines the occurrence of *i* or *u* is not necessarily restricted to the two adjacent consonants, but may also involve other nearby sounds. Typically, *u* environments involve emphatics, labials, velars, and *r* in various combinations; *i* environments involve other consonants. Some examples of common *u* environments follow:

A. Between a labial and an emphatic:

bu̱ṣaṭ	'he beat'
ðaabu̱ṭ	'officer'
ṣu̱far	'he whistled'
Ɛaðu̱m	'bone'

B. Between a labial and a velar:

bu̱qa	'he stayed'
ṭaabu̱x	'having cooked'
ku̱bar	'he grew up'
sagu̱f	'ceiling'

C. Between a labial and *r*:

bu̱ram	'he twisted'
ʔaxaabu̱r	'I telephone'
ru̱baṭ	'he fastened'
zaru̱b	'war'

D. In a sequence C-CC or CC-C, where the consonants adjacent to the vowel are a combination of emphatic, velar, or *r*, and the outside consonant is a labial:

ġu̱rfa	'room'
xu̱ṭba	'engagement'

yrukbuun	'they ride'
ʔaṣurba	'I hit him'

The consonantal environment does not invariably determine the occurrence of *i* or *u* – there are numbers of instances where one may be found in the environment typical of the other – but its tendency to do so is an important feature of the language.

When final in a word, *i* and *u* are entirely independent of each other. There is no free variation between them, they are unaffected by environment, and they are frequently in contrast (notably in imperative forms like the last examples below):

bali	'yes'	*ʒilu*	'sweet, pretty'
yumṣi	'he signs'	*ʕuṣu*	'member'
šuufi	'look F'	*šuufu*	'look P'

3. STRESS

Stress, the relative loudness or force of one syllable over others in the same word, is of two kinds in Iraqi. In the great majority of words,[1] stress is determined by and can be predicted from the word's consonant-vowel structure; this is automatic stress. In certain types of words, however, stress deviates in some way from this norm; it is then called non-automatic stress.

3.1 AUTOMATIC STRESS

Automatic stress is predictable according to the automatic stress formula, as follows:

> Stress is on the syllable containing that long vowel, or short vowel followed by two consonants or a double consonant, which is nearest the end of the word; in the absence of such a vowel, stress is on the next-to-last syllable in two-syllable words and on the third-from-last in all others.

Stress on last syllable

Ɛalée	'on him'
šaafóo	'they saw him'
limnáa	'we blamed him'
xalldáa	'he let him'
nṭiini-yydáa	'give it to me'
maríiδ̣	'sick'
čaakúuč	'hammer'
taƐbdán	'tired'
dazzéet	'I sent'
win-nás	'and the people'
maζáll	'place'
yiζmárr	'he blushes'
raζ-adízz	'I'm going to send'

[1] Forms joined with hyphens are considered single words in determining stress.

Stress on next-to-last syllable

náadi	'club'	*nísa*	'he forgot'
bádla	'suit'		
sálla	'basket'		
sallátha	'her basket'		
káatib	'clerk'	*kítab*	'he wrote'
šúkran	'thanks'		
gáṣṣat	'she cut'		
ƹiráaqi	'Iraqi'		
stilámna	'we received'		
barhánna	'we proved'		
dazzát-la	'she sent to him'		

Stress on third-from-last syllable

ƹáalami	'world-'	*šárika*	'company'
mádrasa	'school'		
musáaƹada	'assistance'		
mumáθθila	'actress'		

In three-syllable words of certain particular consonant-vowel arrangements, stress may follow the automatic stress formula or it may vary, falling sometimes on the next-to-last and sometimes on the third-from-last syllable:

$\mathrm{CvC}\overset{i}{\mathrm{u}}\mathrm{CCvC}$

ʔíbinha	or	*ʔibínha*	'her son'
ġúruftak	or	*ġurúftak*	'your room'

Most such words consist of a stem of the pattern $\mathrm{CvC}\overset{i}{\mathrm{u}}\mathrm{C}$- or $\mathrm{CvC}\overset{i}{\mathrm{u}}\mathrm{CC}$- with a pronoun suffix (9.1.2).

$\underline{\text{CvCC}\overset{\text{i}}{\text{u}}\text{Cv(C)}}$

míxtilif	or	*mixtílif*	'different'
tíštiri	or	*tištíri*	'she buys'

Most such words are imperfect or participle forms of Class VII and VIII verbs (5.1.1.7, 5.1.1.8).

3.2 NON-AUTOMATIC STRESS

Non-automatic stress is found in words containing certain prefixes and suffixes, and in a few words ending in *-aa*.

A. In the second-person masculine singular and first-person singular of perfect-tense verbs, when no pronoun suffix is attached, stress is on the syllable preceding the suffix *-it:*

darrásit	'you M/I taught'
ftikárit	'you M/I thought'
tarjámit	'you M/I translated'

(If a pronoun suffix is attached to such forms, either the *i* is dropped or stress is shifted to it, resulting either way in automatic stress:

darrásta	'you M/I taught him'
darrasítha	'you M/I taught her')

B. In words consisting of a perfect-tense third-person masculine verb stem ending in *-aC*, or a perfect-tense third-person feminine verb stem, which always ends in *-at*, and one of the pronoun suffixes *-a* 'him', *-ak* 'you M', or *-ič* 'you F', the stress is on the syllable preceding the suffix:

xaabára	'he phoned him'
xaabráta	'she phoned him'

In words consisting of a noun stem ending in *-aC* and one of the pronoun suffixes *-a* 'his', *-ak* 'your M', *-ič* 'your F', or *-i* 'my', the stress varies. It may fall on the syllable preceding the suffix, as above, or on the first syllable according to the automatic stress rule:

baláma	or	*bálama*	'his boat'
qalámi	or	*qálami*	'my pencil'

C. In words ending in the dual suffix *-een* 'two', the stress usually falls on the preceding syllable in two-syllable words, on the third syllable from the end in words of three or more syllables:

béeteen	'two houses'
čálbeen	'two dogs'
šárikteen	'two companies'
mántiqteen	'two zones'
ʒámmaameen	'two baths'

D. The negative prefixes *ma–* and *la–* 'not' are usually stressed:

má–yriid	'he doesn't want'
má–aʒibbhum	'I don't like them'
má–nšuuf	'we don't see'
lá–truuʒ	'don't go M'
lá–tibqiin	'don't stay F'

E. In words containing the interrogative prefix *š–* 'what', the stress is usually on the first following vowel, even when that is a helping vowel:

š–ítriid	'what do you M want'
š–túquṣdiin	'what do you F mean'

F. In words containing one of the prepositional prefixes *b–* 'in', *l–* 'to', and *mn–* 'from', the stress is usually on the first following vowel, even when that is a helping vowel:

bíl–beet	'in the house'
b–ámriika	'in America'
líl–madrasa	'to the school'
l–báġdaad	'to Baghdad'
mnís–šaariƐ	'from the street'
mn–ífluusak	'from your money'

G. In a few words ending in *aa*, stress is on a preceding syllable (see 1.2.2 C, Footnote):

ʔíδaa	'if'
ʔílaa	'up to, until'

Hereafter in this book, stress will be indicated by the stress mark '´' only in the cases of non-automatic stress described in A, B, and G above.

PART TWO
MORPHOLOGY

4. INTRODUCTION TO MORPHOLOGY

The preceding three chapters dealt with the sounds of Iraqi. The following six chapters will deal with the classification and forms of Iraqi words. As an introduction, this chapter presents some general comments on word structure.

4.1 STEMS

An Iraqi word usually consists either of a stem alone, for example *yoom* 'day', or of a stem plus one or more affixes, for example *yoomeen* 'two days'. Some stems, like *yoom*, can occur either alone or with an affix; others never have an affix, for example *tara* 'or, else'. Both these types are free stems. A third type, called bound stems, consists of stems which never occur without an affix, for example *-ktib* in *yiktib* 'he writes'. From the point of view of their internal structure, stems may be simple or complex. A complex stem is one which itself consists of a stem plus one or more affixes and to which, as a whole, other affixes are or may be attached. For example, the word *šifitha* 'I saw her' consists of the stem *šifit* 'I saw' and the suffix *-ha* 'her'; and the stem *šifit*, in turn, is a complex stem consisting of the (simple) stem *šif-* 'saw' and the suffix *-it* 'first person singular subject'. A simple stem is one which cannot be further analyzed into stem and affix. Simple stems, finally, fall into two categories: those which consist of a root and a pattern, and solid stems. The system of roots and patterns is a central feature of Iraqi morphology and is discussed in some detail below.

4.1.1 Roots and patterns

The great majority of Iraqi words consist of, or include, a stem which consists of two major elements, a root and a pattern. The most common kind of root (see 4.1.1.1 below for other kinds) consists of three consonants in a certain order, for example *d r s*.

Roots have a general sort of meaning, usually corresponding to the concepts expressed in English by nouns, verbs, or adjectives; and words containing the same root commonly have meanings related in some way to the same concept. For example, the root *d r s* is associated with the general concept of "studying"; words containing that root may be expected to have something to do with that idea:

diras	'he studied'
ʔadrus	'I study'
daris	'lesson'
diraasa	'study'
darras	'he taught'
mudarris	'teacher'
madrasa	'school'

The individual consonants of a root are called root consonants, or radicals. In a given root, the radicals occur in the same order relative to each other. Two, but not more, may occur together; any two, or all, may be separated by vowels or consonants which are not part of the root. Examples of other roots are *ṣ n ε* (general meaning of "manufacturing") in *ṣinaaεa* 'industry' and *maṣnaε* 'factory'; *k t b* (general meaning of "writing") in *kitab* 'he wrote', *ktaab* 'book', and *maktaba* 'library'; and *ḥ m r* (general meaning of "redness") in *ʔaḥmar* 'red', *ḥamaar* 'red color', and *ḥmarr* 'he turned red, blushed'.

A pattern is a set of one or more vowels, and in some cases also one or more consonants, occurring in combination with the consonants of a root. For example, in the word *diras* 'he studied', the root is *d r s*, and the pattern consists of a short vowel *i* between the first and second radicals and a short vowel *a* between the second and third. Whereas roots have general lexical meanings, patterns have grammatical meanings. For example, the pattern just described for *diras* has the meaning 'Class I verb, perfect tense'. The same pattern also occurs in the words *rikab* 'he rode', *difaε* 'he paid', *εiraf* 'he knew', and many others. Some patterns consist not simply of one or more vowels between the radicals, like that of *diras*, but of these plus one or more affixes. Patterns of this sort are called pattern complexes. (See 4.1.1.4 below for description.) For example, the word *maṣnaε* 'factory' has the root *ṣ n ε*, and a pattern consisting of a prefix *ma-* and a vowel *a* between the second and third radicals. This pattern has roughly the meaning 'place where the activity indicated by the root is conducted'; it also occurs in the words *maṭεam* 'restaurant', *malεab* 'playground', *masbaḥ* 'swimming place', and many others.

A root and a pattern together form a stem. These are interdependent: neither can occur without the other. The general lexical meaning of the root and the grammatical meaning of the pattern intersect to form the specific meaning of the stem as a whole.

4.1.1.1 Root types

Roots are classified in two ways: according to the number of radicals and according to the kinds of radicals. A few stems have biliteral roots, consisting of only two radicals, for example *ʔax* 'brother' and *sana* 'year'. A slightly larger group is formed by stems which have multiliteral roots, consisting of five or more radicals, for example *barnaamaj* 'program'. Most stems, however, have either triliteral roots, consisting of three radicals, or quadriliteral roots, consisting of four. Those with triliteral roots are by far the most numerous of all.

A. Triliteral roots

Triliteral roots are classified as strong or weak. Strong roots are those which do not vary in the particular way described below for weak roots. An example of a strong root is *d r s* as illustrated in the list of words in the introductory part of 4.1.1. Weak roots are those in which one or more of the radical elements is unstable ("weak"). In different words of the same weak root, a given weak radical may appear as *ʔ*, *w*, or *y*, or it may be represented by vowel length, or it may be absent altogether.[1] Examples of weak roots are *s V g* and *b n V* (the symbol V

[1] In the traditional analysis of Classical Arabic, the weak radical in roots of this sort is considered, by one criterion or another, to be specifically one of the consonants *ʔ*, *w* or *y*. Thus the two roots illustrated above are cited as *s w g* and *b n y*, and in dictionaries are alphabetized accordingly. Roots containing *ʔ* are sometimes considered weak and sometimes treated as a special category.

represents the weak radical). Among the words built on the first root are *saayiq* 'driver', *suwwaaq* 'drivers', *saaq* 'he drove' (weak radical represented by vowel length; compare *diras* 'he studied'), and *siqna* 'we drove' (weak radical absent; compare *dirasna* 'we studied'). Among the words built on the second root are *bnaaya* 'a building', *binaa?* 'construction', and *bina* 'he built' (weak radical absent; compare *diras* 'he studied'). Both strong and weak roots are further divided into subclasses, as follows.

Strong roots are classified as sound or double. Sound roots are those in which the second and third radicals are not identical. In a small number of sound roots the first and third radicals are identical, and in an even smaller number the first and second are identical. In the great majority, however, all are different. Examples of sound roots are: *d r s* in *diras* 'he studied', *k t b* in *kaatib* 'clerk', and *ṣ n ʕ* in *ṣinaaʕa* 'industry'. Double roots are those in which the second and third radicals are identical; these are fairly numerous. Examples are: *f k k* in *fakk* 'he opened', *h m m* in *htimaam* 'concern', and *ṭ b b* in *?aṭibbaa?* 'doctors'.

Weak roots are classified, according to the position of the unstable radical, as weak-first, weak-middle, or weak-last; there are also a few with two weak radicals, and these are termed doubly weak. Weak-first roots are those in which the first radical is unstable. Examples are *V k l* in *?akal* 'he ate' and *maakil* 'having eaten' *V ṣ f* in *wuṣaf* 'he described' and *ṣifa* 'adjective', and *V b s* in *yibas* 'it M dried' and *teebas* 'it F dries'. Weak-first roots, however, differ from other weak roots in being considerably more stable: in general the first radical of a weak-first root appears consistently as *?*, or *w*, or *y*, in most words of that root. Hereafter in this book, therefore, words with weak-first roots will be treated not as a separate category, but together with one of the other types, and in the indication of roots as such the first radical will be represented as *?*, *w*, or *y* as the case may be. Thus the three roots illustrated above will be written as *? k l*, *w ṣ f*, and *y b s* respectively. When variation does occur, it will be noted as a special case. Weak-middle roots are those in which the middle radical is unstable. In these there is considerable variation in the form taken by the weak radical. Examples are: *š V f* in *šaayif* 'having seen', *šawwaf* 'he showed', and *šifit* 'I saw'; *ṭ V r* in *ṭiyyaara* 'airplane', *ṭeer* 'bird', and *ṭirit* 'I flew'; and *d V r* in *daa?ira* 'office', *?idaara* 'administration', and *mudiir* 'director'. Weak-last roots are those in which the last radical is unstable; here too there is considerable variation. Examples are: *š r V* in *šarwa* 'purchase' and *štira* 'he bought'; *m l V* in *malyaan* 'full' and *yimli* 'he fills'; and *b d V* in *btidaa?i* 'elementary', *bidaaya* 'beginning, first part', and *yibtidi* 'he begins'. Doubly weak roots are those in which there are two or more unstable elements, for example *š V V* in *šii* 'thing' and *?ašyaa?* 'things'; and *č V V* in *čuwa* 'he burned' and *čawya* 'a burn'. However, in most cases of doubly weak roots, only the last radical is unstable; hereafter, therefore, these cases will be treated along with weak-last roots, and the relatively stable middle radical will be represented as *w* or *y* as the case may be. Thus the second root above will be written *č w V*. Any variation will be noted as a special case.

The consonant *?* may play two kinds of role in the root system. It may be (along with *w*, *y*, vowel length, and absence) one of the forms assumed by the unstable radical in a weak root, as illustrated above. Or it may be, in its own right, one of the radicals of a strong root and thus remain stable as *?* in all words of that root, for example *s ? l* in *si?al* 'he asked', *saa?il* 'having asked', and *tsa??al* 'he asked around'.[1] (See also 4.1.1.2.)

[1] There is a related weak root *s V l*, as in *saayil* 'beggar' and *tsawwal* 'he went around begging'.

B. Quadriliteral roots

Quadriliteral roots, like triliterals, are classified as strong or weak.

Strong quadriliteral roots are further divided into two subclasses: sound and reduplicated. Sound roots are those in which the first and third radicals are not identical respectively to the second and last. In most sound roots all four radicals are different; examples are *t r j m* in *tarjam* 'he translated' and *h n d s* in *handas* 'he designed'. In a few, the first and third are identical, for example *d h d r* in *dahdar* 'he rolled'. Reduplicated roots are those in which the first and second radicals are identical respectively to the third and the last. Examples are: *b q b q* in *baqbaq* 'it bubbled' and *n f n f* in *nafnuuf* 'dress'.

Weak quadriliteral roots are those in which the second or the last radical is unstable. (The first and third radicals of quadriliteral roots are always stable.) Examples of weak-second roots are *š V ṭ n* in *šayṭaan* or *šiiṭaan* 'devil' and *šeeṭana* 'devilishness, mischief'; and *m V l s* in *moolas* 'it became worn'. Weakness in the second radical of a quadriliteral root usually takes the form of vowel length in the vowels *ee, oo, ii,* or *uu*. No common examples of weak-last roots (when there is no other weak radical in the root; see below) have been noted. Slightly more common are doubly weak roots in which both the second and the last radicals are weak, for example *ẓ V m V* in *ẓooma* 'he circled, went around'. Weakness in the last radical of a quadriliteral root usually takes the form of absence of the radical.

The types of roots described in the preceding sections are shown in tabular form below, with an example of a word containing each type.

Triliteral

Strong

Sound	*d r s*	*diras*	'he studied'
Double	*s d d*	*sadd*	'he closed'

Weak

Weak-middle	*š V f*	*šaaf*	'he saw'
Weak-last	*b n V*	*bina*	'he built'
Doubly weak	*j V V*	*jaa*	'he came'

Quadriliteral

Strong

Sound	*t r j m*	*tarjam*	'he translated'
Reduplicated	*d g d g*	*dagdag*	'he pounded'

Weak

Weak-second	*n V š n*	*neešan*	'he aimed'
Doubly weak	*ẓ V m V*	*ẓooma*	'he circled'

4.1.1.2 Root alternants

A given root may have different forms when combined with different patterns; such forms are alternants of the root. Weak roots characteristically have alternants, as described in 4.1.1.1, for example the root *s V q* has the form *s y q* in *saayiq* 'driver' and the form *s w q* in *suwwaaq* 'drivers'. In such cases the difference between the forms of the alternants is due to the typical variations of a weak radical. A few roots, strong and weak, have two or more alternants which differ because of variation in one of the strong radicals. This kind of variation, unlike that of a weak radical, follows no set pattern; the facts must be noted for each root. However, the most numerous cases involve variation between the consonants *č* and *k* and the consonants *g* and *q*. Some examples are: *č b r/k b r* in *čibiir* 'big' and *ʔakbar* 'bigger'; *č V n/k V n* in *čaan* 'he was' and *ykuun* 'he is'; *g l b/q l b* in *galub* 'heart' and *qalbi* 'cordial; cardiac'; and *s d s/s t t* in *saadis* 'sixth' and *sitta* 'six'. In some instances there may be variation in a single word, for example *č V n/k V n* in *čaan* or *kaan* 'he was'. The words in such a pair usually differ stylistically, the one more closely resembling a Classical word (here *kaan*) being considerably more formal.

Some roots have two or more alternants of which one is a strong root with *ʔ* as a strong radical, and the other(s) a weak root with the usual manifestations of weakness. An example is the root *r ʔ s/r V s*: The strong alternant *r ʔ s* occurs in the words *raʔiis* 'president, chief' and *traʔʔas* 'to be head of'; a weak alternant occurs in *raas* '(person's) head'. In some instances there may be variation in a single word between a strong and a weak alternant; this is especially common when the last radical of a root is involved. An example is the root *h d ʔ/h d V*, as in *haadiʔ* or *haadi* 'calm'. The words in such a pair usually differ stylistically, the one with *ʔ* being the more formal.

4.1.1.3 Symbolization of roots and patterns

As illustrated in the preceding section, specific roots are shown in this book as groups of consonant letters, for example *d r s*. A weak radical in a root is symbolized by a capital *V*, as for example in the root *š V f*.

Specific patterns are indicated within a framework of symbols representing the radicals of any root. For example, *diras* 'he studied', *rikab* 'he rode', *ʕiraf* 'he knew', and many others, all have a pattern consisting of a short *i* after the first radical and a short *a* after the second; this pattern is conveniently symbolized *FiMaL*, a formula in which the symbols *F*, *M*, and *L*, represent respectively the first, middle and last radical of any triliteral sound root. Thus it can be stated that the word *diras* has the root *d r s* and the pattern *FiMaL*. It is sometimes useful to indicate that a given pattern (or pattern alternant; see 4.1.1.5 below) applies only to double roots; then the symbols *FDD* are used as framework instead of *FML*; for example, the word *sadd* 'he closed' has the root *s d d* and the pattern *FaDD*. Similarly, in the case of weak roots, when the weakness takes the form of vowel length or absence, the consonant symbol in the position of the weak radical is omitted from the framework; for example, the word *šaaf* 'he saw' has the root *š V f* and the pattern *FaaL*, and the word *nisa* 'he forgot' has the root *n s V* and the pattern *FiMa*.

Patterns which apply to quadriliteral roots are symbolized in the same way, except that the symbols used in the framework are *F*, *S*, *T*, and *L*, representing the first, second, third, and last radicals respectively. For example *tarjam* 'he translated': root t r j m, pattern *FaSTaL*. For reduplicated roots, when appropriate, the symbols *FDFD* are used, for example *dagdag* 'he pounded': root d g d g, pattern *FaDFaD;* and for weak roots the *S* or *L* is omitted, for example *neešan* 'he aimed': root n V š n, pattern *FeeTaL*.

When it is useful to refer to the general consonant-vowel structure of a word without regard to whether the consonants are radicals or (part of) an affix, the symbol *C* is used to indicate any consonant. For example, the word *maṣnaƐ* 'factory' is based on the triliteral root ṣ n Ɛ and has the pattern *maFMaL*, and the word *darzan* 'dozen' is based on the quadriliteral root d r z n and has the pattern *FaSTaL;* but both can be said to have the general pattern *CaCCaC*. The symbol *C* may also be used together with specific root symbols to indicate any consonant of an affix; for example, the general pattern of both *maṣnaƐ* and *ʔaẓmar* 'red' (root ẓ m r) might be represented as *CaFMaL*. Similarly, the symbols *v* and *vv* may be used to represent respectively any short or long vowel; for example the general pattern of both *maṣnaƐ* and *burnuṣ* 'bathrobe' (root b r n ṣ) can be represented as *CvCCvC;* that of both *xaabar* 'he phoned' (root x b r) and *neešan* 'he aimed' (root n V š n) as *CvvCvC* .

4.1.1.4 Pattern types

A simple pattern is one which consists solely of one or more vowels distributed among the consonants of a root, for example the patterns *FiMaL* in *diras* 'he studied' and *FaMiL* in *daris* 'lesson'. A pattern complex is a combination of a simple pattern and one or more affixes which has the same sort of grammatical meaning as does a simple pattern, and which, as a unit, combines with a root to form a stem, for example the pattern complex *maFMaL* in *maṣnaƐ* 'factory' (root ṣ n Ɛ). The affix in a pattern complex may be any of the following:

(1) A prefix, for example *ʔa-* in the pattern *ʔaFMaL*, as in *ʔaẓmar* 'red' (root ẓ m r); and *ma-* in the pattern *maFMaL,* as in *maṣnaƐ* 'factory' (root ṣ n Ɛ).

(2) An infix. There are two common types of infix in Iraqi patterns. One is the consonant *t* immediately following the first radical, for example in the pattern *FtiMaL*, as in *ftiham* 'he understood' (root f h m). The other type consists of a repetition or doubling of the middle or the last radical, for example, the doubling of the middle radical in the pattern *FaMMaL,* as in *baddal* 'he changed' (root b d l), and the doubling of the last radical in the pattern *FMaLL*, as in *ẓmarr* 'he grew red' (root ẓ m r).

(3) A suffix, for example *-aan* in the pattern *FaMLaan*, as in *taƐbaan* 'tired' (root t Ɛ b).

(4) A combination, for example the prefix *ʔa-* and the suffix *-aaʔ* in the pattern *ʔaFMiLaaʔ*, as in *ʔaṣdiqaaʔ* 'friends' (root ṣ d q).

4.1.1.5 Pattern alternants

A given pattern may have different forms, called pattern alternants, depending on the root-type with which it occurs. For example, there is a pattern which has the form *FiMaL* when it occurs with triliteral sound roots such as d r s: *diras* 'he studied'. When it occurs with other root types, however, it has different forms. For example, with a triliteral double root, such as s d d, it has the alternant *FaDD* (that is, a short vowel *a* after the first radical, and nothing between the identical middle and last radicals), as in *sadd* 'he closed'. With a triliteral weak-middle root, such as *š V f*, it has the alternant *FaaL*, as in *šaff* 'he saw'; and with a triliteral weak-last root, such as *n s V*, it has the alternant *FiMa*, as in *nisa* 'he forgot'. These different alternants are shown in tabular form below:

Root-type

Triliteral	Root	Pattern alternant	Word	
Sound	*d r s*	*FiMaL*	*diras*	'he studied'
Double	*s d d*	*FaDD*	*sadd*	'he closed'
Weak-middle	*š V f*	*FaaL*	*šaaf*	'he saw'
Weak-last	*n s V*	*FiMa*	*nisa*	'he forgot'

In one sense these alternants in a set like this are all (except the first and the last) different patterns, as they clearly consist of different vowels. In another sense, however, they can all be considered manifestations of the same pattern, as the differences between them are determined solely by the type of root with which they occur, and as they all have the same grammatical meaning mentioned earlier for *diras*: 'Class I verb, perfect tense'. In this book they will be referred to in both ways, as appropriate. For example it may be convenient in one place to speak of "the pattern *FaaL*" meaning that particular alternant; and in another place to speak of "the pattern *FiMaL*", meaning any or all of the alternants *FiMaL*, *FaDD*, *Faal*, and *FiMa* (using the sound-root alternant *FiMaL* as a cover term for the whole set). The context will make clear which sense is intended.

Some patterns have another kind of alternant which occurs, not with certain root-types as above, but with certain individual roots. For example, the pattern *FiMaL* as in *diras* 'he studied' has an alternant *FaMaL*, with *a* as the first vowel, which occurs with the specific root *ʔ k l* (and, as it happens, with only one other), as in *ʔakal* 'he ate'. In a listing of patterns or pattern alternants such as that shown above, alternants of this kind are separated by a comma: *FiMaL, FaMaL*.

Finally, there is a third kind of pattern alternant which is determined neither by the root-type nor by the specific root, as above, but by the nature of the particular consonants in a given root. For example, *diras* 'he studied' has *i* as the first vowel (*FiMaL*) while *ṭubax* 'he cooked' has *u* (*FuMaL*). These are alternants of the same pattern. The difference between them is due to the fact that in some contexts the vowels *i* and *u* play a complementary role, the former occurring only between certain kinds of consonants and the latter only between certain other kinds (see 2.6). Alternants of this sort will be shown separated by a slant line: *FiMaL/FuMaL*.

As a summary of the foregoing facts, the complete set of alternants of the pattern *FiMaL* is shown below:

Root-type

Triliteral	Pattern alternants
Sound	*FiMaL/FuMaL, FaMaL*
Double	*FaDD*
Weak-middle	*FaaL*
Weak-last	*FiMa/FuMa*

4.1.2 Solid stems

Solid stems are those which cannot be analyzed as containing a root and a pattern; they are relatively few in number. Some can have prefixes or suffixes added to them, and are then subject to the kind of stem variation described in 4.1.3 below, but other than that they are all invariable sequences of consonants and vowels. Most solid stems are to be found among the particles, such as pronouns, prepositions, and conjunctions (though not all particles are solid stems), and among words borrowed from other languages.[1] Some examples:

ʔiẓna	'we'	*ʔiiraan*	'Iran'
bass	'only'	*ʔuuteel*	'hotel'
loo	'if'	*raadyo*	'radio'
haaδa	'this'	*ṗaaysikil*	'bicycle'

4.1.3 Stem alternants

A given stem, regardless of whether it is simple or complex, solid or composed of a root and a pattern, may have slightly different forms in different contexts; these varying forms are stem alternants. The occurrence of one alternant or another generally depends on whether the stem in question occurs as an independent word or with an affix, and, if the latter, what kind of affix. Variation in the forms of stems is of considerable importance in Iraqi morphology and will be described for individual cases in subsequent chapters. This section deals with the major types.

Some stem variation is due to overall phonological considerations which apply throughout the language:

A. Variation involving stress

In most cases, the position of stress in an Iraqi word is automatically determined by the general consonant-vowel shape of the word as a whole regardless of its stem-affix structure (see automatic stress formula, 3.1). Thus, in different

---

[1] It is important to note here that numbers of words originally borrowed from non-Arabic languages are not solid stems, but have been adapted to the root-and-pattern system. A typical example is the borrowed word *filim* 'film, movie', which happens to fit a very common Iraqi pattern. The root *flm* recurs with the plural pattern *ʔaFMaaL*, in *ʔaflaam* 'films'. Other examples are *ḇanḡ* 'bank' and *ḇunuuḡ* 'banks'; *biḻaf* 'he bluffed' and *yiḇḻif* 'he bluffs'; and *šuuṯ* 'a kick, a shot' (as in soccer) and *šaw̄waṯ* 'he kicked'. Foreign words are used as Iraqi verbs *only* if they can be adapted to the root-and-pattern system.

words containing the same stem, stress may fall on different syllables of the stem or on an affix, for example (stems underlined):

yúᶜruf	'he knows'	*muᶜállim*	'teacher'
yuᶜrúfna	'he knows us'	*muᶜallímhum*	'their teacher'
		muᶜallimíin	'teachers'

This kind of variation is automatic and will not be noted in detail hereafter.

B. Variation involving a double consonant

A double consonant can occur in Iraqi - that is, a consonant can be pronounced double - only when a vowel immediately follows; when a consonant, or nothing, follows, it automatically becomes single (see 2.2). Thus, many stems have one alternant containing a double consonant sound and another containing a single consonant sound, depending on what follows. Some examples (stems underlined):

Double sound		Single sound[1]	
saddat	'she closed'	*sadd*	'he closed'
sadd il-baab	'he closed the door'	*sadd ᶜeena*	'he closed his eye(s)'
dabbur	'arrange M'	*dabbri*	'arrange F'
ᶜammi	'my uncle'	*ᶜammna*	'our uncle'
xaaṣṣa	'special F'	*xaaṣṣ*	'special M'

This kind of variation too is automatic and will not generally be noted hereafter.

C. Variation involving assimilation

When two consonants come together in a word, one may assimilate to the other, that is, become more like it in some respect (see 2.5). Thus, a stem may have one alternant in which there is no assimilation, and another in which one of the consonants is assimilated either to a consonant in an affix or (through loss or shift of a stem vowel; see 4.1.3.1 below) to another consonant in the stem. Some examples (stems underlined):

A voiced consonant may become voiceless before a voiceless consonant:

ḥisadna	*ḥisatti*
'we envied'	'you F envied'

[1] In this book the convention is followed of spelling such stems with a double *letter* not only when they contain a double sound, as in the left-hand list, but also when they contain a single sound, as in the right-hand list. In the latter case, single-consonant pronunciation is in any event automatic; and double-letter spelling is useful in showing that the stem in question contains a potentially doubled consonant (i.e., when a vowel follows).

A voiceless consonant may become voiced before a voiced consonant:

ẕisadna	*ẕizdat*
'we envied'	'she envied'

An *l* may become *n* before *n*:

ʔakalti	*ʔakanna*
'you F ate'	'we ate'

Variation due to assimilation will not generally be noted hereafter. Moreover, when the consonant affected by assimilation happens to be a root consonant, as it is in the examples above, the assimilation will not be indicated by the spelling; thus the three forms on the right above will be written *ẕisadti*, *ẕisdat* and *ʔakalna*.

D. Variation involving *ʔ*

The consonant sound *ʔ* at the beginning of a form is frequently dropped when anything immediately precedes. Thus, some stems have alternants which differ by the presence or absence of an initial *ʔ*. Examples (stems underlined):

ʔiidi	*b-iidi*
'my hand'	'in my hand'
ʔaxuuya	*w-axuuya*
'my brother'	'and my brother'
ʔukul	*d-ukul*
'eat M'	'eat M'
ʔariid	*ma-ariid*
'I want'	'I don't want'

Variation of this sort will not be noted hereafter.

The stem variation described in the next two subsections differs in two respects from the kind just illustrated: (1) It may be partially restricted by phonological considerations (see 4.1.3.1 A) but is not entirely determined by them; (2) It involves the latter part of stems and thus generally depends on the presence or absence of suffixes specifically. In the discussion of this kind of variation, here and in subsequent chapters, the independent form of the stem -- that is, the alternant which occurs without a suffix -- is taken as the basic alternant, and the others are described in terms of variation in that form.

4.1.3.1 Variation involving a stem vowel

The independent form of some stems ends in a single consonant preceded by a short vowel; the latter is a stem vowel, for example the second *a* in *waƐad* 'promise' and *txarraj* 'he graduated', the *i* in *daris* 'lesson' and *ybaddil* 'he changes', and the (second) *u* in *gaḷub* 'heart' and *yuεruf* 'he knows'. With a suffix beginning with a consonant, the form of such stems generally remains unchanged:

waεad	'promise'	*waεadna*	'our promise'
txarraj	'he graduated'	*txarrajna*	'we graduated'
gaḷub	'heart'	*gaḷubha*	'her heart'

With a suffix beginning with a vowel, however, the stem may occur in a form without the stem vowel (loss), or with a different stem vowel (change), or with a vowel in a different position (shift). These three types of variation from the independent form are described below.

A. Loss

Two facts about Iraqi phonology, both with only few exceptions (see 2.3), are central to a discussion of stem vowel loss: (1) Iraqi words do not end in two or more (different) consonants; and (2) Iraqi words do not contain clusters of three or more consonants. Thus, in general, a stem vowel is dropped only if its absence would not result in a contravention of one of these statements. Specifically, the stem vowel is usually present in the independent form of a stem, since without it the word would end in two or more consonants; and it is also usually present when the stem is followed by a suffix beginning with a consonant, since without it the word would contain three or more consonants. When the stem is followed by a suffix beginning with a vowel, the stem vowel may be dropped, but this depends in turn on what precedes it. If the stem vowel is preceded by two (different) consonants, it is not dropped, since without it the word would contain a cluster of three consonants:

daftar	'notebook'	*daftareen*	'two notebooks'

If the stem vowel is preceded by a double consonant and followed by the same consonant, it is not dropped. (This is not, as in the case above, because without it the word would contain a cluster of three consonants -- the double consonant would become single before another consonant; see 4.1.3 B above --; it is simply a fact of the language):

yḥaddid	'he limits'	*yḥaddiduun*	'they limit'

If, however, the stem vowel is preceded by a single consonant, or preceded by a double consonant and followed by a different consonant, it can be dropped, since the result is a cluster of no more than two consonants (in the latter case the double consonant becomes single before another consonant; see 4.1.3 B above):

daris	'lesson'	*darseen*	'two lessons'
ybaddil	'he changes'	*ybaddluun*	'they change'

These two examples illustrate the phonological circumstances in which a stem vowel *can* be dropped, but even in such circumstances it is not always true that the stem vowel *is* dropped; the facts must be learned for each case. Other examples:

šaεar	'hair'	*šaεrak*	'your M hair'
waεad	'promise'	*waεdak*	'your M promise'
ʔisim	'name'	*ʔisma*	'his name'
gaḷub	'heart'	*gaḷbič*	'your F heart'
ʒaaδir	'ready M'	*ʒaaδra*	'ready F'
ykassir	'he breaks'	*ykassruun*	'they break'
naδ̣δ̣uf	'clean M'[1]	*naδ̣δ̣fi*	'clean F'[1]

B. Change

A stem vowel *a*, most commonly when preceded by two consonants or a double consonant, may be changed to *i* or *u*, depending on the environment (see 2.6):

staεmal	'he used'	*staεmilaw*	'they used'
xarmaš	'he scratched'	*xarmušat*	'she scratched'
jaddad	'he renewed'	*jaddidaw*	'they renewed'
mʔaθθaθ	'furnished M'	*mʔaθθiθa*	'furnished F'
baddal	'he changed'	*baddilaw*	'they changed'
naδ̣δ̣af	'he cleaned'	*naδ̣δ̣ufat*	'she cleaned'

When preceded by two consonants, as in the first two examples above, the stem vowel *a* may in some cases undergo shift (see C below) instead of change. When preceded by a double consonant and followed by a different consonant, as in the last two examples above, the stem vowel is more commonly dropped (see A above) than changed.

C. Shift

A stem vowel preceded by two consonants may be shifted; that is, when the independent form ends in a sequence *–CCvC*, the stem vowel is dropped from its position after the next-to-last consonant and a vowel is inserted before the next-to-last consonant, resulting in a new sequence *–CvCC–*. The vowel in the original (unshifted) sequence may be *a*, *i*, or *u*, but the vowel in the new sequence is either *i* or *u*, depending on the environment. (The term "shift" is a convenient way of referring to this whole process and is not meant to imply that the stem vowel as such moves from one position to another.) Shift occurs most commonly in imperfect and imperative forms of Class I (or IV) verbs, and in suffixing stems of

[1] Imperatives.

feminine nouns ending in –*a*; occasionally in some perfect and imperfect forms of Class X and quadriliteral verbs. Some examples:

yilbas	'he wears'	*yilibsuun*	'they wear'
yiktib	'he writes'	*yikitbuun*	'they write'
yišrab	'he drinks'	*yišurbuun*	'they drink'
yuεruf	'he knows'	*yuεurfuun*	'they know'
(*sitra*	'jacket')		
sitratha	'her jacket'	*sitirta*	'his jacket'
(*ğurfa*	'room')		
ğurfatha	'her room'	*ğurufta*	'his room'
yxarmuš	'he scratches'	*yxarumšuun*	'they scratch'

4.1.3.2 Variation involving a final vowel

If the independent form of a stem ends in a short vowel, it is usually changed in some way when any suffix is added. The major types of change are as follows.

A. Loss

If the suffix begins with a vowel, the final short vowel of the stem may be dropped:

qira	'he read'	*qirat*	'she read'
yiji	'he comes'	*yijuun*	'they come'
muẓaami	'lawyer'	*muẓaamiin*	'lawyers'
sayyaara	'car'	*sayyaaraat*	'cars'

B. Change involving a semivowel

If the suffix begins with a vowel, the final short vowel of the stem may be dropped and replaced by one of the semivowels *y* and *w*, or have a single or a double semivowel added to it:

raʔi	'opinion'	*raʔyak*	'your opinion'
ẓilu	'sweet M'	*ẓilwa*	'sweet F'
rasmi	'official M'	*rasmiyya*	'official F'
εadu	'enemy'	*εaduwwa*	'his enemy'

C. Lengthening

If the suffix begins with a consonant, or is a zero pronoun suffix (see 9.1.2.1), the final short vowel of the stem may be changed to the corresponding long vowel (lengthened):

qira	'he read'	*qiraaha*	'he read it F'
		qiraa	'he read it M'
ʔanṭi	'I give'	*ʔanṭiik*	'I give (to) you M'
		ʔanṭii	'I give (to) him'
jiibu	'bring P'	*jiibuuhum*	'bring P them'
		jiibuu	'bring P him'

D. Change involving *t*

Most feminine (singular) nouns and participles, and some plural nouns, have independent stem forms ending in *a*. With a suffix beginning with a consonant, such stems have a form consisting of the independent form plus an added *t*:

sayyaara	'car'	*sayyaarathum*	'their car'
ġurfa	'room'	*ġurfathum*	'their room'

With a suffix beginning with a vowel[1], the stem also has a form with *t*, but the preceding *a*, which is now a stem vowel, is subject to loss or shift (see 4.1.3.1):

sayyaarathum	'their car'	*sayyaarti*	'my car'
ġurfathum	'their room'	*ġurufta*	'his room'

4.2 AFFIXES

From the point of view of their position with relation to the stem to which they are attached, affixes are three types. Prefixes are those which precede a stem, for example *ʔa-* in the word *ʔašrab* 'I drink'. Infixes are those which occur within a stem, for example *-t-* in *ftikar* 'he thought'. Suffixes are those which follow a stem, for example *-ni* in *šaafni* 'he saw me'. In this book, when a prefix is cited in isolation, it is written with a hyphen after, or before, or both, as in the examples above, as an indication of its position with relation to a stem.

From the point of view of their grammatical function, affixes are also of three main types. Derivational affixes are those which, when added to a stem, form a new (derived) stem. For example the derivational nisba suffix *-i*, together with the noun stem *šaxiṣ* 'person', forms the derived adjective stem *šaxṣi* 'personal'. As in this example, derivational affixes may serve to derive

[1] Not, however, including the plural suffix *-aat* or the nisba suffix *-i*.

one class of stem (e.g. noun, adjective, verb) from another; but they may also serve to derive a new stem of the same class as the underlying stem. For example, the derivational suffix *-či*, together with the noun stem *qundara* 'shoes', forms the derived noun stem *qundarči* 'shoemaker'. Inflectional affixes are those which occur with verb, noun and adjective stems (including derived stems) and indicate inflectional categories such as person, gender, and number, for example the inflectional prefixes *yi-* and *ni-* in *yiktib* 'he writes' and *niktib* 'we write', the inflectional suffixes *-een* and *-iin* in *yoomeen* 'two days' and *muhandisiin* 'engineers', and the inflectional suffix *-a* in *jidiida* 'new (feminine)' and *taεbaana* 'tired (feminine)'. Syntactic affixes are those which, like independent words, function as elements of a sentence or a phrase, such as prepositions, conjunctions, or objects of a verb or preposition. Examples of these are the prepositional prefix *b-* 'in' in *b-beetna* 'in our house', the prefix *w-* 'and' in *ʔaxuuya w-ṣadiiqa* 'my brother and his friend', and the pronoun suffix *-a* 'him' in *šifta* 'I saw him'.

5. VERBS

5.1 DERIVATION

Iraqi verbs are based on either triliteral or quadriliteral roots, and the two groups have different derivational systems.

5.1.1 Triliteral

Triliteral verbs fall into ten derivational classes (also sometimes called "forms" or "measures"), here arranged and numbered according to the system traditionally used in works on Classical Arabic. The verbs of Class I are simple verbs; those of Classes II through X are derived. (The terms "derivation" and "derived" are used here to indicate not historical development but regular relationships of form and meaning between existing words of the same root. In this sense, the more complex of two forms is considered to be derived from the simpler; the latter is termed the underlying form.) Verbs[1] in each of the derivational classes have distinctive patterns, as described below. Within a class, verbs may have differing patterns (pattern alternants) depending upon whether the root of the verb is sound, double, weak-middle, or weak-last, and upon the nature of the consonants involved (see 4.1.1.5).

5.1.1.1 Class I

The distinguishing feature of Class I verbs is a negative one: they lack the characteristics described below for verbs of Classes II to X. Their patterns are thus generally the shortest and simplest of all the verbs. Two Class I verbs have the pattern *FaMaL*: *ʔaxaδ* 'to take' and *ʔakal* 'to eat'. Other Class I verbs with sound roots have the pattern *FiMaL/FuMaL*; a few weak-middle roots also have *FuMaL*. Those with double roots have *FaDD*; most of those with weak-middle roots have *FaaL*; those with weak-last roots have *FiMa/FuMa*.[2]

Sound roots	*FaMaL, FiMaL/FuMaL*	
ʔxδ	*ʔaxaδ*	'to take'
ʔkl	*ʔakal*	'to eat'
ʔml	*ʔimal*	'to hope'
ktb	*kitab*	'to write'
ybs	*yibas*	'to dry' (intr)
ʔmr	*ʔumar*	'to command'
ṭbx	*ṭubax*	'to cook'
wṣl	*wuṣal*	'to arrive'

[1]The term "verb" here and throughout 5.1 refers to the citation form of the verb, which is the third-person masculine singular form of the perfect tense. See 5.2.1.1, footnote.

[2]For the irregular Class I verb *jaa* 'to come', see 5.2.1.2 E.

Weak-middle roots

A very few verbs of this root-type have the pattern *FuMaL*, all with *w* in the M position.

θVl	*θuwal*	'to confuse, rattle'
ṭVl	*ṭuwal*	'to grow tall'
ƐVj	*Ɛuwaj*	'to bend' (tr)

(In some cases the same root also occurs with the pattern *FaaL*, usually with a different but related meaning, for example *ṭaal* 'to be prolonged'.)

Double roots	*FaDD*	
ẓbb	*ẓabb*	'to like'
ġšš	*ġašš*	'to cheat'
wnn	*wann*	'to moan'

Weak-middle roots	*FaaL*	
xVf	*xaaf*	'to be afraid'
ṭVr	*ṭaar*	'to fly'
šVf	*šaaf*	'to see'

Weak-last roots	*FiMa/FuMa*	
bčV	*biča*	'to cry'
qrV	*qira*	'to read'
ẓyV	*ẓiya*	'to revive' (tr)
bqV	*buqa*	'to stay'
wƐV	*wuƐa*	'to become aware'
čwV	*čuwa*	'to burn' (tr)

Class I contains both transitive and intransitive verbs, of widely varying kinds of meanings. The class as such has no particular meaning.

5.1.1.2 Class II

Class II verbs are characterized by a double middle radical. Those with sound, double, and weak-middle roots have the pattern *FaMMaL*; those with weak-last roots, *FaMMa*. In the case of those with weak-middle roots, the doubled consonant in the M position is *w* in some verbs, *y* in others.

Sound roots	*FaMMaL*	
bdl	*baddal*	'to change'
nṣf	*naṣṣaf*	'to clean'
wns	*wannas*	'to amuse'
Double roots		
tmm	*tammam*	'to complete'
qrr	*qarrar*	'to decide'
Weak-middle roots		
xVf	*xawwaf*	'to frighten'
ṣVƐ	*ṣayyaƐ*	'to lose'

Weak-last roots	*FaMMa*	
xlV	*xalla*	'to let'
kfV	*kaffa*	'to be enough'
swV	*sawwa*	'to do'
ẓyV	*ẓayya*	'to greet'

Class II verbs are generally transitive. In fact it is principally the Class II pattern which is used to make transitive verbs from other forms, and the process is still alive and productive: newly coined transitive verbs, if they fit into the triliteral scheme, are almost always in this pattern. Class II verbs are derived from Class I verbs, and from nouns and adjectives of various patterns. In the case of weak-middle roots it is possible to predict to some extent whether *w* or *y* will occur in the M position of the Class II verb (or of the Class III verb; see 5.1.1.3 below). If the underlying form has the pattern *FooL* or *FuuL*, the Class II verb usually has *w*:

ṣooṭ	'voice, vote'	*ṣawwaṭ*	'to vote'
suur	'fence'	*sawwar*	'to fence in'

If *FeeL* or *FiiL* , usually *y* :

ṣeef	'summer'	*ṣayyaf*	'to spend the summer'
ṭiin	'mud'	*ṭayyan*	'to put mud on'

If the underlying form has the pattern *FaaL* it provides no clue in itself, but its plural form if it is a noun or its imperfect form if it is a verb may do so:

baab (*ʔabwaab*	'section' 'sections')	*bawwab*	'to classify'
šaaf (*yšuuf*	'to see' 'he sees')	*šawwaf*	'to show'
ḍaaɛ (*yḍiiɛ*	'to get lost' 'he gets lost')	*ḍayyaɛ*	'to lose'

From Class I verbs

When derived from a Class I verb, a Class II verb is usually transitive, with the general meaning 'to cause (someone or something) to perform the action or undergo the development indicated by the Class I verb'. The underlying Class I verb may be intransitive or transitive; if the latter, the Class II verb may be doubly transitive (i.e., capable of having two objects, for example *darrasni ʔingliizi* 'he taught me English').

Class I		Class II	
tiɛab	'to get tired'	*taɛɛab*	'to tire' (tr)
rijaɛ	'to return' (intr)	*rajjaɛ*	'to return' (tr)
tamm	'to be complete'	*tammam*	'to complete'
xaaf	'to be afraid'	*xawwaf*	'to frighten'
biča	'to cry'	*bačča*	'to make (s-o) cry'
diras	'to study'	*darras*	'to teach'
ɛiraf	'to know'	*ɛarraf*	'to make acquainted, introduce'
libas	'to put on'	*labbas*	'to dress' (tr)

The Class II verb derived from *ʔakal* 'to eat' is usually *wakkal* 'to feed', though the regular *ʔakkal* is also in use.

Some Class II verbs have the general meaning 'to do in an intensified or repetitive way the action indicated by the Class I verb'; some of these are intransitive:

ẓufar	'to dig'	*ẓaffar*	'to dig here and there'
ṭufar	'to jump'	*ṭaffar*	'to jump around'
kisar	'to break'	*kassar*	'to smash'
nigab	'to bore a hole'	*naggab*	'to bore many holes'

From nouns

Although Class II verbs are derived from a number of nouns, there is no one particular relationship of meaning between the two. Some examples:

šamis	'sun'	*šammas*	'to sun'
loon	'color'	*lawwan*	'to color'
xeema	'tent'	*xayyam*	'to set up tents, camp'
ġeem	'clouds'	*ġayyam*	'to become cloudy'
ṣeef	'summer'	*ṣayyaf*	'to spend the summer'
hawa	'air'	*hawwa*	'to air'

From the noun *ʔisim* 'name' is derived, somewhat irregularly, the common Class II verb *samma* 'to name, call'.

From adjectives

Class II verbs derived from adjectives generally have the meaning 'to cause (something) to have the quality indicated by the adjective'.

mariiḍ	'sick'	*marraḍ*	'to make sick'
ṣaẓiiẓ	'correct'	*ṣaẓẓaẓ*	'to correct'
ʔabyaḍ	'white'	*bayyaḍ*	'to make white, bleach'

5.1.1.3 Class III

Class III verbs are characterized by a long vowel *aa* between the first and second radicals. Those with sound, double, and weak-middle roots have the pattern *FaaMaL*; those with weak-last roots, *FaaMa*. In the case of those with weak-middle roots, the consonant in the M position is *w* in some verbs, *y* in others.

Sound roots	FaaMaL	
sʕd	*saaʕad*	'to help'
qrn	*qaaran*	'to compare'
wjh	*waajah*	'to go see, talk with'

Double roots

ʒjj	*ʒaajaj*	'to argue with'

Weak-middle roots

ʒVl	*ʒaawal*	'to attempt'
dVn	*daayan*	'to lend to'

Weak-last roots — *FaaMa*

drV	*daara*	'to take care of'
rwV	*raawa*	'to show to'

Class III contains both transitive and intransitive verbs, but mostly the former. They are derived mainly from Class I verbs. (See 5.1.1.2 above for predictability of *w* or *y* in weak-middle roots.) In some cases a Class III verb with a direct object is equivalent or related in meaning to the corresponding Class I verb with a preposition plus object, for example Class I *biʒaθ il-mawʂuuƐ wiyyaahum* 'he discussed the matter with them' and Class III *baaʒaθhum (bil-mawʂuuƐ)* 'he held a discussion with them (on the matter)'. Two other examples:

Class I		Class III	
ṭilab (šii) min	'to request (s-th) from'	*ṭaalab*	'to demand of, claim from'
Ɛimal (šii) b-	'to do (s-th) to'	*Ɛaamal*	'to treat' (e.g., well, badly)

Aside from this association Class III has no particular meaning as a class.

5.1.1.4 Class IV

Class IV verbs are characterized by a prefix *ʔa-*. (This prefix occurs only in the perfect tense, however; in the imperfect tense the forms of Class IV verbs are identical with those of Class I verbs.) Those with sound roots have the pattern *ʔaFMaL* ; double roots, *ʔaFaDD*; weak-middle roots, *ʔaFaaL*; and weak-last roots *ʔaFMa* .

Sound roots — *ʔaFMaL*

Ɛln	*ʔaƐlan*	'to announce'
wdƐ	*ʔawdaƐ*	'to leave for safekeeping'

Double roots	*ʔaFaDD*	
ṣrr	*ʔaṣarr (ɛala)*	'to insist (on)'

Weak-middle roots	*ʔaFaaL*	
δVɛ	*ʔaδaaɛ*	'to broadcast'
šVr	*ʔašaar*	'to refer'

Weak-last roots	*ʔaFMa*	
lġV	*ʔalġa*	'to cancel'
lqV	*ʔalqa*	'to deliver' (speech)

Class IV verb forms occur relatively rarely in Iraqi, for two reasons. The first is that if a Class IV verb is used at all, it has distinctively Class IV forms only in the perfect, and even in the perfect many speakers tend to use these forms only in the third person, substituting the corresponding Class I forms in the second and first persons. The other reason is that compared to verbs of other classes not many Class IV verbs are used in Iraqi colloquial at all. Some do occur, more commonly in formal speech, but for almost every Class IV verb that might occur there is a verb with the same root of another class, usually I, II, or III, which is more commonly used instead. Class IV verbs are almost all transitive; other than this they have no particular element of meaning in common. A few examples follow, with substitutable verbs of other classes shown in parentheses:

ʔazɛaj (*ziɛaj*)	'to bother, annoy'
ʔarbak (*rubak*)	'to confuse, rattle'
ʔawqaf (*waqqaf*)	'to arrest'
ʔatamm (*tammam*)	'to complete' (tr)
ʔadaar (*daar*)	'to direct'
ʔazaal (*zaal*)	'to remove, erase'
ʔafna (*fina*)	'to annihilate'

5.1.1.5 Class V

Class V verbs are characterized by a prefixed *t–* and a doubled middle radical. Thus, with the addition of the prefix, they have the same patterns as Class II verbs. Those with sound, double, and weak-middle roots have the pattern *tFaMMaL*; those with weak-last roots, *tFaMMa*. In the case of those with weak-middle roots, the doubled consonant in the *M* position is *w* in some verbs, *y* in others. The *t* of the prefix assimilates to certain following consonants as follows:

A. Before *d* and *j* it assimilates as to voice, becoming *d*:

ddaxxal	'to interfere'
djannab	'to avoid'

B. Before *ṭ* it assimilates as to emphasis, becoming *ṭ*:

ṭṭallab	'to be required'

C. Before *θ*, *δ*, and *δ̣* it assimilates completely, becoming respectively *θ*, *δ*, and *δ̣*:

θθabbat	'to be made firm or permanent'
δδakkar	'to remember'
δ̣δ̣amman	'to include'

D. Before *z* and *ṣ* it may assimilate completely, becoming *z* and *ṣ*, or only as to voice and emphasis respectively, becoming *d* and *ṭ*. Before *s* and *š* it may assimilate completely, becoming *s* and *š*, or not at all.[1]

zzawwaj / *dzawwaj*	'to marry'
ṣṣawwar / *ṭṣawwar*	'to suppose, imagine'
ssallam / *tsallam*	'to be delivered'
ššammas / *tšammas*	'to sunbathe'

Sound roots	*tFaMMaL*	
ζsn	*tζassan*	'to improve' (intr)
ṣrf	*ṭṣarraf*	'to behave'

[1] The completely assimilated forms are common in normal-speed speech, especially when not at the beginning of an utterance. In this book, however, the less assimilated forms will be given in lists and paradigms, both forms as appropriate elsewhere.

wns	*twannas*	'to enjoy oneself'
ytm	*tyattam*	'to be orphaned'
Double roots		
ʒdd	*tʒaddad*	'to be fixed, limited'
mdd	*tmaddad*	'to stretch out'
Weak-middle roots		
ʒVl	*tʒawwal*	'to move' (intr)
ƐVn	*tƐayyan*	'to be appointed'
Weak-last roots	*tFaMMa*	
ġdV	*tġadda*	'to have lunch'
rqV	*traqqa*	'to advance, make progress'
swV	*tsawwa*	'to be done'
fyV	*tfayya*	'to get in the shade'

Class V verbs are most commonly derived from Class II verbs and stand in relation to these as medio-passive to transitive or active. (The term medio-passive is used to include both the usual meaning of passive as applied to English: the subject is acted upon by someone or something else; and a reflexive or "middle" meaning: the subject acts upon himself or undergoes a development without an outside agency.) Examples:

Class II		Class V	
baddal	'to change, exchange'	*tbaddal*	'to be exchanged'
ʒassan	'to improve' (tr)	*tʒassan*	'to improve' (intr)
marraṣ̌	'to make sick'	*tmarraṣ̌*	'to become sick'
wannas	'to amuse'	*twannas*	'to enjoy oneself'
samma	'to name, call'	*tsamma*	'to be called'
ġadda	'to give lunch to'	*tġadda*	'to have lunch'

Some may be used in a passive-potential sense (see 5.1.1.7 below), for example *haaδa ma-yitbaddal* 'This can't be changed'.

A few are transitive; when derived from transitive Class II verbs they may differ in meaning from the latter in various ways:

ʒammal	'to place a load on'	*tʒammal*	'to endure, hear'
zawwaj	'to give in marriage'	*tzawwaj*	'to take as wife; to be married'

5.1.1.6 Class VI

Class VI verbs are characterized by a prefixed *t-* and a long vowel *aa* between the first and second radicals. Thus, with the addition of the prefix, they have the same patterns as Class III verbs. Those with sound, double, and weak-middle roots have the pattern *tFaaMaL*; those with weak-last roots, *tFaaMa*. In the case of those with weak middle roots, the consonant in the *M* position is *w* in some verbs, *y* in others. The *t* of the prefix assimilates to certain following consonants in the same ways as those described for the Class V *t-* prefix in 5.1.1.5 above.

Sound roots	*tFaaMaL*	
xbr	*txaabar*	'to talk on the telephone'
rhn	*traahan*	'to bet'
wƐd	*twaaƐad*	'to make an appointment'
Double roots		
ʒbb	*tʒaabab*	'to become good friends'
Weak-middle roots		
ƐVn	*tƐaawan*	'to cooperate'
dVn	*ddaayan*	'to borrow'
Weak-last roots	*tFaaMa*	
bhV	*tbaaha*	'to brag'
rṣ̌V	*traaṣ̌a*	'to reach an agreement'
swV	*tsaawa*	'to become equal'

Class VI verbs are most commonly derived from Class III verbs. Where the latter usually are transitive and indicate an action directed by one person toward another, for example *xaabə́ra* 'he telephoned him', Class VI verbs are intransitive and imply mutual action. If a Class VI verb has a singular subject it is frequently followed by a preposition, usually *wiyya* 'with', and the pronoun suffix or noun object indicating the other person, for example *txaabar wiyyaa* 'he talked on the phone with him'. If it has a plural subject the mutuality of the action is implicit, for example *txaabraw* 'they talked on the phone (with each other)'. Some other examples:

Class III		Class VI	
ʒaasab	'to call to account'	*tʒaasab*	'to settle accounts'
daanaš	'to ask advice from'	*ddaanaš*	'to talk things over'
ṣaafaʒ	'to shake hands with'	*tṣaafaʒ*	'to shake hands'

Some Class VI verbs bear a medio-passive relationship to the corresponding Class III verbs, like that of Class V to Class II:

jaawab	'to answer'	*djaawab*	'to be answered'
Ɛaaqab	'to punish'	*tƐaaqab*	'to be punished'
qaaran	'to compare'	*tqaaran*	'to be compared'

Some may be used in a passive-potential sense (see 5.1.1.7 below), for example *has-suʔaal ma-yidjaawab.* 'This question cannot be answered'.

A few are transitive, for example *tʒaaša* 'to avoid' and *ddaayan* 'to borrow'.

5.1.1.7 Class VII

Class VII verbs are characterized by a prefixed *n-*. They have, with the addition of this prefix, the same patterns as Class I verbs except for *FaMaL*. Those with sound roots have the pattern *nFiMaL/nFuMaL*; a few with weak-middle roots also have *nFuMaL*. Those with double roots have *nFaDD*; most of those with weak-middle roots have *nFaaL*; and those with weak-last roots have *nFiMa/nFuMa*.

Sound roots	*nFiMaL/nFuMaL*	
drs	*ndiras*	'to be studied'
jbr	*njubar*	'to be forced'
wzn	*nwuzan*	'to be weighed'
Weak-middle roots[1]		
θVl	*nθuwal*	'to be rattled, confused'
ƐVj	*nƐuwaj*	'to be bent'
Double roots	*nFaDD*	
ʒll	*nʒall*	'to be solved'
ġšš	*nġašš*	'to be cheated'

[1] See also 5.1.1.1.

Weak-middle roots	*nFaaL*	
xVn	*nxaan*	'to be deceived'
šVl	*nšaal*	'to be picked up'
Weak-last roots	*nFiMa/nFuMa*	
lgV	*nliga*	'to be found'
nsV	*nnisa*	'to be forgotten'
ṭwV	*nṭuwa*	'to be folded'

Class VII verbs are usually derived from transitive Class I verbs, of which they are the passive equivalents. These are extremely common.

Class I		Class VII	
diras	'to study'	*ndiras*	'to be studied'
kital	'to kill'	*nkital*	'to be killed'
ʒall	'to solve'	*nʒall*	'to be solved'
dazz	'to send'	*ndazz*	'to be sent'
šaal	'to carry'	*nšaal*	'to be carried'
nisa	'to forget'	*nnisa*	'to be forgotten'

(The Class VII verb derived from *ʔaxaδ* 'to take' is either *nʔixaδ* or *nnixaδ* 'to be taken'; that derived from *ʔakal* 'to eat' is *nʔikal*, *nnikal*, *nwukal*, or *nkaal* 'to be eaten'.)

A second meaning associated with Class VII verbs is that of passive-potential; that is, they may express the idea that the subject is *capable* of being or *ought* to be acted upon in a certain way. In this sense they occur most commonly in the negative. Some examples:

š-šibbaak ma-yinfakk.	'The window can't be opened.'
hal-ašyaaʔ ma-tingaal.	'These things cannot (or must not) be said.'

Class VII verbs used in this sense can be derived from intransitive Class I verbs. In that case, however, they are impersonal verbs used only in the third-person masculine form. For example, from *naam* 'to sleep' is derived *nnaam*:

hal-beet ma-yinnaam bii.	'This house is impossible to sleep in; One cannot (or may not) sleep in this house.'
hal-ġurfa ma-yinnaam biiha.	'This room (etc.)'

A very few Class VII verbs are transitive, for example *ndall* 'to know (the location of)'.

5.1.1.8 Class VIII

Class VIII verbs are characterized by an infixed *-t-* after the first radical. They have, with the addition of this infix, the same patterns as Class I verbs except for *FaMaL*. Those with sound roots have the pattern *FtiMaL/FtuMaL*; double roots, *FtaDD*; weak-middle roots, *FtaaL*; and weak-last roots, *FtiMa/FtuMa*. The *t* of the infix assimilates to certain *preceding* consonants as follows:

A. After one of the emphatics *ṭ*, *ṣ*, and *δ̣*, it assimilates as to emphasis, becoming *ṭ*:

ṭṭilaɛ ɛala	'to observe, have a look at'
ṣṭidam	'to collide'
δ̣ṭirab	'to be uneasy, nervous'

B. After *d* and *z* it assimilates to voice, becoming *d*:

ddiɛa	'to claim'
zdiḥam	'to be crowded'

C. In one verb in which the first radical is *δ*, it assimilates as to voice, becoming *d*, and the radical also becomes *d*. (No other examples of Class VIII verbs with *δ* as the first radical, and none with *θ* as the first radical, have been observed.)

ddixar	'to save, conserve'

In verbs in which the first radical is *w* or (rare) *y*, and in one verb in which the first radical is *ʔ*, these assimilate to the following *t* of the infix, becoming *t*:

wjh	*ttijah (l-)*	'to head (for)'
yqn	*ttiqan*	'to master, know well'
ʔxδ	*ttixaδ*	'to take, adopt' (measures)

In other verbs with initial *ʔ* no assimilation occurs.

Sound roots	*FtiMaL/FtuMaL*	
xlf	*xtilaf*	'to differ'
ɛqd	*ɛtiqad*	'to think, believe'
ṣbr	*ṣṭubar*	'to be patient, wait'
wḥd	*ttiḥad*	'to be united'

Double roots	*FtaDD*	
ḍrr	*ḍṭarr*	'to have to, be compelled to'
hmm	*htamm*	'to become interested'
Weak-middle roots	*FtaaL*	
ʒVj	*ʒtaaj*	'to need'
rVʒ	*rtaaʒ*	'to rest, take it easy'
Weak-last roots	*FtiMa/FtuMa*	
škV	*štika*	'to complain'
šrV	*štira*	'to buy'
ʒwV	*ʒtuwa ɛala*	'to contain'
ʒyV	*ʒtiya*	'to revive' (intr)

Class VIII includes verbs in both the transitive and intransitive categories, and has as a class no particular meaning of its own.

5.1.1.9 Class IX

Class IX verbs are characterized by a doubled last radical. Only verbs of sound and weak-middle roots occur in this class; all have the pattern *FMaLL*. In the case of those with weak-middle roots, the consonant in the *M* position is *w* in some verbs, *y* in others.

Sound roots	*FMaLL*	
xḍr	*xḍarr*	'to turn green'
ṭrš	*ṭrašš*	'to grow deaf'
Weak-middle roots		
sVd	*swadd*	'to turn black'
bVḍ	*byaḍḍ*	'to turn white'

Class IX verbs are derived from adjectives of color and defect (7.2.5), and have the meaning 'to have or acquire a certain color or defect'.

ʔaʒmar	'red'	*ʒmarr*	'to turn red, blush'
ʔaxḍar	'green'	*xḍarr*	'to turn green'
ʔaswad	'black'	*swadd*	'to turn black'

ʔabyaḍ	'white'	*byaḍḍ*	'to turn white'
ʔaṭraš	'deaf'	*ṭrašš*	'to grow deaf'
ʔaṣlaɛ	'bald'	*ṣlaɛɛ*	'to grow bald'

5.1.1.10 Class X

Class X verbs are characterized by a prefixed *sta-* or *sti-*. The prefix is *sta-* when followed by two consonants; when followed by a single consonant it is more commonly *sta-* in some verbs and *sti-* in others, but there is considerable variation. If the following consonant is an emphatic, the consonants *st* of the prefix usually assimilate, becoming *ṣṭ*. Verbs with sound roots have the pattern *staFMaL*, with some minor exceptions and variations noted below; a few with weak-middle roots also have *staFMaL*. Those with double roots have *staFaDD* or *stiFaDD*; most of those with weak-middle roots have *staFaaL* or *stiFaaL*; and those with weak-last roots have *staFMa*, again with some minor variations.

Sound roots	*staFMaL*	
ʔnf	*staʔnaf*	'to appeal' (a case)
ʒsn	*staʒsan*	'to approve'
ɛml	*staɛmal*	'to use'
wrd	*stawrad*	'to import'
yqḍ	*stayqaḍ*	'to wake up, get up'

In some verbs like the last two, which have *w* or *y* as the initial radical, the sequences *aw* and *ay* may become *oo* and *ee* respectively, for example *stoorad* and *steeqaḍ*; these are less formal variants of the regular pattern. One common verb with *ʔ* as the initial radical has the irregular pattern *staaMaL*:

ʔhl	*staahal*	'to deserve'

Weak-middle roots

A few verbs of this root-type have the pattern *staFMaL*, with *w* or *y* in the *M* position:

jVb	*stajwab*	'to question, interrogate'
ṭVb	*ṣṭaṭyab*	'to find tasty'

(In some cases the same root also occurs in the pattern *staFaaL* or *stiFaaL*, usually with a different but related meaning, for example *stajaab -l-* 'to respond to, comply with', and *staṭaab -l-* 'to become pleasant for'.)

Double roots	*staFaDD, stiFaDD*	
ʒqq	*staʒaqq*	'to come due'
mrr	*stimarr*	'to continue'

Weak-middle roots	*staFaaL*, *stiFaaL*	
jVr	*stijaar*	'to seek help'
rVẓ	*staraaẓ*	'to rest'
Weak-last roots	*staFMa*	
θnV	*staθna*	'to except, exempt'
ġnV	*staġna* *ɛan*	'to do without'
wfV	*stawfa*	'to get back' (money owed)

In some verbs like the last one, which have *w* as the initial radical, the sequence *aw* may become *oo*, for example *stoofa*; this is a less formal variant of the regular pattern. (None with initial *y* have been observed.) There is a doubly weak Class X verb with the irregular pattern *stiFa*:

ẓVV	*stiẓa*	'to be shy, ashamed'

Class X includes both transitive and intransitive verbs. As a class it has no one particular meaning, but within it are a few groups of verbs which show regular correspondences of meaning with other verbs, with nouns, or with adjectives. The two principal ones are illustrated below.

(1) 'To say that (something) has (a certain quality)'. Here the association is primarily with adjectives. In some cases there is the implication that something has too much of the quality.

_____[1]	(good)	*staẓsan*	'to approve'
ṣaɛub	'difficult'	*ṣtaṣɛab*	'to find (something) difficult'
ṭuwiil	'long'	*ṣtaṭwal*	'to think that (something) is (too) long'
ṭayyib	'tasty'	*ṣtaṭyab*	'to find tasty'

(2) 'To ask for or try to obtain'. Here the association is primarily with another verb or a noun:

xidam	'to serve'	*staxdam*	'to employ, make use of'
fiham	'to understand'	*stafham*	'to enquire'
nitaj	'to result'	*stantaj*	'to deduce, conclude'
jawaab	'answer'	*stajwab*	'to question, interrogate'

[1]No basic adjective of this root is used; the root appears, however, in *ʔaẓsan* 'better'

5.1.2 Quadriliteral

Quadriliteral verbs fall into three classes. The first comprises the simple quadriliterals; the second, those derived by means of a *t-* prefix; the third, a very small group of the pattern *FSaTaLL.* Within the first two classes, the pattern of verbs may differ according to the root-type.

5.1.2.1 Simple

Simple quadriliteral verbs with sound roots have the pattern *FaSTaL*; so also do a few with weak-second roots. Those with reduplicated roots have the pattern *FaDFaD*; most of those with weak-second roots have *FooTaL* or *FeeTaL*; the few with both weak-second and weak-last roots all have *FooTa*.[1]

Sound roots	*FaSTaL*	
brhn	*barhan*	'to prove'
trjm	*tarjam*	'to translate'
xrmš	*xarmaš*	'to scratch'
ɛnwn	*ɛanwan*	'to address'

Weak-second roots

A very few verbs of this root-type have the pattern *FaSTaL*, with *y* in the *S* position:

ṣVṭr	*ṣayṭar ɛala*	'to control'
hVmn	*hayman ɛala*	'to obtain, have control of'

Reduplicated roots	*FaDFaD*	
dgdg	*dagdag*	'to rap, pound'
rfrf	*rafraf*	'to flutter'
gṣgṣ	*gaṣgaṣ*	'to cut up'

Weak-second roots	*FooTaL*, *FeeTaL*	
ṣVgr	*ṣoogar*	'to insure'
mVls	*moolas*	'to become worn' (threads of screw)
nVšn	*neešan*	'to aim'

[1] Only one simple quadriliteral with only a weak-last root has been noted, *dahda* 'to roll' (tr), and that is a variant form of *dahdar*.

čVwr	*čeewar*	'to beat up'
dVwr	*deewar*	'to turn' (to right or left)
Weak-second and weak-last roots	*FooTa*	
ʔVmV	*ʔooma*	'to motion, gesture'
ʒVmV	*ʒooma*	'to circle, hang around'
ƐVƐV	*ƐooƐa*	'to crow'
lVlV	*loola*	'to sing a lullaby'

Some simple quadriliteral verbs are derived from nouns:

Ɛinwaan	'address'	*Ɛanwan*	'to address'
siiṭaan	'devil'	*šeeṭan*	'to inspire deviltry in'

Some are related in meaning to verbs of triliteral roots with three of the same radicals:

xubaṭ	'to mix, blend'	*xarbaṭ*	'to mix up, mess up'
ṣufar	'to whistle'	*ṣoofar*	'to whistle'
kumaš	'to grab'	*kamkaš*	'to grope around'

Of the reduplicated quadriliterals, many are onomatopoetic:

ṭagṭag	'to crack, rap'
ṭanṭan	'to buzz, hum'
maƐmaƐ	'to bleat'

Many also share the same roots as triliteral double-root verbs and are related to them in meaning. In pairs like the following, the quadriliteral reduplicated-root verb (pattern *FaDFaD*) often means 'to perform repetitively, continuously, or intensively the action indicated by the triliteral double-root verb' (pattern *FaDD*):

dagg	'to knock'	*dagdag*	'to rap, drum'
δabb	'to throw out'	*δabδab*	'to scatter around'
fakk	'to open'	*fakfak*	'to take apart'
gaṣṣ	'to cut'	*gaṣgaṣ*	'to cut up'

5.1.2.2 Derived

Derived quadriliteral verbs are characterized by a prefixed *t–*. Their patterns are the same, with the addition of the prefix, as those of simple quadriliterals, except that no common examples of *tFooTa* have been noted. The *t* of the prefix assimilates to certain following consonants in the same ways as those described for the Class V *t–* prefix in 5.1.1.5 above.

Sound roots	*tFasTaL*	
brhn	*tbarhan*	'to be proved'
trjm	*ttarjam*	'to be translated'
Reduplicated roots	*tFaDFaD*	
gṣgṣ	*tgaṣgaṣ*	'to be cut up'
Weak-second roots	*tFooTaL, tFeeTaL*	
ṣVgr	*ṭṣoogar*	'to be insured'
ẓVmr	*tẓeemar*	'to act like a donkey, stupidly'

Most *t–* prefix quadriliterals are derived from a simple quadriliteral verb. Verbs thus formed are similar to (triliteral) Class V verbs in having the prefix *t–* plus the general pattern *–CaCCaC*. Many also bear the same relationship of meaning to the simple verb from which they are derived as do Class V verbs to the Class I verbs from which they are derived, that of medio-passive to active:

tarjam	'to translate'	*ttarjam*	'to be translated'
ṣoogar	'to insure'	*ṭṣoogar*	'to be insured'

Some are derived directly from nouns; the meaning of these is often 'to be or act like' that noun, often in a derogatory sense:

faylasuuf	'philosopher'	*tfalsaf*	'to speak learnedly or pompously without real knowledge'
zaƐṭuuṭ	'childish person'	*tzaƐṭaṭ*	'to behave childishly'

5.1.2.3 FSaTaLL

These quadriliteral verbs are characterized by a doubled last radical. Only a few are in use; they are:

šmʔz	*šmaʔazz*	'to be disgusted, revolted'
ṭmʔn	*ṭmaʔann*	'to feel reassured'
qšƐr	*qšaƐarr*	'to feel a chill, shudder'

5.1.3 Summary

The following table summarizes the patterns of the verbal system according to root-type and derivational class, and shows the major relationships of meaning among the various classes as follows:

(1) Class IV verbs are rare; Class I (or other) patterns are commonly used instead.

(2) Class II verbs are often the transitive or doubly transitive equivalent of Class I verbs.

(3) Classes in Column (B) are the passive or medio-passive equivalents of those in Column (A): Class VII of Class I (or IV); Class V of Class II; Class VI of Class III; derived (*t-* prefix) quadriliterals of simple.

(4) Class VI verbs also frequently imply mutual action.

(5) Classes in Column (C) are not paired with other classes in an active - passive relationship.

Triliteral	(A)		(B)	(C)	
	I	IV	VII	VIII	X
Sound	*Fa/i/uMaL*	*?aFMaL*	*nFi/uMaL*	*Fti/uMaL*	*staFMaL*
Double	*FaDD*	*?aFaDD*	*nFaDD*	*FtaDD*	*sta/iFaDD*
Weak-middle	*FaaL*	*?aFaaL*	*nFaaL*	*FtaaL*	*sta/iFaaL*
Weak-last	*Fi/uMa*	*?aFMa*	*nFi/uMa*	*Fti/uMa*	*staFMa*
	II		V		
Sound, Double, Weak-middle	*FaMMaL*		*tFaMMaL*		
Weak-last	*FaMMa*		*tFaMMa*		
	III		VI		
Sound, Double, Weak-middle	*FaaMaL*		*tFaaMaL*		
Weak-last	*FaaMa*		*tFaaMa*		
				IX	
Sound, Weak-middle				*FMaLL*	
Quadriliteral	Simple		Derived		
Sound	*FaSTaL*		*tFaSTaL*		
Reduplicated	*FaDFaD*		*tFaDFaD*		
Weak-second	*Foo/eeTaL*		*tFoo/eeTaL*		
Weak-second and -last	*FooTa*				
				FSaTaLL	
Sound				*FSaTaLL*	

5.2 INFLECTION

The inflections of the Iraqi verb indicate distinctions of

TENSE	Perfect Imperfect
MOOD	Indicative Imperative
PERSON	Third Second First
NUMBER	Singular Plural
GENDER	Masculine Feminine

However, not all combinations of these categories occur. The restrictions are: (1) In the perfect tense, there are no imperative forms; (2) in the imperfect tense, there are imperative forms only in the second person; (3) in both tenses, there are distinctively masculine and feminine forms only in the third and second persons singular.[1] Hereafter, therefore, the term "perfect (tense)" will imply "indicative"; the terms "masculine" and "feminine" as applied to verb forms will imply "singular" The following table summarizes the combinations of distinctions[2] which can be indicated by the inflections of a verb. On the left are the abbreviations which will be used hereafter.

<u>Perfect</u>

3 M	Third person masculine
F	" " feminine
P	" " plural
2 M	Second person masculine
F	" " feminine
P	" " plural
1 S	First person singular
P	" " plural

[1] An exception to (3), which applies to some speakers only, will be noted where appropriate.

[2] See also 5.3.1, 5.3.2, 5.3.3 for further distinctions expressed by certain prefixes.

Imperfect

	Indicative	Imperative
3 M	Third person masculine	
F	" " feminine	
P	" " plural	
2 M	Second person masculine	Second person masculine
F	" " feminine	" " feminine
P	" " plural	" " plural
1 S	First person singular	
P	" " plural	

The inflectional forms of a verb which correspond to these combinations of categories can be listed in similar tables, called paradigms. Given below as an example is the complete paradigm of the verb *kitab* 'to write'.

Perfect

3 M	*kitab*	'he wrote'
F	*kitbat*	'she wrote'
P	*kitbaw*	'they wrote'
2 M	*kitábit*	'you M wrote'
F	*kitabti*	'you F wrote'
P	*kitabtu*	'you P wrote'
1 S	*kitábit*	'I wrote'
P	*kitabna*	'we wrote'

Imperfect

	Indicative		Imperative	
3 M	*yiktib*	'he writes'		
F	*tiktib*	'she writes'		
P	*yikitbuun*	'they write'		
2 M	*tiktib*	'you M write'	*ˀiktib*	'write M'
F	*tikitbiin*	'you F write'	*kitbi*	'write F'
P	*tikitbuun*	'you P write'	*kitbu*	'write P'
1 S	*ˀaktib*	'I write'		
P	*niktib*	'we write'		

Note that in the perfect tense the 2 M and 1 S forms are identical, and in the imperfect tense the 3 F and 2 M (indicative) forms are identical. These two facts are true of all verbs.

Every verb form consists of a stem and an inflectional affix. For example, the perfect 3 P form *kitbaw* 'they wrote' consists of stem *kitb-* and inflectional affix *-aw*.

A. Inflectional affixes in verb forms are of three types: (1) suffixes, (2) prefixes, and (3) combinations of prefix and suffix. Affixes of the perfect tense are of the first type; those of the imperfect tense are mostly of the second and third types. Examples (affixes underlined):

(1) *kitabna*	'we wrote'
(2) *niktib*	'we write'
(3) *tikitbuun*	'you P write'

A given affix may have slightly different forms (alternants) when combined with different stems, the differences usually being due to assimilation (2.5) or other phonological considerations (2.3, 2.6). For example:

niktib	'we write'
nšuuf	'we see'

B. Verb stems show a wide variety of different patterns, depending on their derivational class and root-type (5.1), for example (stems underlined):

kitabna	'we wrote'
jarrabna	'we tried'
tεallamna	'we learned'
qtiraẓna	'we suggested'

Most verbs have two main stem forms: (1) a perfect stem, used with the affixes of the perfect tense; and (2) an imperfect stem, used with those of the imperfect tense. For example:

(1) *kitabna*	'we wrote'
(2) *niktib*	'we write'

Each of these, moreover, may have different forms (alternants)[1] when combined with different affixes, for example:

niktib	'we write'
tikitbuun	'you P write'

For the purposes of inflectional description, verb stems are divided into four inflectional types, according to the ending of the perfect-tense 3 M form (the citation form; see 5.2.1.1, footnote). Sound verbs are those which end in a single consonant preceded by the short vowel *a*, for example *kitab* 'to write'; doubled verbs are those which end in a double consonant, for example *dazz* 'to send'; hollow verbs are those which end in a single consonant preceded by the long vowel *aa*, for example *šaaf* 'to see'; and defective verbs are those which end in the short vowel *a*, for example *nisa* 'to forget'. Two points should be noted about this classification: (1) It cuts across the derivational classes described in 5.1. As can be seen from the chart in 5.1.3, verbs of all four inflectional types are found in (derivational) Classes I, IV, VII, VIII, and X; two types (sound and defective) in Classes II, III, V, and VI; one type (doubled) in Class IX; and three types (sound, doubled, and defective) among the quadriliterals. (2) The classification into four inflectional types applies to whole *stems* and should not be confused, despite the partial similarity of

[1] For general comments on stem alternants, see 4.1.3.

terminology, with the classification of *roots* (4.1.1.1). There is, however, some correlation between root-type and inflectional type; this too can be seen from the chart in 5.1.3.

The inflectional system of verbs is described in more detail below. Section 5.2.1 deals with the affixes and stems of the perfect tense; Section 5.2.2 with those of the imperfect.

5.2.1 Perfect tense

5.2.1.1 Inflectional affixes

The inflectional affixes of the perfect tense are all suffixes. Their forms[1] are as follows:

3 M	-∅	'he'
F	*-at*	'she'
P	*-aw*	'they'
2 M	*-(i)t*	'you M'
F	*-ti*	'you F'
P	*-tu*	'you P'
1 S	*-(i)t*	'I'
P	*-na*	'we'

Comments:

A. The 3 M suffix is in fact no suffix at all: in the perfect tense it is the *absence* of a suffix which distinguishes 3 M verb forms from others. Examples from the verb meaning 'to see', perfect stem *šaaf-*:

3 M	*šaaf*	'he saw'
F	*šaaf<u>at</u>*	'she saw'
P	*šaaf<u>aw</u>*	'they saw'

In a case like this, where the absence of something has a positive meaning, it is useful to borrow a mathematical concept and refer to the feature as <u>zero.</u>[2]

[1] Some speakers of Iraqi (though not commonly those in Baghdad) use special third and second person *feminine plural* forms when referring to or addressing two or more females. The perfect-tense suffixes for these forms are: 3FP *-an* 'they FP' and 2 FP *-tan* 'you FP'.

[2] In tables such as the one above, zero is indicated by the symbol ∅; in the representation of actual words it is not indicated at all.

Since its suffix is zero, a 3 M verb form is identical with its own perfect stem. The two are distinguished in this book by the use of a hyphen with stems. For example, the 3 M verb form meaning 'he saw' is written *šaaf;* the perfect stem as such is written *šaaf-*.

The perfect-tense 3 M verb form is the shortest and simplest of all verb forms. For this reason it is used as the <u>citation form</u> of the verb, as the infinitive is used in English, in listing verbs and in referring to a specific verb as opposed to all other verbs. Thus in English it is usual to speak of "the verb <u>to see</u>"; the Iraqi equivalent is "the verb *šaaf*". The actual English meaning of the form *šaaf* is 'he saw'; but when this and other perfect-tense 3 M verb forms are used as citation forms, they are translated by English infinitives: the verb *šaaf* 'to see'.

B. The 2 M and 1 S suffixes are identical in every verb. The form *-t* occurs with stems ending in a vowel (always *ee*):

dazzeet 'you M sent / I sent'

The form *-it* occurs with stems ending in a consonant:

kitábit 'you M wrote / I wrote'

In the latter case, however, when an additional suffix beginning with a vowel is added to the verb form, the vowel of *-it* is dropped:

kitabta 'you M wrote it M / I wrote it M'

Or, if the verb form is immediately followed by another word which begins with a (helping) vowel, the vowel of *-it* is dropped:

kitabt il-maktuub 'you M wrote the letter / I wrote the letter'

C. When one of the suffixes *-(i)t*, *-ti*, or *-tu* follows a stem ending in the emphatic *ṭ*, the *t* of the suffix usually becomes *ṭ* by assimilation (2.5):

rubaṭiṭ 'you M fastened / I fastened'

rubaṭṭa 'you M fastened it M / I fastened it M'

maššaṭṭi 'you F combed'

ṣaffaṭṭu 'you P arranged, put in order'

After a stem ending in one of the emphatics *ṣ*, *ḍ*, *ḷ*, the *t* of the suffix may also become *ṭ* by assimilation, but there is more variation in these cases.

5.2.1.2 Perfect stems

A. Sound verbs

Sound verbs are those which end in a single consonant preceded by the short vowel *a* (the stem vowel), for example *kitab* 'to write'. Before the 3 F and 3 P suffixes *-at* and *-aw*, the stem vowel is either dropped or changed to *i* or *u*, as described below. (See also 4.1.3.1.) Before the suffixes of the second and first persons, the stem remains unchanged except for the position of stress, which falls on the stem vowel throughout. In the case of 2 M and 1 S forms, which have the suffix *-it*, stress in this position constitutes a deviation from the automatic stress formula (3.1, 3.2).

(1) In sound verbs in which the stem vowel is preceded by a single consonant and followed by a different consonant, the stem vowel is dropped before the 3 F and 3 P suffixes *-at* and *-aw*. Before the other suffixes the stem remains unchanged except for stress. In this category are the sound verbs of Classes I, VII,

and VIII; the sound verbs of Classes III and VI except those with a double root; and simple and derived quadriliteral verbs of the *(t)FooTaL* and *(t)FeeTaL* patterns. Examples:

	ʔakal	'to eat'	(Class I)
3 M	*ʔakal*	'he ate'	
F	*ʔaklat*	'she " '	
P	*ʔaklaw*	'they " '	
2 M	*ʔakálit*	'you M ate'	
F	*ʔakalti*	'you F " '	
P	*ʔakaltu*	'you P " '	
1 S	*ʔakálit*	'I ate'	
P	*ʔakalna*	'we " '	
	kitab[1]	'to write'	(Class I)
3 M	*kitab*	'he wrote'	
F	*kitbat*	'she " '	
P	*kitbaw*	'they " '	
2 M	*kitábit*	'you M wrote'	
F	*kitabti*	'you F " '	
P	*kitabtu*	'you P " '	
1 S	*kitábit*	'I wrote'	
P	*kitabna*	'we " '	
	ṭubax[1]	'to cook'	(Class I)
3 M	*ṭubax*	'he cooked'	
F	*ṭubxat*	'she " '	
P	*ṭubxaw*	'they " '	
2 M	*ṭubáxit*	'you M cooked'	
F	*ṭubaxti*	'you F " '	
P	*ṭubaxtu*	'you P " '	
1 S	*ṭubáxit*	'I cooked'	
P	*ṭubaxna*	'we " '	

[1] In second-person and first-person forms of Class I sound verbs which have the pattern *FiMáL–* or *FuMáL–*, the unstressed short *i* or *u* in the first syllable is frequently dropped in normal-speed speech, for example *ktabit*, *ktabti* etc., especially when a preceding word ends in a vowel. In this book the form with the vowel will be used in paradigms, elsewhere either form as appropriate.

	xaabar	'to telephone'	(Class III)
3 M	*xaabar*	'he telephoned'	
F	*xaabrat*	'she " '	
P	*xaabraw*	'they " '	
2 M	*xaabárit*	'you M telephoned'	
F	*xaabarti*	'you F " '	
P	*xaabartu*	'you P " '	
1 S	*xaabárit*	'I telephoned'	
P	*xaabarna*	'we " '	

Other verbs like those illustrated above are:

Class I

ʔaxaδ	'to take'		
tirak	'to leave'	*ʔumar*	'to order'
ʒirag	'to burn'	*buram*	'to twist'
difaƐ	'to pay'	*xubaz*	'to bake'
siʔal	'to ask'	*ṣubaġ*	'to paint'
libas	'to wear'	*Ɛubar*	'to cross'

Class III

ʒaawal	'to try'
daayan	'to lend'
saaƐad	'to help'
Ɛaaraδ̣	'to oppose'

Class VI

ddaayan	'to borrow'
traahan	'to bet'

Class VII

nṭirad	'to be expelled'
nkumaš	'to be caught'

Class VIII

xtilaf	'to differ'
štiġaḷ	'to work'
ɛtiqad	'to think, believe'
ṣṭubar	'to be patient, wait'

Simple quadriliterals

ṣoofar	'to whistle'
deewar	'to turn'

Derived quadriliterals

tṣoogar	'to be insured'
tẓeewan	'to be boorish'

In a few verbs ending in a sequence *-iCaC* (thus only Classes I, VII, and VIII), when the stem vowel is dropped before the 3 F and 3 P suffixes *-at* and *-aw*, the short vowel *i* of the preceding syllable may be changed to *u*. This kind of change most commonly comes about when the last consonant of the stem is a labial which, when the stem vowel is dropped, adjoins the consonants of the preceding syllable and with these constitutes a *u* environment (2.6 D).

	rikab	'to ride'	(Class I)
3 M	*rikab*	'he rode'	
F	*rukbat*	'she " '	
P	*rukbaw*	'they " '	
2 M	*rikábit*	'you M rode'	
F	*rikabti*	'you F " '	
P	*rikabtu*	'you P " '	
1 S	*rikábit*	'I rode'	
P	*rikabna*	'we " '	

Other verbs like *rikab* are:

Class I

xirab	'to break down'
širab	'to drink'
ṣiraf	'to spend'
ġiḍab	'to get angry'

Class VII

nṣiraf	'to be spent'

Class VIII

ṣ̌tirab	'to be uneasy'

(2) In sound verbs in which the stem vowel is preceded by a double consonant and followed by a different consonant, the stem vowel is usually dropped before the 3 F and 3 P suffixes *-at* and *-aw*; the preceding double consonant then becomes single in pronunciation, since it no longer precedes a vowel (2.2.2). Before the other suffixes the stem remains unchanged except for stress. In this category are the sound verbs of Classes II and V except those with a double root.

	baddal	'to change'	(Class II)
3 M	*baddal*	'he changed'	
F	*baddlat*	'she " '	
P	*baddlaw*	'they " '	
2 M	*baddálit*	'you M changed'	
F	*baddalti*	'you F " '	
P	*baddaltu*	'you P " '	
1 S	*baddálit*	'I changed'	
P	*baddalna*	'we " '	

Other verbs like *baddal* are:

Class II

ʔajjal	'to postpone'
xawwaf	'to frighten'
δakkar	'to remind'
zayyan	'to shave'
sajjal	'to register'
ṣaffag	'to applaud'
ṭallaɛ	'to take out'
ɛallam	'to teach'
maššaṭ	'to comb'
naṣ̌ṣ̌af	'to clean'

Class V

tʔaxxar	'to be late'
dzawwaj	'to get married'
tmarraḍ	'to get sick'
tnaffas	'to breathe'
twannas	'to have a good time'

Sometimes in these verbs, however, the stem vowel is not dropped before *-at* and *-aw*, but changed to *i* or *u* (2.6), for example:

3 M	*baddal*	'he changed'	*naḍḍaf*	'he cleaned'
F	*baddilat*	'she changed'	*naḍḍufat*	'she cleaned'
P	*baddilaw*	'they changed'	*naḍḍufaw*	'they cleaned'

Such forms are used by most speakers only in slow or consciously precise speech.

(3) In sound verbs other than those described in (1) and (2) above, the stem vowel is changed to *i* or *u* (2.6) before the 3 F and 3 P suffixes *-at* and *-aw*. Before the other suffixes the stem remains unchanged except for stress. In this category are the sound verbs of Classes IV and X; the sound verbs of Classes II, III, V, and VI which have a double root; and sound simple and derived quadriliterals of the patterns *(t)FaSTaL* and *(t)FaDFaD*.

	staxdam	'to employ'	(Class X)
3 M	*staxdam*	'he employed'	
F	*staxdimat*	'she " '	
P	*staxdimaw*	'they " '	
2 M	*staxdámit*	'you M employed'	
F	*staxdamti*	'you F " '	
P	*staxdamtu*	'you P " '	
1 S	*staxdámit*	'I employed'	
P	*staxdamna*	'we " '	
	xarmaš	'to scratch, claw'	(Quadriliteral)
3 M	*xarmaš*	'he scratched'	
F	*xarmušat*	'she " '	
P	*xarmušaw*	'they " '	
2 M	*xarmášit*	'you M scratched'	
F	*xarmašti*	'you F " '	
P	*xarmaštu*	'you P " '	
1 S	*xarmášit*	'I scratched'	
P	*xarmašna*	'we " '	

Other verbs like those illustrated above are as follows, with the replacing vowel *i* or *u* indicated in parentheses:

Class II

ʔaθθaθ	(*i*)	'to furnish'
baddad	(*i*)	'to waste'
jaddad	(*i*)	'to renew'
ʒaddad	(*i*)	'to limit'
xaf̣f̣af̣	(*u*)	'to lighten'
dallal	(*i*)	'to pamper, spoil'
sabbab	(*i*)	'to cause'

Class III

ʒaajaj	(*i*)	'to argue with'

Class IV

ʔaʒdaθ	(*i*)	'to create, establish'
ʔaƐlan	(*i*)	'to announce, advertise'
ʔanjaz	(*i*)	'to accomplish'

Class V

txaṣṣaṣ	(*i*)	'to specialize'

Class VI

traaṣaṣ	(*i*)	'to move close together'

Class X

stajwab	(*u*)	'to interrogate'
staʒsan	(*i*)	'to approve'
staƐmal	(*i*)	'to use'
stafham	(*i*)	'to enquire'
staqbal	(*i*)	'to go and meet'
stantaj	(*i*)	'to deduce'
stankar	(*i*)	'to denounce, disapprove strongly'

Simple quadriliterals

barhan	*(i)*	'to prove'
xarbaṭ	*(u)*	'to disarrange, mess up'
ṭagṭag	*(i)*	'to pound'
ɛanwan	*(i)*	'to address'
qašmar	*(u)*	'to tease, fool'
handas	*(i)*	'to plan, engineer'

Derived quadriliterals

djabjab	*(i)*	'to be shy, hesitant'
txarbaṭ	*(u)*	'to get mixed up'

In a few verbs in this category (Class X verbs, and quadriliterals of the patterns *(t)FaSTaL*, and not all of those) there is an optional variant of the 3 F and 3 P forms in which the stem vowel is not simply changed but shifted (4.1.3.1), and stress remains, irregularly, on the first syllable, for example:

3 M	*staxdam*	'he employed'	*xarmaš*	'he scratched'
F	*stáxidmat*	'she " '	*xárumšat*	'she " '
P	*stáxidmaw*	'they " '	*xárumšaw*	'they " '

B. Doubled verbs

Doubled verbs are those which end in a double consonant, for example *dazz* 'to send'. Before the 3 F and 3 P suffixes the stem remains unchanged, but before the other suffixes a long vowel *ee* is added. In this category are those verbs of Classes I, IV, VII, VIII, and X which have a double root; all verbs of Class IX; and quadriliteral verbs of the *FSaTaLL* pattern.

	dazz	'to send'	(Class I)
3 M	*dazz*	'he sent'	
F	*dazzat*	'she " '	
P	*dazzaw*	'they " '	
2 M	*dazzeet*	'you M sent'	
F	*dazzeeti*	'you F " '	
P	*dazzeetu*	'you P " '	
1 S	*dazzeet*	'I sent'	
P	*dazzeena*	'we " '	

Other verbs like *dazz* are:

Class I

jarr	'to pull'
ẓabb	'to love, like'
ẓaṭṭ	'to put'
ẓall	'to solve'
rašš	'to sprinkle'
sadd	'to close'
ḍ̣ann	'to suppose'
f̣akk	'to open'
marr	'to pass'
gaẓẓ	'to cough'

Class IV

ʔaṣarr	'to insist'

Class VII

nġašš	'to be cheated'

Class VIII

ḍ̣ṭarr	'to be forced, have to'
htamm (b-)	'to be concerned (with)'

Class IX

ẓmarr	'to become red, blush'
ṣfarr	'to grow yellow, pale'
ṭrašš	'to grow deaf'

Class X

staʕadd	'to get ready'
stimarr	'to continue'

Quadriliteral

ṭmaʔann	'to become reassured'
qšaƐarr	'to feel a chill, shudder'

C. Hollow verbs

Hollow verbs are those which end in a single consonant preceded by the long vowel *aa*, for example *šaaf* 'to see'. In this category are those verbs of Classes I, IV, VII, VIII, and X which have a weak-middle root.

(1) Class I

In Class I hollow verbs the stem remains unchanged before the third-person suffixes, but before the other suffixes the *aa* of the stem is replaced by *i* or *u*. The replacing vowel is *u* in the verbs *baag* 'to steal, rob', *xaaf* 'to be afraid', and *gaam* 'to get up'. In others it is usually *i*; but in *gaal* 'to say', and in verbs in which the adjacent consonants are a labial and a velar or emphatic, there is some variation.

Replacing vowel *i*

	šaaf	'to see'
3 M	*šaaf*	'he saw'
F	*šaafat*	'she " '
P	*šaafaw*	'they " '
2 M	*šifit*	'you M saw'
F	*šifti*	'you F " '
P	*šiftu*	'you P " '
1 S	*šifit*	'I saw'
P	*šifna*	'we " '

Other Class I verbs like *šaaf* are:

baaƐ	'to sell'	*ṭaab*	'to recover, get well'
jaab	'to bring'	*ṭaar*	'to fly'
xaaṭ	'to stir'	*Ɛaaš*	'to live'
raaẓ	'to go'	*faat*	'to pass'
raad	'to want'	*qaas*	'to measure'
zaar	'to visit'	*laam*	'to blame'
saaq	'to drive'	*maat*	'to die'
šaal	'to pick up, carry'	*naam*	'to sleep, lie down'

ṣaar	'to become'	*gaal*	'to say'[1]
ḏaag	'to taste'	*čaan* *kaan*	'to be'[2]

Replacing vowel *u*

	gaam	'to get up'
3 M	*gaam*	'he got up'
F	*gaamat*	'she " " '
P	*gaamaw*	'they " " '
2 M	*gumit*	'you M got up'
F	*gumti*	'you F " " '
P	*gumtu*	'you P " " '
1 S	*gumit*	'I got up'
P	*gumna*	'we " " '

Other Class I verbs like *gaam* are:

baag	'to steal'
xaaf	'to fear'

(2) Others

In hollow verbs other than those of Class I, the stem also remains unchanged before the third-person suffixes, but before the other suffixes a long vowel *ee* is added.[3]

	nlaam	'to be blamed'	(Class VII)
3 M	*nlaam*	'he was blamed'	
F	*nlaamat*	'she " " '	
P	*nlaamaw*	'they were " '	
2 M	*nlaameet*	'you M were blamed'	
F	*nlaameeti*	'you F " " '	
P	*nlaameetu*	'you P " " '	
1 S	*nlaameet*	'I was blamed'	
P	*nlaameena*	'we were " '	

---

[1] In the second and first persons of this verb, besides the regular forms, the following are common: 2 M and 1 S *gitt* (before a vowel or the suffix *-l-*), 2 F *gitti*, 2 P *gittu*, 1 P *ginna*. See also 5.3.6.

[2] For this verb, *čaan* is the usual form, with *činit*, *činti* etc. in the second and first persons. However, *kaan* is also used, especially in slightly formal speech, with either *kinit*, *kinti* etc. or *kunit*, *kunti* etc. in the second and first persons.

[3] This statement probably reflects the most general usage, but some of these verbs have a variant set of second- and first-person forms in which the *aa* of the stem is

Other verbs like *nlaam* are:

Class IV

ˀabaad	'to destroy, wipe out'
ˀaẓaal	'to pension off'
ˀašaar l-	'to refer to'
ˀahaan	'to insult'

Class VII

nbaaɛ	'to be sold'
nbaag	'to be robbed; to be stolen'
nxaan	'to be betrayed'
ndaar	'to turn around' (intr)
nraad	'to be needed, wanted'
nšaaf	'to be seen'
nṣaab	'to be hit, stricken'
nṣaad	'to be caught'

Class VIII

ẓtaaj	'to need'
ẓṭaaṭ	'to take precautions'

[3] replaced by *i* or *u* as in Class I verbs (see (1) above), or, especially in Class IV and Class X verbs, by *a*. For example:

Class VII	*nlimit*	'I was blamed'	instead of	*nlaameet*
	nbugit	'I was robbed'	" "	*nbaageet*
VIII	*ẓtijit*	'I needed'	" "	*ẓtaajeet*
IV	*ˀahánit*	'I insulted'	" "	*ˀahaaneet*
X	*staqálit*	'I resigned'	" "	*staqaaleet*

Such forms are used by some speakers more than by others. Their occurrence and the extent to which they are used instead of the stems in *ee* are unpredictable matters and must be learned for each verb.

xtaar	'to choose'
rtaaẓ	'to rest, take it easy'
ṣṭaad	'to go hunting'

Class X

staθaar	'to provoke'
stajaab l-	'to comply with'
staraaẓ	'to rest'
staġaab	'to gossip about'
stafaad	'to benefit'
staqaal	'to resign'

D. Defective verbs

Defective verbs are those which end in the short vowel *a* (the final vowel), for example *nisa* 'to forget'. Before the 3 F and 3 P suffixes *-at* and *-aw* the final vowel is dropped; before the other suffixes it is replaced by the long vowel *ee*. In this category are all verbs which have a weak-last root. There are such verbs in Classes I through VIII and Class X, and among the quadriliterals.

	nisa[1]	'to forget'	(Class I)
3 M	*nisa*	'he forgot'	
F	*nisat*	'she " '	
P	*nisaw*	'they " '	
2 M	*niseet*	'you M forgot'	
F	*niseeti*	'you F " '	
P	*niseetu*	'you P " '	
1 S	*niseet*	'I forgot'	
P	*niseena*	'we " '	
	buqa[1]	'to stay'	(Class I)
3 M	*buqa*	'he stayed'	
F	*buqat*	'she " '	
P	*buqaw*	'they " '	

[1] In second-person and first-person forms of Class I defective verbs, which have the pattern *FiLee-* or *FuLee-*, the unstressed short *i* or *u* in the first syllable is frequently dropped in normal-speed speech, for example *nseet*, *nseeti* etc. In the verb *niṭa* 'to give', only the shorter forms are common: *nṭeet, nṭeeti* etc. (See footnote under A above.)

2 M	*buqeet*	'you M stayed'
F	*buqeeti*	'you F " '
P	*buqeetu*	'you P " '
1 S	*buqeet*	'I stayed'
P	*buqeena*	'we " '

Other verbs like those illustrated above are:

Class I

bina	'to build'
biča	'to cry'
ẓiča	'to talk'
qira	'to read'
liga	'to find'
mila	'to fill'
niṭa	'to give'
ġufa	'to doze off'
muḍa	'to sign'

Class II

xalla	'to let'
samma	'to call'
sawwa	'to do'
kaffa	'to be enough'
hanna	'to congratulate'
gaḷḷa	'to fry'

Class III

daara	'to look after, take care of'
raawa	'to show'

Class IV

ʔalġa	'to cancel'
ʔalqa	'to deliver' (speech)

Class V

tbanna	'to adopt'
tɛaššа	'to dine'
twaffa	'to pass away, die'

Class VI

tʒaaša	'to avoid'
tlaaga	'to meet, get together'

Class VII

nliga	'to be found'
nluwa	'to be twisted'

Class VIII

xtiba	'to hide' (intr)
štira	'to buy'

Class X

stanga	'to choose'
staθna	'to except'

Quadriliterals

loola	'to sing a lullaby'

E. *jaa*

The verb *jaa* 'to come' has two variant sets of forms in the perfect tense. The less common set, shown on the right below, has the forms of a Class I defective verb like *nisa* (see D above). Within this set, the third-person forms are more common than the others. The forms of the more common set, shown on the left below, are in some respects like those of a defective verb, but the stem is unusual. The 3 F form *jatti* 'she came' has a uniquely irregular inflectional suffix.

3 M	*jaa*	'he came'	*ʔija*
F	*jatti*	'she " '	*ʔijat*
P	*jaw*	'they " '	*ʔijaw*
2 M	*jeet*	'you M came'	*ʔijeet*
F	*jeeti*	'you F " '	*ʔijeeti*
P	*jeetu*	'you P " '	*ʔijeetu*
1 S	*jeet*	'I came'	*ʔijeet*
P	*jeena*	'we " '	*ʔijeena*

5.2.2 Imperfect tense

5.2.2.1 Inflectional affixes

The inflectional affixes of the imperfect tense include prefixes, suffixes, and combinations of prefix and suffix. The basic forms[1] are as follows:

	Indicative		Imperative
3 M	*y(i/u)-*	'he'	
F	*t(i/u)-*	'she'	
P	*y(i/u)- ...-uun*	'they'	
2 M	*t(i/u)-*	'you M'	*ʔ(i/u)-/∅-*
F	*t(i/u)- ...-iin*	'you F'	*ʔ(i/u)-/∅- ...i*
P	*t(i/u)- ...-uun*	'you P'	*ʔ(i/u)-/∅- ...u*
1 S	*ʔ(a)-*	'I'	
P	*n(i/u)-*	'we'	

Comments:

A. In the indicative, the 3 P, 2 F, and 2 P affixes are combinations of prefix and suffix; the others are prefixes only. In the imperative, the 2 M affix is a prefix *ʔ-*, *ʔi-*, or *ʔu-* in some verbs, and zero (no affix) in others; the 2 F and 2 P affixes are combinations of prefix and suffix in some verbs and suffixes only in others.

B. In the indicative, the 3 F and 2 M prefixes are identical in every verb:

3 F	*tiktib*	'she writes'
2 M	*tiktib*	'you M write''

C. In the indicative, the 1 S prefix is *ʔ-* with stems beginning with a vowel (always long), and *ʔa-* elsewhere:

ʔaakul	'I eat'	*ʔaktib*	'I write'
ʔoogaf	'I stop'	*ʔašuuf*	'I see'

D. In the indicative, the prefixes other than 1 S have forms consisting of a consonant alone (*y-*, *t-* , *n-*), or a consonant plus *i* (*yi-*, *ti-* , *ni-*), or a consonant plus *u* (*yu-*, *tu-*, *nu-*). These three types of forms occur as follows:

(1) The forms with a vowel *i* or *u* occur before stems which begin with two consonants.

(a) If the stem has the pattern *-CCuC*, the vowel of the prefix may be *i* or *u*. It tends to be *i* if the consonants of the stem do not constitute a *u* environment (2.6), *u* if they do; but there is considerable variation in both cases:

[1] For those speakers who use them (see 5.2.1.1, footnote 1), the feminine plural affixes for the imperfect tense are: indicative, 3 FP *y(i/u)-...-an* 'they FP' and 2 FP *t(i/u)-...-an* 'you FP'; imperative, 2 FP *ʔ(i/u)-/∅-...-an* 'you FP'.

3 M	*yiskun*	'he lives'
3 F/2 M	*tidrus*	'she studies / you M study'
1 P	*nitruk*	'we leave'
3 M	*yuεruf*	'he knows'
3 F/2 M	*tuṭbux*	'she cooks / you M cook'
1 P	*nuḍbuṭ*	'we adjust'

(b) If the stem has the pattern *-CC(v)*, the vowel of the prefix is generally *i*, but may be *u* if the two stem consonants are a combination of labial, emphatic, or velar:

3 M	*yimši*	'he walks'
3 F/2 M	*tiqra*	'she reads / you M read'
3 P	*yilguun*	'you P find'
3 M	*yumḍi*	'he signs'

(c) Otherwise the vowel of the prefix is *i* :

3 M	*yilbas* *yiktib*	'he wears' 'he writes'
3 F/2 M	*tismaε* *titġadda*	'she hears / you M hear' 'she lunches / you M lunch'
3 P	*yitxarrjuun* *yitbannuun*	'they graduate' 'they adopt'
2 F	*tindalliin* *tiftahmiin*	'you F know' 'you F understand'
2 P	*tistalmuun* *tistanguun*	'you P receive' 'you P choose'
1 P	*niṭḷaε* *niεtiqid*	'we go out' 'we believe'

In those prefixes involving *t* (3 F, 2 M, 2 F, 2 P), if the first consonant of the stem is an emphatic, the *t* of the prefix may become *ṭ* by assimilation (2.5):

tuṭbux	'she cooks / you M cook'
ṭuḍrub	'she hits / you M hit'
tiṭḷaε	'she goes out / you M go out'

(2) The forms with a vowel (*i* or *u*) may also occur before stems of the patterns *-CiCC-* or *-CuCC-*. These are Class I or Class IV verb stems with shifted vowel (5.2.2.2 A (1) (d) and (2) (b)) and are used only with a suffix beginning with a vowel.

(a) If the stem has the pattern *-CuCC-* the vowel of the prefix may be *i* or *u*. As in (1) (a) above, it tends to be *i* if the consonants of the stem do not constitute a *u* environment (2.6), *u* if they do; but there is considerable variation in both cases:

3 P	*yiturkuun*	'they leave'
	yidursuun	'they study'
	yisuknuun	'they live'
2 F	*tuƐurfiin*	'you F know'
2 P	*turukbuun*	'you P ride'
3 P	*yuṭubxuun*	'they cook'

(b) If the stem has the pattern *-CiCC-* the vowel of the prefix is *i*:

3 P	*yisimƐuun*	'they hear'
2 F	*tilibsiin*	'you F wear'
2 P	*tikitbuun*	'you P write'

In all these cases, however, the forms of the prefix without a vowel may also occur, and in two circumstances usually do occur: (1) when a preceding word or prefix ends in a vowel:

3 P	*humma ysimƐuun*	'they hear'
2 F	*ma-tlibsiin*	'you F do not wear'
2 P	*da-tkitbuun*	'you P are writing'

and, (2) in the prefixes involving *t*, when the first consonant of the stem is one to which this *t* usually assimilates (see (3) below) or is itself *t*:

2 F	*ttirsiin*	'you F fill'
	ddursiin	'you F study'
2 P	*ddifƐuun*	'you P pay'
	ṭṭubxuun	'you P cook'

(3) The forms of the prefix without a vowel occur with all stems beginning with a vowel (always long), and with stems beginning with a single consonant (except as described in (2) above, and in the verb *jaa* 'to come', for which see 5.2.2.2 E):

3 M	*yaakul*	'he eats'
	yšuuf [1]	'he sees'

[1] For the sound of *y* plus another consonant at the beginning of a word see 2.3.1.

3 F/2 M	<u>t</u>ooga£	'she falls / you M fall'
	<u>t</u>bii£	'she sells / you M sell'
3 P	<u>y</u>gu<u>ṣṣ</u>uun	'they cut'
	<u>y</u>baddluun	'they change'
2 F	<u>t</u>qarririin	'you F decide'
	<u>t</u>raawiin	'you F show'
2 P	<u>t</u>riiduun	'you P want'
	<u>t</u>xalḷṣuun	'you P finish'
1 P	<u>n</u>saafir	'we go on a trip'
	<u>n</u>tarjum	'we translate'

In those prefixes involving t (3 F, 2 M, 2 F, 2 P), if the first consonant of the stem is one of the following: $d, j, ṭ, \theta, \delta, \dot\delta, z, ṣ, s, š$, the t of the prefix usually assimilates to it (2.5) as follows: Before d or j it assimilates as to voice, becoming d:

<u>d</u>darris   'you M teach'

<u>d</u>jiib   'you M bring'

Before $ṭ$ it assimilates as to emphasis, becoming $ṭ$:

<u>ṭ</u>ṭiib   'you M get well'

Before θ, δ, or $\dot\delta$ it assimilates completely:

<u>θ</u>θiir   'you M arouse'

<u>δ</u>δakkir   'you M remind'

<u>δ̇</u>δ̇inn   'you M suppose'

Before z and $ṣ$ it may assimilate completely, becoming z and $ṣ$, or only as to voice and emphasis respectively, becoming d and $ṭ$. Before s and $š$ it may assimilate completely, or not at all.

<u>z</u>zayyin ⎫
          ⎬ 'you M shave'
<u>d</u>zayyin ⎭

<u>ṣ</u>ṣiir ⎫
       ⎬ 'you M become'
<u>ṭ</u>ṣiir ⎭

<u>s</u>sawwi ⎫
        ⎬ 'you M do'
tsawwi ⎭

<u>š</u>šiil ⎫
       ⎬ 'you M carry'
<u>t</u>šiil ⎭

E. In the imperative, the prefixes have forms consisting of *ʔ–*, *ʔi–*, *ʔu–*, or zero, which occur as follows:

(1) The forms with a vowel occur with Class I and Class IV stems which begin with two consonants.

(a) If the stem has the pattern *–CCuC* the vowel of the prefix may be *i* or *u*. As in the case of the indicative prefixes (D (1) above), it tends to be *i* if the consonants of the stem do not constitute a *u* environment (2.6), *u* if they do; but there is considerable variation. (The following examples are 2 M only: for examples of 2 F and 2 P forms see (2) below.)

2 M	*ʔidrus*	'study M'
	ʔitruk	'leave M'
	ʔuṭbux	'cook M'
	ʔuδ̣but	'adjust M'

(b) If the stem has the pattern *–CC(v)* (i.e., a Class I or Class IV defective stem), the vowel of the prefix is generally *i*, but may be *u* if the two stem consonants are a combination of labial, emphatic, and velar, or *r* and emphatic. In some verbs the vowel of the prefix may be *i* in the 2 M and 2 F, but *u* in the 2 P under the influence of the suffix *u*:

2 M	*ʔimli*	'fill M'	*ʔumδ̣i*	'sign M'
F	*ʔimli*	' " F'	*ʔumδ̣i*	' " F'
P	*ʔimlu*	' " P'	*ʔumδ̣u*	' " P'

2 M	*ʔixṭi*	'step M'
F	*ʔixṭi*	' " F'
P	*ʔuxṭu*	' " P'

(c) Otherwise the vowel of the prefix is *i*. (The following examples are 2 M only; for examples of 2 F and 2 P forms see (2) below.)

2 M	*ʔidfaƐ*	'pay M'
	ʔirkab	'ride, get on M'
	ʔismaƐ	'listen M'
	ʔišrab	'drink M'
	ʔiktib	'write M'
	ʔirsim	'draw M'

(2) The form with a vowel may also occur with stems of the pattern *–CiCC–* and *–CuCC–*, which are Class I or Class IV stems with shifted vowel (5.2.2.2 A (1) (d) and (2) (b)), used only before a suffix beginning with a vowel. It is these shifted stems, rather than the corresponding unshifted stems *–CCaC*, *–CCiC*, *–CCuC*, which are most commonly used in 2 F and 2 P imperative forms of these verbs.

(a) If the stem has the pattern *–CuCC*, the vowel of the prefix may be *i* or *u*. As in the case of the indicative prefixes (D (2) above), it tends to be *i* if the consonants of the stem do not constitute a *u* environment (2.6), *u* if they do; and there is the same variation in both cases:

2 F	*ʔidursi*	'study F'
P	*ʔidursu*	' " P'
2 F	*ʔuṭubxi*	'cook F'
P	*ʔuṭubxu*	' " P'

(b) If the stem has the pattern *-CiCC-* the vowel of the prefix is *i*:

2 F	*ʔidifεi*	'pay F'	*ʔisimεi*	'listen F'
P	*ʔidifεu*	' " P'	*ʔisimεu*	' " P'
2 F	*ʔikitbi*	'write F'	*ʔirismi*	'draw F'
P	*ʔikitbu*	' " P'	*ʔirismu*	' " P'

In all these cases involving a shifted stem, however, the prefix as a whole is optional; that is, the 2 F and 2 P imperative forms may consist of the (shifted) stem and the suffix:

2 F	*dursi*	'study F'	*ṭubxi*	'cook F'
P	*dursu*	' " P'	*ṭubxu*	' " P'
2 F	*difεi*	'pay F'	*kitbi*	'write F'
P	*difεu*	' " P'	*kitbu*	' " P'

(3) The form consisting of *ʔ-* without a vowel occurs with stems which begin with a vowel (always long):

2 M	*ʔoogaf*	'stop M'
F	*ʔoogfi*	' " F'
P	*ʔoogfu*	' " P'

(4) The form *ʔi-* may occur before stems which begin with two consonants other than stems of Classes I and IV:

2 M	*ʔitfaṣṣal*	'please M'
F	*ʔiṣtaεmili*	'use F'
P	*ʔistimirru*	'continue P'

With such stems, however, the prefix is optional, and may be considered as a manifestation of the helping vowel which occurs optionally before any initial consonant cluster (2.3.1). Hereafter such forms will be described and written as having no prefix:

2 M	*tfaṣṣal*	'please M'
F	*ṣtaεmili*	'use F'
P	*stimirru*	'continue P'

(5) No imperative prefix occurs with stems which begin with a single consonant (except as described in (2) above and in the two verbs *ʔaxaδ* 'to take' and *ʔakal* 'to eat', for which see 5.2.2.2 A (1) (a)):

2 M	*ruuȥ*	'go M'	*saaεid*	'help M'
F	*ruuȥi*	' " F''	*saaεdi*	' " F'
P	*ruuȥu*	' " P'	*saaεdu*	' " P'

5.2.2.2 Imperfect stems

In some verbs the imperfect stem is completely predictable from the perfect and in others partially so; details are given below. In doubled and hollow verbs, the imperfect stem itself (as it occurs in the 3 M form) remains unchanged throughout all forms of the imperfect. In sound verbs, when an inflectional suffix beginning with a vowel is added, the stem vowel is subject to loss, change, or shift (4.1.3.1). In defective verbs, when such a suffix is added, the final vowel is subject to loss (4.1.3.2).

A. Sound verbs

(1) Class I

(a) *ʔaxaδ* and *ʔakal*

The two verbs *ʔaxaδ* 'to take' and *ʔakal* 'to eat', which are unique in Class I in having the vowel *a* in the first syllable, have the imperfect stem pattern *-aaMuL*. Their imperative forms are irregular. The stem vowel *u* is dropped before suffixes.

	ʔaxaδ	'to take'		
3 M	*yaaxuδ*	'he takes'		
F	*taaxuδ*	'she " '		
P	*yaaxδuun*	'they take'		
2 M	*taaxuδ*	'you M take'	*ʔuxuδ*	'take M'
F	*taaxδiin*	'you F " '	*ʔuxδi*	' " F'
P	*taaxδuun*	'you P " '	*ʔuxδu*	' " P'
1 S	*ʔaaxuδ*	'I take'		
P	*naaxuδ*	'we " '		
	ʔakal	'to eat'		
3 M	*yaakul*	'he eats'		
F	*taakul*	'she " '		
P	*yaakluun*	'they eat'		
2 M	*taakul*	'you M eat'	*ʔukul*	'eat M'
F	*taakliin*	'you F " '	*ʔukli*	' " F'
P	*taakluun*	'you P " '	*ʔuklu*	' " P'
1 S	*ʔaakul*	'I eat'		
P	*naakul*	'we " '		

(b) Verbs beginning with *w*

Class I sound verbs beginning with *w* have the imperfect stem pattern *-ooMaL*, *-ooMiL*, or *-ooMuL*. As between *a* on the one hand and *i* or *u* on the other, the stem vowel is unpredictable and must be learned for each verb. As between *i* and *u*, the stem vowel depends on the adjacent consonants (2.6), but *u* is rare. The stem vowel is dropped before suffixes. The imperative forms have the prefix *ʔ-*.

Stem pattern *-ooMaL*

	wugaf	'to stop'		
3 M	*yoogaf*	'he stops'		
F	*toogaf*	'she " '		
P	*yoogfuun*	'they " '		
2 M	*toogaf*	'you M stop'	*ʔoogaf*	'stop M'
F	*toogfiin*	'you F " '	*ʔoogfi*	' " F'
P	*toogfuun*	'you P " '	*ʔoogfu*	' " P'
1 S	*ʔoogaf*	'I stop'		
P	*noogaf*	'we " '		

Other verbs like *wugaf* are:

wujaƐ	*yoojaƐ*	'to hurt'
wuram	*yooram*	'to swell'
wuṣal	*yooṣal*	'to arrive'
wugaƐ	*yoogaƐ*	'to fall'

Stem pattern *-ooMiL*

	wuzan	'to weigh' (tr)		
3 M	*yoozin*	'he weighs'		
F	*toozin*	'she " '		
P	*yooznuun*	'they weigh'		
2 M	*toozin*	'you M weigh'	*ʔoozin*	'weigh M'
F	*tooznìin*	'you F " '	*ʔoozni*	'weigh F'
P	*tooznuun*	'you P " '	*ʔooznu*	'weigh P'
1 S	*ʔoozin*	'I weigh'		
P	*noozin*	'we " '		

Other verbs like *wuzan* are:

wuƐad	*yooƐid*	'to promise'
wuldat	*toolid*	'to give birth'

Stem pattern *-ooMuL*

	wuṣaf	'to describe'
3 M	*yooṣuf*	'he describes'
F	*tooṣuf*	'she " '
P	*yooṣfuun*	'they describe'

2 M	*tooṣuf*	'you M describe'	*ʔooṣuf*	'describe M'
F	*tooṣfiin*	'you F " '	*ʔooṣfi*	' " F'
P	*tooṣfuun*	'you P " '	*ʔooṣfu*	' " P'
1 S	*ʔooṣuf*	'I describe'		
P	*nooṣuf*	'we " '		

No other verbs like *wuṣaf* have been noted.

(c) Verbs beginning with *y*

Class I sound verbs beginning with *y* have the imperfect stem pattern *-eeMaL*, *-eeMiL*, or *-eeMuL*. The stem vowel is unpredictable and must be learned for each verb; but the only two common verbs of this type, *yiʔas* 'to despair' and *yibas* 'to dry' (intr), both have the stem vowel *a*. The stem vowel is dropped before suffixes. The imperative forms have the prefix *ʔ-*.

	yiʔas	'to despair'		
3 M	*yeeʔas*	'he despairs'		
F	*teeʔas*	'she " '		
P	*yeeʔsuun*	'they despair'		
2 M	*teeʔas*	'you M despair'	*ʔeeʔas*	'despair M'
F	*teeʔsiin*	'you F " '	*ʔeeʔsi*	' " F'
P	*teeʔsuun*	'you P " '	*ʔeeʔsu*	' " P'
1 S	*ʔeeʔas*	'I despair'		
P	*neeʔas*	'we " '		

(d) Others

All other Class I sound verbs have the imperfect stem patterns *-FMaL*, *-FMiL*, or *-FMuL*. The stem vowel is unpredictable and must be learned for each verb. Before suffixes, the stem vowel is usually[1] shifted (4.1.3.1 C), with resulting stem patterns *-FiML-* or *-FuML-*. (If the unshifted stem is *-FMaL*, the shifted stem is *-FiML-* or *-FuML-* depending on the (new) environment (2.6). If the unshifted stem is *-FMiL*, the shifted stem is usually *-FiML-*. If the unshifted stem is *-FMuL*, the shifted stem is usually *-FuML-*, with variation in a few cases between the two.) In the imperative, the 2 M form has a prefix *ʔi-* or *ʔu-*; the 2 F and 2 P forms may, but need not, have one of these prefixes. (See 5.2.2.1 for the vowels of imperfect prefixes.)

Stem pattern *-FMaL*; shifted stem *-FiML-*

In verbs of this category the vowel of the prefix is *i*.

[1] Less commonly, the stem vowel remains unshifted before suffixes, for example in the verb *libas yilbas* 'to wear': 3 M *yilbasuun* 'they wear', 2 F *tilbasiin* 'you F wear', imperative 2 F *ʔilbasi* 'wear F'. Such forms will not be shown in the paradigms which follow.

	libas	'to wear, put on'		
3 M	*yilbas*	'he wears'		
F	*tilbas*	'she " '		
P	*yilibsuun*	'they wear'		
2 M	*tilbas*	'you M wear'	*ʔilbas*	'wear M'
F	*tilibsiin*	'you F " '	*(ʔi)libsi*	' " F'
P	*tilibsuun*	'you P " '	*(ʔi)libsu*	' " P'
1 S	*ʔalbas*	'I wear'		
P	*nilbas*	'we " '		

Other verbs like *libas* are:

ʒilam	*yiʒlam*	'to dream'
difaƐ	*yidfaƐ*	'to pay; to push'
rijaƐ	*yirjaƐ*	'to come back, go back'
ziƐal	*yizƐal*	'to get angry'
sibaʒ	*yisbaʒ*	'to swim'
sikar	*yiskar*	'to get drunk'
simaƐ	*yismaƐ*	'to hear'
siman	*yisman*	'to get fat'
ṭilaƐ	*yiṭḷaƐ*	'to go out'

Stem pattern *-FMaL*; shifted stem *-FuML-*

In verbs of this category the vowel of the prefix is *i* before the stem *-FMaL* and generally *u* before the shifted stem *-FuML-*, but in the latter case there may be variation between the two.

	rikab	'to ride'		
3 M	*yirkab*	'he rides'		
F	*tirkab*	'she " '		
P	*yurukbuun*	'they ride'		
2 M	*tirkab*	'you M ride'	*ʔirkab*	'ride M'
F	*turukbiin*	'you F " '	*(ʔu)rukbi*	' " F'
P	*turukbuun*	'you P " '	*(ʔu)rukbu*	' " P'
1 S	*ʔarkab*	'I ride'		
P	*nirkab*	'we " '		

Other verbs like *rikab* are:

xirab	*yixrab*	'to break down, collapse'
širab	*yišrab*	'to drink'
riham	*yirham*	'to fit, suit'
ġiḍab	*yiġḍab*	'to get angry'
girab	*yigrab*	'to approach'
fuƐaṣ	*yifƐaṣ*	'to crush'
kubar	*yikbar*	'to grow up'
rubaẓ	*yirbaẓ*	'to win'

Stem pattern *-FMiL*; shifted stem *-FiML-*

In verbs of this category the vowel of the prefix is *i*.

kitab 'to write'

3 M	*yiktib*	'he writes'		
F	*tiktib*	'she " '		
P	*yikitbuun*	'they write'		
2 M	*tiktib*	'you M write'	*ʔiktib*	'write M'
F	*tikitbiin*	'you F " '	*(ʔi)kitbi*	' " F'
P	*tikitbuun*	'you P " '	*(ʔi)kitbu*	' " P'
1 S	*ʔaktib*	'I write'		
P	*niktib*	'we " '		

Other verbs like *kitab* are:

jilaf	*yijlif*	'to scour'
ẓirag	*yiẓrig*	'to burn' (tr)
difan	*yidfin*	'to bury'
ziƐaj	*yizƐij*	'to annoy'
ṣidam	*yiṣdim*	'to bump into'
Ɛijab	*yiƐjib*	'to please'
Ɛizam	*yiƐzim*	'to invite'
ġisal	*yiġsil*	'to wash'

Stem pattern *-FMuL*; shifted stem *-FuML-*

In verbs of this category the vowel of the prefix varies between *u* and *i*. In most cases it is perhaps more commonly *u*, as illustrated in the first set of examples below, and in some more commonly *i*, as illustrated in the second set; but there is variation in both sets. In verbs of the second set, in which the stem consonants do not constitute a *u* environment, there may also be some variation in the shifted stem between *-FuML-* and *-FiML-*.

	rigaṣ	'to dance'		
3 M	*yurguṣ*	'he dances'		
F	*turguṣ*	'she " '		
P	*yurugṣuun*	'they dance'		
2 M	*turguṣ*	'you M dance'	*ʔurguṣ*	'dance M'
F	*turugṣiin*	'you F " '	*(ʔu)rugṣi*	' " F'
P	*turugṣuun*	'you P " '	*(ʔu)rugṣu*	' " P'
1 S	*ʔarguṣ*	'I dance'		
P	*nurguṣ*	'we " '		

Other verbs like *rigaṣ* are:

xiṣam	*yuxṣum*	'to take off' (price)
xiṭab	*yuxṭub*	'to make a speech'
rikaḍ	*yurkuḍ*	'to run'
ṣiqaṭ	*yuṣquṭ*	'to fail'
ṣiraf	*yuṣruf*	'to spend'
ḍirab	*yuḍrub*	'to hit'
ṭilab	*yuṭlub*	'to ask for'
ɛiraf	*yuɛruf*	'to know'
xubaz	*yuxbuz*	'to bake'
xubaṭ	*yuxbuṭ*	'to mix'
ṣubaġ	*yuṣbuġ*	'to paint'
ḍubaṭ	*yuḍbuṭ*	'to adjust, control'
ṭubax	*yuṭbux*	'to cook'
ɛubar	*yuɛbur*	'to cross'

	diras	'to study'		
3 M	*yidrus*	'he studies'		
F	*tidrus*	'she " '		
P	*yidursuun*	'they study'		
2 M	*tidrus*	'you M study'	*ʔidrus*	'study M'
F	*tidursiin*	'you F " '	*(ʔi)dursi*	' " F'
P	*tidursuun*	'you P " '	*(ʔi)dursu*	' " P'
1 S	*ʔadrus*	'I study'		
P	*nidrus*	'we " '		

Other verbs like *diras* are:

tirak	*yitruk*	'to leave'
dixal	*yidxul*	'to enter'
sikat	*yiskut*	'to be silent'
sikan	*yiskun*	'to live, reside'

(2) Class IV

(a) First radical *w*

Class IV sound verbs in which the first radical is *w* have the imperfect stem pattern *-ooMiL*, and are thus indistinguishable in the imperfect from some Class I sound verbs beginning with *w* ((1) (b) above; cf. also D (2) (a) below). The stem vowel is dropped before suffixes. The imperative forms have the prefix *ʔ-*.

	ʔawdaɛ	'to deposit, leave for safekeeping'		
3 M	*yoodiɛ*	'he deposits'		
F	*toodiɛ*	'she " '		
P	*yoodɛuun*	'they deposit'		
2 M	*toodiɛ*	'you M deposit'	*ʔoodiɛ*	'deposit M'
F	*toodɛiin*	'you F " '	*ʔoodɛi*	' " F'
P	*toodɛuun*	'you P " '	*ʔoodɛu*	' " P'
1 S	*ʔoodiɛ*	'I deposit'		
P	*noodiɛ*	'we " '		

Another verb like *ʔawdaɛ* is *ʔawjad yoojid* 'to create'.

(b) Others

All other Class IV sound verbs have the imperfect stem pattern *-FMiL* or *-FMuL*, and are thus indistinguishable in the imperfect from some Class I sound verbs ((1) (d) above). The stem vowel generally depends on the adjacent consonants (2.6) but there is some variation. The stem vowel is dropped before suffixes. In the imperative, the 2 M form has the prefix *ʔi-* or *ʔu-*; the 2 F and 2 P forms may, but need not, have the same prefix. An example:

	ʔaεlan	'to announce, advertise'		
3 M	*yiεlin*	'he announces'		
F	*tiεlin*	'she " '		
P	*yiεilnuun*	'they announce'		
2 M	*tiεlin*	'you M announce'	*ʔiεlin*	'announce M'
F	*tiεilniin*	'you F " '	*(ʔi)εilni*	' " F'
P	*tiεilnuun*	'you P " '	*(ʔi)εilnu*	' " P'
1 S	*ʔaεlin*	'I announce'		
P	*niεlin*	'we " '		

(3) Verbs with *t-* prefix

All sound verbs which bear the derivational prefix *t-* have imperfect stems identical with their perfect stems; the stem vowel is thus always *a*. The stem vowel is dropped before suffixes if it is preceded by a single or a double consonant and followed by a different consonant;[1] otherwise it is changed to *i* or *u* (2.6)[2]. The imperative forms have no prefixes. In this category are sound triliteral verbs of Classes V and VI, and sound quadriliteral verbs of the patterns *tFaSTaL*, *tFaDFaD*, *tFooTaL*, and *tFeeTaL*.

Stem vowel dropped

	txarraj	'to graduate'	(Class V)	
3 M	*yitxarraj*	'he graduates'		
F	*titxarraj*	'she " '		
P	*yitxarrjuun*	'they graduate'		
2 M	*titxarraj*	'you M graduate'	*txarraj*	'graduate M'
F	*titxarrjiin*	'you F " '	*txarrji*	' " F'
P	*titxarrjuun*	'you P " '	*txarrju*	' " P'
1 S	*ʔatxarraj*	'I graduate'		
P	*nitxarraj*	'we " '		

---

[1] When the stem vowel is preceded by a double consonant and followed by a different consonant, as in some Class V verbs, it is sometimes changed to *i* or *u* (2.6) before suffixes instead of being dropped:

3 M	*yitẓammal*	'he endures'
P	*yitẓammiluun*	'they endure'

[2] In some cases only, when the stem vowel is preceded by two consonants and followed by a different consonant, as in some derived quadriliteral verbs, it is sometimes shifted (4.1.3.1 C) before suffixes instead of being simply changed to *i* or *u*:

3 M	*yitxarbaṭ*	'he is confused'
P	*yitxarubṭuun*	'they are confused'

Other verbs like *txarraj* are:

Class V

tˀaxxar	*yitˀaxxar*	'to be late, take long'
tʒassan	*yitʒassan*	'to improve' (intr)
dzawwaj	*yidzawwaj*	'to get married'
tʒammal	*yitʒammal*	'to endure'
trayyag	*yitrayyag*	'to have breakfast'
ṭṣawwar	*yiṭṣawwar*	'to think, suppose'

Class VI

txaabar	*yitxaabar*	'to talk on the phone'
traahan	*yitraahan*	'to bet'
tʕaamal	*yitʕaamal*	'to haggle'

Quadriliterals

ṭṣoogar	*yiṭṣoogar*	'to be insured'
tneešan	*yitneešan*	'to be aimed'

Stem vowel changed to *i*

txaṣṣaṣ 'to specialize' (Class V)

3 M	*yitxaṣṣaṣ*	'he specializes'		
F	*titxaṣṣaṣ*	'she " '		
P	*yitxaṣṣiṣuun*	'they specialize'		
2 M	*titxaṣṣaṣ*	'you M specialize'	*txaṣṣaṣ*	'specialize M'
F	*titxaṣṣiṣiin*	'you F " '	*txaṣṣiṣi*	' " F'
P	*titxaṣṣiṣuun*	'you P " '	*txaṣṣiṣu*	' " P'
1 S	*ˀatxaṣṣaṣ*	'I specialize'		
P	*nitxaṣṣaṣ*	'we " '		

Other verbs like *txaṣṣaṣ* are:

Class V

tʒaddad	*yitʒaddad*	'to be limited'
tʒarrar	*yitʒarrar*	'to be freed'
tmaddad	*yitmaddad*	'to stretch out'

Class VI

tẓaadad	*yitẓaadad*	'to become neighbors'

Quadriliteral

tbarhan	*yitbarhan*	'to be proved'
thandas	*yithandas*	'to be planned, engineered'
tbačbač	*yitbačbač*	'to put on a piteous act' (in asking for s-th)

Stem vowel changed to *u*

txarbaṭ　'to be confused'　(Quadriliteral)

3 M	*yitxarbaṭ*	'he is confused'		
F	*titxarbaṭ*	'she " " '		
P	*yitxarbuṭuun*	'they are " '		
2 M	*titxarbaṭ*	'you M are confused'	*txarbaṭ*	'be confused M'
F	*titxarbuṭiin*	'you F " " '	*txarbuṭi*	' " " F'
P	*titxarbuṭuun*	'you P " " '	*txarbuṭu*	' " " P'
1 S	*ʔatxarbaṭ*	'I am confused'		
P	*nitxarbaṭ*	'we are " '		

Other verbs like *txarbaṭ* are:

Class V

txaḟḟaḟ	*yitxaḟḟaḟ*	'to be lightened, diluted'

Quadriliteral

ttarjam	*yittarjam*	'to be translated'
djamhar	*yidjamhar*	'to gather, crowd'

(4) Classes VII and VIII

Sound verbs of Classes VII and VIII have imperfect stem patterns *-nFiMiL/-nFuMuL* and *-FtiMiL/-FtuMuL* respectively; those with *i* are much more common. The stem vowel *i* or *u* is dropped before suffixes, and the *preceding* vowel *i* or *u* is changed to *a*. The imperative forms have no prefixes.

Stem vowel *i*

qtiraẓ　'to suggest'　(Class VIII)

3 M	*yiqtiriẓ*	'he suggests'
F	*tiqtiriẓ*	'she " '
P	*yiqtarẓuun*	'they suggest'

2 M	*tiqtiriz*	'you M suggest'	*qtiriz*	'suggest M'
F	*tiqtarziin*	'you F " '	*qtarzi*	' " F'
P	*tiqtarzuun*	'you P " '	*qtarzu*	' " P'
1 S	*ʔaqtiriz*	'I suggest'		
P	*niqtiriz*	'we " '		

Other verbs like *qtiraz* are:

Class VII

ndifaƐ	*yindifiƐ*	'to get carried away, go too far'
nṭirad	*yinṭirid*	'to be expelled, fired'
nkisar	*yinkisir*	'to be broken'
nlizam	*yinlizim*	'to be caught'

Class VIII

xtilaf	*yixtilif*	'to differ, disagree'
Ɛtiraf	*yiƐtirif*	'to confess'
ftikar	*yiftikir*	'to think'
ftiham	*yiftihim*	'to understand'
ntixab	*yintixib*	'to elect'

Stem vowel *u*

štiġaḷ 'to work' (Class VIII)

3 M	*yištuġuḷ*	'he works'		
F	*tištuġuḷ*	'she " '		
P	*yištaġḷuun*	'they work'		
2 M	*tištuġuḷ*	'you M work'	*štuġuḷ*	'work M'
F	*tištaġḷiin*	'you F " '	*štaġḷi*	' " F'
P	*tištaġḷuun*	'you P " '	*štaġlu*	' " P'
1 S	*ʔaštuġuḷ*	'I work'		
P	*ništuġuḷ*	'we " '		

Other verbs like *štiġaḷ* are:

Class VII

nƐiraf	*yinƐuruf*	'to become known'
njubar	*yinjubur*	'to be forced'

Class VIII

ẓtifaẓ̧	*yiẓtufuẓ̧ b-*	'to keep, preserve'
ṣṭubar	*yiṣṭubur*	'to wait, be patient'

(5) Others

All sound verbs other than those listed in (1) through (4) above have imperfect stems identical with their perfect stems except for the stem vowel, which is *i* or *u* depending on the adjacent consonants (2.6). The stem vowel is dropped before suffixes if it is preceded by a single or a double consonant and followed by a different consonant;[1] otherwise it remains unchanged.[2] The imperative forms have no prefixes. In this category are sound verbs of Classes II, III, and X, and sound quadriliterals without *t-*.

Stem vowel *i* (dropped)

	baddal	'to change'	(Class II)	
3 M	*ybaddil*	'he changes'		
F	*tbaddil*	'she " '		
P	*ybaddluun*	'they change'		
2 M	*tbaddil*	'you M change'	*baddil*	'change M'
F	*tbaddliin*	'you F " '	*baddli*	' " F'
P	*ybaddluun*	'you P " '	*baddlu*	' " P'
1 S	*ʔabaddil*	'I change'		
P	*nbaddil*	'we " '		

Other verbs like *baddal* are:

Class II

ʔajjal	*yʔajjil*	'to postpone'
ẓassan	*yẓassin*	'to improve' (tr)

---

[1] When the stem vowel is preceded by a double consonant and followed by a different consonant, as in some Class II verbs, it is sometimes retained before suffixes instead of being dropped:

3 M	*ybaddil*	'he changes'
P	*ybaddiluun*	'they change'

[2] In some cases only, when the stem vowel is preceded by two consonants and followed by a different consonant, as in some Class X and simple quadriliteral verbs, it is sometimes shifted (4.1.3.1 C) before suffixes instead of remaining unchanged:

3 M	*yxarmuš*	'he scratches'
P	*yxarumšuun*	'they scratch'

δakkar	*yδakkir*	'to remind'
sajjal	*ysajjil*	'to register'
ṣaddag	*yṣaddig*	'to believe'
ʕallam	*yʕallim*	'to teach'
ʕayyan	*yʕayyin*	'to appoint'

Class III

baalaġ	*ybaaliġ*	'to exaggerate'
ʒaawal	*yʒaawil*	'to try'
daayan	*ydaayin*	'to lend'
saafar	*ysaafir*	'to go on a trip'
qaaran	*yqaarin*	'to compare'

Quadriliterals

ṣoogar	*yṣoogir*	'to insure'
neešan	*yneešin*	'to aim'

Stem vowel *u* (dropped)

	dabbar	'to arrange'		(Class II)
3 M	*ydabbur*	'he arranges'		
F	*ddabbur*	'she " '		
P	*ydabbruun*	'they arrange'		
2 M	*ddabbur*	'you M arrange'	*dabbur*	'arrange M'
F	*ddabbriin*	'you F " '	*dabbri*	' " F'
P	*ddabbruun*	'you P " '	*dabbru*	' " P'
1 S	*ʔadabbur*	'I arrange'		
P	*ndabbur*	'we " '		

Other verbs like *dabbar* are:

Class II

xarrab	*yxarrub*	'to ruin'
daggam	*ydaggum*	'to button'
ṣaffag	*yṣaffug*	'to applaud'
naḍḍaf	*ynaḍḍuf*	'to clean'
fawwar	*yfawwur*	'to boil'

Class III

xaabar	*yxaabur*	'to telephone'
daawam	*ydaawum*	'to last, continue'

Quadriliterals

deewar	*ydeewur*	'to turn'

Stem vowel *i* (retained)

	tammam	'to complete'	(Class II)	
3 M	*ytammim*	'he completes'		
F	*ttammim*	'she " '		
P	*ytammimuun*	'they complete'		
2 M	*ttammim*	'you M complete'	*tammim*	'complete M'
F	*ttammimiin*	'you F " '	*tammimi*	' " F'
P	*ttammimuun*	'you P " '	*tammimu*	' " P'
1 S	*ʔatammim*	'I complete'		
P	*ntammim*	'we " '		

Other verbs like *tammam* are:

Class II

jaddad	*yjaddid*	'to renew'
ẓarrar	*yẓarrir*	'to edit; to free'
sammam	*ysammim*	'to poison'
qarrar	*yqarrir*	'to decide'

Class III

ẓaajaj	*yẓaajij*	'to argue with'

Class X

staẓsan	*yistaẓsin*	'to approve'
staxdam	*yistaxdim*	'to employ'
staɛmal	*yistaɛmil*	'to use'
stafham	*yistafhim*	'to enquire'
staqbal	*yistaqbil*	'to go to meet'

stantaj	*yistantij*	'to deduce'
stankar	*yistankir*	'to denounce, disapprove strongly'

Quadriliterals

barhan	*ybarhin*	'to prove'
ɛarqal	*yɛarqil*	'to hinder'
handas	*yhandis*	'to design'
lablab	*ylablib*	'to cut up; to polish up'

Stem vowel *u* (retained)

xaffaf 'to lighten, dilute' (Class II)

3 M	*yxaffuf*	'he lightens'			
F	*txaffuf*	'she " '			
P	*yxaffufuun*	'they lighten'			
2 M	*txaffuf*	'you M lighten'		*xaffuf*	'lighten M'
F	*txaffufiin*	'you F " '		*xaffufi*	' " F'
P	*txaffufuun*	'you P " '		*xaffufu*	' " P'
1 S	*ʔaxaffuf*	'I lighten'			
P	*nxaffuf*	'we " '			

Other verbs like *xaffaf* are:

Class X

stajwab	*yistajwub*	'to question'

Quadriliteral

tarjam	*ytarjum*	'to translate'
xarbaṭ	*yxarbuṭ*	'to mix up'
xarmaš	*yxarmuš*	'to scratch'
qašmar	*yqašmur*	'to tease'
baqbaq	*ybaqbuq*	'to bubble'

B. Doubled verbs

(1) Class I

Class I doubled verbs have the imperfect stem pattern *-FaDD*, *-FiDD*, or *-FuDD*. The vowel is unpredictable and must be learned for each verb; however there are only one or two common verbs with the *-FaDD* pattern. The stem remains the same in all forms. The imperative forms have no prefixes.

Stem pattern *-FaDD*

	Ɛaδ̣δ̣	'to bite'		
3 M	*yƐaδ̣δ̣*	'he bites'		
F	*tƐaδ̣δ̣*	'she " '		
P	*yƐaδ̣δ̣uun*	'they bite'		
2 M	*tƐaδ̣δ̣*	'you M bite'	*Ɛaδ̣δ̣*	'bite M'
F	*tƐaδ̣δ̣iin*	'you F " '	*Ɛaδ̣δ̣i*	' " F'
P	*tƐaδ̣δ̣uun*	'you P " '	*Ɛaδ̣δ̣u*	' " P'
1 S	*ʔaƐaδ̣δ̣*	'I bite'		
P	*nƐaδ̣δ̣*	'we " '		

Stem pattern *-FiDD*

	sadd	'to close'		
3 M	*ysidd*	'he closes'		
F	*tsidd*	'she " '		
P	*ysidduun*	'they close'		
2 M	*tsidd*	'you M close'	*sidd*	'close M'
F	*tsiddiin*	'you F " '	*siddi*	' " F'
P	*tsidduun*	'you P " '	*siddu*	' " P'
1 S	*ʔasidd*	'I close'		
P	*nsidd*	'we " '		

Other verbs like *sadd* are:

ʒabb	*yʒibb*	'to like, love'
ʒadd	*yʒidd*	'to sharpen'
ʒall	*yʒill*	'to solve; to untie'
dazz	*ydizz*	'to send'
δabb	*yδibb*	'to throw away'
šadd	*yšidd*	'to fasten'
δ̣ann	*yδ̣inn*	'to suppose'
Ɛadd	*yƐidd*	'to count'
hamm	*yhimm*	'to matter, be important'

Stem pattern *-FuDD*

	zaṭṭ	'to put'		
3 M	*yzuṭṭ*	'he puts'		
F	*tzuṭṭ*	'she " '		
P	*yzuṭṭuun*	'they put'		
2 M	*tzuṭṭ*	'you M put'	*zuṭṭ*	'put M'
F	*tzuṭṭiin*	'you F " '	*zuṭṭi*	' " F'
P	*tzuṭṭuun*	'you P " '	*zuṭṭu*	' " P'
1 S	*ʔazuṭṭ*	'I put'		
P	*nzuṭṭ*	'we " '		

Other verbs like *zaṭṭ* are:

jarr	*yjurr*	'to pull'
zakk	*yzukk*	'to scratch'
dagg	*ydugg*	'to knock'
ṭagg	*yṭugg*	'to burst'
ġašš	*yġušš*	'to cheat'
fakk	*yfukk*	'to open'
marr	*ymurr*	'to pass'
maṣṣ	*ymuṣṣ*	'to suck'
gazz	*yguzz*	'to cough'
gaṣṣ	*yguṣṣ*	'to cut'

(2) Class IV

Class IV doubled verbs have the imperfect stem pattern *-FiDD* and are thus indistinguishable in the imperfect from some Class I doubled verbs (B (1) above). The stem remains the same in all forms. The imperative forms have no prefixes.

	ʔaṣarr	'to insist'		
3 M	*yṣirr*	'he insists'		
F	*tṣirr*	'she " '		
P	*yṣirruun*	'they insist'		
2 M	*tṣirr*	'you M insist'	*ṣirr*	'insist M'
F	*tṣirriin*	'you F " '	*ṣirri*	' " F'
P	*tṣirruun*	'you P "	*ṣirru*	' " P'
1 S	*ʔaṣirr*	'I insist'		
P	*nṣirr*	'we " '		

Other verbs like *ʔaṣarr* are:

ʔatamm	*ytimm*	'to complete, fulfill'
ʔaδall	*yδill*	'to subjugate, overpower'

(3) Class X and quadriliteral *FSaTaLL*

Class X doubled verbs and quadriliteral verbs of the pattern *FSaTaLL* have imperfect stems identical with their perfect stems except for the vowels. The patterns are respectively-*stiFiDD* and-*FSaTill*. The stem remains the same in all forms. The imperative forms have no prefixes.

	stimarr	'to continue'	(Class X)	
3 M	*yistimirr*	'he continues'		
F	*tistimirr*	'she " '		
P	*yistimirruun*	'they continue'		
2 M	*tistimirr*	'you M continue'	*stimirr*	'continue M'
F	*tistimirriin*	'you F " '	*stimirri*	' " F'
P	*tistimirruun*	'you P " '	*stimirru*	' " P'
1 S	*ʔastimirr*	'I continue'		
P	*nistimirr*	'we " '		

Other verbs like *stimarr* are:

Class X

staẓaqq	*yistiẓiqq*	'to deserve; to fall due'
stixaff	*yistixiff b-*	'to make fun of'
stiradd	*yistiridd*	'to take back, get back'
staƐadd	*yistiƐidd*	'to be ready, make preparation'
stilaδδ	*yistiliδδ b-*	'to enjoy'

Quadriliteral *FSaTaLL*

šmaʔazz	*yišmaʔizz*	'to be disgusted'
ṭmaʔann	*yiṭmaʔinn*	'to be reassured, unworried'
qšaƐarr	*yiqšaƐirr*	'to shudder; to crawl (skin)'

(4) Others

The other doubled verbs (Class VII doubled, Class VIII doubled, and Class IX) all have imperfect stems identical with their perfect stems; the vowel of the stem is thus always *a*. The stem remains the same in all forms. The imperative forms have no prefixes.

	ndall	'to know (location of)'			(Class VII)
3 M	*yindall*	'he knows'			
F	*tindall*	'she " '			
P	*yindalluun*	'they know'			
2 M	*tindall*	'you M know'	*ndall*	'know M'	
F	*tindalliin*	'you F " '	*ndalli*	' " F'	
P	*tindalluun*	'you P " '	*ndallu*	' " P'	
1 S	*ʔandall*	'I know'			
P	*nindall*	'we " '			

Other verbs like *ndall* are:

Class VII

nẓabb	*yinẓabb*	'to be liked'
nẓall	*yinẓall*	'to be released; to be solved'
ndazz	*yindazz*	'to be sent'
nƐadd	*yinƐadd*	'to be counted'
nġaθθ	*yinġaθθ*	'to be upset, bothered'
nġašš	*yinġašš*	'to be cheated'

Class VIII

ẓtall	*yiẓtall*	'to conquer, occupy'
ṣṭakk	*yiṣṭakk*	'to chatter' (teeth)
ḍṭarr	*yiḍṭarr*	'to be forced, have to'
htamm	*yihtamm*	'to be interested'

Class IX

byaḍḍ	*yibyaḍḍ*	'to turn white'
xrass	*yixrass*	'to be struck dumb'
xraff	*yixraff*	'to grow senile'
zragg	*yizragg*	'to turn blue'
swadd	*yiswadd*	'to turn black'
ṣfarr	*yiṣfarr*	'to turn yellow or pale'

ṣḷaƐƐ	*yiṣḷaƐƐ*	'to grow bald'
ṭrašš	*yiṭrašš*	'to grow deaf'

C. Hollow verbs

(1) Class I

Class I hollow verbs have the imperfect stem pattern *-FaaL*, *-FiiL*, or *-FuuL*. The vowel is unpredictable and must be learned for each verb; the *-FaaL* pattern, however, is much less common than the other two. The stem remains the same in all forms. The imperative forms have no prefixes.

Stem pattern *-FaaL*

naam 'to sleep; to lie down'

3 M	*ynaam*	'he sleeps'		
F	*tnaam*	'she " '		
P	*ynaamuun*	'they sleep'		
2 M	*tnaam*	'you M sleep'	*naam*	'sleep M'
F	*tnaamiin*	'you F " '	*naami*	' " F'
P	*tnaamuun*	'you P " '	*naamu*	' " P'
1 S	*ˀanaam*	'I sleep'		
P	*nnaam*	'we " '		

Other verbs like *naam* are:

baat	*ybaat*	'to spend the night'
xaaf	*yxaaf*	'to be afraid'
ġaar	*yġaar*	'to be jealous'
naal	*ynaal*	'to obtain'
haab	*yhaab*	'to fear, respect'

Stem pattern *-FiiL*

baaƐ 'to sell'

3 M	*ybiiƐ*	'he sells'		
F	*tbiiƐ*	'she " '		
P	*ybiiƐuun*	'they sell'		
2 M	*tbiiƐ*	'you M sell'	*biiƐ*	'sell M'
F	*tbiiƐiin*	'you F " '	*biiƐi*	' " F'
P	*tbiiƐuun*	'you P " '	*biiƐu*	' " P'
1 S	*ˀabiiƐ*	'I sell'		
P	*nbiiƐ*	'we " '		

Other verbs like *baaɛ* are:

jaab	*yjiib*	'to bring'
raad	*yriid* [1]	'to want'
zaad	*yziid*	'to increase' (intr)
šaal	*yšiil*	'to pick up, carry'
ṣaaẓ	*yṣiiẓ*	'to shout'
ṣaar	*yṣiir*	'to become'
ṭaar	*yṭiir*	'to fly'
ɛaaš	*yɛiiš*	'to live'
qaas	*yqiis*	'to measure'
maal	*ymiil*	'to lean'

Stem pattern *-FuuL*

	šaaf	'to see'		
3 M	*yšuuf*	'he sees'		
F	*tšuuf*	'she " '		
P	*yšuufuun*	'they see'		
2 M	*tšuuf*	'you M see'	*šuuf*	'see M'
F	*tšuufiin*	'you F " '	*šuufi*	' " F'
P	*tšuufuun*	'you P " '	*šuufu*	' " P'
1 S	*ʔašuuf*	'I see'		
P	*nšuuf*	'we " '		

Other verbs like *šaaf* are:

baag	*ybuug*	'to steal'
xaaṭ	*yxuuṭ*	'to stir'

[1] In the 3 P, 2 F, and 2 P forms of this verb, which have a suffix *-uun* or *-iin*, variant forms based on a shortened stem *-rd-* are quite common, i.e., *yirduun* 'they want' beside *yriiduun*, *tirdiin* 'you F want' beside *triidiin*, and *tirduun* 'you P want' beside *triiduun*. The same shortened stem *-rd* also occurs in a variant of the 1 S form, when it is followed by another 1 S imperfect (in the latter the *ʔ* of the prefix is usually dropped), for example, *ʔard ašuufak* 'I want to see you' instead of *ʔariid ašuufak*.

raaẓ	*yruuẓ* [1]	'to go'
zaar	*yzuur*	'to visit'
saaq	*ysuuq*	'to drive'
ḍaag	*yḍuug*	'to taste'
faat	*yfuut*	'to pass'
laam	*yluum*	'to blame'
maat	*ymuut*	'to die'
gaal	*yguul* [2]	'to say'
gaam	*yguum*	'to get up'
čaan/kaan	*ykuun* [3]	'to be'

(2) Class IV

Class IV hollow verbs have the imperfect stem pattern *-FiiL*, and are thus indistinguishable in the imperfect from some Class I hollow verbs (see (1) above). The stem remains the same in all forms. The imperative forms have no prefixes.

	ʔadaar	'to direct, administer'		
3 M	*ydiir*	'he directs'		
F	*ddiir*	'she " '		
P	*ydiiruun*	'they direct'		
2 M	*ddiir*	'you M direct'	*diir*	'direct M'
F	*ddiiriin*	'you F " '	*diiri*	' " F'
P	*ddiiruun*	'you P " '	*diiru*	' " P'
1 S	*ʔadiir*	'I direct'		
P	*ndiir*	'we " '		

---

[1] In the 3 P, 2 F and 2 P of *raaẓ* there are variant forms based on a shortened stem *-rẓ-*; i.e. *yirẓuun* 'they go' beside *yruuẓuun*, *tirẓiin* 'you F go' beside *truuẓiin*, and *tirẓuun* 'you P go' beside *truuẓuun*.

[2] In the 3 P, 2 F, and 2 P of *gaal* there are variant forms based on a shortened stem *-gl-*; i.e. *yugluun* 'they say' beside *yguuluun*, *tugliin* 'you F say' beside *tguuliin*, and *tugluun* 'you P say' beside *tguuluun*. Also see 5.3.6 for forms of this verb before suffix *-l-* 'to'.

[3] The verb *čaan* 'to be', which in the perfect tense has two variant sets of forms, one beginning with *č* and one with *k* (see 5.2.1.2 C), has in the imperfect tense only one possible stem: *-kuun*.

Other verbs like *ʔaθaar* are:

ʔazaal	*yziil*	'to remove'
ʔasaaʔ	*ysiiʔ l–*	'to wrong, harm'
ʔaqaam	*yqiim*	'to establish, found'

(3) Class X

Class X hollow verbs have the imperfect stem pattern *–stiFiiL*.[1] The stem remains the same in all forms. The imperative forms have no prefix.

staraaz 'to rest'

3 M	*yistiriiz*	'he rests'		
F	*tistiriiz*	'she " '		
P	*yistiriizuun*	'they rest'		
2 M	*tistiriiz*	'you M rest'	*stiriiz*	'rest M'
F	*tistiriiziin*	'you F " '	*stiriizi*	' " F'
P	*tistiriizuun*	'you P " '	*stiriizu*	' " P'
1 S	*ʔastiriiz*	'I rest'		
P	*nistiriiz*	'we " '		

Other verbs like *staraaz* are:

stajaab	*yistijiib l–*	'to respond to, comply with'
stašaar	*yistišiir*	'to consult'
staʕaad	*yistiʕiid*	'to regain'
staʕaar	*yistiʕiir (min)*	'to be ashamed (of)'
stafaad	*yistifiid*	'to benefit (from)'
staqaal	*yistiqiil*	'to resign'

(4) Others

The other hollow verbs (Class VII and Class VIII) have imperfect stems identical with their perfect stems; the vowel of the stem is thus always *aa*. The stem remains the same in all forms. The imperative forms have no prefixes.

rtaaz 'to rest, take it easy' (Class VIII)

3 M	*yirtaaz*	'he rests'
F	*tirtaaz*	'she " '
P	*yirtaazuun*	'they rest'

[1] A few also have a variant pattern *–staFaaL̆*.

2 M	*tirtaaʒ*	'you M rest'	*rtaaʒ*	'rest M'
F	*tirtaaʒiin*	'you F " '	*rtaaʒi*	' " F'
P	*tirtaaʒuun*	'you P " '	*rtaaʒu*	' " P'
1 S	*ʔartaaʒ*	'I rest'		
P	*nirtaaʒ*	'we " '		

Other verbs like *rtaaʒ* are:

Class VII

nbaaƐ	*yinbaaƐ*	'to be sold'
njaab	*yinjaab*	'to be brought'
nδaaƐ	*yinδaaƐ*	'to be broadcast'
nraad	*yinraad*	'to be needed, wanted'
nšaal	*yinšaal*	'to be picked up, carried'
nṣaad	*yinṣaad*	'to be caught'
nδ̣aaf	*yinδ̣aaf*	'to be added'
nhaan	*yinhaan*	'to be insulted'

Class VIII

ʒtaaj	*yiʒtaaj*	'to need'
ʒtaar	*yiʒtaar*	'to be at a loss'
xtaar	*yixtaar*	'to select'
Ɛtaad	*yiƐtaad*	'to get accustomed'
ltaaf	*yiltaaf*	'to turn'

D. Defective verbs

(1) Class I

(a) Verbs beginning with *w*

Class I defective verbs which begin with *w* have the imperfect stem pattern *-ooMa* or *-ooMi*. (Cf. Class I sound verbs beginning with *w* in A (1) (b) above.) The final vowel is unpredictable and must be learned for each verb. The final vowel is dropped before suffixes. The imperative forms have the prefix *ʔ-*.

Stem pattern *-ooMa*

	wuƐa	'to beware, become aware'
3 M	*yooƐa*	'he bewares'
F	*tooƐa*	'she " '
P	*yooƐuun*	'they beware'

2 M	*tooƐa*	'you M beware'	*ʔooƐa*	'beware M'
F	*tooƐiin*	'you F " '	*ʔooƐi*	' " F'
P	*tooƐuun*	'you P " '	*ʔooƐu*	' " P'
1 S	*ʔooƐa*	'I beware'		
P	*nooƐa*	'we " '		

Another verb like *wuƐa* is:

wuha	*yooha*	'to fade, grow weak' (of enthusiasm)

Stem pattern *-ooMi*

	wuqa	'to protect'
3 M	*yooqi*	'he protects'
F	*tooqi*	'she " '
P	*yooquun*	'they protect'

2 M	*tooqi*	'you M protect'	*ʔooqi*	'protect M'
F	*tooqiin*	'you F " '	*ʔooqi*	' " F'
P	*tooquun*	'you P " '	*ʔooqu*	' " P'
1 S	*ʔooqi*	'I protect'		
P	*nooqi*	'we " '		

Other verbs like *wuqa* are:

wila	*yooli*	'to overpower, get' (at a weak moment)
wuša (b-)	*yooši*	'to inform (on)'
wufa b-	*yoofi*	'to keep' (a promise)

(b) Others

All other Class I defective verbs have the imperfect stem pattern *-FMa*, *-FMi*, or *-FMu*. The vowel is unpredictable and must be learned for each verb; the *-FMu* pattern, however, is extremely rare. The final vowel is dropped before suffixes. The imperative forms have the prefix *ʔi-* or *ʔu-*.

Stem pattern *-FMa*

	qira	'to read'
3 M	*yiqra*	'he reads'
F	*tiqra*	'she " '
P	*yiqruun*	'they read'

2 M	*tiqra*	'you M read'	*ʔiqra*	'read M'
F	*tiqriin*	'you F " '	*ʔiqri*	' " F'
P	*tiqruun*	'you P " '	*ʔiqru*	' " P'

| 1 S | *ʔaqra* | 'I read' |
| P | *niqra* | 'we " ' |

Other verbs like *qira* are:

difa	*yidfa*	'to get warm'
xiša	*yixša*	'to be afraid'
z̧ima	*yiz̧ma*	'to get hot'
ṣiz̧a	*yiṣz̧a*	'to get sober'
nisa	*yinsa*	'to forget'
buqa	*yibqa*	'to stay'
ġufa	*yiġfa*	'to doze off'

Stem pattern *-FMi*

| | *bina* | 'to build' |

3 M	*yibni*	'he builds'
F	*tibni*	'she " '
P	*yibnuun*	'they build'

2 M	*tibni*	'you M build'	*ʔibni*	'build M'
F	*tibniin*	'you F " '	*ʔibni*	' " F'
P	*tibnuun*	'you P " '	*ʔibnu*	' " P'

| 1 S | *ʔabni* | 'I build' |
| P | *nibni* | 'we " ' |

Other verbs like *bina* are:

bida	*yibdi*	'to begin'
biča	*yibči*	'to cry'
jira	*yijri*	'to flow'
z̧iba	*yiz̧bi*	'to crawl' (baby)
z̧iča	*yiz̧či*	'to talk'
liga	*yilgi*	'to find'
mila	*yimli*	'to fill'

niṭa	*yinṭi*	'to give'
giδa	*yigδi*	'to finish'
muδa	*yimδi*	'to sign'

Stem pattern *-FMu*

	nima	'to grow'		
3 M	*yinmu*	'he grows'		
F	*tinmu*	'she " '		
P	*yinmuun*	'they grow'		
2 M	*tinmu*	'you M grow'	*ʔinmu*	'grow M'
F	*tinmiin*	'you F " '	*ʔinmi*	' " F'
P	*tinmuun*	'you P " '	*ʔinmu*	' " P'
1 S	*ʔanmu*	'I grow'		
P	*ninmu*	'we " '		

No other examples of full verbs like *nima* have been found, and even in this verb some speakers use a final *i* instead. A trace of the *-FMu* stem occurs, however, in the first-person verb forms *ʔarju* 'I hope' and *nirju* 'we hope', and the common expressions *ʔarjuuk*, *ʔarjuuč*, *ʔarjuukum* 'please; I beg of you', all of which are forms of an otherwise rare verb *rija* 'to hope; to beg'.

(2) Class IV

(a) First radical *w*

Class IV defective verbs in which the first radical is *w* have the imperfect stem pattern *-ooMi* and are thus indistinguishable in the imperfect from Class I defective verbs beginning with *w* (D (1) (a) above). (Cf. Class IV sound verbs with *w* as first radical in A (2) (a) above.) The final vowel is dropped before suffixes. The imperative forms have the prefix *ʔ-*.

	ʔawẓa (-l-)	'to inspire (s-o)'		
3 M	*yooẓi*	'he inspires'		
F	*tooẓi*	'she " '		
P	*yooẓuun*	'they inspire'		
2 M	*tooẓi*	'you M inspire'	*ʔooẓi*	'inspire M'
F	*tooẓiin*	'you F " '	*ʔooẓi*	' " F'
P	*tooẓuun*	'you P " '	*ʔooẓu*	' " P'
1 S	*ʔooẓi*	'I inspire'		
P	*nooẓi*	'we " '		

(b) Others

All other Class IV defective verbs have the imperfect stem pattern *-FMi* and are thus indistinguishable in the imperfect from some Class I defective verbs

((1) (b) above). The final vowel is dropped before suffixes. The imperative forms have the prefix *ʔi–*.

	ʔalġa	'to cancel'		
3 M	*yilġi*	'he cancels'		
F	*tilġi*	'she " '		
P	*yilġuun*	'they cancel'		
2 M	*tilġi*	'you M cancel'	*ʔilġi*	'cancel M'
F	*tilġiin*	'you F " '	*ʔilġi*	' " F'
P	*tilġuun*	'you P " '	*ʔilġu*	' " P'
1 S	*ʔalġi*	'I cancel'		
P	*nilġi*	'we " '		

Other verbs like *ʔalġa* are:

ʔalqa	*yilqi*	'to deliver' (a speech)
ʔamla	*yimli*	'to dictate' (a letter)

(3) Verbs with *t–* prefix

All defective verbs which bear the derivational prefix *t–* (Classes V and VI) have imperfect stems identical with their perfect stems; the final vowel is thus always *a*.[1] The final vowel is dropped before suffixes. The imperative forms have no prefix.

	tbanna	'to adopt'	(Class V)	
3 M	*yitbanna*	'he adopts'		
F	*titbanna*	'she " '		
P	*yitbannuun*	'they adopt'		
2 M	*titbanna*	'you M adopt'	*tbanna*	'adopt M'
F	*titbanniin*	'you F " '	*tbanni*	' " F'
P	*titbannuun*	'you P " '	*tbannu*	' " P'
1 S	*ʔatbanna*	'I adopt'		
P	*nitbanna*	'we " '		

Other verbs like *tbanna* are:

<u>Class V</u>

tʒadda	*yitʒadda*	'to challenge'
txaffa	*yitxaffa*	'to wear a disguise'
tsamma	*yitsamma*	'to be called'

---

[1] This is also true of sound verbs with *t–* prefix; see A (3) above.

tšakka	*yitšakka*	'to complain'
tƐašša	*yitƐašša*	'to dine'
tġadda	*yitġadda*	'to lunch'
twaffa	*yitwaffa*	'to pass away, die'
twalla	*yitwalla*	'to take over, assume'

Class VI

tbaaha	*yitbaaha*	'to brag'
tʒaaša	*yitʒaaša*	'to avoid, dodge'
traaḍa	*yitraaḍa*	'to agree' (mutually)
tƐaaṭa	*yitƐaaṭa*	'to carry' (line of goods)
tlaaga	*yitlaaga*	'to get together, meet'

(4) Others

All other defective verbs have imperfect stems identical with their perfect stems except for the final vowel, which is *i*. The final vowel is dropped before suffixes. The imperative forms have no prefixes. In this category are the defective verbs of Classes II, III, VII, VIII, and X, and defective quadriliterals of the pattern *FooTa*.

	xalla	'to let, allow'	(Class II)	
3 M	*yxalli*	'he lets'		
F	*txalli*	'she " '		
P	*yxalluun*	'they let'		
2 M	*txalli*	'you M let'	*xalli*	'let M'
F	*txalliin*	'you F " '	*xalli*	' " F'
P	*txalluun*	'you P " '	*xallu*	' " P'
1 S	*ʔaxalli*	'I let'		
P	*nxalli*	'we " '		

Other verbs like *xalla* are:

Class II

dalla	*ydalli*	'to direct'
rabba	*yrabbi*	'to raise, bring up'
samma	*ysammi*	'to name, call'
sawwa	*ysawwi*	'to do'

ṣaffa	*yṣaffi*	'to refine'
ġaṭṭa	*yġaṭṭi*	'to cover'
wadda	*ywaddi*	'to take' (someone somewhere)
gaḷḷa	*ygaḷḷi*	'to fry'

Class III

daara	*ydaari*	'to look after, take care of'
raawa	*yraawi*	'to show'
saawa	*ysaawi*	'to equal'
laaga	*ylaagi*	'to meet'

Class VII

nʒina	*yinʒini*	'to bow, bend over, be bent'
nƐina	*yinƐini*	'to be meant'
nqira	*yinqiri*	'to be read'
nliga	*yinligi*	'to be found'
nnisa	*yinnisi*	'to be forgotten'

Class VIII

xtiba	*yixtibi*	'to hide'
ddiƐa	*yiddiƐi*	'to claim'
štika	*yištiki*	'to complain'
ntiha	*yintihi*	'to finish' (intr)

Class X

starƐa	*yistarƐi*	'to attract' (attention)
staġna	*yistaġni Ɛan*	'to do without'
stafta	*yistafti*	'to take a poll of'
stawla	*yistawli*	'to take over'

Quadriliterals

ʔooma	*yʔoomi*	'to beckon, gesture'
ʒooma	*yʒoomi*	'to circle, hang around'
loola -l-	*ylooli*	'to sing a lullaby to'

E. *jaa*

The verb *jaa* (or *ʔija*; see 5.2.1.2 E) 'to come' has the imperfect stem *-ji*. The stem vowel is dropped before suffixes. The imperative forms are based on a totally different stem *taƐaal-;* they have no prefixes.

	jaa	'to come'		
3 M	*yiji*	'he comes'		
F	*tiji*	'she " '		
P	*yijuun*	'they come'		
2 M	*tiji*	'you M come'	*taƐaal*	'come M'
F	*tijiin*	'you F " '	*taƐaali*	' " F'
P	*tijuun*	'you P " '	*taƐaalu*	' " P'
1 S	*ʔaji*	'I come'		
P	*niji*	'we " '		

5.3 VERBAL AFFIXES

This section deals with the prefixes and suffixes which occur with perfect and imperfect verb forms. It includes some syntactical as well as morphological information.

5.3.1 Future prefix *raʒ-* 'going to'

The prefix *raʒ-* (or *raaʒ-*, with a long vowel) is used with imperfect indicative verb forms. It has the specific meaning of future action. The English equivalents are usually going to or will with a verb, and occasionally a present tense form with future meaning. A *raʒ-* construction is made negative by the negative prefix *ma-* 'not', preceding the *raʒ-*. Examples:

ʔaani mitʔakkid huwwa raʒ-yinjaʒ.	'I'm sure he's going to succeed.'
raʒ-abaṭṭil imnit-tadxiin.	'I'm going to give up smoking.'
ʔiʒsib šgadd raʒ-itkallif.	'Figure out how much it's going to cost.'
raʒ-asawwiiha ṣ-ṣubuʒ.	'I'm going to do it in the morning.'
minu raʒ-yidfaƐ kull haaδa?	'Who's going to pay all this?'
ma-raʒ-yiji.	'He's not going to come.'
ma-raʒ-agul-lak.	'I'm not going to tell you.'

raʒ-nooṣal l-ihnaak ib-xilaal saaƐa.	'We'll get there in an hour.'
ʔiʒna raʒ-inkuun ihnaak raabiƐ yoom mniš-šahar.	'We'll be there on the fourth day of the month.'
had-duwa raʒ-yxaffuf il-alam.	'This medicine will ease the pain.'
raʒ-insaafir l-isbuuƐ ij-jaay.	'We're leaving next week.'
raʒ-itruuʒ lil-ʒafla?	'Are you going to the party?'

5.3.2 Progressive prefix *da-*

The prefix *da-* is used with imperfect indicative verb forms. (When it occurs with a first-person singular verb form, e.g. *ʔadrus* 'I study', usually the initial *ʔ* of the verb is dropped, and the short *a* of the prefix and that of the verb are pronounced together as a long *aa*, for example *da-adrus* 'I'm studying'.) A *da-* construction is made negative by the negative prefix *ma-*, preceding the *da-*.

The prefix *da-* has the general meaning of continuing, repeated, or habitual action. For continuing action - action going on at a given time - the usual English equivalent is an -ing phrase (e.g. is writing); for habitual action, a present tense form (e.g. works, doesn't work); in some cases the English translation might be either of these. A number of Iraqi verbs which often have the *da-* prefix are translated by English verbs which seldom or never enter into -ing phrases; among these are some common verbs having to do with mental processes, for example *gidar* 'to be able', *Ɛiraf* and *dira* 'to know', *ftiham* 'to understand', *šaaf* 'to see', and *raad* 'to want'. (See also 12.1.2.) Examples:

da-yiktib maktuub.	'He's writing a letter.'
š-da-tsawwi?	'What are you doing?'
minu yidri š-da-yṣiir ihnaak?	'Who knows what's going on there?'
l-ʒanafiyya da-tnaggiṭ.	'The faucet's dripping.'
da-aʒaawil aṭalliƐ it-tapaduur imnil-buṭil.	'I'm trying to get the cork out of the bottle.'
ʔinta hassa da-tištuġul ib-daaʔirt il-bariid?	'Are you working at the post office now?'
haaδa bass da-yḍayyiƐ wakta.	'He's just wasting his time.'
haδoola kulši ma-da-yitƐallmuun ib-hal-madrasa.	'They're not learning anything at that school.'
da-yištaġluun ib-jidd bil-mašruuƐ ij-jidiid.	'They're working hard on the new project.'
da-tišƐur mariiḍa.	'She feels (or is feeling) ill.'
l-waaridaat da-tziid Ɛaṣ-ṣaadiraat has-sana.	'Imports exceed exports this year.'

haaδa da-yƐaawinhum ihwaaya b-šuġuḷhum.	'He helps them a lot in their work.'
ruuz šuuf šuu š-da-yṣiir bid-daaʔira min ʔinta ma-mawjuud.	'Go see what goes on in the office when you're not there.'
ʔiδni da-toojaƐni.	'My ear aches (hurts me).'
ma-da-aƐruf iš-da-yriid.	'I don't know what he wants.'
ma-da-adri luweeš mistaƐjil Ɛaleeha halgadd.	'I don't know why you're in such a hurry about it.'
minu gal-lak huwwa da-yriid ybaṭṭil min šuġḷa?	'Who told you he wanted to quit his job?'
ma-da-aftihim luweeš yriiduun yfukkuun šaariƐ ihnaak.	'I don't understand why they want to open up a road there.'
ʔaku fadd šii ġaḷaṭ laakin ma-da-agdar algii.	'There's something wrong but I can't find it.'

5.3.3 Prefix *d(i)-*

The prefix *d(i)-* is used with imperative verb forms. With imperatives beginning with *ʔi-* or *ʔu-* the prefix has the form *d-* and the *ʔ-* of the imperative is dropped, for example *d-imši* 'go away'. With imperatives beginning with any other consonant, the prefix has the form *di-*, for example *di-guul* 'say'.

The meaning of this prefix with an imperative cannot be indicated by any one English equivalent. It adds to the simple imperative a note of cajolery or impatience which might be rendered in English in various ways. The word *Ɛaad* frequently occurs after an imperative with this prefix; it too has no single English translation, but serves to intensify the sense of the imperative. Some examples follow.

di-guulha.	'Come on, say it!' 'Go on now, say it.' 'Say it, for heaven's sake.'
d-ukul.	'Go ahead, eat.' 'Please eat.'
di-ruuz Ɛaad.	'Go on, go!'

5.3.4 Negative prefixes *ma-* and *la-*

Verbs are made negative by the prefixes *ma-* and *la-*.[1] These prefixes usually have a somewhat stronger stress and higher pitch than the stressed syllable of the form to which they are prefixed (see 3.2).

[1] Independent forms *maa* and *laa* are sometime heard in slow, precise speech, but the prefix forms are the normal ones.

The prefix *ma-* is used with perfect and imperfect indicative verb forms. (When it occurs with an imperfect first-person singular form, e.g. *ʔariid*, usually the initial *ʔ* of the verb is dropped, and the short *a* of the prefix and that of the verb are pronounced together as a long *aa*, for example *ma-ariid* 'I don't want'.)

ma-šaaf	'he did not see'
ma-ftihámit	'I/you M did not understand'
ma-yšuuf	'he does not see'
ma-agdar	'I can't'

When *ma-* is used with a *raz-* construction (5.3.1 above) or a *da-* construction (5.3.2 above), it precedes these prefixes:

ma-raz-yiji	'he's not going to come'
ma-da-agdar	'I can't'

The prefix *la-* is used with second-person imperfect *indicative* verb forms to form negative commands. (Imperative forms are used only for positive commands.) Compare the following sets:

	Imperative (Positive command)		*la-* with imperfect (Negative command)	
2 M	*ruuz*	'go M'	*la-truuz*	'don't go M'
F	*ruuzi*	' " F'	*la-truuziin*	' " " F'
P	*ruuzu*	' " P'	*la-truuzuun*	' " " P'

First-person plural and third-person imperfect indicative verb forms also may occur with prefix *la-*, usually after *xalli* or *xal-* 'let' (5.3.5 below), or in indirect commands. However, with these persons, *ma-* may be used instead.

1 P	*xal-la-nruuz.* *xal-ma-nruuz.*	'Let's not go.'
	xal-la-ništirii. *xal-ma-ništirii.*	'Let's not buy it.'
3 M	*gul-la la-yruuz.* *gul-la ma-yruuz.*	'Tell him not to go.'
F	*xal-la-taakul halgadd.* *xal-ma-taakul halgadd.*	'Have her not eat so much.'
P	*gul-lhum la-yšuufuun hal-filim.*	'Tell them not to see that film.'

5.3.5 Prefix *xal-* 'let'

The prefix *xal-* is used with imperfect indicative verb forms. (It is a shortened form of *xalli*, an imperative form of the verb *xalla* 'to let, allow', which is used in the same way and with the same meanings.) It occurs most commonly with the first person plural, and then corresponds to the English let's with a verb:

xal-naaxuδ taksi.	'Let's take a taxi.'
xal-niktib-la maktuub.	'Let's write him a letter.'

The verb in such cases is sometimes preceded by the prefix *da-* (5.3.2 above), with *xal-* preceding the whole construction:

xal-da-nruuẓ.	'Let's go.'
xal-da-naakul.	'Let's eat.'

The prefix may also occur with persons other than first-person plural; it then corresponds to English let or have with a pronoun object and a verb:

xal-yiẓči šgadd-ma yriid.	'Let him talk as much as he wants.'
xal-taakul fawaakih ihwaaya.	'Have her eat a lot of fruit.'

For negative *xal-* constructions see 5.3.4 above.

5.3.6 Prepositional suffix *-l-*

The suffix *-l-* 'to, for' is used with verb forms of any tense or mood. It occurs only in combination with a pronoun suffix (9.1.2), as follows:

3	M	*-la*	'to / for him'
	F	*-(i)lha*	' " " her'
	P	*-(i)lhum*	' " " them'
2	M	*-lak*	'to / for you M'
	F	*-lič*	' " " you F'
	P	*-(i)lkum*	' " " you P'
1	S	*-li*	'to / for me'
	P	*-(i)lna*[1]	' " " us'

The (*i*) noted in four of the above forms occurs only when the verb stem ends in a consonant:

dazz-ilhum ifluus.	'He sent them money.'
dazzoo-lhum ifluus	'They sent them money.'

If the verb stem ends in a vowel, the vowel becomes long when *-l-* plus a pronoun suffix is added, just as it does when a pronoun suffix alone is added. Similarly,

[1] In this form the *l* usually assimilates to the *n*: *-(i)nna*.

if the verb stem ends in *-aw*, this changes to *-oo-* ; if it ends in *-uun* or *-iin* the final *n* is dropped (9.1.2.2).

jiibi	'bring F'
jiibii-li	'bring F (to) me'
jiibu	'bring P'
jiibuu-lha	'bring P (to) her'
jaabaw	'they brought'
jaaboo-lhum	'they brought (to) them'
yjiibuun	'they bring'
yjiibuu-li	'they bring (to) me'
djiibiin	'you F bring'
djiibii-li	'you F bring (to) me'

The verb *gaal* 'to say, tell' has some special forms when the suffix *-l-* is attached. When the verb form ends in *-aal* or *-uul*, (1) the long vowel is shortened, and (2) if the suffix *-l-* is followed by a pronoun suffix beginning with a consonant, the final *-l* of the verb form is either doubled, in which case it is followed by the helping vowel, or combined with the suffix *-l-* into a single sound. In the perfect tense, the forms of the second and first persons may be regular, but more commonly are: 2 M and 1 S *gitt*, 2 F *gitti*, 2 P *gittu*, and 1 P *ginna* (these forms also occur elsewhere).

gaal	'he said'	*gilit*	'you M/I said'
gal-la	'he told him'	*gilit-la* / *gitt-la*	'you M/I told him'
nguul	'we say'	*gitt-ilhum*	'you M/I told them'
ngul-la	'we tell him'		
ngull-ilhum / *ngul-lhum*	'we tell them'		

Following are two complete paradigms illustrating all the forms of *-l-* plus a pronoun suffix, the first with a verb stem ending in a consonant and the second with a verb stem ending in a vowel.

jaab	'he brought'
jaab-la	'he brought (to) him'
jaab-ilha	'" " " her'
jaab-ilhum	'" " " them'
jaab-lak	'he brought (to) you M'
jaab-lič	'" " " you F'
jaab-ilkum	'" " " you P'
jaab-li	'he brought (to) me'
jaab-ilna	'" " " us'

jaabaw (stem jaaboo-)	'they brought'
jaaboo-la	'they brought (to) him'
jaaboo-lha	' " " " her'
jaaboo-lhum	' " " " them'
jaaboo-lak	'they brought (to) you M'
jaaboo-lič	' " " " you F'
jaaboo-lkum	' " " " you P'
jaaboo-li	'they brought (to) me'
jaaboo-lna	' " " " us'

5.3.7 Suffix stem *-yyaa-*

When two pronoun suffixes occur with a verb, the first is added directly to the verb stem or to the verb stem plus *-l-* (5.3.6), and the second is added to a stem *-yyaa-*, which is itself added to the first pronoun suffix:

jiib-li l-gahwa	'Bring me the coffee.'
jiib-li-yyaaha	'Bring me it F.'

The form *-yyaa-* has no meaning in itself; its function is only that of a stem for a second pronoun suffix.

5.3.7.1 Forms of *-yyaa-* plus pronoun suffix

Since *-yyaa-* is a stem which ends in a vowel, the pronoun suffixes attached to it are in the forms appropriate to vowel stems, including zero (absence of any suffix) for the third person masculine (9.1.2.1). All the possible forms of *-yyaa-* plus suffix are listed below, but only the three third-person forms are common, the others occurring rarely or never.[1]

3 M	*-yyaa*	'him'
F	*-yyaaha*	'her'
P	*-yyaahum*	'them'
2 M	*-yyaak*	'you M'
F	*-yyaač*	'you F'
P	*-yyaakum*	'you P'
1 S	*-yyaaya*	'me'
P	*-yyaana*	'us'

When this suffix is preceded by a consonant a helping vowel *i* (2.4) occurs at the beginning: *jiib-ilhum-iyyaaha* 'bring it F to them.'

[1] Another kind of construction, usually involving the independent preposition *ʔil-* 'to', is used instead. For example, instead of *dazzoo-la-yyaak* 'they sent you to him', one says *dazzook ʔila*.

5.3.7.2   Uses

As stated above, *-yyaa-* occurs whenever two pronoun suffixes are used with a verb.

A. Some verbs may have a double object, the first a pronoun suffix and the second either a noun or a second pronoun suffix. Of these the most common is *niṭa* 'to give'. If the second object is a noun, *-yyaa-* does not occur:

> *raz̧-anṭiik haṣ-ṣuura.*   'I'm going to give you M this picture.'

But if the second object is a pronoun suffix, *-yyaa-* occurs as its stem:

> *raz̧-anṭiik-iyyaaha.*   'I'm going to give it F to you.'

Note that in either case the first object is the one corresponding to what in English is sometimes called "indirect object": in the example above, the person *to whom* something is given.

B. A great many verbs have a suffixed *-l-* plus pronoun suffix (5.3.6). If a noun follows as the object of the verb, *-yyaa-* does not occur:

> *raz̧-ajiib-ilkum iṣ-ṣuura.*   'I'm going to bring you P the picture.'

But if a pronoun suffix occurs instead of the noun, *-yyaa-* is used as its stem, and this is by far the most frequent use of *-yyaa-* : after a suffixed *-l-* plus pronoun suffix:

> *raz̧-ajiib-ilkum-iyyaaha.*   'I'm going to bring it F to you P.'

Note that in Iraqi the *-l-* with its suffix is always first, though in the English translations the corresponding pronoun is not always first. Additional examples follow:

dizz-li-yyaa.	'Send it M to me.'
dizz-li-yyaaha.	'Send it F to me.'
dizz-li-yyaahum.	'Send them to me.'
raz̧-inxallii-lkum-iyyaaha bil-garaaj.	'We'll leave it F in the garage for you P.'
ʔiqraa-li-yyaa bit-talafoon.	'Read it M to me on the telephone.'
la-tinsiin itz̧aδδrii-nna-yyaahum.	'Don't forget F to get them ready for us.'
tigdar taaxuδ-li-yyaaha?	'Can you take it F for me?'

5.3.7.3 Special forms of pronoun suffixes before *-yyaa*

The third-person masculine pronoun 'him', which everywhere else has the form *-a* (after a consonant) or zero (after a long vowel), has a special form *h* which occurs only before *-yyaa-*

nṭeeta	'I gave to him'
nṭeeth-iyyaa	'I gave it to him'
ʔanṭii	'I give to him'
ʔanṭiih-iyyaa	'I give it to him'
njiib-la	'we bring to him'
njiib-ilh-iyyaa	'we bring it to him'

The third-person feminine pronoun suffix 'her', which everywhere else has the form *-ha*, may lose its final vowel before *-yyaa* and thus become identical with the masculine form:

nṭeetha	'I gave to her'
nṭeeth-iyyaa	'I gave it to her'
ʔanṭiiha	'I give to her'
ʔanṭiih-iyyaa	'I give it to her'
njiib-ilha	'we bring to her'
njiib-ilh-iyyaa	'we bring it to her'

The combinations of suffix *-l-* plus the second-person masculine and feminine pronoun suffixes, i.e. *-lak* 'to you M' and *-lič* 'to you F', usually have the forms *-(i)lk-* and *-(i)lč* before *-yyaa*, the initial *i* in each case occurring only if preceded by a consonant. Note the parallel between these alternants and those of the third person masculine form, *-la* and *-(i)lh-*:

njiib-la	'we bring to him'
njiib-lak	'we bring to you M'
njiib-lič	'we bring to you F'
njiib-ilh-iyyaa	'we bring it to him'
njiib-ilk-iyyaa	'we bring it to you M'
njiib-ilč-iyyaa	'we bring it to you F'

5.3.7.4 Agreement of pronoun suffixes attached to *-yyaa-*

When *h* occurs as an alternant of the third-person masculine or feminine pronoun suffix before *-yyaa-*, as described in 5.3.7.3 above, the *-yyaa* is invariable, regardless of the gender of its antecedent. There is thus no contrast in form in sets like the following four.

ʔabuuk yriid il-qaamuus.	'Your father wants the dictionary.'
jiib-ilh-iyyaa.	Bring it M to him.
ʔabuuk yriid ij-jariida.	'Your father wants the newspaper.'
jiib-ilh-iyyaa.	Bring it F to him'

ʔuṃṃak itriid il-qaamuus. *jiib-ilh-iyyaa.*	'Your mother wants the dictionary.' Bring it M to her.
ʔuṃṃak itriid ij-jariida. *jiib-ilh-iyyaa.*	'Your mother wants the newspaper.' Bring it F to her.

In other cases the pronoun suffix with *-yyaa-* agrees with its antecedent according to the usual rules of pronoun agreement (11.2.2):

ween il-qaamuus? *jiib-li-yyaa.*	'Where's the dictionary? Bring it M to me.'
ween ij-jariida? *jiib-li-yyaaha.*	'Where's the newspaper? Bring it F to me.'

6. NOUNS

6.1 DERIVATION

6.1.1 Verbal nouns

A verbal noun[1] is a noun which is derived from a verb and has the general meaning 'action' or 'state' indicated by that verb. English equivalents are often nouns ending in such elements as -ing, -ness, -tion, -al, -ance, for example 'studying', 'bashfulness', 'addition', 'removal', 'appearance'; or they may be nouns not marked by any particular endings, for example 'anger', 'work', 'talk'. Verbal nouns thus generally have an abstract meaning; but many of them also have a specialized concrete meaning, frequently indicating the physical result of the action indicated, for example 'act of wounding' or 'wound' and 'act of reporting' or 'report'.

The pattern of a verbal noun depends upon the derivational class and root-type of the verb from which it is derived. Verbal nouns of Class I triliteral verbs exhibit a number of different patterns; the other classes have only one or two patterns each.

6.1.1.1 Class I

The most common Class I verbal noun patterns are illustrated below. Those in B through E are common only for sound verbs, but one or two examples of other types are also shown below in each group. Each of the groups E through G illustrates two patterns, one with and one without the final *-a* shown in parentheses; which pattern applies is a matter to be learned for each word.

A.

Verb	Verbal noun
Sound	*FaMiL/FaMuL*
Doubled	*FaDD*
Hollow	*FooL, Feel*
Defective	*FaMi*

This is a common pattern for verbal nouns of sound verbs, and the most common for those of doubled, hollow, and defective verbs. Examples:

Sound verbs

ʔakal	'to eat'	*ʔakil*	'eating; food'
jiraẓ	'to wound'	*jariẓ*	'wounding; wound'
ṣiraf	'to spend'	*ṣaruf*	'spending, outlay'
ṭubax	'to cook'	*ṭabux*	'cooking'

[1] The Arabic term, also used in some English texts, is *maṣdar*.

Doubled verbs

z̧all	'to solve'	*z̧all*	'solution'
sadd	'to close, block'	*sadd*	'blocking; dam'
šakk	'to doubt'	*šakk*	'doubt'
gaṣṣ	'to cut'	*gaṣṣ*	'cutting'

Hollow verbs. If the imperfect of the verb (shown below in parentheses) has the vowel *uu*, the verbal noun generally has *oo* ; if *ii*, it generally has *ee*; if *aa*, it has *oo* or *ee* unpredictably.

laam (*yluum*)	'to blame'	*loom*	'blame'
maat (*ymuut*)	'to die'	*moot*	'death'
baaε (*ybiiε*)	'to sell'	*beeε*	'selling'
ṣaad (*yṣiid*)	'to hunt'	*ṣeed*	'hunting'
naam (*ynaam*)	'to sleep'	*noom*	'sleep'
naal (*ynaal*)	'to acquire'	*neel*	'acquiring'

Defective verbs

biča	'to cry'	*bači*	'crying'
z̧iča	'to talk'	*z̧ači*	'talk, talking'
miša	'to walk'	*maši*	'walking'
čuwa	'to burn'	*čawi*	'burning'

B.   Verb   Verbal noun

Sound	*FiMiL*
Doubled	*FiDD*
Hollow	*FiiLa*

Sound verbs

siman	'to get fat'	*simin*	'fatness'
libas	'to wear'	*libis*	'wearing'

Doubled verbs

ġašš	'to cheat'	*ġišš*	'cheating'

Hollow verbs

ʒaar (*yʒiir*)	'to be perplexed'	*ʒiira*	'perplexity'
Ɛaaš (*yƐiiš*)	'to live'	*Ɛiiša*	'living, life'
ġaar (*yġaar*)	'to be jealous'	*ġiira*	'jealousy'

C. Verb — Verbal noun

Verb	Verbal noun
Sound	*FuMuL*
Doubled	*FuDD*

Sound verbs

ʒufaẓ	'to memorize'	*ʒufuẓ*	'memorizing'
širab	'to drink'	*šurub*	'drinking'
ẓiƐaf	'to lose weight'	*ẓuƐuf*	'loss of weight'

Doubled verbs

ʒabb	'to like, love'	*ʒubb*	'love'

D. Verb — Verbal noun

Verb	Verbal noun
Sound, Doubled	*FaMaL*

Sound verbs

tiƐab	'to be tired'	*taƐab*	'tiredness'
ġirag	'to drown'	*ġarag*	'drowning'
furaʒ	'to be happy'	*faraʒ*	'happiness'

Doubled verbs

mall	'to be bored'	*malal*	'boredom'

E. Verb — Verbal noun

Verb	Verbal noun
Sound, Doubled	*FuMuuL(a)*

Sound verbs

ẓiḍar	'to attend'	*ẓuḍuur*	'attendance'
ṭumaẓ	'to be ambitious'	*ṭumuuẓ*	'ambition'
sihal	'to be easy'	*suhuula*	'ease'

Doubled verbs

marr	'to pass'	*muruur*	'passing; traffic'

F. Verb — Verbal noun

All types — *FaMaaL(a)*

Sound verbs

simaẓ	'to permit'	*samaaẓ*	'permission'
silam	'to be safe'	*salaama*	'safety'

Doubled verbs

jaff	'to dry' (intr)	*jafaaf*	'dryness'

Hollow verbs. The constants in the M position is generally *w*.

raaj (*yruuj*)	'to sell well' (intr)	*rawaaj*	'success on the market'

Defective verbs. The consonant in the L position is *ʔ* if final and generally *w* if followed by *-a*.

rija	'to request'	*rajaaʔ*	'requesting'
rixa	'to be loose, slack'	*raxaawa*	'slackness'
niqa	'to be pure' (water)	*naqaawa*	'purity'

G. Verb — Verbal noun

All types — *F(i)MaaL(a)*

The short *i* shown in parentheses is optional or more commonly absent in some nouns of this pattern.

Sound verbs

nibaẓ	'to bark'	*nibaaẓ*	'barking'
kitab	'to write'	*kitaaba*	'writing'

Hollow verbs. The consonant in the M position is *y*.

ṣaaʒ (*yṣiiʒ*)	'to shout'	*ṣiyaaʒ*	'shouting'
saaq (*ysuuq*)	'to drive'	*siyaaqa*	'driving'

Defective verbs. The consonant in the L position is *ʔ* if final and generally *y* if followed by *-a*.

bina	'to build'	*binaaʔ*, *binaaya*	'building' (activity)
qira	'to read'	*qiraaya*	'reading'

H. Others

Some other patterns, less common than those above, are illustrated by the following examples.

jaa	'to come'	*jayya*[1]	'coming'
ṭaar (*yṭiir*)	'to fly'	*ṭayaraan*	'flying, aviation'
nisa	'to forget'	*nisyaan*	'forgetting'
baat	'to stay overnight'	*beetuuta*[1]	'overnight stay'
jaabat	'she gave birth'	*jeebuuba*[1]	'birth, delivery'

I. Class IV pattern

Some Class I verbs have verbal nouns with a Class IV pattern, rather than one of the Class I patterns listed above. (The Class IV pattern is described in 6.1.1.4 below; see also 5.1.1.4 for general comments on Class IV verbs.) Some examples:

ziƐaj	'to bother'	*ʔizƐaaj*	'bother'
ṣarr	'to insist'	*ʔiṣraar*	'insistence'
wuƐaz	'to order'	*ʔiiƐaaz*	'order'
daar	'to administer'	*ʔidaara*	'administration'
liġa	'to cancel'	*ʔilġaaʔ*	'cancellation'

6.1.1.2 Class II

Two verbal noun patterns are associated with Class II verbs.

---

[1]Also used as instance noun (6.1.2).

A. Verb — Verbal noun

Verb	Verbal noun
Sound	*taFMiiL*
Defective	*taFMiya*

This is the usual pattern for Class II verbal nouns.

Sound verbs

ʔajjal	'to postpone'	*taʔjiil*	'postponement'
baddal	'to change'	*tabdiil*	'changing'
ʒassan	'to improve' (tr)	*taʒsiin*	'improvement'
waʒʒad	'to unify'	*tawʒiid*	'unification'
ṣaʒʒaʒ	'to correct'	*taṣʒiiʒ*	'correction'
ʒawwal	'to transfer'	*taʒwiil*	'transfer'
Ɛayyan	'to appoint'	*taƐyiin*	'appointment'

Defective verbs

rabba	'to breed, raise'	*tarbiya*	'raising; education'
ṣaffa	'to refine'	*taṣfiya*	'refining'
qawwa	'to strengthen'	*taqwiya*	'strengthening'

B. Verb — Verbal noun

Verb	Verbal noun
Sound	*tFiMMiL/tFuMMiL/tFuMMuL*
Defective	*tFiMMi/tFuMMi*

Some speakers use quite a few verbal nouns of this pattern instead of, or interchangeably with, those in A above. Other speakers use them only seldom, and then usually in a phrase involving both the verb and the verbal noun, for example *kassára tkissir* (literally 'he broke him a breaking') 'he gave him a good beating'. The initial *t* in nouns of this pattern assimilates to certain following consonants in the same ways as those described in 5.1.1.5 for the initial *t* of Class V verbs. Some examples follow.

Sound verbs

baṭṭal	'to quit'	*tbuṭṭil*	'quitting'
sallam	'to deliver'	*tsillim*	'delivery'
Ɛabbas	'to frown'	*tƐibbis*	'frowning'
kammaš	'to grab' (repetitively)	*tkummuš*	'grabbing'

dallal	'to spoil' (a child)	*ddillil*	'spoiling'
bayyan	'to appear'	*tbiyyin*	'appearing'
mawwat	'to kill, beat up'	*tmuwwit*	'killing, beating up'

Defective verbs

ẓašša	'to stuff, fill'	*tẓišši*	'stuffing, filling'
našša	'to starch'	*tnišši*	'starching'

6.1.1.3 Class III

There are two verbal noun patterns, of which the first is more common.

A. Verb	Verbal noun
Sound	*muFaaMaLa*
Defective	*m(u)FaaMaa(t)*

Sound verbs. Examples:

baalaġ	'to exaggerate'	*mubaalaġa*	'exaggeration'
saaƐad	'to help'	*musaaƐada*	'help'
qaabal	'to meet, talk with'	*muqaabala*	'interview'
ẓaajaj	'to argue'	*muẓaajaja*	'argument'
ẓaawal	'to attempt'	*muẓaawala*	'attempt'
qaawam	'to resist'	*muqaawama*	'resistance'

Defective verbs. The pattern has the alternant *m(u)FaaMaa(t)*. In some it is *mFaaMaa*, for example *mdaaraa* 'taking care of, looking after'. (The final *t* occurs when the noun has attached to it a pronoun suffix: *mdaaraathum* 'taking care of them', or is followed by another noun in annexion: *mdaaraat ij-jihaal* 'taking care of the children'.) Examples:

daara	'to take care of'	*mdaaraa*	'taking care of'
saawa	'to level' (ground)	*msaawaa*	'leveling'
laaga	'to find, meet'	*mlaagaa*	'meeting'

In some verbal nouns a short *u* occurs after the *m*; the final *t* may then also occur even when there is no pronoun suffix or noun in annexion. Sometimes, for the same verb, there may be a verbal noun *mFaaMaa* corresponding to one meaning of the verb, and a verbal noun *muFaaMaat* corresponding to another; compare the second example above with the second example below.

baara	'to compete with'	*mubaaraat*	'competition'
saawa	'to be equal to'	*musaawaat*	'equality'
Ɛaada	'to antagonize'	*muƐaadaat*	'antagonizing'

B. Verb	Verbal noun
All types	*FiMaaL*

Some Class III verbal nouns have this pattern along with (occasionally instead of) that listed in A above. The two different verbal nouns may correspond to different meanings of the verb.

jaadal	'to debate with'	*jidaal* (*mujaadala*)	'debate'
xaalaf	'to disagree with; to break' (rule)	*xilaaf* (*muxaalafa*	'disagreement' 'violation')
daafaƐ	'to defend'	*difaaƐ* (*mudaafaƐa*)	'defense'
Ɛaatab	'to reproach'	*Ɛitaab* (*muƐaataba*)	'reproach'

6.1.1.4 Class IV

Class IV verbs differ in form from Class I verbs only in the perfect tense, and even there most of them have alternative and more commonly used Class I or other forms (see 5.1.1.4). The Class IV verbal noun pattern, on the other hand, is not uncommon. It is associated with Class IV verbs, with those Class I (or, less commonly, II or III) verbs which are alternative forms of Class IV verbs, and also with a number of verbs which were Class IV at an earlier stage of the language but have forms of other classes today. Thus for a given Class I verb it is impossible to predict whether the verbal noun will have one of the Class I patterns listed in 6.1.1.1 above, or a Class IV pattern; the facts must be learned for each verb. (However, Class I verbs in which the last vowel of the *imperfect* is *a* or *aa* generally do not have Class IV verbal nouns.)

The Class IV verbal noun pattern is shown below. In the examples, the verb forms are identified by roman numerals as Class I, II, III, or IV.

Verb	Verbal noun
Sound, Doubled, Defective	*ʔiFMaaL*
Weak first radical	*ʔiiMaaL*
Hollow	*ʔiFaaLa*

Verbal nouns of sound, doubled, and defective verbs (except those with a weak first radical, for which see below) have the alternant *ʔiFMaaL*. Examples:

Sound verbs

I	*jubar*	'to force'	*ʔijbaar*	'forcing'
IV	*ʔajbar*			
I	*ʒiraj*	'to embarrass'	*ʔiʒraaj*	'embarrassment'
IV	*ʔaʒraj*			
I	*ziɛaj*	'to annoy'	*ʔizɛaaj*	'annoyance'
IV	*ʔazɛaj*			
IV	*ʔaδ̣har*	'to reveal'	*ʔiδ̣haar*	'revealing'
I	*ɛilan*	'to announce, advertise'	*ʔiɛlaan*	'announcement, advertisement'
IV	*ʔaɛlan*			
I	*filas*	'to go bankrupt'	*ʔiflaas*	'bankruptcy'
IV	*ʔaflas*			
I	*himal*	'to neglect'	*ʔihmaal*	'neglect'
IV	*ʔahmal*			

Doubled verbs

I	*ṣarr*	'to insist'	*ʔiṣraar*	'insistence'
IV	*ʔaṣarr*			

Defective verbs. In the verbal noun, the consonant in the L position is *ʔ*.

I	*xifa*	'to conceal'	*ʔixfaaʔ*	'concealment'
IV	*ʔaxfa*			
I	*liġa*	'to cancel'	*ʔilġaaʔ*	'cancellation'
IV	*ʔalġa*			
I	*fina*	'to destroy'	*ʔifnaaʔ*	'destruction'
IV	*ʔafna*			

Weak first radical. If the corresponding verb has *ʔ*, *w*, or *y* as its first radical, the verbal noun has the alternant *ʔiiMaaL*.

III	*ʔaaman*	'to believe, have faith'	*ʔiimaan*	'belief, faith'
IV	*ʔawjaz*	'to make brief'	*ʔiijaaz*	'making brief'
IV	*ʔawraθ*	'to make (s-o) an heir'	*ʔiiraaθ*	'making (s-o) an heir'
II	*waṣṣal*	'to transmit'	*ʔiiṣaal*	'transmission'
I	*wuɛaz*	'to order'	*ʔiiɛaaz*	'order'
IV	*ʔawɛaz*			

Hollow verbs. Verbal nouns of hollow verbs have the alternant *ʔiFaaLa*.

I	*daar*	'to administer'	*ʔidaara*	'administration'
IV	*ʔadaar*			
I	*δaaɛ*	'to broadcast'	*ʔiδaaɛa*	'broadcasting'
IV	*ʔaδaaɛ*			
I	*jaaz*	'to permit'	*ʔijaaza*	'permit, license'
IV	*ʔajaaz*			

6.1.1.5 Class V

A. Verb — Verbal noun

Sound	*taFaMMuL*
Defective	*taFaMMi*

This is the usual pattern for Class V verbal nouns.

Sound verbs

tbajjaʒ	'to brag'	*tabajjuʒ*	'bragging'
tṣarraf	'to behave'	*taṣarruf*	'behavior'
tɛajjab	'to be amazed'	*taɛajjub*	'amazement'
txaṣṣaṣ	'to specialize'	*taxaṣṣuṣ*	'specialty'
traddad	'to hesitate'	*taraddud*	'hesitation'
tṣawwar	'to imagine'	*taṣawwur*	'imagination'

Defective verbs

tbanna	'to adopt'	*tabanni*	'adoption'
traqqa	'to advance, get ahead'	*taraqqi*	'advancement'

B. Verb — Verbal noun

Sound	*tFiMMiL/tFuMMiL/tFuMMuL*
Defective	*tFiMMi/tFuMMi*

This pattern is associated with some Class V verbs instead of, or interchangeably with, the one in A above. It is identical with the Class II verbal noun pattern described in 6.1.1.2 B, and the remarks on form and usage made there also apply here. Some examples follow.

Sound verbs

tšammas	'to sunbathe'	*tšimmis*	'sunbathing'

Defective verbs

tšakka	'to complain'	*tšikki*	'complaining'
tmaṭṭa	'to stretch, give'	*tmuṭṭi*	'stretching'

6.1.1.6 Class VI

Verb	Verbal noun
Sound	*taFaaMuL*
Defective	*taFaaMi*

This is the only pattern for Class VI verbal nouns.

Sound verbs

djaasar	'to be impertinent'	*tajaasur*	'impertinence'
traajaƐ	'to retreat'	*taṛaajuƐ*	'retreat'
ṭṣaadam	'to conflict'	*taṣaadum*	'conflict'
traaṣaṣ	'to move (closer) together'	*taraaṣuṣ*	'moving together'
tƐaawan	'to cooperate'	*taƐaawun*	'cooperation'
tbaayan	'to contrast'	*tabaayun*	'contrast'

Defective verbs

tbaaha	'to boast'	*tabaahi*	'boasting'
tzaaša	'to avoid'	*tazaaši*	'avoiding'

6.1.1.7 Class VII

Verb	Verbal noun
All types	*(ʔi)nFiMaaL*

This is the only pattern for Class VII verbal nouns. The form with the initial *ʔi-* here and in the patterns of verbal nouns of Classes VIII, IX, X and *FSaTaLL* verbs (6.1.1.8, 9, 10, 13 below) is a variant, occurring most commonly at the beginning of an utterance; examples in this book are cited in the form without *ʔi-*.

Sound verbs

nziƐaj	'to be upset, annoyed'	*nziƐaaj*	'upset feeling'
nfijar	'to explode'	*nfijaar*	'explosion'

nqisam	'to be divided'	*nqisaam*	'division, split'
nkisar	'to be broken, defeated'	*nkisaar*	'defeat'

Doubled verbs

nʒaṭṭ	'to decline'	*nʒiṭaaṭ*	'decline'
nʒall	'to be dissolved'	*nʒilaal*	'dissolution, disbanding'

Hollow verbs. In the verbal noun, the consonant in the M position is *y*.

nhaar	'to collapse'	*nhiyaar*	'collapse'

Defective verbs. In the verbal noun, the consonant in the L position is *ʔ*; these verbal nouns are rare.

nʒina	'to bow'	*nʒinaaʔ*	'bowing'

6.1.1.8 Class VIII

Verb	Verbal noun
All types	*(ʔi)FtiMaaL*

This is the only pattern for Class VIII verbal nouns. (For the initial *ʔi–* see 6.1.1.7.) If, in the verb, the *–t–* infix assimilates to the preceding consonant (5.1.1.8), the same assimilation occurs in the verbal noun.

Sound verbs

ttijah	'to lean, tend'	*ttijaah*	'tendency, leaning'
jtimaƐ	'to gather, assemble'	*jtimaaƐ*	'assembly, meeting'
ʒtifal	'to celebrate'	*ʒtifaal*	'celebration'
xtilaf	'to differ, disagree'	*xtilaaf*	'disagreement'
zdiʒam	'to become crowded'	*zdiʒaam*	'crowded state'
Ɛtiraf	'to confess'	*Ɛtiraaf*	'confession'
qtiraʒ	'to suggest'	*qtiraaʒ*	'suggestion'
ntixab	'to elect'	*ntixaab*	'election'

Doubled verbs

ʒtall	'to occupy'	*ʒtilaal*	'occupation'
δ̣ṭarr	'to have to, be forced to'	*δ̣ṭiraar*	'compulsion'
htamm	'to be interested'	*htimaam*	'interest, concern'

Hollow verbs. In the verbal noun, the consonant in the M position is *y*.

ẓtaaj	'to need'	*ẓtiyaaj*	'need'
xtaar	'to select'	*xtiyaar*	'selection'
rtaaẓ	'to rest'	*rtiyaaẓ*	'resting, rest'
zdaad	'to increase'	*zdiyaad*	'increase'

Defective verbs. In the verbal noun, the consonant in the L position is *ʔ*.

xtiba	'to hide oneself'	*xtibaaʔ*	'hiding'
ddiɛa	'to claim'	*ddiɛaaʔ*	'claim'
rtiša	'to be bribed'	*rtišaaʔ*	'bribery'
ɛtida	'to encroach, assault'	*ɛtidaaʔ*	'aggression'
ntiha	'to end'	*ntihaaʔ*	'end'

6.1.1.9 Class IX

Verb	Verbal noun
Doubled [1]	*(ʔi)FMiLaaL*

This is the pattern for Class IX verbal nouns, but it is restricted to those which refer to color, and even there is somewhat uncommon. (For the initial *ʔi-* see 6.1.1.7.) Two examples:

ẓmarr	'to turn red'	*ẓmiraar*	'act of turning red'
swadd	'to turn black'	*swidaad*	'act of turning black'

The nouns which are most closely associated with Class IX verbs, and with the related adjectives of color and defect (7.2.5), are illustrated below. Those referring to colors are of the pattern *FaMaaL*; the others mostly *FaMaL*. These nouns generally mean not 'act of becoming -----', but 'quality of being -----'.

ẓmarr	'to become red'	*ẓamaar*	'redness, red color'
xḍarr	'to become green'	*xaḍaar*	'greenness'
swadd	'to become black'	*sawaad*	'blackness'
byaḍḍ	'to become white'	*bayaaḍ*	'whiteness'

[1] Class IX contains only doubled verbs.

ṣlaƐƐ	'to become bald'	*ṣalaƐ*	'baldness'
ṭrašš	'to become deaf'	*ṭaraš*	'deafness'

6.1.1.10 Class X

Verb	Verbal noun
Sound Doubled Defective	*(ʔi)stiFMaaL*
Weak first radical	*(ʔi)stiiMaaL*
Hollow	*(ʔi)stiFaaLa*

This is the only pattern for Class X verbal nouns. (For the initial *ʔi-* see 6.1.1.7.) Those of sound, doubled, and defective verbs (except those with a weak first radical, for which see below) have the alternant *stiFMaaL*. Examples:

Sound verbs

staḥsan	'to approve'	*stiḥsaan*	'approval'
staxdam	'to employ'	*stixdaam*	'employing'
staƐmal	'to use'	*stiƐmaal*	'use'

Doubled verbs

staxaff b-	'to make light of'	*stixfaaf b-*	'making light of'
stiƐadd (l-)	'to prepare (for)'	*stiƐdaad*	'preparation'

Defective verbs. In the verbal noun, the consonant in the L position is *ʔ*.

staθna	'to except'	*stiθnaaʔ*	'exception'
staġna Ɛan	'to do without'	*stiġnaaʔ*	'doing without'

Weak first radical. If the corresponding verb has *ʔ* as the first radical, the verbal noun pattern may have the alternant *stiFMaaL*, as above, or *stiiMaaL*. If the verb has *w* as the first radical, the verbal noun is *stiiMaaL* in most cases, either *stiiMaaL* or *stiFMaaL* in one or two. If the verb has *y* as the first radical, the verbal noun is *stiiMaaL*, but these are rare.

staʔjar	'to rent'	*stiʔjaar* *stiijaar*	'renting'
staʔnaf	'to appeal' (at law)	*stiʔnaaf* *stiinaaf*	'appeal'
stawθaq min	'to trust'	*stiiθaaq*	'trust'
stawrad	'to import'	*stiiraad*	'importing'

stawṣaz̧	'to enquire about'	*stiiṣaaz̧*	'enquiry'
stawṭan	'to settle in' (a place)	*stiiṭaan* *stiwṭaan*[1]	'settling'
stawfa	'to collect' (debt)	*stiifaaʔ*	'collecting'
stayqaṣ	'to wake, get up'	*stiiqaaṣ*	'getting up'

Hollow verbs. The verbal noun has the alternant *stiFaaLa*.

stajaab	'to comply with'	*stijaaba*	'compliance'
staraaz̧	'to rest'	*stiraaz̧a*	'rest'
staqaal	'to resign'	*stiqaala*	'resignation'

6.1.1.11 Simple quadriliterals

A. Verb — Verbal noun

Sound	*FaSTaLa*
Weak second radical	*FooTaLa, FeeTaLa*

This is the usual pattern for the verbal nouns of simple quadriliteral verbs.

Sound verbs. These include verbs of both sound and reduplicated root-types.

xarbaṭ	'to mix up, mess up'	*xarbaṭa*	'mixing up'
ɛarqal	'to hinder, hamper'	*ɛarqala*	'hindering'
handas	'to design, engineer'	*handasa*	'engineering'
baqbaq	'to bubble'	*baqbaqa*	'bubbling'
θarθar	'to talk a lot, chatter'	*θarθara*	'chattering'
ṭabṭab	'to pound'	*ṭabṭaba*	'pounding'

Weak second radical. Sound verbs of the pattern *FooTaL* or *FeeTaL* have verbal nouns *FooTaLa* or *FeeTaLa* respectively.

ṣoofar	'to whistle'	*ṣoofara*	'whistling'
neešan	'to aim'	*neešana*	'aiming'

No verbal nouns of this pattern from defective quadriliteral verbs have been noted.

[1] One of the very rare occurrences of the sequence *iw*; see 2.1.

B. Verb / Verbal noun

Verb	Verbal noun
Sound	*tFiSTiL/tFuSTiL/tFuSTuL*
Weak second radical	*tFvvTiL/tFvvTuL*
Defective	*tFooTi, tFuuTi*

This pattern is associated with some quadriliteral verbs in addition to the pattern in A above. Some speakers use the forms of A as a general rule, and restrict their use of B to constructions involving both the verb and the corresponding verbal noun, for example *xarmušatni l-bazzuuna txurmuš* (literally 'The cat scratched me a scratching') 'The cat scratched me up badly'. Other speakers use the forms of B more freely. (Compare 6.1.1.2 A and B above.) The initial *t* in nouns of this pattern assimilates to certain following consonants in the same ways as described in 5.1.1.5.

Sound verbs. These include verbs of both sound and reduplicated root-types.

dahdar	'to roll' (tr)	*ddihdir*	'rolling'
xarbaṭ	'to mix up, mess up'	*txurbuṭ*	'mixing up'
dagdag	'to rap'	*ddigdig*	'rapping'
baqbaq	'to bubble'	*tbuqbuq*	'bubbling'

Weak second radical. Sound verbs of the pattern *FooTaL* may have verbal nouns *tFooTiL/tFooTuL* or *tFuuTiL/tFuuTiL*, with variation between the two in some cases. Sound verbs of the pattern *FeeTaL* may have verbal nouns *tFeeTiL/tFeeTuL* or *tFiiTiL/tFiiTuL*, also with variation between the two in some cases.

doozas	'to become inflamed, swollen' (boil)	*ddoozis*	'inflammation'
jooɛar	'to bray; to talk loudly'	*djuuɛir*	'braying'
deewar	'to turn'	*ddeewir*	'turning'
neešan	'to aim'	*tniišin*	'aiming'

Defective verbs. Defective quadriliteral verbs of the pattern *FooTa* (others are very rare) may have verbal nouns *tFooTi* or *tFuuTi*, with variation between the two in some cases. There are only a few.

ʔooma	'to motion, gesture'	*tʔoomi*	'motioning'
loola	'to sing a lullaby'	*tluuli*	'singing a lullaby'

6.1.1.12 Derived quadriliterals

The pattern *taFaSTuL* is peculiar to verbal nouns of derived quadriliteral verbs, but it is used in only a few cases, for example:

djamhar	'to form a crowd'	*tajamhur*	'forming a crowd'
tqahqar	'to retreat, back down'	*taqahqur*	'retreat'

In most cases these verbal nouns have the same patterns as those of simple quadriliterals (6.1.1.11 A and B above). Examples:

tmaqlaj	'to simper, be coy'	*maqlaja* } *tmiqlij* }	'simpering'
djabjab	'to hold back, be shy'	*jabjaba* } *djibjib* }	'holding back'
ṭṭooṭaẓ	'to stagger'	*ṭooṭaẓa*	'staggering'
tmeedan	'to become citified'	*tmeedin*	'becoming citified'

6.1.1.13 FSaTaLL verbs

Two verbs of this small category have verbal nouns in common use; the pattern is *(ʔi)FSiTLaaL*. (For the initial *ʔi-* see 6.1.1.7.)

šmaʔazz	'to be disgusted'	*šmiʔzaaz*	'disgust'
ṭmaʔann	'to be calm, reassured'	*ṭmiʔnaan*	'calmness'

6.1.2 Instance nouns

Instance nouns[1] are derived from certain verbal nouns (6.1.1) by the addition of the suffix *-a*. Whereas verbal nouns have the general meaning 'action or state indicated by the verb', instance nouns mean 'a particular instance of such action' or 'a particular period of such a state'. For example: verbal noun *ḍarub*, '(general action of) hitting, striking', instance noun *ḍarba* 'a (single act of) hitting, a blow'; verbal noun *taƐab* '(state of) tiredness', instance noun *taƐba* 'a spell of tiredness'. Instance nouns are feminine in gender, and have regular dual (*ḍarubteen* 'two blows') and feminine sound plural forms (*ḍarbaat* 'blows').

Class I instance nouns are formed by the addition of the suffix *-a* to the verbal nouns of the patterns *FvMvL* (with loss of stem vowel), *FaDD*, *FooL*, or *FeeL*, and *FaMi* (with change of final *i* to *y* or *w*); their patterns are thus *FvMLa*, *FaDDa*, *FooLa* or *FeeLa*, and *FaMya* or *FaMwa*. For example:

Verbal noun		Instance noun	
baliƐ	'swallowing'	*balƐa*	'a swallow'
dafur	'kicking'	*dafra*	'a kick'
gariṣ	'pinching'	*garṣa*	'a pinch'

[1] Also called "nouns of single instance".

ḍiẓik	'laughter'	*ḍiẓka*	'a laugh'
sukur	'drunkenness'	*sukra*	'a period of drunkenness'
gaẓẓ	'coughing'	*gaẓẓa*	'a cough'
noom	'sleep'	*nooma*	'a (period of) sleep'
beeƐ	'selling'	*beeƐa*	'a sale'
bači	'crying'	*bačya*	'a spell of crying'
čawi	'burning'	*čawya*	'a burn'
badi	'beginning'	*badwa*	'a beginning'

(In a few cases the vowel of the instance noun differs from that of the corresponding verbal noun, for example *ṭalab* 'requesting', *ṭulba* 'a request'.)

These are the usual patterns for instance nouns even when the corresponding verbal nouns have totally different patterns:

Verbal noun		Instance noun	
ṣraax	'yelling'	*ṣarxa*	'a yell'
ġiyaab	'absence'	*ġeeba*	'an absence'
rawaaẓ	'going'	*rooẓa*	'an (act of) going'

Instance nouns of derived verbs are less common. They are also formed by the addition of *-a* to the corresponding verbal noun. Some examples:

Verbal noun		Instance noun	
taṭmiis	'dipping'	*taṭmiisa*	'a dip'
taƐbiis	'frowning'	*taƐbiisa*	'a frown'
nẓinaaʔ	'bowing'	*nẓinaaʔa*	'a bow'
ntikaas	'regression'	*ntikaasa*	'a regression, relapse'

Instance nouns are not formed from verbal nouns which themselves end in *a* or from verbal nouns of the pattern *tCvCCvC*.

6.1.3 Unit nouns

Unit nouns[1] are derived from collectives (6.2.1 B) by the addition of the suffix *-a* or *-aaya* and bear to them much the same relationship as instance nouns bear to

[1] Also called "nouns of unity" from the Latin nomen unitatis.

verbal nouns (6.1.2 above). Whereas a collective noun indicates a substance or material in the mass, or a collection of objects viewed as a totality without reference to the individual members, a unit noun refers to a specific quantity of the substance or to an individual member of the collection. For example: collective *xišab* 'wood', unit noun *xišba* 'piece of wood'; collective *dijaaj* 'chicken' (viewed as a kind of food) or 'chickens' (as a species), unit noun *dijaaja* 'a(n individual) chicken'; collective *beeḏ̣* 'eggs' (in general), unit noun *beeḏ̣a* 'an egg'. It should be noted that although some collectives are best translated by an English singular noun ('wood'), some by a plural noun ('eggs'), and some by either according to the context ('chicken(s)'), the varying English translations are determined by the structure of English and should not be taken as reflecting similar distinctions among Iraqi collectives.

Unit nouns are feminine in gender, and have regular dual (*dijaajteen* 'two chickens') and sound feminine plural forms (*ʔarbaɛ-dijaajaat* 'four chickens'). Although feminine in gender, unit nouns may refer to living creatures of either sex. The example used above, *dijaaja*, usually does imply 'hen', as there is a common special word *diič* 'rooster', but the unit nouns referring to lower life-forms such as fish or insects carry no implication as to actual sex.

A. Suffix *-a*

The suffix *-a* is used to form unit nouns from collectives which do not themselves end in *a*. The examples below are grouped according to the kind of stem change which occurs when *-a* is added.

(1) Stems ending in *-vvC*, *-DD*, *-CC*: no change.

baṭṭiix	'melons'	*baṭṭiixa*	'a melon'
tiffaaẓ	'apples'	*tiffaaẓa*	'an apple'
jaam	'glass' (in sheets)	*jaama*	'a sheet of glass, pane'
jooz	'nuts'	*jooza*	'a nut'
riiš	'feathers'	*riiša*	'a feather'
ġeem	'clouds'	*ġeema*	'a cloud'
filliin	'cork'	*filliina*	'a cork'
yaaquut	'rubies'	*yaaquuta*	'a ruby'
ḅagg	'bugs, gnats'	*ḅagga*	'a bug, gnat'
naarinj	'(sour) oranges'	*naarinja*	'a (sour) orange'

(2) Stems of pattern *FvMvL*: stem vowel is dropped.[1]

[1] When the stem vowel is *a*, there are a few exceptions: *tanak* 'tin', *tanaka* 'piece of tin; can'.

ruṭab	'(fresh) dates'	*ruṭba*	'a (fresh) date'
šaƐar	'hair'	*šaƐra*	'a hair'
simač	'fish'	*simča*	'a fish'
laʒam	'meat'	*laʒma*	'piece of meat'
namil	'ants'	*namla*	'an ant'
warid	'flowers'	*warda*	'a flower'
guṭin	'cotton'	*guṭna*	'piece of cotton'
tamur	'dates'	*tamra*	'a date'
gamuḷ	'lice'	*gamḷa*	'a louse'

(3) Quadriliterals and multiliteral stems: in some, no change; in a few, final consonant is doubled.

sfarjal	'quinces'	*sfarjala*	'a quince'
marmar	'marble'	*marmara*	'a piece of marble'
mišmiš	'apricots'	*mišmiša*	'an apricot'
duƐbul	'marbles' (in game)	*duƐbulla*	'a marble'
Ɛugrug	'frogs'	*Ɛugrugga*	'a frog'

(4) Stems ending in *i*: *yy* is added.

raggi	'watermelons'	*raggiyya*	'a watermelon'
nuumi	type of fruit	*nuumiyya*	one such fruit
kaahi	type of pastry	*kaahiyya*	'a piece of *kaahi*'

(5) Stems ending in *u*: in some, *u* is changed to *w*; in others, *ww* is added.

ʒaṣu	'pebbles, gravel'	*ʒaṣwa*	'a pebble'
liilu	'pearls'	*liiluwwa*	'a pearl'

B. Suffix *-aaya*

The suffix *-aaya* is used with collectives which themselves end in *a*, and with some others.

(1) Stems ending in *a*: the *a* is dropped.

ṭamaaṭa[1]	'tomatoes'	*ṭamaaṭaaya*	'a tomato'
mqawwa	'cardboard'	*mqawwaaya*	'a piece of cardboard'
nuwa	'pits, seeds'	*nuwaaya*	'a pit, seed'
puteeta[1]	'potatoes'	*puteetaaya*	'a potato'

(2) Other stems: For many unit nouns of the types described in A above, there are alternative forms with the suffix *-aaya* instead of simply *-a*, for example *tiffaaẓaaya* 'an apple' beside *tiffaaẓa*. In such cases the two forms are usually interchangeable in the singular, but in the plural the form based on the shorter singular is more common: *tlat-tiffaaẓaat* 'three apples'. Other examples:

baṭṭiix	'melons'	*baṭṭiixa, baṭṭiixaaya*	'a melon'
ẓabb	'seeds; pills'	*ẓabba, ẓabbaaya*	'a seed; a pill'
xoox	'peaches'	*xooxa, xooxaaya*	'a peach'
warid	'flowers'	*warda, wardaaya*	'a flower'
mišmiš	'apricots'	*mišmiša, mišimšaaya*[2]	'an apricot'

6.1.4 Feminine nouns in sex-gender pairs

Feminine nouns referring to female creatures are derived, by the addition of the suffix *-a*, from certain masculine nouns referring to the corresponding male creatures. Together the two constitute a sex-gender pair (6.2.1 A). These pairs refer to human beings and some forms of animals. The examples below are grouped according to the kind of stem change undergone by the stem when *-a* is added.

A. Stems ending in *-vvC*, *-CC*, *-DD*: no change.

xaaḷ	'maternal uncle'	*xaaḷa*	'maternal aunt'
zamiil	'colleague M'	*zamiila*	'colleague F'
ẓṃaal	'donkey M'	*ẓṃaala*	'donkey F'
ṭabiib	'doctor M'	*ṭabiiba*	'doctor F'
fannaan	'artist M'	*fannaana*	'artist F'
ṭabbaax	'cook M'	*ṭabbaaxa*	'cook F'
ɛamm	'paternal uncle'	*ɛamma*	'paternal aunt'

---

[1] Also used as a unit noun.

[2] Note vowel shift.

B. Stems of pattern *FvMvL*: stem vowel is dropped.

baǧaḷ	'mule M'	*baǧḷa*	'mule F'
ṣaxaḷ	'billy-goat'	*ṣaxḷa*	'nanny-goat'
čalib	'dog'	*čalba*	'bitch'

C. Stems of pattern *FaaMiL/FaaMuL* (Class I active participle pattern): stem vowel is dropped in some cases, retained in others.

xaadim	'servant M'	*xaadma*	'servant F'
jaahil	'child M'	*jaahla*	'child F'
ṣaaʒib	'owner M'	*ṣaaʒba*	'owner F'
raaqiṣ	'dancer M'	*raaqiṣa*	'dancer F'
kaatib	'clerk M'	*kaatiba*	'clerk F'

D. Stems of derived participle patterns ending in *-vC*: stem vowel is usually retained.

muƐallim	'teacher M'	*muƐallima*	'teacher F'
mumaθθil	'actor'	*mumaθθila*	'actress'
muṣ̌ammid	'male nurse'	*muṣ̌ammida*	'nurse'
muwaṣ̌ṣ̌af	'civil servant M'	*muwaṣ̌ṣ̌afa*	'civil servant F'
mulaaʒiṣ̌	'supervisor M'	*mulaaʒiṣ̌a*	'supervisor F'
mustaxdam	'employee M'	*mustaxdama*	'employee F'

E. Stems of active participle patterns ending in *i*: *y* is added.

muǧanni	'singer M'	*muǧanniya*	'singer F'
muʒaami	'lawyer M'	*muʒaamiya*	'lawyer F'

F. Other stems ending in *i*: *yy* is added.

dukkanči	'shopkeeper M'	*dukkančiyya*	'shopkeeper F'
ʒajji	'pilgrim to Mecca M'	*ʒijjiyya*[1]	'pilgrim to Mecca F'
moosiiqi	'musician M'	*moosiiqiyya*	'musician F'
muṭi	'donkey M'	*muṭiyya*	'donkey F'

[1] Note also vowel change.

G. Stems ending in *u*: in some, *u* is changed to *w*; in others, *ww* is added.

ɛuḍu	'member M'	*ɛuḍwa*	'member F'
ɛadu	'enemy M'	*ɛaduwwa*	'enemy F'

H. Stems ending in *a*: the *a* is lengthened to *aa* and *y* is added.

mulla	'mullah M'	*mullaaya*	'mullah F'

6.1.5 Nouns in *-či*

A considerable number of nouns can be derived from other nouns by the addition of the suffix *-či*, with stem changes in some cases. The nouns ending in *-či* most commonly refer to persons of certain trades or occupations; some refer to persons of a certain character or personality. These nouns have plural forms ending in *-čiyya* (see 6.2.2.3 A (2) (b)). The examples given below are grouped according to the major types of change undergone by the stem when *-či* is added.

A. No change: generally, one-syllable words of pattern *CvvC*, two-syllable words ending in *a* except *wa*, words ending in *-uC*.

teel	'wire'	*teelči*	'wire-, screen-seller'
titin	'tobacco'	*titinči*	'tobacconist'
xaan	'warehouse'	*xaanči*	'man in charge of warehouse'
saaɛa	'watch'	*saaɛači*	'watch dealer, repairman'
saxta	'lie'	*saxtači*	'cheater, faker'
pooṣṭa	'post-office; mail'	*pooṣṭači*	'postman'
šakar	'sugar'	*šakarči*	'confectioner'
čurak	kind of bun	*čurakči*	'baker of *čurak*'
čaay	'tea'	*čaayči*	'tea vendor'

B. Shift of final *wa* to *aw*: a few words of pattern *CaCwa*.

daɛwa	'lawsuit'	*daɛawči*	'frequent complainer'
ɛalwa	'grain warehouse'	*ɛalawči*	'manager of grain warehouse'
gahwa	'coffee (-house)'	*gahawči*	'coffee-house proprietor'

C. Loss of final *a*: words of three or more syllables ending in *a*.

doošama	'upholstery'	*doošamči*	'upholsterer'
ɛarabaana	'carriage'	*ɛarabanči* [1]	'carriage-driver'
qundara	'shoes'	*qundarči*	'shoemaker'

D. Shortening of vowel in last syllable: words of two or more syllables ending in *-vvC*.

bistaan	'orchard, grove'	*bistanči*	'orchard-tender'
ʒammaam	'bath'	*ʒammamči*	'bath-house proprietor'
ɛarḍaʒaal	'petition'	*ɛarḍaʒalči*	'public scribe'
kabaab	'skewered meat, kabob'	*kababči*	'kabob-seller'

E. A few forms show vowel change or shift.

ʔuuti	'(pressing) iron'	*ʔuutači*	'presser'
dumbug	'drum'	*dumbagči*	'drummer'
ṭurši	'pickles'	*ṭuruščí*	'pickle-seller'

6.1.6 Nouns of participle form

An important category of derived nouns consists of those words which have the patterns of active or passive participles (7.1.1), but are frequently used as nouns rather than as adjectives, and in some cases have specialized noun meanings. For example, the form *maktuub* is a Class I passive participle meaning 'written'; it is also a noun with the specialized meaning 'letter' (epistle).

Participle nouns which refer to human beings occur in pairs, a masculine form and a feminine form, used according to the sex of the person concerned, for example *kaatib* 'clerk (male)', *kaatiba* 'clerk (female)'. Of those which refer to inanimate objects or concepts, some have the masculine form of the participle, for example *ṭaabiq* 'floor, story'; some have the feminine form, for example *ɛaaṣima* 'capital' (city); and in a few cases both forms occur, with different specialized meanings, for example *majmuuɛ* 'total' and *majmuuɛa* 'a collection' (e.g. of stamps).

In some cases there is a distinction in form between the participle as such (used as adjective or verb) and the participle noun, in that the former may begin with the prefix *m-* or *mi-* and the latter with *mu-*, for example: participle *mɛallim* 'having taught', participle noun *muɛallim* 'teacher'.

Some further examples are given below.

---

[1] Note also shortening of long *aa*.

	Active		Passive	
Class I	*taajir*	'merchant, businessman'	*manduub*	'delegate'
	waajib	'duty'	*maḥṣuul*	'profit; crop'
	ʕaaṣifa	'storm'	*maqṣuura*	'booth; box (in theatre)'
Class II	*muʔallif*	'author'	*muraššaḥ*	'candidate'
	mzayyin	'barber'	*mḥajjar*	'railing, fence'
	muxaddir	'anesthetic'		
Class III	*mulaazim*	'lieutenant'		
	muraabi	'money-lender'		
Class IV	*mujrim*	'criminal'	*mulḥaq*	'attaché'
	mudiir	'director'		
	muhimma	'assignment'		
Class VIII	*muktašif*	'explorer'	*muʔtamar*	'conference'
	muddaʕi	'plaintiff'	*mujtamaʕ*	'society'
Class X	*mustawrid*	'importer'	*mustaxdam*	'employee'
	mustadʕi	'applicant'	*mustašaar*	'advisor, counsellor'
			mustaqbal	'future'
			mustaʕmara	'colony'
Quadriliteral	*muhandis*	'engineer'		

6.1.7 Feminine nisba nouns

There is a large category of nouns which have the form of feminine nisba adjectives (ending in *-iyya*; see 7.1.3) but have specialized noun meanings. Some of these nouns refer to concrete objects, and some to places of certain activities. Most, however, refer to abstract concepts; these frequently have English equivalents with endings such as -tion, -ity, -dom, -ism.

In some cases there is both a nisba adjective and a feminine nisba noun; the latter is then identical with the feminine form of the adjective, for example *šaxṣi* (feminine *šaxṣiyya*) 'personal', and *šaxṣiyya* 'personality'. In other cases there is no corresponding nisba adjective, and the feminine nisba noun is derived directly, by the addition of the ending *-iyya*, from some other related word. Among these related words are nouns, adjectives, (including comparatives and participles), and a few uninflected words. In the examples which follow, the right-hand column shows the feminine nisba noun; the left-hand column shows the nisba adjective or other related word from which the noun is derived.

ʔafḍal	'more favorable'	*ʔafḍaliyya*	'preference, priority'
ʔaqall	'fewer'	*ʔaqalliyya*	'minority'
ʔakθar	'more'	*ʔakθariyya*	'majority'
ʔahamm	'more important'	*ʔahammiyya*	'importance'
barqi	'telegraphic'	*barqiyya*	'telegram'
jinis [1]	'type, class'	*jinsiyya*	'nationality'
zeen	'good'	*zeeniyya*	'a favor'
štiraaki	'socialist(ic)'	*štiraakiyya*	'socialism'
šiyuuʕi	'communist(ic)'	*šiyuuʕiyya*	'communism'
ṣaydali	'pharmacist'	*ṣaydaliyya*	'pharmacy'
ʕuḍu	'member'	*ʕuḍwiyya*	'membership'
qunṣul	'consul'	*qunṣuliyya*	'consulate'
čam, kam	'how many'	*kammiyya*	'quantity'

6.2 INFLECTION

6.2.1 Gender

Nouns in Iraqi fall into two grammatical classes, called masculine and feminine. A noun's membership in one or the other of these classes is called its gender. In most nouns which refer to the larger species of living creatures, masculine or feminine gender corresponds to male or female sex; but in other nouns gender is only a grammatical classification. The gender of a noun, together with its number (6.2.2), determines the pronouns used to refer to it, the form of the adjectives used to modify it, and the form of the verbs of which it is the subject. (See 11.2).

Some nouns occur in pairs, one masculine and one feminine, with meanings related in specific ways. In most such pairs the feminine noun is formed by adding the ending *-a* to the masculine, often with some change in the stem of the latter. There are three important groups of such pairs:

A. Sex-gender pairs

These are the nouns, referred to above, in which masculine or feminine gender corresponds to male or female sex. They include nouns referring to human beings and to certain of the larger animals.

---

[1] The corresponding nisba adjective *jinsi* means 'sexual'.

Male beings (Masculine)		Female beings (Feminine)	
ra?iis	'chief'	*ra?iisa*	'female chief'
ẕmaal	'donkey'	*ẕmaala*	'female donkey'
ɛamm	'paternal uncle'	*ɛamma*	'paternal aunt'
kaatib	'clerk'	*kaatiba*	'female clerk'
malik	'king'	*malika*	'queen'
mudiir	'director'	*mudiira*	'directress'
mumaθθil	'actor'	*mumaθθila*	'actress'
čalib	'dog'	*čalba*	'bitch'

Some pairs of nouns with similar relationships of meaning have partially or completely different stems. In most such pairs the feminine noun ends in a consonant.

?ab	'father'	*?umm*	'mother'
?ax	'brother'	*?uxut*	'sister'
?ibin	'son'	*binit*	'daughter'
ẕṣaan	'horse'	*faras*	'mare'
rijjaal	'man'	*mara*	'woman'

B. Collective and unit nouns

A collective noun is one which refers to a substance, a material, or a kind of plant or creature in a mass or as a type, without any specification of number. Most collectives are masculine in gender[1] and grammatically singular, though some are best translated by plural English forms. The corresponding unit noun (6.1.3) refers to a single unit or piece of the designated material, or a single plant or creature. Unit nouns end in *-a*. In most cases they are grammatically feminine but may refer to a creature of either sex.

Collective nouns (Masculine)		Unit nouns (Feminine)	
baṭṭ	'ducks'	*baṭṭa*	'a duck'
tamur	'dates'	*tamra*	'date'
tiffaaẕ	'apples'	*tiffaaẕa*	'apple'

[1] A few collectives are themselves feminine, and the corresponding unit nouns are also feminine: *faaṣuuliyya* 'beans' *faaṣuuliyyaaya* 'a bean' (see 6.1.3).

xišab	'wood'	*xišba*	'piece of wood'
dijaaj	'chicken'	*dijaaja*	'a chicken'
simač	'fish'	*simča*	'a fish'

C. Verbal and instance nouns

Certain nouns derived from verbs have the meaning 'action indicated by the verb'. These are verbal nouns (6.1.1). Many of them have feminine counterparts ending in *-a*, with the meaning 'a single action of the type indicated'; these are instance nouns (6.1.2).

Verbal nouns (Masculine)		Instance nouns (Feminine)	
ḍarub	'hitting'	*ḍarba*	'a blow'
rigiṣ	'dancing'	*rigṣa*	'a dance'
liɛib	'playing'	*liɛba*	'a game'

6.2.2 Number

Nouns are inflected for number. There are three numbers: singular, dual, and plural.

6.2.2.1 Singular

Singular nouns occur in many widely varying patterns. In nouns which have broken plurals, the singular pattern as a whole sometimes determines the plural form; such patterns are listed in 6.2.2.3 B. In the inflection of nouns for dual (6.2.2.2) and for sound plural (6.2.2.3 A), only the ending of the singular is important. Listed below are examples of singular nouns with different patterns and types of endings, with indications of the extent to which a noun's gender may be predicted from its ending.

A. Nouns ending in a consonant

Most such nouns are masculine, but there are also a few very common feminine ones.

Masculine		Feminine	
beet	'house'	*ʔiid*	'hand'
ʒabil	'rope'	*binit*	'daughter'
ṣaff	'class'	*rijil*	'leg'
qalam	'pencil'	*šamis*	'sun'
maktuub	'letter'		
muhandis	'engineer'		

B. Nouns ending in *-a*

The great majority of these nouns are feminine. Of the masculine ones, all are from weak-last roots (4.1.1.1) and most have the pattern *FvMa*. There are also feminine nouns of the pattern *MiLa*; these are from roots beginning with *w*.

Masculine		Feminine	
biča	'crying'	*tijaara*	'commerce'
duwa	'medicine'	*xaaḷa*	'maternal aunt'
sira	'turn'	*daraja*	'degree'
ġada	'lunch'	*safra*	'trip'
mustašfa [1]	'hospital'	*šaxṣiyya*	'personality'
		ṭooba	'ball'
		fikra	'idea'
		muʒaasaba	'accounting'
		hiba	'donation, gift' (root *whb*)

C. Nouns ending in *-i*

These nouns are all masculine.

jundi	'soldier'
ʒaraami	'thief'
raʔi	'opinion'
naadi	'club'

D. Nouns ending in *-u*

There are very few of these nouns. They are all masculine.

ɛadu	'enemy'
ɛuḍu	'member'
faru	'fur'
filu	'colt'

[1] May also be feminine.

E. Nouns ending in *-o*

A few nouns borrowed from other languages end in *-o*. They are masculine.

ḅaanyo	'bath tub'
raadyo	'radio'
ṃaayo	'bathing-suit'

6.2.2.2 Dual

Dual number means 'two of the item indicated'.[1] It is formed by the suffix *-een*, added to the singular. The singular stem may undergo certain changes when *-een* is added; the most common types of stem change are described below. (See also 4.1.3.1 and 4.1.3.2.)

A. Nouns ending in a consonant

(1) In nouns of the patterns *FvMiL/FvMuL* and *FaaMiL/FaaMuL*, the stem vowel is dropped:

Singular		Dual	
daris	'lesson'	*darseen*	'two lessons'
gaḅur	'grave'	*gaḅreen*	'two graves'
jisir	'bridge'	*jisreen*	'two bridges'
quful	'lock'	*qufleen*	'two locks'
kaatib	'clerk'	*kaatbeen*	'two clerks'
ḍaabuṭ	'officer'	*ḍaabṭeen*	'two officers'

(2) In nouns of the pattern *FvMaL* the stem vowel is dropped if the preceding consonant is *ʔ*, *ḥ*, *ε*, *x*, *ġ*, or *h*:

Singular		Dual	
baḥar	'sea'	*baḥreen*	'two seas'
waεad	'promise'	*waεdeen*	'two promises'
taxat	'bench'	*taxteen*	'two benches'
baġaḷ	'mule'	*baġḷeen*	'two mules'
kahaf	'cave'	*kahfeen*	'two caves'

[1] See 8.1.1 B for another way of expressing the same meaning.

Otherwise the stem vowel is retained:

qalam	'pencil'	*qalameen*	'two pencils'
nafar	'person'	*nafareen*	'two persons'
jibal	'mountain'	*jibaleen*	'two mountains'

(3) Three feminine nouns which end in a consonant, and refer to parts of the body that come in pairs, have two dual forms each. One is regularly formed by the addition of *-een* to the singular stem (in one case with loss of stem vowel); in the other a *t* is added to the stem before *-een*:

Singular		Dual	
rijil	'leg'	*rijleen* *rijilteen*	'two legs'
ʔiid	'hand'	*ʔiideen* *ʔiidteen*	'two hands'
ʕeen	'eye'	*ʕeeneen* *ʕeenteen*	'two eyes'

The forms *rijleen* and *ʔiideen* are also used as the *plurals* of *rijil* and *ʔiid* respectively (6.2.2.3 B (24) (b)). (The plural of *ʕeen* is *ʕyuun*.)

(4) In other nouns there is generally no stem change:

Singular		Dual	
muʕallim	'teacher'	*muʕallimeen*	'two teachers'
mulaaẓiḍ	'supervisor'	*mulaaẓiḍeen*	'two supervisors'
muxtabar	'laboratory'	*muxtabareen*	'two laboratories'
qaalab	'mold'	*qaalabeen*	'two molds'
goošar	'basket'	*goošareen*	'two baskets'
sadd	'dam'	*saddeen*	'two dams'
jayš	'army'	*jayšeen*	'two armies'
maktuub	'letter'	*maktuubeen*	'two letters'
qanaat	'canal'	*qanaateen*	'two canals'
mawʕid	'appointment'	*mawʕideen*	'two appointments'

B. Nouns ending in *-a*

The changes in the stem of a noun ending in *-a* depend upon its gender.

(1) Masculine nouns

In masculine nouns ending in *-a*, a *y* or, less commonly, a *w* is added before the suffix *-een*; some nouns may have either. The *-a* of the stem may be lengthened to *aa*, more commonly in nouns of the pattern *FvMa* than in others:

Singular		Dual	
ġada	'lunch'	*ġadaayeen*	'two lunches'
sira	'row; turn'	*siraayeen*	'two rows; two turns'[1]
malha	'nightclub'	*malhayeen*	'two nightclubs'
mustašfa	'hospital'	*mustašfayeen*	'two hospitals'

(2) Feminine nouns

In feminine nouns the final *-a* is replaced by *t* when *-een* is added. There may also be other changes, as follows:

(a) When the *-a* is preceded by *iyy*, by *iy*, or by *y* preceded by another consonant, these are changed to *ii*:

Singular		Dual	
jinsiyya	'nationality'	*jinsiiteen*	'two nationalities'
tarbiya	'education'	*tarbiiteen*	'two educations'
qarya	'village'	*qariiteen*	'two villages'
kunya	'nickname'	*kuniiteen*	'two nicknames'

(b) When the *-a* is preceded by *uww*, by *uw*, or by *w* preceded by another consonant, these are changed to *uu*:

Singular		Dual	
juwwa	'flower-bed'	*juuteen*	'two flower-beds'
quwwa	'strength'	*quuteen*	'two strengths'
gahwa	'coffee(-house)'	*gahuuteen*	'two coffee(-house)s'
daʕwa	'lawsuit'	*daʕuuteen*	'two lawsuits'

[1] But *sitra siraaween* 'double-breasted jacket'.

šarwa	'purchase'	*šaruuteen*	'two purchases'
labwa	'lioness'	*labuuteen*	'two lionesses'
čiswa	'pair of swimming trunks'	*čisuuteen*	'two pairs of swimming trunks'

(c) When the *-a* is preceded by two consonants of which the second is not *y* or *w*, a short vowel *i* or *u* is inserted between them. (This is an instance of vowel shift as described in 4.1.3.1 C.) Generally the vowel inserted is *i* if the preceding vowel is *i*, *u* if the preceding vowel is *u*, and *i* or *u* depending on the adjacent consonants if the preceding vowel is *a* (2.6):

Singular		Dual	
sitra	'coat'	*sitirteen*	'two coats'
ċilba	'can'	*ċilibteen*	'two cans'
fikra	'idea'	*fikirteen*	'two ideas'
ʔubra	'needle'	*ʔuburteen*	'two needles'
ẓufra	'hole'	*ẓufurteen*	'two holes'
ġurfa	'room'	*ġurufteen*	'two rooms'
ẓafla	'party'	*ẓafilteen*	'two parties'
safra	'trip'	*safirteen*	'two trips'
ḍarba	'a blow'	*ḍarubteen*	'two blows'
gamḷa	'louse'	*gamuḷteen*	'two lice'

(d) When the *-a* is preceded by a double consonant, except in the sequences *iyy* and *uww*, the double consonant is changed to a single consonant (in pronunciation, but is still written double; see 4.1.3 B):

Singular		Dual	
ẓayya	'snake'	*ẓayyteen*	'two snakes'
salla	'basket'	*sallteen*	'two baskets'
šiqqa	'apartment'	*šiqqteen*	'two apartments'
muhimma	'assignment'	*muhimmteen*	'two assignments'

(e) In cases other than those specified above, there is no further change:

Singular		Dual	
ʒadiiqa	'park'	*ʒadiiqteen*	'two parks'
daraja	'degree'	*darajteen*	'two degrees'
sana	'year'	*santeen*	'two years'
šarika	'company'	*šarikteen*	'two companies'
ṣuura	'picture'	*ṣuurteen*	'two pictures'
wizaara	'ministry'	*wizaarteen*	'two ministries'

C. Nouns ending in *-i*

In a few nouns of this type the final *-i* is replaced by *y*. This group is limited to, but does not include all, nouns of the pattern *FvMi*. A common one is:

Singular		Dual	
raʔi	'opinion'	*raʔyeen*	'two opinions'

In other nouns ending in *-i*, the final *-i* is retained and *yy* added:

Singular		Dual	
ġabi	'fool'	*ġabiyyeen*	'two fools'
jaabi	'collector'	*jaabiyyeen*	'two collectors'
muʒaami	'lawyer'	*muʒaamiyyeen*	'two lawyers'
naadi	'club	*naadiyyeen*	'two clubs'

D. Nouns ending in *-u*

In most nouns of the pattern *FvMu*, the final *-u* is replaced by *w*:

Singular		Dual	
bahu	'hall'	*bahween*	'two halls'
ɛuḏu	'member'	*ɛuḏween*	'two members'

In a few of these, and in those of other patterns ending in *-u*, the *-u* is retained and *ww* added:

Singular		Dual	
ɛadu	'enemy'	*ɛaduwween*	'two enemies'

mad£u [1]	'invited guest'	*mad£uwween*	'two invited guests'
biibimattu	'parrot'	*biibimattuwween*	'two parrots'

E. Nouns ending in *-o*

In these nouns *ww* is added:

Singular		Dual	
raadyo	'radio'	*raadyowween*	'two radios'
ɱaayo	'bathing-suit'	*ɱaayowween*	'two bathing-suits'

6.2.2.3 Plural

There are two major types of plurals in Iraqi. The first is formed by the addition of a suffix to the singular, in some cases with minor changes in the stem of the latter; this is called a sound plural. The other consists of a form with a pattern (4.1.1) different from that of the singular; this is called a broken plural. The latter category includes a few nouns whose plurals show both a suffix and a change in pattern.

A. Sound plurals

Three suffixes are used to form sound plurals: *-iin*, *-a*, and *-aat*.

(1) The suffix *-iin*

This suffix is used to form the plural of a great many masculine nouns referring to male persons, and is traditionally called the masculine sound plural suffix. It is used with four major categories listed below. Some of these nouns also have alternative plurals; in such cases the latter are given in parentheses. Any stem changes made when *-iin* is added are noted for each category.

(a) Nouns of participle form

Nouns which have the form of participles (except Class I active participles, for which see 6.2.2.3 B (7)), and refer to male persons, have plurals in *-iin*. The great majority of nouns with plurals in *-iin* are of this type. In those which end in *-i*, the *-i* is dropped when *-iin* is added.

Singular		Plural
mas?uul	'responsible person'	*mas?uuliin*
manduub	'delegate'	*manduubiin*
mumaθθil	'actor'	*mumaθθiliin*
mukawwi	'dry-cleaner'	*mukawwiin*

[1] Also *mad£i*.

muslim	'Moslem'	*muslimiin (slaam)*
muδiiε	'announcer'	*muδiiεiin*
muẓaasib	'accountant'	*muẓaasibiin*
muẓaami	'lawyer'	*muẓaamiin*
muxtaṣṣ	'expert'	*muxtaṣṣiin*
mustašaar	'counsellor'	*mustašaariin*
muhandis	'engineer'	*muhandisiin*

There are a few exceptions; a common one is

mudiir	'director'	*mudaraa?*

(b) Nouns of nisba form

Most nouns which have the nisba ending *-i*, and refer to persons, have plurals in *-iin*. In these the final *-i* is retained, and *yy* is added:

Singular		Plural
baġdaadi	'Baghdadi'	*baġdaadiyyiin (bġaadda)*
suuri	'Syrian'	*suuriyyiin*
εiraaqi	'Iraqi'	*εiraaqiyyiin*
qawmi	'nationalist'	*qawmiyyiin*

(c) Nouns of pattern *FaMMaaL*

Nouns of this pattern referring to human beings generally have the meaning 'person of a certain profession or characteristic type of behavior'. Those which indicate behavior have plurals in *-iin*:

Singular		Plural
šarraab	'heavy drinker'	*šarraabiin*
fattaan	'tattle-tale'	*fattaaniin*
kaδδaab [1]	'liar'	*kaδδaabiin*

Of those which indicate profession, some have plurals in *-iin* exclusively, some may have either plurals in *-iin* or another kind of plural, and some have another kind of plural exclusively; the plural form must be learned for each noun. Besides *-iin*, the kinds of plural found with these nouns are the suffix *-a* and a broken

[1] More commonly *čaδδaab, čaδδaabiin.*

plural of the pattern *FMaaMiiL* or, more rarely, *FMaaFMa*. The following list includes examples of nouns which have plurals exclusively or optionally in *-iin*, with the second plural form in parentheses where appropriate:

Singular		Plural
bayyaaƐ	'salesman'	*bayyaaƐiin (bayyaaƐa)*
ʒaddaad	'blacksmith'	*ʒaddaadiin (ʒdaaʒda)*
xabbaaz	'baker'	*xabbaaziin (xbaabiiz)*
ṣabbaaġ	'shoe-shine boy'	*ṣabbaaġiin (ṣbaabiiġ)*
ṭayyaar	'flier'	*ṭayyaariin*
ġawwaaṣ	'diver'	*ġawwaaṣiin*
farraaš	'office-boy'[1]	*farraašiin (fraariiš)*
fallaaʒ	'peasant'	*fallaaʒiin*

(d) Nouns of pattern *FiMMiiL*

Nouns of this pattern referring to human beings generally have the meaning 'person of a certain type of behavior'. Such nouns have plurals in *-iin*.

Singular		Plural
sikkiir	'heavy drinker'	*sikkiiriin*
šiġġiil	'hard worker'	*šiġġiiliin*

(2) The suffix *-a*

The plural suffix *-a* is used to form the plural of three categories of nouns referring to male persons, most having to do with trades or professions.

(a) Nouns of pattern *FaMMaaL*

Most nouns of this pattern which refer to male persons have a plural in *-iin*, some with an alternative broken plural (see 1 (c) above). A few, however, have a plural in *-a*, some also with alternate plurals in *-iin*:

Singular		Plural
baʒʒaar	'sailor'	*baʒʒaara*
dayyaan	'creditor'	*dayyaana*
kaššaaf	'scout'	*kaššaafa*

[1] More precisely: a school or office employee who runs errands, brings coffee, does odd jobs.

bayyaaɛ	'salesman'	*bayyaaɛa (bayyaaɛiin)*
zarraaɛ	'farmer'	*zarraaɛa (zarraaɛiin)*

(b) Nouns ending in *-či*

Nouns ending in the derivational suffix *-či* (6.1.5) all have plurals in *-a*. The stem adds *yy* before the *-a*:

Singular		Plural
ʔuutači	'presser'	*ʔuutačiyya*
ɛarabanči	'carriage-driver'	*ɛarabančiyya*
qundarči	'cobbler'	*qundarčiyya*
čarxači	'night guard'	*čarxačiyya*

(c) Others

Besides those ending in the suffix *-či* (see (b) above), a few other nouns ending in *-i* and referring to male persons have plurals in *-a*. These do not include nouns of participle form (see (1) (a) above) or nisbas referring to geographical origin (see (1) (b) above). The stem adds *yy* before the *-a*:

Singular		Plural
ẓaraami	'thief'	*ẓaraamiyya*
sarsari	'hoodlum'	*sarsariyya*

A few nouns which do not end in *-i* in the singular have similar plural forms ending in *-iyya*:

Singular		Plural
ẓakam	'referee'	*ẓakamiyya*
qabṭaan	'(ship's) captain'	*qabṭaaniyya*
moosiiqaar	'musician'	*moosiiqaariyya*
muxtaar	a neighborhood official	*muxtaariyya*

(3) The suffix *-aat*

This suffix is used to form the plural of a great many feminine nouns and for that reason is traditionally called the <u>feminine sound plural suffix</u>; its use, however, is not restricted to feminine nouns. Listed below are the main categories of nouns which have plurals in *-aat*. When *-aat* is added to a feminine noun ending in *a*, the final *a* is dropped (not replaced by *t* as in the dual). Other stem changes are noted below, where applicable.

(a) Feminine members of sex-gender pairs (6.2.1 A)

Feminine nouns ending in *-a* which refer to female persons or animals, and have masculine counterparts of approximately the same form without the final *-a*, have plurals in *-aat*.

Singular		Plural
ṭabbaaxa	'female cook'	*ṭabbaaxaat*
malika	'queen'	*malikaat*
mumaθθila	'actress'	*mumaθθilaat*

(b) Unit nouns (6.2.1 B)

Unit nouns for the most part are feminine and end in *-a*. These have plurals in *-aat*.

Singular		Plural
beeẓa	'an egg'	*beeẓaat*
ʒabba	'a seed'	*ʒabbaat*
dijaaja	'a chicken'	*dijaajaat*
simča	'a fish'	*simčaat*
ṣaxra	'a rock'	*ṣaxraat*
ṣammuuna	'loaf of bread'	*ṣammuunaat*
faʒma	'piece of coal'	*faʒmaat*
namla	'an ant'	*namlaat*
čimaaya	'a truffle'	*čimaayaat*

(c) Instance nouns (6.2.1 C)

Instance nouns are feminine and end in *a*; the majority have plurals in *-aat*:

Singular		Plural
dafra	'kick'	*dafraat*
ẓarba	'blow'	*ẓarbaat*
rigṣa	'dance'	*rigṣaat*
safra	'trip'	*safraat*

laɛna	'curse'	*laɛnaat*
liɛba	'game'	*liɛbaat*

(d) Nouns of verbal noun patterns (6.1.1)

Most nouns which have the patterns of verbal nouns other than Class I, whether feminine and ending in *a* or not, have plurals in *-aat*. The exceptions are nouns of the patterns *taFMiiL* and *taFMiya* (Class II verbal nouns); some of these have plurals in *-aat*, some broken plurals of the patterns *taFaaMiiL* and *taFaaMi*, and some either these broken plurals or *-aat*:

Singular		Plural
taʔxiir	'delay'	*taʔxiiraat*
tazdiid	'limitation'	*tazdiidaat*
tamriin	'drill'	*tamriinaat (tamaariin)*
mujaadala	'debate'	*mujaadalaat*
musaabaqa	'contest'	*musaabaqaat*
ʔiɛlaan	'announcement'	*ʔiɛlaanaat*
ʔiḍbaara	'dossier'	*ʔiḍbaaraat*
taṣarruf	'behavior'	*taṣarrufaat*
taṣaadum	'conflict'	*taṣaadumaat*
ɛtiraaḍ	'objection'	*ɛtiraaḍaat*

(e) Nouns of participle patterns (6.1.6)

Most feminine nouns which end in *-a* and have the patterns of participles have plurals in *-aat*. Among these are a great many nouns which are the feminine members of sex-gender pairs (see (a) above):

Singular		Plural
kaatiba	'female clerk'	*kaatibaat*
mumaθθila	'actress'	*mumaθθilaat*

Nouns of Class I participle patterns which are not members of such pairs have plurals in *-aat* in some cases and broken plurals in others:

Singular		Plural
qaaṣifa	'bomber plane'	*qaaṣifaat*
majmuuɛa	'collection'	*majmuuɛaat (majaamiiɛ)*
maqṣuura	'booth'	*maqṣuuraat*

In the case of most nouns of participle patterns other than Class I, feminine nouns and masculine nouns not referring to persons have plurals in *-aat*: [1]

Singular		Plural
muʔassasa	'foundation'	*muʔassasaat*
mustaɛmara	'colony'	*mustaɛmaraat*
miswadda	'rough draft'	*miswaddaat*
muhimma	'assignment'	*muhimmaat*
muʔtamar	'conference'	*muʔtamaraat*
mẓajjar	'railing'	*mẓajjaraat*
muẓarrik	'engine'	*muẓarrikaat*
muẓiiṭ	'ocean'	*muẓiiṭaat*

(f) Feminine nisba nouns

Nouns which have the form of feminine nisbas (ending in *-iyya*) have plurals in *-aat*:

Singular		Plural
barqiyya	'telegram'	*barqiyyaat*
baṭṭaaniyya	'blanket'	*baṭṭaaniyyaat*
jamɛiyya	'association'	*jamɛiyyaat*
ṣaydaliyya	'pharmacy'	*ṣaydaliyyaat*
qunṣuliyya	'consulate'	*qunṣuliyyaat*
kammiyya	'quantity'	*kammiyyaat*

(g) Feminine nouns of various patterns

Most feminine nouns of the following patterns have plurals in *-aat*:

FvMMaaLa

Singular		Plural
sayyaara	'car'	*sayyaaraat*
ṭiyyaara	'airplane'	*ṭiyyaaraat*

[1] A few feminine nouns of the pattern *muFiiLa* have a plural *maFaayiL* (see B (10) below), for example *muṣiiba* 'disaster', plural *maṣaayib*.

fattaaẓa	'can-opener'	*fattaaẓaat*
laƐƐaaba	'toy'	*laƐƐaabaat*

FvMaaLa

Singular		Plural
sulaala	'dynasty'	*sulaalaat*
šahaada	'certificate'	*šahaadaat*
wizaara	'ministry'	*wizaaraat*

FaMaLa

Singular		Plural
tanaka	'can'	*tanakaat*
ẓaraka	'movement'	*ẓarakaat*
Ɛaqaba	'obstacle'	*Ɛaqabaat*

FaMaat

This pattern is the alternant of *FaMaLa* (above) in words of weak-last roots. In these nouns the final sequence *-aat* of the singular is replaced by *-aw* or *-ay* when the plural suffix *-aat* is added:

Singular		Plural
ʔadaat	'instrument'	*ʔadawaat*
fataat	'girl'	*fatayaat*
qanaat	'canal'	*qanawaat*

FaMLa

Singular		Plural
badla	'suit'	*badlaat*
ṭabla	'ashtray'	*ṭablaat*
ġalṭa	'mistake'	*ġalṭaat*

FaaLa

Singular		Plural
saaẓa	'courtyard'	*saaẓaat*

saaƐa	'hour'	*saaƐaat*
Ɛaada	'habit'	*Ɛaadaat*

FeeLa

Singular		Plural
beeƐa	'sale'	*beeƐaat*
ṣeeda	'a catch, prize'	*ṣeedaat*
čeela	a measure	*čeelaat*

FooLa

Singular		Plural
jooga	'group' (of people)	*joogaat*
ṭooba	'ball'	*ṭoobaat*

(h) Masculine nouns of various patterns

Some masculine nouns of various other patterns have plurals in *-aat*. Among these are Class I verbal nouns which do not have broken plurals, and most nouns borrowed from other languages. When *-aat* is added, if the word ends in *-iC* or *-uC* the stem vowel is usually dropped unless the result would be three consecutive consonants; if in *-a*, the vowel is lengthened to *aa*, and *y* or *w* is added; if in *-i*, *yy* is added; if in *-u* or *-o*, *ww* is added:

Singular		Plural
bayaan	'proclamation'	*bayaanaat*
talafoon	'telephone'	*talafoonaat*
ʒammaam	'bath'	*ʒammaamaat*
zaar	'die' (in games)	*zaaraat*
šaah	'shah; (chess) king'	*šaahaat*
ṗaaṣ	'bus'	*ṗaaṣaat*
ṗlakk	'(spark-) plug'	*ṗlakkaat*
ṭaḷab	'request'	*ṭaḷabaat*
ṭubar	'cleaver'	*ṭubaraat*
yalag	'vest'	*yalagaat*

paaysikil	'bicycle'	*paaysiklaat*
sira	'row'	*sirawaat (sirayaat)*
ġada	'lunch'	*ġadaayaat*
taksi	'taxi'	*taksiyyaat*
skamli	'chair'	*skamliyyaat*
biibimattu	'parrot'	*biibimattuwwaat*
raadyo	'radio'	*raadyowwaat*
pyaano	'piano'	*pyaanowwaat*

B. Broken plurals

A broken plural is a plural form which has a pattern (4.1.1) differing from that of the singular. There are a great many different plural patterns, of which about a dozen are fairly common. For many nouns there is no way to predict from the singular form whether the plural is a sound plural or a broken plural, or, if the latter, what pattern. In general, therefore, the plural of each noun must be learned with the singular. However, as far as the broken plural is concerned, certain singular patterns tend to be associated with specific plural patterns - in a few cases exclusively so - and a knowledge of these associations can help to lighten the burden of memorizing individual plurals. The numbered headings below are the most common broken plural patterns; under each plural are given the singular patterns with which it is most frequently associated. Some nouns have more than one plural form; alternative forms are shown in parentheses where appropriate.

(1) Plural pattern *ˀaFMaaL*

This is one of the most common plurals for nouns of the singular patterns *FvMvL*, *FvvL*, and *FvMv*. Some nouns may have in the plural either this pattern or the pattern *FMaaL* (see (2) below).

(a) Singular *FvMvL*

Singular		Plural
xaṭar	'danger'	*ˀaxṭaar*
sabab	'cause'	*ˀasbaab*
qadam	'foot'	*ˀaqdaam*
qalam	'pencil'	*ˀaqlaam*
maθal	'proverb'	*ˀamθaal*
watad	'peg'	*ˀawtaad*

ratil	'(military) column'	*ʔartaal*
šaxiṣ	'person'	*ʔašxaaṣ*
jisim	'body'	*ʔajsaam*
jinis	'kind'	*ʔajnaas*
ẓilim	'dream'	*ʔaẓlaam*
siƐir	'price'	*ʔasƐaar*
ṭifil	'child'	*ʔaṭfaal*
filim	'film'	*ʔaflaam (flaam)*
qisim	'part'	*ʔaqsaam*
ẓukum	'sentence' (of court)	*ʔaẓkaam*
ṣubuġ	'paint'	*ʔaṣbaaġ*
Ɛumur	'age'	*ʔaƐmaar*

There are a few nouns in this category which begin with ʔ. In the plural of such nouns the ʔ is lost and the pattern becomes *ʔaaMaaL*.

ʔaθar	'trace, ruin'	*ʔaaθaar*
ʔalam	'pain'	*ʔaalaam*
ʔamal	'hope'	*ʔaamaal*

(b) Singular *FvvL*

These are nouns with a weak middle radical. It appears in the plural as *w* or *y*. In nouns of pattern *FaaL*, *FuuL*, and *FooL* it is usually *w*; in *FiiL*, *y*; there are some exceptions. (For nouns of pattern *FeeL* see (3) below.)

Singular		Plural
ẓaal	'situation'	*ʔaẓwaal*
maal	'property, fortune'	*ʔamwaal*
buuq	'bugle'	*ʔabwaaq*
door	'role'	*ʔadwaar*
ṣooṭ	'voice; vote'	*ʔaṣwaaṭ*

jiil	'generation'	*ʔajyaal*
Ɛiid	'feastday'	*ʔaƐyaad*

(c) Singular *FvMv*

These are nouns with a weak last radical. It appears in the plural as *ʔ*.

Ɛadu	'enemy'	*ʔaƐdaaʔ (Ɛidwaan)*
Ɛuḍu	'member'	*ʔaƐḍaaʔ*

A few nouns with a doubly weak root have this plural; the weak middle radical appears in the plural as *w* or *y*. Only the following is common:

šii	'thing'	*ʔašyaaʔ*

(2) Plural pattern *FMaaL*

This is also a common plural for nouns of the singular patterns *FvMvL* and *FvvL*. Some nouns may have in the plural either this pattern or the pattern *ʔaFMaaL* (see (1) above). A few have either *FMaaL* or *FMaaLa* (see examples in (b) below).

(a) Singular *FvMvL*

Singular		Plural
balam	'rowboat'	*blaam*
jaraṣ	'bell'	*jraaṣ*
qafaṣ	'cage'	*qfaaṣ*
qalam	'pencil'	*qlaam (ʔaqlaam)*
naƐal	'sole'	*nƐaal*
jibal	'mountain'	*jbaal*
jimal	'camel'	*jmaal*
sabiƐ	'lion'	*sbaaƐ*
čalib	'dog'	*člaab*
qufal	'lock'	*qfaal*

(b) Singular *FvvL*

These are nouns with a weak middle radical. It appears in the plural as *w* or *y*; see (1) (b) above.

Singular		Plural
baab	'door'	*bwaab* (*ʔabwaab*, *buub*)
xaaḷ	'maternal uncle'	*xwaaḷ*
naab	'tusk'	*nyaab*
buuq	'horn, bugle'	*bwaaq* (*ʔabwaaq*)
suug	'market'	*swaag* (*swaaga*)
muus	'razor blade'	*mwaas*
θoob	'shirt'	*θyaab*
ẓooš	'house'	*ẓwaaš*
ẓooδ̣	'pool'	*ẓwaaδ̣*
fiil	'elephant'	*fyaal* (*fyaala*)
ṗiiṗ	'drum' (container)	*ṗyaaṗ* (*ṗiiṗaat*)
čiis	'sack'	*čyaas*

(3) Plural pattern *F(u)MuuL/F(i)MuuL*

This is primarily a plural for nouns of the singular patterns *FvMvL*, *FvDD*, and *FeeL*. For a given noun there may be some variation between the forms with and without the short vowel, but in general the vowel is absent in the more common everyday words, present in the more abstract or learned words. Some nouns may have in the plural either *FMuuL* or *FMuuLa*.

(a) Singular *FvMvL*

Singular		Plural
šaεab	'people'	*šεuub*
ṣaẓan	'plate'	*ṣẓuun*
faẓal	'male'	*fẓuul* (*fẓuula*)
naġaḷ	'bastard'	*nġuuḷ* (*nġuuḷa*)
jaδir	'root'	*jδuur*
ẓalig	'mouth'	*ẓluug*
daris	'lesson'	*druus*
ṣaṭiẓ	'roof'	*ṣṭuuẓ*

ṣaṭir	'line'	*ṣṭuur (ṣṭuura)*
faṭir	'crack'	*fṭuur (fṭuura)*
darub	'road'	*druub*
ḍaruf	'envelope'	*ḍruuf*
ṭabuḷ	'drum'	*ṭbuuḷ (ṭbuula)*
gaḷub	'heart'	*gḷuub*
ʕaqid	'contract'	*ʕuquud*
ʕahid	'era'	*ʕuhuud*
faẓiṣ	'examination'	*fuẓuuṣ*
qarin	'century'	*quruun*
wafid	'delegation'	*wufuud*

(b) Singular *FvDD*

Singular		Plural
tall	'hill'	*tluul (tlaal)*
jidd	'grandfather'	*jduud*
sadd	'dam'	*sduud (sdaad)*
šaṭṭ	'river'	*šṭuuṭ*
ṣaff	'class'	*ṣfuuf*
čaff	'glove'	*čfuuf*
sinn	'tooth'	*snuun*
ẓadd	'limit'	*ẓiduud*
ẓaqq	'right'	*ẓuquuq*
fann	'art'	*finuun*

(c) Singular *FeeL*

These are nouns with a weak middle radical. It appears in the plural as *y*.

Singular		Plural
beet	'house'	*byuut*
teel	'wire'	*tyuul (tyuula)*

xeeṭ	'thread'	*xyuuṭ*
deen	'debt'	*dyuun*
seer	'strap'	*syuur (syuura)*
šeex	'sheikh, chief'	*šyuux*
ṭeer	'bird'	*ṭyuur*
ʕeen	'eye'	*ʕyuun*
meez	'table'	*myuuz (myuuza, meezaat)*

(4) Plural pattern *FuuL*

This is the plural for a few nouns of the singular pattern *FaaL*.

Singular		Plural
baab	'door'	*buub (bwaab)*
daar	'house'	*duur*
raas	'head'	*ruus*
ṭaag	'arch'	*ṭuug*
faas	'axe'	*fuus*
qaaṭ	'suit'	*quuṭ*

(5) Plural pattern *FiMaL*

This is the most common plural for nouns of the patterns *FiMLa*, *FiDDa*, and *FiiLa*, except those which are femine members of sex-gender pairs, or unit nouns, or instance nouns (6.2.2.3 A (3) (a), (b), (c)). For some nouns there may be variation between *FiMaL* and *FuMaL* (see (6) below).

(a) Singular *FiMLa* or *FiDDa*

Singular		Plural
sitra	'coat'	*sitar*
ṣidfa	'coincidence'	*ṣidaf*
ʕilba	'box, can'	*ʕilab*
firqa	'team'	*firaq*
firča	'brush'	*firač*
jiθθa	'corpse'	*jiθaθ*
ʕilla	'defect'	*ʕilal*

(b) Singular *FiiLa*

These are nouns with a weak middle radical; it appears in the plural as *y*.

Singular		Plural
ziila	'trick'	*ziyal*
fiina	'fez'	*fiyan*
qiima	'cost'	*qiyam*

(6) Plural pattern *FuMaL*

This is the most common plural for nouns of the pattern *FuMLa*, *FuDDa*, and *FuuLa*, with the same exceptions noted in (5) above. For some nouns there may be variation between *FuMaL* and *FiMaL*.

(a) Singular *FuMLa* or *FuDDa*

Singular		Plural
ʔubra	'needle'	*ʔubar*
buqča	'bundle'	*buqač*
jumla	'sentence'	*jumal*
dugma	'button'	*dugam*
ġurfa	'room'	*ġuraf*
nusxa	'copy'	*nusax*
nuqṭa	'point, dot'	*nuqaṭ*
nugra	'hole'	*nugar*
quṃṃa	'peak'	*quṃaṃ*

(b) Singular *FuuLa*

These are nouns with a weak middle radical; it appears in the plural as *w*.

Singular		Plural
duuba	'barge'	*duwab*
ṣuura	'picture'	*ṣuwar*
ɛuuda	'stick'	*ɛuwad*
fuuṭa	'head scarf'	*fuwaṭ*

(7) Plural pattern *FuMMaaL/FiMMaaL*

This is the usual plural for those nouns of the pattern *FaaMiL/FaaMuL* (the Class I active participle pattern; see 6.1.6) which refer to human males of a certain profession or occupation.

Singular		Plural
taajir	'merchant'	*tijjaar*
ɀaaris	'guard'	*ɀurraas*
ɀaakim	'judge'	*ɀukkaam*
ṣaaniƐ	'houseboy'	*ṣinnaaƐ*
ẟaabuṭ	'officer'	*ẟubbaaṭ*
ẟaalim	'tyrant'	*ẟullaam*
ṭaalib	'student'	*ṭullaab*
Ɛaamil	'worker'	*Ɛummaal*
kaatib	'clerk'	*kuttaab*
kaafir	'unbeliever'	*kuffaar*

If the middle consonant of the singular is *ʔ* or *y*, the doubled middle consonant of the plural is *w*.

zaayir	'visitor'	*zuwwaar*
saayiq	'driver'	*suwwaaq*
qaaʔid	'commander'	*quwwaad*
naaʔib (*naayib*)	'deputy'	*nuwwaab*

(8) Plural pattern *FuMaat*

This is the plural for a small group of masculine nouns which have the singular pattern *FaaMi* (Class I active participle, weak last radical) and refer to human males of certain occupations.

Singular		Plural
jaabi	'tax collector'	*jubaat*
daaƐi	'advocate'	*duƐaat*
saaƐi	'rural postman'	*suƐaat*
haawi	'amateur'	*huwaat*

(9) Plural pattern *FuMaLaa?*

This is the usual plural for those nouns of the pattern *FaMiiL*, and a few of the pattern *FaaMiL/FaaMuL*, which refer to human males of a certain profession or occupation.

(a) Singular *FaMiiL*

Singular		Plural
?amiin	'executor, custodian'	*?umanaa?*
ẓaliif	'ally'	*ẓulafaa?*
ra?iis	'chief, head'	*ru?asaa?*
zaƐiim	'leader'	*zuƐamaa?*
safiir	'ambassador'	*sufaraa?*
waziir	'minister' (of state)	*wuzaraa?*
wakiil	'agent'	*wukalaa?*

(b) Singular *FaaMiL*

Singular		Plural
šaaƐir	'poet'	*šuƐaraa?*
Ɛaalim	'scientist'	*Ɛulamaa?*

(10) Plural pattern *C(a)CaaCiC/C(a)CaaCuC*

This is primarily a plural for masculine or feminine nouns which have four (in a few cases five) consonants and a short vowel between the last two; for certain mostly feminine nouns which have three consonants and a long vowel between the last two; and for certain nouns of the general pattern *CvvCvC(a)*.

(a) Singular *CvCCvC(a)*

In this category the four consonants of the singular may be a prefix consonant and three radicals, or four radicals (quadriliterals). In the former group the most common prefix is *mv–*; in a few cases *ta–*.

Singular		Plural
mablaġ	'amount'	*mabaaliġ*
markab	'boat'	*maraakub*
maƐraḍ	'exhibition'	*maƐaariḍ*

mazkama	'court'	*mazaakim*
madrasa	'school'	*madaaris*
mazraƐa	'farm'	*mazaariƐ*
majlis	'council'	*majaalis*
manṭiqa	'area'	*manaaṭiq*
mawhiba	'talent'	*mawaahib*
mizraf	'drill' (tool)	*mazaaruf*
miƐṭaf	'overcoat'	*maƐaaṭuf*
mirwaza	'fan'	*maraawiz*
minḍada	'desk'	*manaaḍid*
tajruba	'experiment'	*tajaarub*

Examples of quadriliterals:

ʔarnab	'rabbit'	*ʔaraanib*
xanjar	'dagger'	*xanaajir*
xandaq	'ditch'	*xanaadiq*
darzan	'dozen'	*daraazin*
čarčaf	'lining, cover'	*čaraačif*
burnuṣ	'bathrobe'	*baraaniṣ*
dunbug	'drum'	*danaabug*
qunṣul	'consul'	*qanaaṣil*
dinbila	'abscess, wen'	*danaabil*
qunbula	'bomb'	*qanaabil*

(b) Singular *CvCvvC(a)*

Most nouns in this category end in *-iiCa*, but there are also a few others. In most, also, the three consonants are all radicals, but there are a few in which the first is a prefix and the other two are the first and last radicals of a weak-middle stem (for example *muṣiiba* and *manaara* below). In the plural of all these nouns a *y* appears as the next-to-last consonant.

Singular		Plural
ʒabiib	'sweetheart'	*ʒabaayib*
jariida	'newspaper'	*jaraayid*
ʒadiiqa	'park'	*ʒadaayiq*
xariiṭa	'map'	*xaraayiṭ*
daqiiqa	'minute'	*daqaayiq*
εaruus	'bride'	*εaraayis*
muṣiiba	'disaster'	*maṣaayib (mṣaayib)*
manaara	'minaret'	*manaayir*

The plural of *jigaara* 'cigarette' has *i* as the first vowel: *jigaayir*.

(c) Singular *CvvCvC*

One group in this category consists of nouns of the Class I active participle pattern *FaaMiL/FaaMuL* which do not refer to human beings. In the plural a *w* appears as the second consonant; the short *a* is generally present.

Singular		Plural
daafiε	'motive'	*dawaafiε*
saaʒil	'coast'	*sawaaʒil*
šaariε	'street'	*šawaariε*
ṭaabiq	'story, floor'	*ṭawaabiq*
faaṣil	'partition'	*fawaaṣil*
ʒaadiθa	'incident'	*ʒawaadiθ*
raabiṭa	'bond, tie'	*rawaabiṭ*
εaaṣima	'capital'	*εawaaṣim*
qaaεida	'principle'	*qawaaεid*

In nouns with weak-middle roots there may be some variation between *y* and *ʔ* in both singular and plural.

saaʔil	'liquid'	*sawaaʔil*
εaayiq (εaaʔiq)	'obstacle'	*εawaayiq (εawaaʔiq)*

daaʔira (daayira)	'office'	*dawaaʔir (dawaayir)*
qaaʔima	'list'	*qawaaʔim*

Other nouns in this category are those of the singular patterns *CaaCaC*, *CooCaC*, and *CeeCaC*. In the plural of the first two a *w* appears as the second consonant; in that of the third, a *y*. The short *a* is generally absent.

xaatam	'ring'	*xwaatim*
qaalab	'mold, form'	*qwaalib*
doošag	'mattress'	*dwaašig*
koosaj	'shark'	*kwaasij*
goošar	kind of basket	*gwaašir*
beeraq	'banner'	*b(a)yaariq*
šeebag	'rolling-pin'	*šyaabug*

(d) Others

A few nouns of longer singular patterns also have this plural. Some have four consonants and a short vowel between the last two:

Singular		Plural
numuuδaj	'sample, model'	*namaaδij*

Some end in *-vvCa*; in these a *y* appears as the next-to-last consonant. Among them are several compounds of which the second element is *-xaana* 'house, place'. Most of these have alternative plurals in *-aat*.

Ɛarabaana	'carriage'	*Ɛarabaayin*
xastaxaana	'hospital'	*xastaxaayin (xastaxaanaat)*

A few have five consonants. In the plural of these, one of the consonants is dropped:

barnaamaj	'program'	*baraamij*

(11) Plural pattern

This pattern is the same as the preceding with the addition of the final *a*. It is the plural for a few nouns which have four or more consonants in the singular (either all radicals, or three radicals and a prefix), mostly of foreign origin.

Singular		Plural
ʔustaaδ	'professor'	*ʔasaatiδa*
ṣaydali	'pharmacist'	*ṣayaadila*

faylasuuf	'philosopher'	*falaasifa*
daktoor (*diktoor*)	'doctor'	*dakaatra*
mzayyin	'barber'	*mzaayna*

(12) Plural pattern *C(a)CaaCi*

This is the alternant of the pattern *CaCaaCiC* (see (10) above) for certain nouns with a weak-last root. It is also used for a few nouns with the patterns *CvCCi* and *CuuCi(yya)*.

(a) Singular *FvMwa*

Some nouns of this singular pattern have a sound plural in *-aat*; others have the broken plural illustrated below; a few may have either.

Singular		Plural
balwa	'trouble'	*balaawi*
daƐwa	'lawsuit' [1]	*daƐaawi*
Ɛalwa	'warehouse'	*Ɛalaawi*
karwa	'fare, charge'	*karaawi*
gahwa	'coffee-shop'	*gahaawi*
čilwa	'kidney'	*č(a)laawi*

(b) Singular *maFMa*

These are nouns formed by the prefix *ma-* and a stem with a weak-last root.

Singular		Plural
majra	'riverbed; gutter'	*majaari*
marƐa	'pasture'	*maraaƐi*
maƐna	'meaning'	*maƐaani*
maġza	'intention, purpose'	*maġaazi*
malha	'nightclub'	*malaahi*

[1] In meaning 'invitation', plural is *daƐwaat*.

(c) Singular *taFMiya*

These are nouns of the pattern of Class II verbal nouns with a weak-last root. Most have plurals in *-aat*; a few have the plural illustrated below.

Singular		Plural
taƐziya	'condolence'	*taƐaazi*
tahniya	'congratulation'	*tahaani*

(d) Singular *FaaMi* or *FaaM(i)ya*

These are nouns which have the pattern of Class I active participles with a weak-last root, and do not refer to human beings. In the plural a *w* appears as the second consonant, as in the plural described in (10) (c) above. For these nouns the plural most commonly lacks the short *a*; there are some exceptions.

Singular		Plural
šaadi	'monkey'	*šwaadi*
šaaṭi	'bank, beach'	*šwaaṭi*
naadi	'club'	*nawaadi*
ʒaašya	'edge'	*ʒwaaši*
saagya [1]	'irrigation ditch'	*swaagi*

(e) Singular *CvCCi*

In the plural the short *a* is generally present.

Singular		Plural
burġi	'screw'	*baraaġi (burġiyyaat)*
surgi	'bolt'	*saraagi (surgiyyaat)*
kursi	'chair'	*karaasi*

(f) Singular *CuuCi* or *CuuCiyya*

There are very few of these nouns. In the plural a *w* appears as the second consonant, and the short *a* is generally absent.

Singular		Plural
buuri	'pipe'	*bwaari (buuriyyaat)*
quuri	'teapot'	*qwaari*

[1] Also *saajya*, plural *swaaji*.

zuuliyya	'rug'	*zwaali*
quuṭiyya	'packet, box, can'	*qwaaṭi*

(13) Plural pattern *C(a)CaaCiiC*

This is the usual broken plural for masculine or feminine nouns which have four consonants (either all radicals, or a prefix and three radicals) and a long vowel between the last two, and for those which have three consonants and a long vowel both before and after the second (cf. (10) above). It is also used for a few nouns of the singular pattern *mFaDD(a)*. The short *a* shown in parentheses in the heading is present in the plurals of some of these nouns, absent in others, optional in still others; these facts must be learned for each noun. However, a general statement as to its probable occurrence is given for each group below.

(a) Singular *CvFMvvL(a)*

These are nouns consisting of a sound triliteral stem with a prefix. The majority are nouns with the patterns of Class I passive participles (*maFMuuL*) and Class II verbal nouns (*taFMiiL*). The plurals generally have the short *a* after the first consonant.

Singular		Plural
marsuum	'decree'	*maraasiim*
masjuun	'prisoner'	*masaajiin*
mašruuƐ	'project'	*mašaariiƐ*
maktuub	'letter'	*makaatiib*
mawḍuuƐ	'subject'	*mawaaḍiiƐ*
majmuuƐa	'collection'	*majaamiiƐ*
taṣriiḥ	'statement'	*taṣaariiḥ (taṣriiḥaat)*
taqriir	'report'	*taqaariir*
taqwiim	'calendar'	*taqaawiim*
tamriin	'drill'	*tamaariin (tamriinaat)*
miqdaar	'quantity'	*maqaadiir*
miqyaas	'measure'	*maqaayiis*

(b) Singular *FvMMvvL(a)*

These are nouns of triliteral root, with a doubled middle radical. The plurals generally lack the short *a* after the first consonant.

Singular		Plural
ʒammaal	'porter'	*ʒmaamiil (ʒammaaliin)*
xabbaaz	'baker'	*xbaabiiz (xabbaaziin)*
dukkaan	'shop'	*dkaakiin*
ṣabbaaġ	'shoeshine boy'	*ṣbaabiiġ (ṣabbaaġiin)*
bazzuuna	'cat'	*bzaaziin*
balluuƐa	'drain'	*blaaliiƐ*
sijjaada	'rug'	*sjaajiid (sijjaadaat)*
siččiina	'knife'	*sčaačiin*

(c) Singular *FvSTvvL(a)*

These are nouns of quadriliteral root. The presence or absence of the short *a* in the plurals is not predictable.

Singular		Plural
barmiil	'barrel'	*baraamiil*
burhaan	'proof'	*baraahiin*
bismaar	'nail'	*bsaamiir*
tilmiiδ	'student'	*talaamiiδ*
danbuus	'pin'	*danaabiis*
ṣanduug	'box'	*ṣ(a)naadiig*
Ɛifriit	'demon'	*Ɛafaariit*
finjaan	'cup'	*f(a)naajiin*
jarθuuma	'germ'	*jaraaθiim*

(d) Singular *CvvCvvC(a)*

These include nouns of both triliteral and quadriliteral roots. In the plural a *w* or *y* appears as the second consonant. The short *a* is absent in most cases.

Singular		Plural
taabuut	'coffin'	*twaabiit*
taariix	'date; history'	*tawaariix*

jooraab	'sock'	*jwaariib*
diilaab (duulaab)	'cupboard'	*dwaaliib*
šiiṭaan	'devil'	*šyaaṭiin*
ṭaaẓuuna	'mill'	*ṭwaaẓiin*
maaɛuun	'plate'	*mwaaɛiin* [1]
miizaan	'scales'	*mwaaziin*
čaakuuč	'hammer'	*čwaakiič*

An important exception is *diinaar* 'dinar' (the Iraqi unit of currency), plural *d(i)naaniir*.

(e) Singular *mFaDD(a)*

A few nouns consisting of an *m* prefix and a stem with a double root have this plural; most also have plurals in *-aat*. The plurals generally lack the short *a*.

Singular		Plural
mjarr	'drawer'	*mjaariir (mjarraat)*
mxadda	'cushion'	*mxaadiid (mxaddaat)*
mhaffa	'fan'	*mhaafiif (mhaffaat)*

(14) Plural pattern *FuMuL/FiMiL/FuMiL*

A small number of nouns, most of which have a long vowel before the final consonant, have this plural pattern. There may be some variation between *i* and *u* in the plural, except that the combination *FiMuL* does not occur, and *FuMuL* is more common as the plural of the first group below.

(a) Singular *FvMiiL(a)*

Singular		Plural
sifiina	'(sailing) ship'	*sufun (sifin)*
ṭariiq	'way, road'	*ṭuruq*
ṭariiqa	'way, method'	*ṭuruq*
madiina	'city'	*mudun*

[1] Or, irregularly, *mmaaɛiin*.

(b) Singular *FMaaL*

Singular		Plural
ʒzaam	'belt'	*ʒizim*
fraaš	'bed, bedding'	*furiš (fraašaat)*
ktaab	'book'	*kutub*

The noun *walad* 'boy' also has this plural: *wulid*.

(15) Plural pattern *F(a)Maaya*

This is the plural for a few nouns, mostly feminine and ending in *-ya*. Some also have plurals in *-aat*.

(a) Singular *F(a)Miyya*

Singular		Plural
zwiyya [1]	'corner'	*zwaaya*
qaḍiyya	'case, matter'	*qaḍaaya*
hadiyya	'gift'	*hadaaya*

(b) Singular *FvMya*

Singular		Plural
ʒayya	'snake'	*ʒyaaya (ʒayyaat)*
niθya	'female'	*nθaaya*

(16) Plural pattern *ʔaFMiLa*

This is the plural for some masculine nouns with a long vowel *aa*, *ii*, or *uu* before the final consonant.

Singular		Plural
jihaaz [2]	'appliance'	*ʔajhiza*
damaaġ	'brain'	*ʔadmiġa*
raṣiif	'dock'	*ʔarṣifa*

[1] The related, more technical word *zaawiya* 'angle' has the plural *zawaaya*.

[2] The form *jhaaz* plural *jhaazaat* has the specialized meaning 'thing for use in a woman's household after her marriage'.

slaaz	'weapon'	*ʔasliza*
Ɛamuud	'pillar'	*ʔaƐmida*
miθaal	'example'	*ʔamθila*

(17) Plural pattern *ʔaFiDDa*

This pattern is the alternant of the preceding pattern (*ʔaFMiLa*) for nouns with a double root. This is thus the plural for nouns of the pattern *F(v)DvvD*.

Singular		Plural
janiin	'fetus'	*ʔajinna*
daliil	'evidence'	*ʔadilla*
šuƐaaƐ	'ray'	*ʔašiƐƐa*

(18) Plural pattern *ʔaFMiLaaʔ*

This is the plural for only a few nouns of the pattern *FaMiiL* or *FaMi*. It is more common as an adjective plural (see 7.2.2).

(a) Singular *FaMiiL*

Singular		Plural
ṣadiiq	'friend'	*ʔaṣdiqaaʔ*
qariib	'relative'	*ʔaqribaaʔ*

(b) Singular *FaMi*

These are nouns with a weak last radical. A *y* appears as the consonant before the long *aa*.

Singular		Plural
ġabi	'fool'	*ʔaġbiyaaʔ*

(19) Plural pattern *ʔaFiDDaaʔ*

This is the alternant of the preceding pattern (*ʔaFMiLaaʔ*) for nouns with a double root. It is thus the plural for some nouns of the pattern *FaDiiD* (and for adjectives of the same pattern; see 7.2.2).

Singular		Plural
daliil	'guide'	*ʔadillaaʔ*
šaqiiq	'full brother'	*ʔašiqqaaʔ*
ṭabiib	'doctor'	*ʔaṭibbaaʔ*

(20) Plural pattern *FiMLaan/FuMLaan*

This is the plural for a number of nouns of various patterns.

(a) Singular *F(v)MvvL*

Singular		Plural
ʒaṣiir(a)	'straw mat'	*ʒiṣraan*
xaliij	'bay'	*xiljaan*
šujaaƐ	'brave man'	*šujƐaan*
ṣaliib	'cross'	*ṣulbaan*
ġraab	'crow'	*ġurbaan*
qaṭiiƐ	'flock, herd'	*qiṭƐaan*
nisiib	'son-in-law'	*nisbaan*

(b) Singular *FaaMiL*

Singular		Plural
raahib	'monk'	*ruhbaan*

(c) Singular *FaaMi*

In these nouns a *y* appears as the third consonant.

Singular		Plural
raaƐi	'shepherd'	*riƐyaan*

(d) Singular *FvMv*

Here too a *y* appears as the third consonant.

Singular		Plural
ṣibi	'young boy'	*ṣibyaan*

(e) Others

Singular		Plural
blaad	'country'	*buldaan*
Ɛurbi	'nomadic Arab'	*Ɛurbaan* [1]
Ɛirriis	'bridegroom'	*Ɛirsaan*

[1] Specifically: 'camps of nomads, bedouins'.

The noun *ʔax* 'brother' has the plural *ʔixwaan* (or *ʔuxwa*); the noun *mara* 'woman' has the plural *niswaan*.

(21) Plural pattern *FiiLaan*

This is the alternant of the preceding pattern *(FiMLaan/FuMLaan)* for a few nouns, with a weak-middle root, of the pattern *FvvL*.

Singular		Plural
taaj	'crown'	*tiijaan (tuuj)*
jaar	'neighbor'	*jiiraan*[1]
saaq	'leg, calf'	*siiqaan*
naar	'fire'	*niiraan*
θoor	'bull'	*θiiraan*
ẓuut	'whale'	*ẓiitaan*

(22) Others

There are other plural patterns, but most of them are limited to two or three nouns each. Examples are:

FaMiiL

ɛabid	'slave; Negro'	*ɛabiid*

ʔaFMuL

saham	'(stock) share'	*ʔashum*

FaMaLa

saaẓir	'magician'	*saẓara*

FaMLa

ʔasiir	'prisoner'	*ʔasra*

(23) The counting plural

There is a small group of nouns which have one or more broken plural forms for general use, and also a special <u>counting plural</u> form. The latter begins with *t*, and is used only after one of the numerals from one to ten (8.1). The following are the most common:

---

[1] Also used as singular.

Singular		General plural	Counting plural
ʔalif	'thousand'	*ʔaalaaf (ʔluuf)*	*taalaaf*
ḍraaƐ	'forearm'[1]	*ʔaḍruƐ*	*tuḍruƐ*
zooj	'pair'	*ʔazwaaj*	*tizwaaj*
šahar	'month'	*ʔašhur (šhuur)*	*tušhur*
mann	a weight	*ʔamnaan*	*timnaan*
yoom	'day'	*ʔayyaam*	*tiyyaam*

The fractions from one-third to one-tenth are also in this category; for these see 8.3. Examples of counting plural:

tlat-taalaaf	'three thousand'
ʔarbaƐ-tizwaaj	'four pairs'
xamis-tušhur	'five months'
sabiƐ-timnaan	'seven *mann*'
θman-tiyyaam	'eight days'
tlat-tarbaaƐ	'three-fourths'

(24) Miscellaneous plural forms

Listed below are some common nouns with unusual or unpredictable plurals.

(a) Family relationships

Singular		Plural
ʔab	'father'	*ʔaabaaʔ (ʔabbahaat)*
ʔax	'brother'	*ʔuxwa (ʔixwaan)*[2]
ʔibin	'son'	*ʔabnaaʔ*
ʔuxut	'sister'	*xawaat*
ʔumm	'mother'	*ʔummahaat*
binit	'daughter'	*banaat*

[1] Used as a measure of length.

[2] Usually *ʔuxwa* means (real) 'brothers'; *ʔixwaan*, 'friends, colleagues, gentlemen'.

(b) Parts of body

Singular		Plural
ʔiδin (ʔiiδaan)[1]	'ear'	*ʔiiδaan (ʔiiδaanaat)*
ʔiid	'hand, arm'	*ʔiideen*[2]
ʔiṣbiƐ	'finger; toe'	*ʔaṣaabiƐ*
δ̣raaƐ	'arm'	*ʔaδ̣ruƐ (δ̣raaƐaat)*
rijil	'foot, leg'	*rijleen*[2]

(c) Others

Singular		Plural
ʔisim	'name'	*ʔasmaaʔ (ʔasaami)*
jigaara	'cigarette'	*jigaayir*
diinaar	'dinar'	*d(i)naaniir*
rijjaal	'man'	*riyaajiil*
sana	'year'	*sniin*
sbuuƐ	'week'	*ʔasaabiiƐ*
šii	'thing'	*ʔašyaaʔ*
qarya	'village'	*qura*
m̩ara	'woman'	*niswaan*
walad	'boy'	*wulid*

6.3 NOUN PREFIXES

Three types of prefixes are primarily associated with nouns (though some occur with other forms as well): the article prefix, the demonstrative prefix, and several preposition prefixes.

6.3.1 The article prefix

The Iraqi equivalent of the English definite article the is a prefix.[3] It has two forms.

---

[1] In the singular, *ʔiδin* is used for 'sense of hearing, ear' (e.g. for music); *ʔiiδaan* for (physical) 'ear'. In the plural, either of the forms listed can mean (physical) 'ears'.

[2] These are dual in form but are either dual or plural in use. See 6.2.2.2 A (3).

[3] For occurrence of the article prefix with adjectives, see 11.2.1.1, 13.6.

A. The *l–* form. One form of the article prefix is the consonant *l–*, which occurs with words beginning with the following consonant sounds:

ʔ	*ʔakil*	'food'	*l–ʔakil*	'the food'
b	*beet*	'house'	*l–beet*	'the house'
ʒ	*ʒaliib*	'milk'	*l–ʒaliib*	'the milk'
x	*xeel*	'horses'	*l–xeel*	'the horses'
ε	*εinab*	'grapes'	*l–εinab*	'the grapes'
ġ	*ġada*	'lunch'	*l–ġada*	'the lunch'
f	*fikra*	'idea'	*l–fikra*	'the idea'
q	*qisim*	'part'	*l–qisim*	'the part'
k	*kaatib*	'clerk'	*l–kaatib*	'the clerk'
m	*mooz*	'bananas'	*l–mooz*	'the bananas'
h	*hawa*	'air'	*l–hawa*	'the air'
w	*wakit*	'time'	*l–wakit*	'the time'
y	*yoom*	'day'	*l–yoom*	'the day'
p	*paaṣ*	'bus'	*l–paaṣ*	'the bus'
g	*guṭin*	'cotton'	*l–guṭin*	'the cotton'

The article prefix also has the *l–* form before words beginning with a consonant cluster (2.3) of which the first consonant is one of those above. A helping vowel then automatically occurs before the cluster: [1]

blaam	'rowboats'	*l–iblaam*	'the rowboats'
bnayya	'girl'	*l–ibnayya*	'the girl'
byuut	'houses'	*l–ibyuut*	'the houses'
fluus	'money'	*l–ifluus*	'the money'
qmaaš	'cloth'	*l–iqmaaš*	'the cloth'
mraaya	'mirror'	*l–imraaya*	'the mirror'

---

[1] When a helping vowel occurs after the article, as here and in some cases in B below, one may also occur before the article, for example *il–iblaam* 'the rowboats', *il–ittifaaq* 'the agreement'. This vowel does not occur after another vowel; it does occur after the preposition prefixes *b–*, *l–*, and *mn–* (see 6.3.3); otherwise it is optional.

B. The doubled form. The other form of the article prefix occurs with words beginning with the remaining consonant sounds, and in each case consists of the same consonant as the one with which the word begins.[1] It should be noted that these consonants are all those which are produced by the tip or front of the tongue:

t	*timman*	'rice'	*t-timman*	'the rice'
θ	*θoob*	'shirt'	*θ-θoob*	'the shirt'
j	*junṭa*	'suitcase'	*j-junṭa*	'the suitcase'
d	*diinaar*	'dinar'	*d-diinaar*	'the dinar'
δ	*δibbaan*	'flies'	*δ-δibbaan*	'the flies'
r	*rukkaab*	'passengers'	*r-rukkaab*	'the passengers'
z	*zibid*	'butter'	*z-zibid*	'the butter'
s	*sana*	'year'	*s-sana*	'the year'
š	*šahar*	'month'	*š-šahar*	'the month'
ṣ	*ṣuura*	'picture'	*ṣ-ṣuura*	'the picture'
δ̣	*δ̣aabuṭ*	'officer'	*δ̣-δ̣aabuṭ*	'the officer'
ṭ	*ṭooba*	'ball'	*ṭ-ṭooba*	'the ball'
l	*leela*	'night'	*l-leela*	'the night'
n	*naar*	'fire'	*n-naar*	'the fire'
č	*čaakuuč*	'hammer'	*č-čaakuuč*	'the hammer'

When prefixed to a word beginning with a consonant cluster of which the first consonant is one of those in B above, the form of the article depends upon whether the cluster is separable or not. A non-separable cluster is one which is never separated by any vowel. In general one must learn what words begin with non-separable clusters, but it is helpful to remember that among them are all verbal nouns of Classes VII through X (6.1.1). When prefixed to such words, the article prefix has the *l-* form, and a helping vowel occurs before the cluster:

ttifaaq	'agreement'	*l-ittifaaq*	'the agreement'
jtimaaε	'meeting'	*l-ijtimaaε*	'the meeting'
stiεmaal	'use'	*l-istiεmaal*	'the use'
skamli	'chair'	*l-iskamli*	'the chair'

[1] The *l-* form is also occasionally heard with a noun beginning with one of these, for example *l-junṭa*, *l-zibid*, but not as a general rule.

With other words, the article may have either the *l-* form, in which case the helping vowel occurs before the cluster, or the doubled form, in which case a shoı vowel occurs between the two consonants of the cluster:

ṭyuur	'birds'	*l-iṭyuur* *ṭ-ṭiyuur*	'the birds'
jbaal	'mountains'	*l-ijbaal* *j-jibaal*	'the mountains'
sniin	'years'	*l-isniin* *s-siniin*	'the years'
ṭbuul	'drums'	*l-iṭbuul* *ṭ-ṭubuul*	'the drums'

6.3.2 The demonstrative prefix

The Iraqi equivalent of the English demonstrative adjectives this and these may be independent words *haaδa*, *haaδi*, *(ha)δool*, followed by a noun with the article prefix, for example *haaδa l-meez* 'this table' (see 13.2). Another equivalent is a prefix, in which the element *ha* of the independent demonstratives is combined with the following article prefix, for example *hal-meez* 'this table'. Like the article prefix itself, the demonstrative prefix has two forms. One is a form *hal-*, which occurs before the same consonants as does the *l-* form of the article prefix (6.3.1); the other is a doubled form *hat-*, *haθ-*, *haj-*, *had-* and so on, which occurs before the same consonants as does the doubled form of the article prefix. Some examples:

l-ʔakil	'the food'	*hal-ʔakil*	'this food'
l-fikra	'the idea'	*hal-fikra*	'this idea'
l-mooz	'the bananas'	*hal-mooz*	'these bananas'
l-ibnayya	'the girl'	*hal-ibnayya*	'this girl'
l-ifluus	'the money'	*hal-ifluus*	'this money'
θ-θoob	'the shirt'	*haθ-θoob*	'this shirt'
r-rukkaab	'the passengers'	*har-rukkaab*	'these passengers'
s-sana	'the year'	*has-sana*	'this year'
l-ijtimaaε	'the meeting'	*hal-ijtimaaε*	'this meeting'
l-iskamli	'the chair'	*hal-iskamli*	'this chair'
l-isniin	'the years'	*hal-isniin* *has-siniin*	'these years'

6.3.3 Preposition prefixes [1]

A. *b-* 'in, at, by means of'

This preposition occurs only as a prefix:

baġdaad	'Baghdad'	*b-baġdaad*	'in Baghdad'
sayyaarti	'my car'	*b-sayyaarti*	'in my car'
čaakuuč	'hammer'	*b-čaakuuč*	'with a hammer'

When the following word begins with a consonant cluster, a helping vowel precedes:

fluusak	'your money'	*b-ifluusak*	'with your money'

The prefix *b-* combines with the article prefix as follows:

l-beet	'the house'	*bil-beet*	'in the house'
l-qiṭaar	'the train'	*bil-qiṭaar*	'on the train'
l-iktaab	'the book'	*bil-iktaab*	'in the book'
j-junṭa	'the suitcase'	*bij-junṭa*	'in the suitcase'
n-naar	'the fire'	*bin-naar*	'in the fire'

B. *l-* 'to, for'

This preposition prefix is identical in form with the article prefix and, like it, occurs in both an *l-* form and a doubled form depending on the following consonant (see 6.3.1):

baġdaad	'Baghdad'	*l-baġdaad*	'to Baghdad'
beetna	'our house'	*l-beetna*	'to our house'
ɛammi	'my uncle'	*l-ɛammi*	'to my uncle'
jaasim	'Jaasim'	*j-jaasim*	'to Jaasim'
ṣadiiqi	'my friend'	*ṣ-ṣadiiqi*	'to my friend'

When the following word begins with a consonant cluster, a helping vowel precedes:

ttifaaqna	'our agreement'	*l-ittifaaqna*	'to our agreement'
spaanya	'Spain'	*l-ispaanya*	'to Spain'

---

[1] See also 9.1.2.2 B and 10.1.1.

The prefix *l-* combines with the article prefix as follows:

l-beet	'the house'	*lil-beet*	'to the house'
l-Ɛiraaq	'Iraq'	*lil-Ɛiraaq*	'to Iraq'
l-maṭaar	'the airport'	*lil-maṭaar*	'to the airport'
l-ijtimaaƐ	'the meeting'	*lil-ijtimaaƐ*	'to the meeting'
j-jaamiƐa	'the university'	*lij-jaamiƐa*	'to the university'
ṣ-ṣaff	'the class'	*liṣ-ṣaff*	'to the class'
n-naadi	'the club'	*lin-naadi*	'to the club'

C. *mn-* 'from, of'

This is a prefix form of the independent preposition *min*. In this form it occurs before words beginning with two consonants (which are thus preceded by a helping vowel), and in combination with the article prefix:

fluusi	'my money'	*mn-ifluusi*	'from my money'
l-beet	'the house'	*mnil-beet*	'from the house'
l-Ɛiraaq	'Iraq'	*mnil-Ɛiraaq*	'from Iraq'
l-ijtimaaƐ	'the meeting'	*mnil-ijtimaaƐ*	'from the meeting'
š-šaariƐ	'the street'	*mniš-šaariƐ*	'from the street'
n-naas	'the people'	*mnin-naas*	'from the people'

D. *Ɛa-* 'on, at, against'

This is a prefix form of the independent preposition *Ɛala*. It occurs only in combination with the article prefix, as follows:

l-meez	'the table'	*Ɛal-meez*	'on the table'
l-gaaƐ	'the ground'	*Ɛal-gaaƐ*	'on the ground'
l-iqtiraaẓ	'the suggestion'	*Ɛal-iqtiraaẓ*	'about the suggestion'
ṣ-ṣaṭiẓ	'the roof'	*Ɛaṣ-ṣaṭiẓ*	'on the roof'
n-naar	'the fire'	*Ɛan-naar*	'on the fire'

7. ADJECTIVES

7.1 DERIVATION

This section deals with the derivation of active and passive participles (7.1.1), *FaMLaan* adjectives (7.1.2), nisba adjectives (7.1.3) and comparatives (7.1.4). Ordinal adiectives are treated in 8.2.

7.1.1 Participles

Participles are adjectives derived from verbs and closely related to them in meaning. They are sometimes called "verbal adjectives". Participles are of two kinds, active and passive. The general meaning of an active participle (AP) is 'in a certain state as a result of having performed the action indicated by the verb', or simply 'in the state indicated by the verb'. The English form which best translates an AP in a given context usually depends on the translation of the corresponding verb. For example, if the verb is translated 'to be ---', 'to become ---', 'to turn ---', 'to get ---', or 'to grow ---', with an adjective (such as 'cold', 'red', 'perplexed') in the blank, then the AP is usually translated by the adjective alone:

Verb		AP	
burad	'to be, get cold'	*baarid*	'cold'
xaaf	'to be afraid'	*xaayif*	'afraid'
ʒaar	'to be perplexed'	*ʒaayir*	'perplexed'
ʒmarr	'to turn red'	*miʒmarr*	'red'

(In the last example the AP *miʒmarr* means 'red' with the implication 'having changed to red from some other state', and thus differs from the color adjective *ʔaʒmar*, which means 'red' with no implication of change.) In some cases an AP can be translated by an English -ing form:

Verb		AP	
raaʒ	'to go'	*raayiʒ*	'going'
jaa	'to come'	*jaay*	'coming'
giƐad	'to sit (down)'	*gaaƐid*	'sitting'
wugaf	'to stand; to stop'	*waaguf*	'standing; not moving'
libas	'to wear; to put on'	*laabis*	'wearing'

In still other cases the AP is best translated by an English perfect verb phrase (a form of to have plus a past participle): [1]

[1] Note that in these cases the AP does *not* correspond to the English progressive construction consisting of to be plus an -ing form. Thus *ʔaani qaari l-maqaal* does not mean 'I am reading the article', but 'I have read the article'. (See 12.1.3).

ṭilaɛ	'to go out'	*ween ɛali? ṭaaliɛ.* 'Where's Ali? He has gone out.' (That is, he is in the state resulting from his having gone out; he is out.)
šaaf	'to see'	*ʔaani šaayif kull il-ʔašyaaʔ il-muhimma hnaa.* 'I've seen all the important things here. (That is, I am now in the state of having seen...)

When AP's of this sort are given in lists or as isolated entries, they will be translated as 'having gone out', 'having seen', 'having bought', and so on.

The general meaning of a passive participle (PP) is 'having undergone the action indicated by the verb'. The usual English equivalent is a past participle form:

Verb		PP	
minaɛ	'to forbid'	*mamnuuɛ*	'forbidden'
sadd	'to close'	*masduud*	'closed'
nisa	'to forget'	*mansi*	'forgotten'
baddal	'to change'	*mbaddal*	'changed'

Participles are basically adjectives, with the inflections and the syntactic properties of adjectives. Some may have specialized adjective meanings differing from the expected participle meanings as described above. For example, the common AP form *šaaṭir*, with the same root as the (uncommon) verb *šiṭar* 'to split', has the specialized meaning 'clever' (corresponding to a sense in which the verb is no longer used); and the PP form *masʔuul*, from *siʔal* 'to ask', has the specialized meaning 'responsible'. In addition, many participles have specialized meanings as nouns (6.1.6), in which case they have the inflectional and syntactic properties of nouns. Some examples are the AP's *jaahil* 'child' and *muɛallim* 'teacher', and the PP's *maktuub* 'letter' and *mujallad* 'volume' (book). Participles with specialized meanings frequently differ slightly in form from those with participle meanings.

With some general exceptions, the forms of participles are predictable from the derivational class and stem-type (sound, doubled, hollow, or defective) of the corresponding verb. Class I participles have special patterns (see 7.1.1.1 below). All others (see 7.1.1.2 to 7.1.1.13) consist of a prefix *m-*, *mi-* or *mu-* and a stem which is identical, except for vowels, to the imperfect stem of the verb (Class IV participles show some exceptions; see 7.1.1.4).

In active participles, the prefix is *m-* before stems beginning with one consonant: *ɛallam* 'to teach', AP *mɛallim* 'having taught'. Before stems beginning with two consonants it is generally *mi-*, but may also be *mu-* in a *u* environment (2.6) or as a stylistic variant in formal words: *tɛallam* 'to learn', AP *mitɛallim* 'having learned'; *ḍṭarr* 'to be obliged to, have to', AP *muḍṭarr* '(having been) obliged to'. The stem is identical to that of the imperfect except that when the latter ends in *-aC* or *-a*, the active participle stem ends in *-iC/-uC* or *-i*, for example (imperfect forms given in parentheses):

Verb		AP	
ɛallam (*yɛallim*)	'to teach'	*mɛallim*	'having taught'
tɛallam (*yitɛallam*)	'to learn'	*mitɛallim*	'having learned'
tġadda (*yitġadda*)	'to have lunch'	*mitġaddi*	'having had lunch'

Active participles with specialized meanings generally have the prefix *mu-* rather than *m-*, and stems ending in *-iC* rather than *-uC*:

Verb		AP		Specialized	
ɛallam (*yɛallim*)	'to teach'	*mɛallim*	'having taught'	*muɛallim*	'teacher'
naẓẓaf (*ynaẓẓuf*)	'to clean'	*mnaẓẓuf*	'having cleaned'	*munaẓẓif*	'cleanser'

In passive participles, the prefix is *m-* before stems beginning with one consonant: *naẓẓaf* 'to clean', PP *mnaẓẓaf* 'cleaned'. Before stems beginning with two consonants it is *mu-*: *staɛmal* 'to use', PP *mustaɛmal* 'used'. The stem is identical to that of the imperfect with two exceptions: (1) when the latter ends in *-iC/-uC* or *-i*, the passive participle stem ends in *-aC* or *-a*, for example:

Verb		PP	
θallaj (*yθallij*)	'to chill'	*mθallaj*	'chilled'
naẓẓaf (*ynaẓẓuf*)	'to clean'	*mnaẓẓaf*	'cleaned'
samma (*ysammi*)	'to name'	*msamma*	'named'

and (2) when in the imperfect stem the vowel before the last vowel is *i* or *u*, the corresponding vowel in the passive participle is *a*, for example:

Verb		PP	
ʒtiqar (*yiʒtiqir*)	'to despise'	*muʒtaqar*	'despised'

Passive participles with specialized meanings generally have the prefix *mu-* rather than *m-*:

Verb		PP		Specialized	
jallad (*yjallid*)	'to bind'	*mjallad*	'bound'	*mujallad*	'volume'

xaṭṭaṭ (*yxaṭṭiṭ*)	'to draw lines on'	*mxaṭṭaṭ*	'lined'	*muxaṭṭaṭ*	'blueprint, layout'

7.1.1.1 Class I

Participles of Class I verbs have the following patterns:

Verb	AP	PP
Sound	*FaaMiL/-uL*	*maFMuuL*
Doubled	*FaaDD*	*maFMuuL*
Hollow	*FaaMiL*	*maFMuuL*
Defective	*FaaMi*	*maFMi*

Examples:

Sound verbs		AP	PP
ẓisab	'to count'	*ẓaasib*	*maẓsuub*
simaƐ	'to hear'	*saamiƐ*	*masmuuƐ*
širab	'to drink'	*šaarub*	*mašruub*
ṭubax	'to cook'	*ṭaabux*	*maṭbuux*

Doubled verbs

δabb	'to throw out'	*δaabb*	*maδbuub*
sadd	'to close'	*saadd*	*masduud*

Hollow verbs. In the active participle, the consonant in the M position is generally *y*, but may be *ʔ* in a few cases, mostly those with specialized meanings. In the passive participle, the consonant in the M position is *y*.

šaal	'to pick up, carry'	*šaayil*	*mašyuul*
δ̣aag	'to taste'	*δ̣aayig*	*maδ̣yuug*

Defective verbs

bina	'to build'	*baani*	*mabni*
nisa	'to forget'	*naasi*	*mansi*
muδ̣a	'to sign'	*maaδ̣i*	*mamδ̣i*

Three Class I verbs have irregular active participles; the third, being intransitive, has no passive participle:

ʔaxaδ	'to take'	*maaxiδ*	*maʔxuuδ*

ʔakal	'to eat'	*maakil*	*maʔkuul*
jaa	'to come'	*jaay*	———

The verb *niṭa* 'to give' has either a regular Class I active participle *naaṭi* or a Class IV active participle *minṭi*. In place of a passive participle form, the active participle of the Class VII verb *nniṭa* 'to be given' is used: *minniṭi* 'given'.

7.1.1.2 Class II

Participles of Class II verbs have the following patterns:

Verb	AP	PP
Sound	*mFaMMiL/–uL*	*mFaMMaL*
Defective	*mFaMMi*	*mFaMMa*

Examples (imperfect forms in parentheses):

Sound verbs		AP	PP
baddal (*ybaddil*)	'to change'	*mbaddil*	*mbaddal*
dabbar (*ydabbur*)	'to arrange'	*mdabbur*	*mdabbar*
ẓaddad (*yẓaddid*)	'to limit'	*mẓaddid*	*mẓaddad*
ɛayyan (*yɛayyin*)	'to appoint'	*mɛayyin*	*mɛayyan*
fawwar (*yfawwur*)	'to boil'	*mfawwur*	*mfawwar*
Defective verbs			
samma (*ysammi*)	'to name, call'	*msammi*	*msamma*
sawwa (*ysawwi*)	'to do, make'	*msawwi*	*msawwa*

7.1.1.3 Class III

Participles of Class III verbs have the following patterns:

Verb	AP	PP
Sound	*mFaaMiL/–uL*	*mFaaMaL*
Defective	*mFaaMi*	*mFaaMa*

Examples (imperfect forms in parentheses):

Sound verbs		AP	PP
Ɛaaqab (*yƐaaqib*)	'to punish'	*mƐaaqib*	*mƐaaqab*
ḍaaƐaf (*yḍaaƐuf*)	'to double'	*mḍaaƐuf*	*mḍaaƐaf*
naawaš (*ynaawuš*)	'to hand'	*mnaawuš*	*mnaawaš*
Defective verbs			
daara (*ydaari*)	'to take care of'	*mdaari*	*mdaara*
raawa (*yraawi*)	'to show'	*mraawi*	*mraawa*

7.1.1.4 Class IV

Participles of Class IV verbs differ from other participles in having the prefix *mu-*, rather than *m-*, before stems beginning with a single consonant, and, in the case of those from sound and defective verbs with first radical *w*, in having a different long vowel *uu* from that of the imperfect form of the verb *oo*. The patterns are as follows:

Verb	AP	PP
Sound	*miFMiL/muFMiL*	*muFMaL*
First radical *w*	*muuMiL*	*muuMaL*
Doubled	*muFiDD*	*muFaDD*
Hollow	*muFiiL*	*muFaaL*
Defective	*miFMi/muFMi*	*muFMa*
First radical *w*	*muuMi*	*muuMa*

Used as participles proper, these forms are somewhat uncommon, as are Class IV verbs themselves (see 5.1.1.4). A few examples (imperfect forms in parentheses):

Sound verbs		AP	PP
ʔadraj (*yidrij*)	'to enter' (as item on list)	*midrij*	*mudraj*
First radical *w*			
ʔawfad (*yoofid*)	'to send as a delegate'	*muufid*	*muufad*

Doubled verbs		AP	PP
ʔaṣarr (ɛala) (yṣirr)	'to insist (on)'	*muṣirr*	*muṣarr* [1]
ʔaɛadd (yɛidd)	'to prepare' (tr)		*muɛadd*

Hollow verbs

ʔaqaal	'to dismiss' (from office)	*muqiil*	*muqaal*

Defective verbs. For the passive participles, the Class I pattern *maFMi* is generally used instead of *muFMa*.

ʔafša (yifši)	'to reveal' (secret)	*mifši*	*(mafši)*

First radical *w*

ʔawẓa (-l-) b- (yooẓi)	'to inspire (in)'	*muuẓi*	*muuẓa* [2]

As nouns and adjectives with specialized meanings, however, the Class IV participle forms are fairly common. These generally have *mu-* as the prefix in all cases. Some examples:

Active participle forms

mujrim	'criminal' (noun)
muxliṣ	'sincere'
muḍẓik	'funny'
muujib	'necessity, reason'
muuẓiš	'desolate, lonesome' (place)
muhimm	'important'
mudiir	'director'
muriiẓ	'comfortable'
muɛdi	'contagious'

Passive participle forms

mulẓaq	'attaché'

[1] In *muṣarr ɛalee* (thing) 'insisted on'.

[2] In phrases *muuẓa ʔila* (person) 'inspired' or *muuẓa bii* (thing) 'inspired'.

muṭḷaq	'absolute'
muujaz	'brief, short'
muraad	'objective, goal'

7.1.1.5 Class V

Participles of Class V verbs have the following patterns:

Verb	AP	PP
Sound	*mitFaMMiL/-uL*	*mitFaMMaL*
Defective	*mitFaMMi*	*mitFaMMa*

Passive participle forms are rare. Examples (imperfect forms in parentheses):

Sound verbs		AP	PP
tʔaxxar (*yitʔaxxar*)	'to be delayed'	*mitʔaxxir*	
tƐammad (*yitƐammad*)	'to intend'	*mitƐammid*	*mitƐammad*
tšarraf (*yitšarraf*)	'to be ḥonored'	*mitšarruf*	
txaṣṣaṣ (*yitxaṣṣaṣ*)	'to specialize'	*mitxaṣṣiṣ*	
trayyag (*yitrayyag*)	'to have breakfast'	*mitrayyig*	
dzawwaj (*yidzawwaj*)	'to marry'	*midzawwij*	
Defective verbs			
tšakka (*yitšakka*)	'to complain'	*mitšakki*	
tġadda (*yitġadda*)	'to have lunch'	*mitġaddi*	

7.1.1.6 Class VI

Participles of Class VI verbs have the following patterns:

Verb	AP	PP
Sound	*mitFaaMiL/-uL*	*mitFaaMaL*
Defective	*mitFaaMi*	*mitFaaMa*

Passive participle forms are rare. Examples (imperfect forms in parentheses):

Sound verbs		AP
tƐaamal (*yitƐaamal*)	'to haggle'	*mitƐaamil*
tẓaarab (*yitẓaarab*)	'to fight'	*mitẓaarub*
traaṣaṣ (*yitraaṣaṣ*)	'to crowd together'	*mitraaṣiṣ*
ddaayan (*yiddaayan*)	'to borrow'	*middaayin*
tƐaawan (*yitƐaawan*)	'to cooperate'	*mitƐaawin*
Defective verbs		
tbaaha (*yitbaaha*)	'to brag'	*mitbaahi*
tlaaga (*yitlaaga*)	'to get together, meet'	*mitlaagi*

7.1.1.7 Class VII

Participles of Class VII verbs have the following patterns:

Verb	AP	PP
Sound	*minFiMiL/minFuMuL*	*munFaMaL*
Doubled	*minFaDD*	*munFaDD*
Hollow	*minFaaL*	*munFaaL*
Defective	*minFiMi/minFuMi*	*munFaMa*

Passive participle forms are limited to a few words of specialized meanings. Examples of active participles (imperfect forms in parentheses):

Sound verbs		AP
nfijar (*yinfijir*)	'to explode, erupt'	*minfijir*
njiraẓ (*yinjiriẓ*)	'to be wounded'	*minjiriẓ*
nxubaṣ (*yinxubuṣ*)	'to be agitated, flustered'	*minxubuṣ*
Doubled verbs		
nẓall (*yinẓall*)	'to be solved'	*minẓall*

nƐadd (*yinƐadd*)	'to be counted'	*minƐadd*

Hollow verbs

nẓaaš (*yinẓaaš*)	'to be mown'	*minẓaaš*
nhaar (*yinhaar*)	'to collapse'	*minhaar*

Defective verbs

nẓina (*yinẓini*)	'to be bent over'	*minẓini*
nluwa (*yinluwi*)	'to be twisted'	*minluwi*

However, in the case of Class VII verbs which are the passive equivalents of Class I verbs, the Class I passive participle is generally used instead, for example the AP for *nbaaƐ* 'to be sold' would be *minbaaƐ* 'sold' but instead one normally says *mabyuuƐ* 'sold', the PP of the corresponding Class I verb *baaƐ* 'to sell'.

7.1.1.8 Class VIII

Participles of Class VIII verbs have the following patterns:

Verb	AP	PP
Sound	*miFtiMiL/miFtuMuL*	*muFtaMaL*
Doubled	*miFtaDD*	*muFtaDD*
Hollow	*miFtaaL*	*muFtaaL*
Defective	*miFtiMi/miFtuMi*	*muFtama*

Passive participle forms are not very common except in specialized meanings. Examples (imperfect forms in parentheses):

Sound verbs		AP	PP
ẓtiqar (*yiẓtiqir*)	'to despise'	*miẓtiqir*	*muẓtaqar*
qtiraẓ (*yiqtiriẓ*)	'to suggest'	*miqtiriẓ*	*muqtaraẓ*

Doubled verbs

ẓtall (*yiẓtall*)	'to conquer, occupy'	*miẓtall*	*muẓtall*
ṣṭarr (*yiṣṭarr*)	'to be obliged to, have to'	*muṣṭarr*[1]	

[1] For vowel of prefix see 7.1.1, p. 220.

Hollow verbs

ẓtaaj (*yiẓtaaj*)	'to need'	*miẓtaaj*	
xtaar (*yixtaar*)	'to select'	*mixtaar*	*muxtaar* (a neighborhood official)
rtaaẓ (*yirtaaẓ*)	'to rest; to be content'	*mirtaaẓ*	

Defective verbs.

štira (*yištiri*)	'to buy'	*mištiri*	
ntiha (*yintihi*)	'to end'	*mintihi*	*muntaha* ('end')

7.1.1.9 Class IX

Class IX verbs are all intransitive and have no passive participles. The active participle pattern is:

AP

miFMaLL

Examples (imperfect forms in parentheses):

Verb		AP
ẓmarr (*yiẓmarr*)	'to turn red; to blush'	*miẓmarr*
xẓarr (*yixẓarr*)	'to turn green'	*mixẓarr*
swadd (*yiswadd*)	'to turn black'	*miswadd*
xraff (*yixraff*)	'to grow senile'	*mixraff*
ṭrašš (*yiṭrašš*)	'to grow deaf'	*miṭrašš*

7.1.1.10 Class X

Participles of Class X verbs have the following patterns:

Verb	AP	PP
Sound	*mistaFMiL/-uL*	*mustaFMaL*
Doubled	*mistiFiDD*	*mustaFaDD*

	AP	PP
Hollow	*mistiFiiL*[1]	*mustaFaaL*
Defective	*mistaFMi*	*mustaFMa*

Examples (imperfect forms in parentheses):

Sound verbs		AP	PP
staʒsan (*yistaʒsin*)	'to approve'	*mistaʒsin*	*mustaʒsan*
staɛmal (*yistaɛmil*)	'to use'	*mistaɛmil*	*mustaɛmal*
stajwab (*yistajwub*)	'to question, interrogate'	*mistajwub*	*mustajwab*
Doubled verbs			
stiʒaqq (*yistiʒiqq*)	'to deserve'	*mistiʒiqq*	*mustaʒaqq*
stamadd (*yistimidd*)	'to derive' (one's power, authority)	*mistimidd*	*mustamadd*
Hollow verbs			
staraaʒ (*yistiriiʒ*)	'to rest'	*mistiriiʒ* or *mistiraaʒ*	
staɛaar (*yistiɛiir*)	'to take out' (library book)	*mistiɛiir*	*mustaɛaar*
Defective verbs			
staθna (*yistaθni*)	'to exclude, except'	*mistaθni*	*mustaθna*
stawfa (*yistawfi*)	'to get back' (a loan)	*mistawfi*	*mustawfa*
stiʒa (*yistiʒi*)	'to be ashamed'	*mistiʒi*	

7.1.1.11 Simple quadriliterals

Participles of simple quadriliteral verbs have the following patterns:

Verb	AP	PP
Sound	*mFaSTiL/-uL*	*mFaSTaL*
Weak second radical	*mFooTiL/-uL*, *mFeeTiL/-uL*	*mFooTaL*, *mFeeTaL*
Defective	*mFooTi*	*mFooTa*

[1] Or, in some cases, *mistaFaaL*. See 5.2.2.2 C (3) for same variation in imperfect.

Examples (imperfect forms in parentheses):

Sound verbs. These include verbs of both sound and reduplicated root-types.

		AP	PP
handas (*yhandis*)	'to design, engineer'	*mhandis*	*mhandas*
xarbaṭ (*yxarbuṭ*)	'to mix up, mess up'	*mxarbuṭ*	*mxarbaṭ*
lamlam (*ylamlim*)	'to gather up, collect'	*mlamlim*	*mlamlam*
fakfak (*yfakfuk*)	'to take apart'	*mfakfuk*	*mfakfak*

Weak second radical. The long vowel in the participles is the same as in the corresponding verb.

doolab (*ydoolib*)	'to trick, fool'	*mdoolib*	*mdoolab*
deewar (*ydeewur*)	'to turn'	*mdeewur*	*mdeewar*

Defective verbs. Defective quadriliteral verbs of the pattern *FooTa* (others are rare) have active participles *mFooTi*; the passive participles are seldom used.

ʔooma (*yʔoomi*)	'to gesture, motion'	*mʔoomi*
loola (*ylooli*)	'to sing a lullaby'	*mlooli*

7.1.1.12 Derived quadriliterals

These verbs are generally intransitive and lack passive participles. The active participle patterns are as follows:

Verb	AP
Sound	*mitFaSTiL/-uL*
Weak second radical	*mitFooTiL/-uL*, *mitFeeTiL/-uL*

Examples (imperfect forms in parentheses):

Sound verbs. These include verbs of both sound and reduplicated root-types.

		AP
ddahdar (*yiddahdar*)	'to roll' (intr)	*middahdir*

txarbaṭ (*yitxarbaṭ*)	'to be mixed up'	*mitxarbuṭ*
tnaʒnaʒ (*yitnaʒnaʒ*)	'to clear one's throat'	*mitnaʒniʒ*

Weak second radical. The long vowel in the participle is the same as in the corresponding verb.

tṣoogar (*yitṣoogar*)	'to be insured, assured'	*mitṣoogir*
tʒeewan (*yitʒeewan*)	'to become rough, boorish'	*mitʒeewin*

7.1.1.13 FSaTaLL verbs

The few verbs of this category (all doubled verbs) have participles of the following patterns:

AP	PP
miFSaTiLL/ muFSaTiLL	*muFSaTaLL*

The passive participles are rarely used. Two examples of active participles (imperfect forms in parentheses):

šmaʔazz (*yišmaʔizz*)	'to be disgusted'	*mišmaʔizz*
ṭmaʔann (*yiṭmaʔinn*)	'to be reassured, confident'	*muṭmaʔinn*

7.1.2 FaMLaan adjectives

Adjectives of the pattern *FaMLaan* are derived from certain Class I verbs, almost all intransitive. Most of these adjectives refer to transitory physical or emotional states; most apply only to living beings; most bear the same relationship of meaning to the corresponding verbs as do active participles. In the case of some verbs, the active participle form is lacking, and the *FaMLaan* adjective occurs instead, for example *kubar* 'to grow big', *kabraan* 'having grown big, grown up'. In some cases both active participle and *FaMLaan* forms occur, but are used differently, for example *burad* 'to be cold', *baarid* 'cold' (of things, weather) *bardaan* 'cold' (of a person's physical sensations). The most common of these adjectives are shown below. (For their inflection see 7.2.1 and 7.2.2 H.)

From sound verbs

burad	'to get cold'	*bardaan*	'cold'
tiεab	'to get tired'	*taεbaan*	'tired'

tilaf	'to get exhausted'	*talfaan*	'exhausted'
ʒilam	'to dream'	*ʒalmaan*	'dreaming, having dreamed'
xijal	'to be embarrassed'	*xajlaan*	'embarrassed'
xidar	'to get numb'	*xadraan*	'numb, asleep' (limb)
xirab	'to break down'	*xarbaan*	'broken down, not functioning' (thing); 'unwell' (person)
xiṣar	'to lose' (game)	*xaṣraan*	'losing, having lost'
xiḷaṣ	'to be finished'	*xaḷṣaan*	'finished, all gone' (thing); 'free (of), no longer concerned (with)' (person)
δibal	'to droop'	*δablaan*	'drooping, wilted' (flower, person)
riʒam	'to be merciful'	*raʒmaan*	'merciful' (only God)
ziƐal	'to get angry'	*zaƐlaan*	'angry'
zihag	'to get fed up'	*zahgaan*	'fed up'
sikar	'to get drunk'	*sakraan*	'drunk'
sihar	'to stay up' (at night)	*sahraan*	'staying up, having stayed up'
siman	'to get fat'	*samnaan*	'having grown fat'
šibaƐ	'to be full' (of food)	*šabƐaan*	'full' (of food)
δ̣iƐaf	'to get thin'	*δ̣aƐfaan*	'having grown thin'
Ɛijaz	'to be bored'	*Ɛajzaan*	'bored'
Ɛirag	'to sweat'	*Ɛargaan*	'sweating'
Ɛiṭaš	'to get thirsty'	*Ɛaṭšaan*	'thirsty'
ġiδ̣ab	'to be furious'	*ġaδ̣baan*	'furious'
ġufal	'to be inattentive'	*ġaflaan*	'inattentive'
ġiḷaṭ	'to make a mistake'	*ġaḷṭaan*	'mistaken, wrong'
furaʒ	'to be happy'	*farʒaan*	'happy'
kubar	'to grow big'	*kabraan*	'grown big, grown up'

______[1]		*kaslaan*	'lazy'
niεas	'to get sleepy'	*naεsaan*	'sleepy'
wujaε	'to ache, hurt'	*wajεaan*	'sick'
hilak	'to be ruined'	*halkaan*	'very poor; exhausted' (person); 'broken down' (thing)

From hollow verbs. The adjectives have *w* or *y* in the M position; the last example is irregular.

ṭaal or *ṭuwal*	'to grow tall'	*ṭawlaan*	'grown tall'
ṭaab	'to get well'	*ṭaybaan*	'well again, healed'
jaaε	'to get hungry'	*juuεaan*	'hungry'

From defective verbs. The adjectives have *y* in the L position.

ʒima	'to get hot'	*ʒamyaan*	'hot'
difa	'to get warm'	*dafyaan*	'warm'
εima	'to become blind'	*εamyaan*	'having become blind'
ġufa	'to fall asleep'	*ġafyaan*	'having fallen asleep'
mila	'to fill'	*malyaan*	'full'
giδ̣a	'to be finished, at end of life or strength'	*gaδyaan*	'finished, done for'

7.1.3 Nisba adjectives

Nisba adjectives are derived from nouns and, to a much smaller extent, from adjectives and prepositions. The meaning of a nisba, with reference to the word from which it is derived, is commonly 'pertaining to', 'having the nature of', 'having the color of', or 'native, resident of'. A nisba consists of a stem and a suffix *-i*. In the great majority of cases this suffix is added directly to the singular (or, rarely, the plural) stem, with only the stem changes appropriate to the addition of any suffix beginning with a vowel. In other cases, however, when the nisba suffix is added, the stem is changed in other ways; such nisbas end in *-aaʔi*, *-awi*, *-aawi*, or *-aani*.

A. Nisbas ending in *-i*

The suffix *-i* is added to the stem. The examples below are grouped according to the kind of change, if any, which occurs in the stem when *-i* is added.

[1] There is no underlying Class I verb; there is a related Class VI verb *tkaasal* 'to be lazy'.

Loss of stem vowel. In words of the general pattern *FvMvL*, a stem vowel *i* or *u* is dropped; a stem vowel *a* is usually dropped if preceded by *ʔ, ẓ, x, ε, ġ, h*.

ʔaṣil	'origin'	*ʔaṣli*	'original'
šaxiṣ	'person'	*šaxṣi*	'personal'
εilim	'science'	*εilmi*	'scientific'
ramuḷ	'sand'	*ramḷi*	'sandy'
baẓar	'sea'	*baẓri*	'naval'
šahar	'month'	*šahri*	'monthly'

No change. In other words ending in a consonant, there is generally no change in the stem.

ʔabad	'eternity'	*ʔabadi*	'eternal'
ʔasaas	'basis'	*ʔasaasi*	'basic'
btidaaʔ	'beginning'	*btidaaʔi*	'elementary'
qtiṣaad	'economics'	*qtiṣaadi*	'economic'
kahrabaaʔ	'electricity'	*kahrabaaʔi*	'electrical'
markaz	'center'	*markazi*	'central'
maẓall	'place'	*maẓalli*	'local'

Loss of feminine *-a*. In feminine nouns ending in *-a*, the final *-a* is dropped.

ʔaala	'machine'	*ʔaali*	'mechanical'
ʔiḍaafa	'addition'	*ʔiḍaafi*	'additional'
ẓaqiiqa	'truth, reality'	*ẓaqiiqi*	'true, real'
ḍaruura	'necessity'	*ḍaruuri*	'necessary'
εaada	'habit, custom'	*εaadi*	'usual, customary'
moosiiqa	'music'	*moosiiqi*	'musical'

B. Nisbas ending in *-aaʔi*

In the case of certain nouns ending in *-a*, including both masculine and feminine nouns, the final *-a* is lengthened and *-ʔ-* added before the nisba suffix *-i*.

masa	'evening'	*masaaʔi*	'evening' (adj.)

kastana [1]	'chestnuts'	*kastanaaʔi*	'chestnut-colored, light brown'
gahwa	'coffee'	*qahwaaʔi* [2]	'coffee-colored, brown'
hawa	'air'	*hawaaʔi*	'air-, aerial'

C. Nisbas ending in *-awi*

In some nouns ending in *-a*, the *-a* is retained and *-w-* added before the nisba suffix *-i*. This group of nouns includes, but is not restricted to, some feminine and collective nouns of the pattern *CvCa*.

ʔaasya	'Asia'	*ʔaasyawi*	'Asian'
beeḍ̣a	'egg'	*beeḍ̣awi*	'oval'
riʔa	'lung'	*riʔawi*	'pulmonary'
sana	'year'	*sanawi*	'yearly, annual'
fawḍ̣a	'anarchy'	*fawḍ̣awi*	'anarchist(ic)'
kura	'ball'	*kurawi*	'ball-shaped'
luġa	'language'	*luġawi*	'linguistic'

D. Nisbas ending in *-aawi*

Some nouns have nisbas ending in *-aawi*. Most such nouns end in *-a*; before the nisba suffix *-i* the *-a* is lengthened and *-w-* added.

baṣra	'Basra'	*baṣraawi*	'from Basra'
l-ʒilla	'Hilla'	*ʒillaawi*	'from Hilla'
ṣafʒa	'side'	*ṣafʒaawi*	'sideways'
fransa	'France'	*fransaawi* [3]	'French'
kiimya	'chemistry'	*kiimyaawi*	'chemical'
namsa	'Austria'	*namsaawi*	'Austrian'

[1] Or *kastaana*.

[2] See also F below.

[3] More commonly *fransi*.

E. Nisbas ending in *-aani*

A small group of words, themselves with no *n* in their independent forms, have nisbas ending in *-aani*. This group includes some prepositions, several nouns of the pattern *FaDD*, and a few others.

barra	'outside'	*barraani*	'outside; irrelevant'
jawwa	'under'	*jawwaani*	'lower; inner'
foog	'over'	*foogaani*	'upper; outer'
wara	'behind'	*warraani* [1]	'rear, hind'
giddaam	'in front of'	*giddaami*	'front'
ʒaqq	'right'	*ʒaqqaani*	'just, honest'
šaṭṭ	'river'	*šaṭṭaani*	'located by the river'
waṣaṭ	'middle'	*waṣṭaani*	'middle' (adj)

F. Nisbas with internal change

In each of the groups described in A-E above are found nisbas whose stems differ from the underlying word in some feature besides the ending. Examples:

beet	'house'	*bayti*	'household-, domestic'
damm	'blood'	*damawi*	'bloody' (war)
sima	'sky'	*samaawi*	'blue'
šiffa	'lip'	*šafawi*	'oral, lip-'
gaḷub	'heart'	*qalbi*	'heart-; cordial'
gahwa	'coffee'	*qahwaaʔi*	'coffee-colored, brown'
l-muuṣil	'Mosul'	*miṣlaawi*	'from Mosul'
ʔiid	'hand'	*yadawi*	'manual'

7.1.4 Comparatives

Iraqi comparatives are generally equivalent in meaning to English comparative words or phrases such as <u>bigger</u> and <u>more important</u>, or superlative words or phrases such as <u>biggest</u> and <u>most important</u>. Comparatives are derived for the most part from simple adjectives, but also from some derived adjectives, including participles, and from a few nouns. Regardless of the form of the underlying

[1] See also F below.

word, comparatives have the following pattern, with predictable variations depending on root-type:

Sound	*ʔaFMaL*
Double	*ʔaFaDD*
Weak-middle	*ʔaFMaL*
Weak-last	*ʔaFMa*

Sound roots

ʔamiin	'trustworthy'	*ʔaʔman*	'more trustworthy'
basiiṭ	'easy'	*ʔabsaṭ*	'easier'
θigiil	'heavy'	*ʔaθgal*	'heavier'
ṣaƐub	'difficult'	*ʔaṣƐab*	'more difficult'
waṣix	'dirty'	*ʔawṣax*	'dirtier'
šaaṭir	'smart'	*ʔašṭar*	'smarter'
waasiƐ	'broad'	*ʔawsaƐ*	'broader'
yaabis	'dry'	*ʔaybas*	'dryer'
mašhuur	'famous'	*ʔašhar*	'more famous'
muxliṣ	'sincere'	*ʔaxlaṣ*	'more sincere'
kaδδaab[1]	'liar; lying'	*ʔakδab*	'more of a liar'
kaslaan	'lazy'	*ʔaksal*	'lazier'
ʒmaar	'ass, stupid person'	*ʔaʒmar*	'more of an ass'

Double roots

jidiid	'new'	*ʔajadd*[1]	'newer'
qaliil	'few'	*ʔaqall*	'fewer'
murr	'bitter'	*ʔamarr*	'bitterer'
ʒaarr	'hot'	*ʔaʒarr*	'hotter'
muhimm	'important'	*ʔahamm*	'more important'

[1] Or *čaδδaab.*

[2] A few comparatives with double roots, of which this is the most common, have either the form *ʔaFaDD* or *ʔaFMaL*: *ʔajadd* or *ʔajdad.*

Weak-middle roots. In these comparatives the consonant in the M position may be *w* or *y*, but it is not possible to predict which it will be from the form of the underlying word.

xayyir	'good, charitable'	*ʔaxyar*	'more charitable'
rayyiḍ	'accommodating'	*ʔarwaḍ*	'more accommodating'
ḍayyig	'narrow'	*ʔaḍyag*	'narrower'
ṭayyib	'good, tasty'	*ʔaṭyab*	'tastier'
xaayif	'afraid'	*ʔaxwaf*	'more afraid'
laayiq	'suitable'	*ʔalyaq*	'more suitable'
muriiz	'convenient'	*ʔaryaz*	'more convenient'
mufiid	'useful'	*ʔafyad*	'more useful'

Weak-last roots

δaki	'clever, bright'	*ʔaδka*	'cleverer'
qawi	'strong'	*ʔaqwa*	'stronger'
zilu	'sweet; pretty'	*ʔazla*	'sweeter; prettier'
ɛaali	'high'	*ʔaɛla*	'higher'
ġaali	'expensive'	*ʔaġla*	'more expensive'
haadi	'quiet'	*ʔahda*	'quieter'

In a few cases the comparative, while always conforming to the pattern illustrated above, may have radicals which differ in some respect from those of the underlying word, or be based on a different root altogether, for example:

zangiin	'rich'	*ʔazgan*	'richer'
čibiir	'big'	*ʔakbar*	'bigger'
zeen	'good'	*ʔazsan*	'better'

The adjective *kaθiir* 'much, many' is a somewhat formal word, but its comparative, *ʔakθar* 'more' is common. Both *ʔakθar* and *ʔazyad* (or the variant form *ʔdzeed*) 'more' are used as the comparative of the very common particle *hwaaya* 'much, many, a lot of, lots of'. Also, both *ʔakθar* and *ʔazyad* (or *ʔdzeed*) are used in phrases expressing the comparative of adjectives for which there is no *ʔaFMaL* pattern[1] (see 13.4.2), for example *juuɛaan ʔazyad* 'hungrier'.

---

[1] These include most derived adjectives.

7.1.5 Adjectives ending in *-sizz*

Adjectives are derived from some nouns by the addition of the suffix *-sizz* (or, with a few nouns, *-ṣiẓẓ*) 'lacking in, -less'. (See 7.2.6 E for inflection.) Examples:

ʔadab	'manners, politeness'	*ʔadabsizz*	'lacking in manners'
ɛaar	'shame, disgrace'	*ɛaarṣiẓẓ*	'shameless, brazen'

7.2 INFLECTION

Adjectives[1] are inflected for gender and number. They differ from nouns in respect to gender, in that adjectives are inflected for gender, a given adjective having a masculine form in some contexts and a feminine form in others, whereas nouns have inherent gender, some nouns being masculine and some feminine regardless of the context. Adjectives are similar to nouns in having both sound and broken plurals, in having the same singular and broken plural patterns, and in having the same inflectional suffixes.

Adjectives of participle patterns, with few exceptions, have sound plurals (7.2.1, 7.2.3). *FaMLaan* adjectives all have sound plurals; some also have broken plurals (7.2.2 H). Nisba adjectives generally have sound plurals (7.2.1 E); some referring to nationality or city origin have broken plurals (7.2.4). Adjectives of the pattern *ʔaFMaL* which refer to color have broken plurals; those which refer to defects have both sound and broken plurals (7.2.5). Of the other adjectives, some have sound plurals, some broken plurals, some both; the facts must be learned for each case (7.2.1, 7.2.2, 7.2.6).

7.2.1 Inflectional suffixes

The masculine singular form of the adjective is the basic form, and has no inflectional suffix, for example *zeen* 'good', *jidiid* 'new', *farzaan* 'happy', *ɛiraaqi* 'Iraqi'.

The feminine singular is formed from the masculine singular by the addition of the suffix *-a*[2], with stem changes as described below, for example *zeena*, *jidiida*, *farzaana*, *ɛiraaqiyya*.

The masculine and the feminine duals are formed from the masculine and feminine singulars, respectively, by the addition of the suffix *-een*, with stem changes as described for nouns in 6.2.2.2, for example *ɛiraaqiyyeen* and *ɛiraaqiiteen*. However, dual forms of adjectives are quite rare (see 11.2.1.2) and will not be included in subsequent examples.

The masculine sound plural is formed from the masculine singular by the addition of the suffix *-iin*, with stem changes as described below, for example *zeeniin*, *farzaaniin*, *ɛiraaqiyyiin*. Some adjectives have a broken plural instead of or along with the sound masculine plural.

---

[1] Not including comparatives and a few other forms; see 7.2.6.

[2] Except in adjectives of color and defect; see 7.2.5.

The feminine sound plural is formed from the feminine singular by the replacement of the final *-a* with the suffix *-aat*, for example *zeenaat*, *farzaanaat*, *εiraaqiyyaat*. However, the use of feminine sound plural adjectives is more restricted than that of masculine sound or broken plural adjectives (see 11.2.1.2). Since their forms are always predictable from the form of the feminine singular, they will not be included in subsequent examples.

The inflectional suffixes described above are shown in tabular form below:

	Singular	Dual	Sound plural
Masculine		-een	-iin
Feminine	-a		-aat

The stem changes which may occur when these suffixes are added are similar to those described for nouns (see 6.2). The examples given below summarize the types of changes which most commonly apply to adjectives. (Only forms involving the feminine singular suffix *-a* and the masculine sound plurals suffix *-iin* are illustrated. In the rare instances when the dual suffix *-een* is used with an adjective, the stem changes are like those described for dual nouns in 6.2.2.2; and the stem forms with the feminine sound plural suffix *-aat* are the same in each case as those with *-a*. For adjectives which have only broken plurals, these are shown in parentheses. Adjectives which do not refer to human beings generally lack a plural form.)

A. If the masculine singular form ends in a double consonant or a single consonant preceded by a long vowel, there is no change:

M	F	P	
faṣṣ	*faṣṣa*	*faṣṣiin*	'rude'
zaadd	*zaadda*		'sharp'
qadiir	*qadiira*	*qadiiriin*	'capable'
taεbaan	*taεbaana*	*taεbaaniin*	'tired'

B. If the masculine singular form ends in *-iC* or *-uC*:

(1) If the stem vowel is preceded by a doubled consonant and followed by the same consonant, there is no change:

M	F	P	
mqarrir	*mqarrira*	*mqarririin*	'having decided'

(2) If the stem vowel is preceded by two consonants and followed by a consonant identical with the first of the two, there is no change:

M	F	P	
mlamlim	*mlamlima*	*mlamlimiin*	'having gathered up'
mfakfuk	*mfakfuka*	*mfakfukiin*	'having taken apart'

(3) If the stem vowel is preceded by two consonants and followed by a consonant different from both, there is usually no change, but in some cases the stem vowel may be shifted (4.1.3.1):

M	F	P	
mistaƐjil	*mistaƐjila*	*mistaƐjiliin*	'in a hurry, urgent'
mxarbuṭ	*mxarbuṭa* (*mxarubṭa*)	*mxarbuṭiin* (*mxarubṭiin*)	'having mixed up'

(4) If the stem vowel is preceded by a single consonant and followed by the same consonant, there is usually no change, but in some cases the stem vowel may be dropped:

M	F	P	
mʒaadid	*mʒaadida*		'bordering on'
mitraaṣiṣ	*mitraaṣiṣa* (*mitraaṣṣa*)	*mitraaṣiṣiin* (*mitraaṣṣiin*)	'crowded together' (with)

(5) If the stem vowel is preceded by a single or a doubled consonant and followed by a different consonant, it is dropped:

M	F	P	
šaris	*šarsa*	*šarsiin*	'rough, crude'
laabis	*laabsa*	*laabsiin*	'wearing'
midzawwij	*midzawwja*	*midzawwjiin*	'married'

In active participles of Class VII and VIII, when the stem vowel *i* or *u* is dropped, as above, the preceding *i* or *u* is changed to *a*:

M	F	P	
minziƐij	*minzaƐja*	*minzaƐjiin*	'annoyed'
minxubuṣ	*minxabṣa*	*minxabṣiin*	'flustered'
miƐtimid	*miƐtamda*	*miƐtamdiin*	'dependent'

C. In passive participles ending in *-aC*, there is variation. In somewhat formal speech, or in certain words with formal or learned connotations, there may be no change:

M	F	P	
mθaqqaf	*mθaqqafa*	*mθaqqafiin*	'cultured'

More commonly, the stem vowel *a* is changed to *i* or *u* (4.1.3.1), or, under the conditions stated in B above, is dropped. In such cases the feminine and plural passive participles have the same forms as the corresponding active participles:

M	F	P	
mʔaθθaθ	*mʔaθθiθa*		'furnished'
mballal	*mballila*	*mballiliin*	'soaking wet'
mdallal	*mdallila*	*mdalliliin*	'coddled, babied'
mʔakkad	*mʔakkda*		'definite, sure'
mrattab	*mrattba*	*mrattbiin*	'organized'

D. In passive participles ending in *-a*, this is changed to *-aay-* before the feminine suffix *-a* or the plural suffix *-iin*:

M	F	P	
msamma	*msammaaya*	*msammaayiin*	'named'
mdaara	*mdaaraaya*	*mdaaraayiin*	'cared for'

E. If the masculine singular form ends in *-i*:

(1) In active participles, the *-i* is replaced by *-y-* before the feminine suffix *-a* (or, if it is preceded by two (different) consonants, *y* is added), and dropped before the plural suffix *-iin*:

M	F	P	
baaqi	*baaqya*	*baaqiin*	'remaining'
msawwi	*msawwya*	*msawwiin*	'having done'
muġri	*muġriya*	*muġriin*	'attractive'

In active participles of Class VII and VIII, when the final *-i* is replaced by *-y-* as above, the preceding *i* or *u* is changed to *a*:

M	F	P	
minzini	*minzanya*	*minziniin*	'bent over'
mištiri	*mištarya*	*mištiriin*	'having bought'

(2) In other adjectives ending in *-i*, including Class I passive participles and nisbas, *-yy-* is added before both suffixes:

M	F	P	
ðaki	*ðakiyya*	(*ʔaðkiyyaaʔ*)	'clever'
qawi	*qawiyya*	(*ʔaqwiyyaaʔ*)	'strong'

mabli	*mabliyya*	*mabliyyiin*	'blamed'
mansi	*mansiyya*	*mansiyyiin*	'forgotten'
baġdaadi	*baġdaadiyya*	*baġdaadiyyiin* (*bġaadda*)	'Baghdadi'
ɛiraaqi	*ɛiraaqiyya*	*ɛiraaqiyyiin*	'Iraqi'
qaṣdi	*qaṣdiyya*		'intentional'
miṣri	*miṣriyya*	*miṣriyyiin*	'Egyptian'

F. If the masculine singular form ends in *-u*, this is replaced by *-w-*:

M	F	P	
ʒilu	*ʒilwa*	*ʒilwiin*	'sweet; pretty'
kafu	*kafwa*	(*ʔakiffaaʔ*)	'capable'

7.2.2 Broken plural patterns

The broken plural patterns of adjectives are the same as those of nouns, but there are not as many in common use. The most common are listed in the sections which follow. In the columns headed "Singular", only masculine forms are given. For many adjectives there are sound plural as well as broken plural forms, or a second broken plural form; these are shown in parentheses when they occur among the examples below.

A. Plural pattern *FMaaL*

This is the plural pattern for a large number of very common adjectives of various singular patterns.

(1) Singular *FvMiiL*

Singular	Plural	
ɛariiḍ	*ɛraaḍ*	'wide'
ġamiij	*ġmaaj*	'deep'
našiiṭ	*nšaaṭ*	'lively'
naḍiif	*nḍaaf*	'clean'
biɛiid	*bɛaad*	'far'
θigiil	*θgaal*	'heavy'
simiin	*smaan*	'fat'

čibiir	*kbaar*[1]	'big'
ṭuwiil	*ṭwaal*	'long'
xasiis	*xsaas*	'mean, low'
šaẓiiẓ	*šẓaaẓ*	'stingy'
Ɛaziiz	*Ɛzaaz* (*ʔaƐizzaaʔ*)	'dear'

(2) Singular *FaMiL/FaMuL, FaDD*

Singular	Plural	
jalif	*jlaaf*	'rude, coarse'
xašin	*xšaan*	'blunt, rough'
sabiƐ	*sbaaƐ*	'brave'
ḍaxum	*ḍxaam*	'huge'
faḍḍ	*fḍaaḍ* (*faḍḍiin*)	'rude'

(3) Singular *FMayyiL*

Singular	Plural	
ṣġayyir	*ṣġaar*	'little'
gṣayyir	*gṣaar*	'short'

B. Plural pattern *ʔaFMaaL*

This is a plural pattern for some adjectives of the *FaMiL/FaMuL, FvDD* patterns. In some cases there is variation between the two plurals.

Singular	Plural	
naḍil	*ʔanḍaal*	'vile'
faḍḍ	*ʔafḍaaḍ* (*fḍaaḍ*)	'rude'
ẓurr	*ʔaẓraar*	'free'

The plural of *ẓayy* 'alive' is *ʔaẓyaaʔ*.

[1] Note *č* in singular, *k* in plural.

C. Plural pattern *FuMaLaa?*

This is a plural for some adjectives of the *FaMiiL* pattern which refer to people. In some cases there may be variation between the two forms *FuMaLaa?* and *FuMaLa*.

Singular	Plural	
baxiil	*buxalaa?* (*buxala*)	'stingy'
baṣiiṭ	*buṣaṭaa?* (*buṣaṭa*)	'simple'
baliid	*buladaa?* (*bulada*)	'stupid'
taƐis or *taƐiis*	*tuƐasaa?* (*tuƐasa*)	'miserable'
saƐiid	*suƐadaa?* (*suƐada*)	'happy'
Ɛaδ̣iim	*Ɛuδ̣amaa?* (*Ɛuδ̣ama*)	'grand'
qadiim	*qudamaa?*	'ancient'
la?iim	*lu?amaa?*	'mean, cruel'
ḷaṭiif	*ḷuṭafaa?*	'pleasant'

D. Plural pattern *?aFMiLaa?*

This is the plural for a number of adjectives of the *FaMi* pattern (weak-last roots). A *y* appears in the L position.

Singular	Plural	
bari [1]	*?abriyaa?*	'innocent'
dani	*?adniyaa?*	'low, base'
δaki	*?aδkiyaa?*	'clever, bright'
qawi	*?aqwiyaa?*	'strong'
ṣaxi	*?aṣxiyaa?*	'generous'
ġabi	*?aġbiyaa?*	'stupid'

[1] Also *barii?*.

E. Pattern *ʔaFiDDaaʔ*

This plural pattern is an alternant of the preceding, used for adjectives of the pattern *FaDiiD* (double root), and irregularly for one common adjective of the *FaMu* pattern.

(1) Singular *FaDiiD*

Singular	Plural	
xasiis	*ʔaxissaaʔ* (*xsaas*)	'mean, low'
daqiiq	*ʔadiqqaaʔ* (*daqiiqiin*)	'fine, precise'
šadiid	*ʔašiddaaʔ* (*šadiidiin*)	'strict, firm; strong'
ṣaʒiiʒ	*ʔaṣiʒʒaaʔ*	'healthy'
ƹaziiz	*ʔaƹizzaaʔ* (*ƹzaaz*)	'dear'

(2) Singular *FaMu*

Singular	Plural	
kafu	*ʔakiffaaʔ*	'capable'

F. Pattern *FiMMaL/FuMMaL*

This is the pattern for a few adjectives, mostly of the singular pattern *FvMiiL*.

Singular	Plural	
jidiid	*jiddad*	'new'
ƹatiig	*ƹittag*	'old'
fuṭiir	*fuṭṭar*	'inept'
wakiʒ	*wukkaʒ*	'bullying'

G. *FaMLa*, *FiMLa*, *FuMLa*

These are the plural patterns for a few adjectives, mostly of the singular pattern *FvMiiL*.

Singular	Plural	
mariiḍ	*marḍa*	'sick'
jariiʒ	*jarʒa*	'wounded'

ġašiim	*ġišma (ġiššam)*	'uninitiated, ignorant'
faqiir	*fuqra (fuqaraaʔ)*	'poor; well-behaved'

H. Pattern *FMaaLa*

This is an alternative plural (besides the sound plural) for certain adjectives of the *FaMLaan* pattern. (For list of these see 7.1.2):

Singular	Plural	
taɛbaan	*tɛaaba*	'tired'
zaɛlaan	*zɛaala*	'angry'
sakraan	*skaara*	'drunk'
šabɛaan	*šbaaɛa*	'full' (of food)
ɛaṭšaan	*ɛṭaaša*	'thirsty'
kaslaan	*ksaala*	'lazy'
naɛsaan	*nɛaasa*	'sleepy'
wajɛaan	*wjaaɛa*	'sick'
halkaan	*hlaaka*	'exhausted; poor'
juuɛaan	*jwaaɛa*	'hungry'

7.2.3 Inflection of participles

Most adjectives with the patterns of active or passive participles have sound plurals, as illustrated in 7.2.1 above. However, a few adjectives of the Class I active participle pattern have broken plurals of one of the patterns illustrated in 7.2.2, for example:

Singular	Plural	
šaaṭir	*šuṭṭar (šuṭṭaar)*	'clever'
baaʔis	*buʔasaaʔ*	'miserable'
ʒaafi	*ʒiffaay*	'barefoot'

A few with passive participle patterns have plurals of the *C(a)CaaCiiC* pattern:

Singular	Plural	
majnuun	*majaaniin*	'crazy'
mxabbaḷ	*mxaabiiḷ*	'crazy'

mṣaḷḷax	*mṣaaḷiix*	'naked'

7.2.4 Inflection of nisbas

The feminine singular of all nisba adjectives (7.1.3) is regularly formed from the masculine singular by the addition of *-yy-* and the feminine suffix *-a*, for example *ɛilmi* 'scientific' (masculine), *ɛilmiyya* 'scientific' (feminine). The sound plurals are also regularly formed, by the addition of *-yy-* and the suffixes *-iin* and *-aat*, for example *ɛiraaqi* 'Iraqi' (masculine singular), *ɛiraaqiyyiin* (masculine sound plural) *ɛiraaqiyyaat* (feminine sound plural).

Most nisba adjectives, if they have plural forms at all, have sound plurals. There are some however, which have broken plurals, especially those which are used as nouns, for example *ʔajnabi* 'foreign, foreigner', plural *ʔajaanib*. There is one fairly large group of nisbas in particular, those which refer to regions, countries, cities, or towns, or to ethnic or religious groups, which show various irregularities of both derivation and plural inflection. The most important of these are listed below in four groups, according to the type of plural. Within each group some words may have more than one plural; the alternative forms are shown in parentheses. Each entry consists of two or more lines, the first showing the place-name (a noun) from which the nisba is derived, and the lower ones showing the masculine singular and the plural form(s) of the nisba. (The feminine singular and feminine sound plural, which are predictable, are not shown.)

Besides being an adjective, the masculine singular form of these nisbas is also used as a noun to mean (where applicable) the language, for example *tiḥči ʔingiliizi?* 'Do you speak English?'; and all forms are also used as nouns to mean persons, for example *l-ʔameerkaani* 'the American', *l-ʔingiliizi* 'the Englishman', *l-ɛarab* 'the Arabs'.

A. Sound plural in *-iin*

ʔaasya	'Asia'	
ʔaasyawi	'Asian'	*ʔaasyawiyyiin*
ʔiiraan	'Iran'	
ʔiiraani [1]	'Iranian'	*ʔiiraaniyyiin*
ʔiirlanda	'Ireland'	
ʔiirlandi	'Irish'	*ʔiirlandiyyiin*
ʔiiṭaalya	'Italy'	
ʔiiṭaali	'Italian'	*ʔiiṭaaliyyiin* (*ṭilyaan*)
ʔooruṗṗa	'Europe'	
ʔooruṗṗi	'European'	*ʔooruṗṗiyyiin*
l-ʔardun	'Jordan'	
ʔarduni	'Jordanian'	*ʔarduniyyiin*

[1] Or *ɛijmi*; see D below.

ʔafriiqya	'Africa'	
ʔafriiqi	'African'	*ʔafriiqiyyiin*
l-ʔafġaan	'Afghanistan'	
ʔafġaani	'Afghan'	*ʔafġaaniyyiin*
ʔisraaʔiil	'Israel'	
ʔisraaʔiili	'Israeli'	*ʔisraaʔiiliyyiin*
baljiika	'Belgium'	
baljiiki	'Belgian'	*baljiikiyyiin*
biḷġaarya	'Bulgaria'	
biḷġaari	'Bulgarian'	*biḷġaariyyiin*
tuunis	'Tunisia'	
tuunisi	'Tunisian'	*tuunisiyyiin*
l-jazaaʔir	'Algeria'	
jazaaʔiri	'Algerian'	*jazaaʔiriyyiin*
l-ʒilla	'Hilla' [1]	
ʒillaawi	'from Hilla'	*ʒillaawiyyiin*
danimaark	'Denmark'	
danimaarki	'Danish'	*danimaarkiyyiin*
ruumaanya	'Rumania'	
ruumaani	'Rumanian'	*ruumaaniyyiin*
s-suudaan	'Sudan'	
suudaani	'Sudanese'	*suudaaniyyiin*
l-Ɛarabiyya s-suƐuudiyya	'Saudi Arabia'	
suƐuudi	'Saudi Arabian'	*suƐuudiyyiin*
s-suwiid	'Sweden'	
swiidi	'Swedish'	*swiidiyyiin*
swiisra	'Switzerland'	
swiisri	'Swiss'	*swiisriyyiin*
suurya	'Syria'	
suuri	'Syrian'	*suuriyyiin*
ṣ-ṣiin	'China'	
ṣiini	'Chinese'	*ṣiiniyyiin*
l-Ɛiraaq	'Iraq'	
Ɛiraaqi	'Iraqi'	*Ɛiraaqiyyiin*

[1] City in Iraq.

faḷaṣṭiin	'Palestine'	
faḷaṣṭiini	'Palestinian'	*faḷaṣṭiiniyyiin*
fillanda	'Finland'	
fillandi	'Finnish'	*fillandiyyiin*
fransa	'France'	
fransi	'French'	*fransiyyiin*
kárbalaa	'Karbala' [1]	
karbalaaʔi	'from Karbala'	*karbalaaʔiyyiin*
l-ikweet	'Kuwait'	
kweeti	'Kuwaiti'	*kweetiyyiin*
liibya	'Libya'	
liibi	'Libyan'	*liibiyyiin*
labnaan	'Lebanon'	
labnaani	'Lebanese'	*labnaaniyyiin*
maraakiš	'Morocco'	
maraakiši	'Moroccan'	*maraakišiyyiin*
miṣir	'Egypt'	
miṣri	'Egyptian'	*miṣriyyiin*
n-najaf	'Najaf' [1]	
najafi	'from Najaf'	*najafiyyiin*
n-narwiič	'Norway'	
narwiiči	'Norwegian'	*narwiičiyyiin*
n-namsa	'Austria'	
namsaawi	'Austrian'	*namsaawiyyiin*
hangaarya	'Hungary'	
hangaari	'Hungarian'	*hangaariyyiin*
hooḷanda	'Holland'	
hooḷandi	'Dutch'	*hooḷandiyyiin*
l-yaaḅaan	'Japan'	
yaaḅaani	'Japanese'	*yaaḅaaniyyiin*
l-yaman	'Yemen'	
yamaani	'Yemen'	*yamaniyyiin*
yooġoslaafya	'Yugoslavia'	
yooġoslaafi	'Yugoslav'	*yooġoslaafiyyiin*

[1] City in Iraq.

paakistaan	'Pakistan'	
pakistaani	'Pakistani'	*paakistaaniyyiin*
purtuġaal	'Portugal'	
purtuġaali	'Portuguese'	*purtuġaaliyyiin*
pooḷanda	'Poland'	
pooḷandi	'Polish'	*pooḷandiyyiin*
čiikosloovaakya	'Czechoslovakia'	
čiikosloovaaki	'Czech'	*čiikoslovaakiyyiin*

B. Sound plural in *-a*

A few adjectives are derived from the names of cities or towns by the addition of the suffix *-li* instead of *-i*. These have plurals ending in *-a*, before which *-yy-* is added to the singular:

ʔarbiil	'Irbil'	
ʔarbiilli	'from Irbil'	*ʔarbiilliyya* (*ʔarbiilliyyiin*)
l-iʕmaara	'Amara'	
ʕmaaratli	'from Amara'	*ʕmaaratliyya*
karkuuk	'Kirkuk'	
karkuukli	'from Kirkuk'	*karkuukliyya*

Two nisba adjectives referring to branches of the Muslim faith also have plurals in *-a*; in these the *-i* of the singular is dropped:

sinni	'Sunni'	*sinna*
šiiʕi	'Shiite'	*šiiʕa*

C. Plural like singular, minus *-i*

The plural of some nisbas is formed by dropping the final *-i* of the singular form; some also have sound plurals.

ʔarmiinya	'Armenia'	
ʔarmani	'Armenian'	*ʔarman*
ʔaḷḅaanya	'Albania'	
ʔaḷḅaani	'Albanian'	*ʔaḷḅaan*
ʔaḷmaanya	'Germany'	
ʔaḷmaani	'German'	*ʔaḷmaan*
ʔameerka	'America'	
ʔameerkaani / *ʔameerki*	'American'	*ʔameerkaan* (*ʔameerkaaniyyiin*) (*ʔameerkiyyiin*)

or *ʔamriika*	'America'	
ʔamriiki	'American'	*ʔamriikaan* (*ʔamriikaaniyyiin*) (*ʔamriikiyyiin*)
ʔingiltara	'England'	
ʔingiliizi	'English'	*ʔingiliiz*
ruusya	'Russia'	
ruusi	'Russian'	*ruus*
spaanya	'Spain'	
spaani	'Spanish'	*spaan* (*spaaniyyiin*)
ɛarabi	'Arab(ic)'	*ɛarab*
l-yuunaan	'Greece'	
yuunaani	'Greek'	*yuunaan* (*yuunaaniyyiin*)

D. Broken plural

l-baṣra	'Basra'	
baṣraawi	'from Basra'	*bṣaarwa* (*baṣraawiyyiin*)
baġdaad	'Baghdad'	
baġdaadi	'Baghdadi'	*bġaadda* (*baġdaadiyyiin*)
l-muuṣil	'Mosul'	
miṣḷaawi	'from Mosul'	*mṣaaḷwa*
turkiya	'Turkey'	
turki	'Turkish'	*ʔatraak* (*turk*)
l-ʒabaša	'Ethiopia'	
ʒabaši	'Ethiopian'	*ʔaʒbaaš*
š-šaam	'Damascus'	
šaami	'Damascene'	*šwaam* (*šaamiyyiin*)
ʔiiraan	'Iran'	
ɛijmi	'Persian'[1]	*ɛajam*
kurdi	'Kurdish'	*kraad* (*kurd*)

[1] See also A above.

l-hind	'India'	
hindi	'Indian'	*hnuud*

7.2.5 Adjectives of color and defect

A number of adjectives share with comparatives (7.1.4) the pattern *ʔaFMaL*. These are called adjectives of color and defect, since most of them refer to colors and to physical or mental defects or weaknesses. Unlike comparatives, these adjectives are inflected for gender and number. The feminine forms have the patterns *FaMLa* and, for weak-middle roots, *FooLa* or *FeeLa*. Those referring to colors have exclusively a broken plural; those referring to defects may have a broken plural, but most may also have a sound plural in *-iin*. The most common are listed below:

A. Colors

Sound roots

M	F	P	
ʔaʒmar	*ʒamra*	*ʒumur*	'red'
ʔaxḍar	*xaḍra*	*xuḍur*	'green'
ʔazrag	*zarga*	*zurug*	'blue'
ʔasmar	*samra*	*sumur*	'brunette'
ʔašgar	*šagra*	*šugur*	'blond'
ʔaṣfar	*ṣafra*	*ṣufur*	'yellow'

Weak-middle roots

M	F	P	
ʔaswad	*sooda*	*suud*	'black'
ʔabyaḍ	*beeḍa*	*biiḍ*	'white'

B. Defects

Sound roots. Besides broken plurals, these also have sound plurals of the pattern *FaMLiin*.

M	F	P	
ʔaxras	*xarsa*	*xurus* (*xarsiin*)	'mute, dumb'
ʔadġam	*daġma*	*duġum* (*daġmiin*)	'gloomy-looking'

ʔaṣlaƐ	*ṣalƐa*	*ṣuluƐ* (*ṣalƐiin*)	'bald'
ʔaṭraš	*ṭarša*	*ṭuruš* (*ṭaršiin*)	'deaf'
ʔaƐraj	*Ɛarja*	*Ɛirij* (*Ɛarjiin*)	'lame'
ʔaƐmaš	*Ɛamša*	*Ɛimiš* (*Ɛamšiin*)	'myopic'
ʔaƐḍab	*Ɛaḍba*	*Ɛuḍub* (*Ɛaḍbiin*)	'paralysed in one hand or arm'
ʔamlas	*malsa*	*milis* (*malsiin*)	'smooth'
ʔamḷaṭ		*muḷuṭ* (*maḷṭiin*)	'beardless, hairless'
ʔačqal	*čaqla*	*čuqul* (*čaqliin*)	'cross-eyed'

Weak-middle roots. Besides broken plurals, these also have sound plurals of the pattern *FooLiin*.

ʔaθwal	*θoola*	*θuul* (*θooliin*)	'stupid, dense'
ʔaẓwal	*ẓoola*	*ẓuul* (*ẓooliin*)	'cross-eyed'
ʔaƐwaj	*Ɛooja*	*Ɛuuj* (*Ɛoojiin*)	'bent; crooked'
ʔaƐwar	*Ɛoora*	*Ɛuur* (*Ɛooriin*)	'one-eyed'
ʔaƐwaṣ	*Ɛooṣa*	*Ɛuuṣ* (*Ɛooṣiin*)	'squinting'
ʔahwaj	*hooja*	*huuj* (*hoojiin*)	'rash'

Weak-last root

ʔaƐma	*Ɛamya*	*Ɛimi*	'blind'

7.2.6 Special cases

A. Comparatives

Comparatives are not inflected for gender or number. See 7.1.4 and 13.4.

B. *laax* 'other'

This common word has the feminine form *lux*, and no plural form. These have the same meaning as the related but less commonly used words *ʔaaxar*, feminine *ʔuxra*, plural *ʔaaxariin* 'other'. See also 13.6.

meez laax	'another table'
bnayya lux	'another girl'
kutub lux	'other books'

C. *xooš* 'good'

The particle *xooš*, which usually corresponds in meaning to the English adjective 'good', precedes the noun it modifies and is not inflected for gender or number. See also 13.3.3.

xooš walad	'a good boy, nice guy'
xooš ibnayya	'a good girl'
xooš muwaḍḍafiin	'good civil servants'
xooš filim	'a good movie'
xooš tanḍiif	'a good cleaning'

D. Invariables

There are a few other adjectives, of various patterns and meanings, which are not inflected for gender or number. These are most commonly used as predicates, rather than attributively in a noun-adjective phrase. Some examples:

buhul	'slow-witted, dense'
taaza	'fresh' (food, news)
talaf	'useless, on last legs'
jalab	'shoddy, of low quality'
ʒalal	'weak, lacking in strictness'
xaam	'crude' (oil); 'raw, green' (person)
siʒig	'exhausted, worn out'
šalal	'crippled'
ṣirf	'pure, 100%'
ɛadam	'useless, no good' (things)

ɛijba	'amazing, unusual'
ġaḷaṭ	'in error, false'
falla	'marvelous, beautiful'
kibaar	'dignified; stuck-up'
yaṣaġ	'forbidden'
čuruk	'shoddy, defective; morally low'
parakanda	'sloppy, slovenly, disorganized'

E. Adjectives ending in *-sizz*

Derived adjectives ending in *-sizz* or *-ṣiẓẓ* (7.1.5) are not inflected for gender, but have a plural form ending in *-iyya*.

M/F	P	
ʔadabsizz	*ʔadabsizziyya*	'lacking in manners'
ɛaarṣiẓẓ	*ɛaarṣiẓẓiyya*	'shameless, brazen'

8. NUMERALS

This chapter deals with the morphology and some aspects of the syntax of numerals, including cardinals, ordinals, and fractions.

8.1 CARDINALS

8.1.1 Numerals 1 through 10

waaẓid	(F *wiẓda*)	'one'
θneen	(F *θinteen*)	'two'
tlaaθa		'three'
ʔarbaɛa		'four'
xamsa		'five'
sitta		'six'
sabɛa		'seven'
θmaanya		'eight'
tisɛa		'nine'
ɛašra		'ten'

A. The numeral for 'one' has a masculine form *waaẓid* and a feminine form *wiẓda*. The former is used in abstract counting and figuring, and in referring to a specific masculine noun. The latter is used only in referring to a specific feminine noun. When the noun is mentioned, it precedes the numeral.

waaẓid, θneen, tlaaθa ...	'One, two, three ... '
waaẓid w-xamsa sitta.	'One and five are six.'
(čam beet?) waaẓid.	'(How many houses?) One.'
(čam jigaara?) wiẓda.	'(How many cigarettes?) One.'
beet waaẓid	'one house'
jigaara wiẓda	'one cigarette'

B. The numeral for 'two' has a masculine form *θneen* and a feminine form *θinteen*. The former is used in abstract counting and figuring, and in referring to a specific masculine noun. Either may be used in referring to a specific feminine noun.

θneen w-xamsa sabɛa.	'Two and five are seven.'
(čam beet?) θneen.	'(How many houses?) Two.'

(čam jigaara?) $\begin{cases} \theta neen \\ \theta inteen. \end{cases}$ '(How many cigarettes?) Two.'

To express the equivalent of 'two ---s', where the noun is mentioned, all the following arrangements are used:

    (1) The dual form of the noun alone:

        beeteen   'two houses'

        bnayyteen   'two girls'

    (2) For masculine nouns, the dual form of the noun followed by *θneen*:[1]

        beeteen iθneen   'two houses'

    (3) For feminine nouns, the dual form of the noun followed by either *θneen* or *θinteen*: [1]

        $\left.\begin{array}{l} \textit{bnayyteen iθneen} \\ \textit{bnayyteen θinteen} \end{array}\right\}$ 'two girls'

    (4) For masculine nouns, the plural form of the noun either preceded or followed by *θneen*:

        $\left.\begin{array}{l} \textit{byuut iθneen} \\ \textit{θneen ibyuut} \end{array}\right\}$ 'two houses'

    (5) For feminine nouns, the plural form of the noun either preceded or followed by either *θneen* or *θinteen*:

        $\left.\begin{array}{l} \textit{banaat iθneen} \\ \textit{θneen banaat} \\ \textit{banaat θinteen} \\ \textit{θinteen banaat} \end{array}\right\}$ 'two girls'

    C. In the case of the numerals from 'three' to 'ten', the forms listed above (the <u>independent</u> forms) are used in abstract counting and figuring and referring to a specific noun of either gender.

        tlaaθa w-sitta tisɛa.   'Three and six are nine.'

        (čam beet?) xamsa.   '(How many houses?) Five.'

        (čam jigaara?) xamsa.   '(How many cigarettes?) Five.'

---

[1] These combinations are generally used when the speaker wishes to emphasize the fact that there are *two*.

When the noun is mentioned, it is plural and follows the numeral. The numeral then has a special combining form, as follows:

tlaθ-	'three'
ʔarbaε-	'four'
xam(i)s-	'five'
sitt-	'six'
sab(i)ε-	'seven'
θman-	'eight'
tis(i)ε-	'nine'
εaš(i)r-	'ten'

The stem vowel *i*, shown in parentheses in the list above, occurs only when the following noun begins with a (single) consonant. The final *θ* of *tlaθ-* 'three' is often assimilated completely to a following *t*, *ṭ*, *d*, *δ*, *δ̣*, *s*, *ṣ*, *ƶ*, *š*, and partially (to *d*) to a following *j*; the final *tt* of *sitt-* 'six' is sometimes assimilated completely to a following *ṭ*, *d*, *θ*, *δ*, *δ̣*, *s*, *ṣ*, *ƶ*, *š* and partially (to *dd*) to a following *j*. Some examples:

tlaθ-isniin	'three years'
tlaθ-maʒallaat	'three places'
tlat-talaamiiδ	'three students'
tlad-dinaaniir	'three dinars'
tlad-jigaayir	'three cigarettes'
ʔarbaε-isniin	'four years'
ʔarbaε-kutub	'four books'
xams-isniin	'five years'
xamis-marraat	'five times'
sitt-isniin	'six years'
sitt-marraat	'six times'
sidd-dinaaniir	'six dinars'
siss-saaεaat	'six hours'
sabε-isniin	'seven years'

sabiƐ-ṣafẓaat	'seven pages'
θman-isniin	'eight years'
θman-ġuraf	'eight rooms'
tisƐ-isniin	'nine years'
tisiƐ-saaƐaat	'nine hours'
Ɛašr-isniin	'ten years'
Ɛašir-daqaayiq	'ten minutes'

8.1.2 Numerals 11 through 99

The numerals from 11 through 19, and multiples of ten from 20 to 90 are as follows:

daƐaš or *ʔidaƐaš*	'eleven'
θṇaƐaš [1]	'twelve'
ṭḷaṭṭaƐaš	'thirteen'
ʔarḅaaṭaƐaš	'fourteen'
xṃuṣṭaƐaš	'fifteen'
ṣiṭṭaƐaš	'sixteen'
ṣḅaaṭaƐaš	'seventeen'
θṃunṭaƐaš	'eighteen'
ṭṣaaṭaƐaš	'nineteen'
Ɛišriin	'twenty'
tlaaθiin	'thirty'
ʔarbaƐiin	'forty'
xamsiin	'fifty'
sittiin	'sixty'
sabƐiin	'seventy'
θmaaniin	'eighty'
tisƐiin	'ninety'

[1] Note unusual emphatic *n* here, and emphasis in subsequent teens.

Numbers between the multiples of ten from 21 to 99 are expressed by phrases consisting of a units number (in its masculine or its independent form) followed by a tens number, the latter having the prefix *w-* 'and':

waazid w-Ɛišriin	'twenty-one'
θneen w-Ɛišriin	'twenty-two'
tlaaθa w-Ɛišriin	'twenty-three'
waazid w-itlaaθiin	'thirty-one'
θneen w-itlaaθiin	'thirty-two'
tlaaθa w-itlaaθiin	'thirty-three'
ʔarbaƐa w-arbaƐiin	'forty-four'
xamsa w-arbaƐiin	'forty-five'
sitta w-xamsiin	'fifty-six'
sabƐa w-xamsiin	'fifty-seven'
θmaanya w-sittiin	'sixty-eight'
θmaanya w-sabƐiin	'seventy-eight'
tisƐa w-iθmaaniin	'eighty-nine'
tisƐa w-tisƐiin	'ninety-nine'

When a noun is mentioned with one of these numerals, the noun is singular and follows the numeral:

daƐaš yoom	'eleven days'
xṃuṣṭaƐaš sana	'fifteen years'
tlaaθiin daqiiqa	'thirty minutes'
waazid w-itlaaθiin saaƐa	'thirty-one hours'
θneen w-xamsiin diinaar	'fifty-two dinars'
tlaaθa w-sabƐiin ṣafza	'seventy-three pages'

8.1.3 The hundreds

The word for 'hundred' is a feminine noun *miyya*, with a dual form *miiteen.* [1] Multiples of one hundred from 300 to 900 are expressed by a phrase consisting

[1] It has a plural *miyyaat*, used not after other numerals, but in an indefinite sense: *miyyaat imnin-naas* 'hundreds of people'.

of a units numeral in its combining form and the singular form of *miyya*:

miyya	'hundred, one hundred'
miiteen	'two hundred'
tlaθ-miyya	'three hundred'
ˀarbaε-miyya	'four hundred'
xamis-miyya	'five hundred'
sitt-miyya	'six hundred'
sabiε-miyya	'seven hundred'
θman-miyya	'eight hundred'
tisiε-miyya	'nine hundred'

Numbers between the multiples of hundred are expressed by phrases consisting of the hundreds number followed by a units number or a tens number or a combination, each with the prefix *w-* 'and':

miyya w-xamsa	'105'
miiteen w-sitta	'206'
tlaθ-miyya w-tisεa	'309'
ˀarbaε-miyya w-daεaš	'411'
xamis-miyya w-ṣiṭṭaεaš	'516'
sitt-miyya w-εišriin	'620'
sabiε-miyya w-waaẓid w-itlaaθiin	'731'
θman-miyya w-iθneen w-arbaεiin	'842'
tisiε-miyya w-xamsa w-sittiin	'965'

When a noun is mentioned with one of these numerals the noun is singular and follows the numeral. The word *miyya* immediately preceding a noun has a special combining form *miit-*. [1]

miit-diinaar	'100 dinars'
miiteen diinaar	'200 dinars'

[1]The final *-t* may assimilate to following sounds as described for *sitt-* in 8.1.1 C above: *miid-diinaar* '100 dinars'.

tlaθ-miit-sana	'300 years'
tlaθ-miyya w-ʕišriin sana	'320 years'

8.1.4 The thousands

The word for 'thousand' is a masculine noun *ʔalif*[1], with a dual form *ʔalfeen*. It has a counting plural (6.2.2.3 B (23)) *taalaaf*, used only after one of the numerals from three through ten.[2] Like any noun, it is singular after any numeral above ten.

ʔalif	'1000'
ʔalfeen	'2000'
tlat-taalaaf	'3000'
ʔarbaʕ-taalaaf	'4000'
xamis-taalaaf	'5000'
sitt-taalaaf	'6000'
sabiʕ-taalaaf	'7000'
θman-taalaaf	'8000'
tisiʕ-taalaaf	'9000'
ʕašir-taalaaf	'10,000'
daʕaš ʔalif	'11,000'
θn̩aʕaš ʔalif	'12,000'
xm̩us̩t̩aʕaš ʔalif	'15,000'
ʕišriin ʔalif	'20,000'
xamsa w-itlaaθiin ʔalif	'35,000'
miit-ʔalif	'100,000'
miiteen ʔalif	'200,000'
tlaθ-miit-ʔalif	'300,000'

---

[1] Commonly also *ʔalf*.

[2] Elsewhere its plural is either *ʔaalaaf* or *ʔluuf*: *šifna ʔluuf imnin-naas.* 'We saw thousands of people.'

ʔarbaƐ-miyya w-xamsiin ʔalif	'450,000'
xamis-miyya w-xamsa w-sabƐiin ʔalif	'575,000'

When a noun is mentioned, it is singular and follows the numeral.

ʔalif diinaar	'1000 dinars'
miit-ʔalif sana	'100,000 years'

8.1.5 The millions and billions

The word for 'million' is a masculine noun *milyoon*, with a dual form *milyooneen* and a plural *malaayiin*. Like any noun, it is plural after one of the numerals from three to ten and singular after any higher numeral.

milyoon	'million, one million'
milyooneen	'two million'
tlaθ-malaayiin	'three million'
ʔarbaƐ-malaayiin	'four million'
xamis-malaayiin	'five million'
sitt-malaayiin	'six million'
sabiƐ-malaayiin	'seven million'
θman-malaayiin	'eight million'
tisiƐ-malaayiin	'nine million'
Ɛašir-malaayiin	'ten million'
daƐaš milyoon	'eleven million'
ʔarḅaaṭaƐaš milyoon	'fourteen million'
Ɛišriin milyoon	'twenty million'
xamsa w-xamsiin milyoon	'fifty-five million'
miit-milyoon	'a hundred million'
miiteen milyoon	'two hundred million'
sitt-miit milyoon	'six hundred million'

When a noun is mentioned, it is singular and follows the numeral:

tlaθ-malaayiin diinaar '3,000,000 dinars'

The word for 'billion' is a masculine noun *bilyoon*, with a dual form *bilyooneen* and a plural *balaayiin*. It is counted exactly like *milyoon* above.[1]

8.1.6 Complex combinations

In combinations of the major elements of numbers (billions, millions, thousands, hundreds, units (or teens), and tens) a units number precedes a tens number (8.1.2) but in all other cases the larger element precedes the smaller. Each major element except the first has the prefix *w-* 'and'.

Millions	Thousands	Hundreds	Units	Tens	
			xamsa	*w-sittiin*	65
		miyya	*w-xamsa*	*w-sittiin*	165
		miiteen	*w-xamsa*	*w-sittiin*	265
		tlaθ-miyya	*w-xamsa*	*w-sittiin*	365
	ʔalif	*w-itlaθ-miyya*	*w-xamsa*	*w-sittiin*	1,365
	ʔalfeen	*w-itlaθ-miyya*	*w-xamsa*	*w-sittiin*	2,365
	tlat-taalaaf	*w-itlaθ-miyya*	*w-xamsa*	*w-sittiin*	3,365
	daɛaš ʔalif	*w-itlaθ-miyya*	*w-xamsa*	*w-sittiin*	11,365
	ʔarbaɛiin ʔalif	*w-itlaθ-miyya*	*w-xamsa*	*w-sittiin*	40,365
	θneen w-xamsiin ʔalif	*w-itlaθ-miyya*	*w-xamsa*	*w-sittiin*	52,365
	tlaθ-miyya w-iθneen w-xamsiin ʔalif	*w-itlaθ-miyya*	*w-xamsa*	*w-sittiin*	352,365
xamsa w-sabɛiin milyoon	*w-itlaθ-miyya w-iθneen w-xamsiin ʔalif*	*w-itlaθ-miyya*	*w-xamsa*	*w-sittiin*	75,352,365

[1] Some speakers follow the system in which *bilyoon* 'billion' is 1,000,000,000. Others follow the system in which *milyaar* 'milliard' is 1,000,000,000, and *bilyoon* 'billion' is 1,000,000,000,000.

8.1.7 Summary of numeral-noun constructions

A. For nouns with the simple numeral *waaẓid* (F *wiẓda*) 'one', see 8.1.1 above.

With compound numbers ending in one, all of the following constructions are used:

tlaθ-miyya w-diinaar (waaẓid) *tlaθ-miit diinaar w-waaẓid* *tlaθ-miit diinaar w-diinaar* *tlaθ-miyya w-waaẓid diinaar*	'301 dinars'

B. For nouns with the simple numeral *θneen* (F *θinteen*) 'two', see 8.1.1 above.

With compound numbers ending in two, both of the following constructions are used:

tlaθ-miyya w-diinaareen *tlaθ-miit diinaar w-diinaareen*	'302 dinars'

C. Immediately following any numeral from three through ten the noun follows and is plural.

sabiƐ-makaatiib	'seven letters'
miyya w-sabiƐ-makaatiib	'a hundred and seven letters'

D. Immediately following any numeral over ten, the noun follows and is singular.

daƐaš diinaar	'eleven dinars'
xamsa w-Ɛišriin diinaar	'twenty five dinars'
miit-diinaar	'a hundred dinars'
ʔalif diinaar	'a thousand dinars'

8.2 ORDINALS

8.2.1 From first to tenth

There are distinctive forms in Iraqi only for the ordinals from first to tenth. These are listed below, together with the corresponding cardinals. Note that (1) *ʔawwal* 'first' is based on a different root from the corresponding cardinal *waaʒid* 'one' and has a different pattern from the other ordinals; (2) the other ordinals have the Class I active participle pattern *FaaMiL* or *FaaMi*; and (3) the roots in *θaaliθ* 'third' and *saadis* 'sixth' have different forms from those of the corresponding cardinals. As adjectives, ordinals have feminine forms, listed below; *ʔawwal* also has plural forms *ʔuwal* or *ʔawaaʔil*.

Cardinals		Ordinals M	F	
waaʒid	'one	*ʔawwal*	*ʔuula*	'first'
θneen	'two'	*θaani* [1]	*θaanya*	'second'
tlaaθa	'three'	*θaaliθ*	*θaalθa*	'third'
ʔarbaƐa	'four'	*raabiƐ*	*raabƐa*	'fourth'
xamsa	'five'	*xaamis*	*xaamsa*	'fifth'
sitta	'six'	*saadis*	*saadsa*	'sixth'
sabƐa	'seven'	*saabiƐ*	*saabƐa*	'seventh'
θmaanya	'eight'	*θaamin*	*θaamna*	'eighth'
tisƐa	'nine'	*taasiƐ*	*taasƐa*	'ninth'
Ɛašra	'ten'	*Ɛaašir*	*Ɛaašra*	'tenth'

8.2.2 Above tenth

The function of ordinals above tenth may be served by the corresponding cardinals, following the noun. Both noun and numeral may have the article prefix, or the noun may lack it:

(l-)qaaṭ il-arḅaaṭaƐaš — 'the fourteenth floor'

Such constructions, however, are not common. Usually, where a high ordinal might be used in English, the Iraqi sentence contains a cardinal in another kind of construction:

haay ṣaar xamsiin marra gitt-lak. — 'This is the fiftieth time I've told you' (More literally: 'This makes fifty times that I've told you.')

8.3 FRACTIONS

8.3.1 From half to tenth

There are distinctive forms only for the fractions one-half to one-tenth inclusive. These forms are nouns, with dual inflections in *-een* (6.2.2.2) and

[1] Also means 'next; remaining, other'; in this sense has a sound plural *θaaniin*.

broken plurals (6.2.2.3 B). Except for *nuṣṣ* 'half', they all have the pattern *FuMuL* (or, as a variant, *FiMiL*) and the same radicals as the corresponding ordinals (8.2). The singular and dual forms are listed below; where a variant form *FiMiL* occurs it is given in parentheses under the singular and can apply to the dual as well:

nuṣṣ	'(one-) half'	*nuṣṣeen*	'two halves'
θuluθ (*θiliθ*)	'(one-) third'	*θulθeen*	'two-thirds'
rubuƐ	'(one-) fourth, quarter'	*rubƐeen*	'two-fourths'
xumus	'(one-) fifth'	*xumseen*	'two-fifths'
sudus (*sidis*)	'(one-) sixth'	*sudseen*	'two-sixths'
subuƐ	'(one-) seventh'	*subƐeen*	'two-sevenths'
θumun (*θimin*)	'(one-) eighth'	*θumneen*	'two-eighths'
tusuƐ	'(one-) ninth'	*tusƐeen*	'two-ninths'
Ɛušur (*Ɛišir*)	'(one-) tenth'	*Ɛušreen*	'two-tenths'

The plural of *nuṣṣ* 'half' is *nṣaaṣ:*

tlaθ-inṣaaṣ	'three halves'

The other fractions have two plural forms. One is *taFMaaL* (sometimes *tiFMaaL*). This is a counting plural (6.2.2.3 B (23)); it occurs only after one of the numerals from <u>three</u> to <u>ten</u>, most commonly after <u>three</u>:

tlat-tarbaaƐ	'three-fourths'
tlat-taxmaas	'three-fifths'
ʔarbaƐ-taxmaas	'four-fifths'

The other plural is *(ʔ)aFMaaL* (sometimes *(i)FMaaL*); this may occur after one of the numbers from <u>three</u> to <u>ten</u> or elsewhere:

ʔarbaƐ-axmaas	'four-fifths'
xams-asdaas	'five-sixths'
sabƐ-aθmaan	'seven-eights'
tisƐ-aƐšaar	'nine-tenths'

8.3.2 Above tenth

Fractions above tenth are expressed by a phrase consisting of a cardinal number and the preposition *ɛala* 'on' followed by another cardinal number:

waaẓid ɛala daɛaš	'one eleventh'
θneen ɛala xmuṣṭaɛaš	'two fifteenths'
tlaaθa ɛala ɛišriin	'three twentieths'
ʔarbaɛa ɛala xamsa w-ɛišriin	'four twenty-fifths'

Instead of *ɛala*, some speakers use the preposition *min* 'of, from' in these constructions:

waaẓid min daɛaš	'one eleventh'

9. PRONOUNS

9.1 PERSONAL

The personal pronouns reflect in their forms the same distinctions of person, gender, and number as do the verbs (see 5.2). They occur as independent words and as suffixes.

9.1.1 Independent

The forms of the independent personal pronouns are as follows:

3 M	*huwwa*	'he, it M'
F	*hiyya*	'she, it F'
P	*humma*	'they'
2 M	*ʔinta*	'you M'
F	*ʔinti*	'you F'
P	*ʔintu*	'you P'
1 S	*ʔaani*	'I'
P	*ʔiḥna*	'we'

Some speakers also use a third-person feminine plural form *hinna* 'they F' and a second-person feminine plural form *ʔintan* 'you FP' when referring to or addressing two or more female persons, but these forms are not common in Baghdad. See 11.2.2 for pronoun agreement.

The chief uses of the independent personal pronouns are:

(1) As the subject or the predicate of an equational sentence (11.1.1):

huwwa b-baġdaad.	'He's in Baghdad.'
ʔaani taʕbaan kulliš.	'I'm very tired.'
haaḏa huwwa.	'This is he.'

(2) Optionally, or for emphasis, as the subject of a verbal sentence (11.1.2):

ʔaani ʔafaḍḍil čaay.	'I prefer tea.'
ʔiḥna ma-naakul laḥam xanziir.	'We don't eat pork.'

(3) As the topic of a topical sentence (11.1.3):

ʔinta š-biik?	'What's the matter with you?'

9.1.2 Pronoun suffixes

Pronoun suffixes occur with noun, preposition, verb, and active participle stems (and also with a small number of other stems; for these see 9.1.2.2 E below.) With noun stems they correspond to English possessives: *beetna* 'our house'; with preposition, verb, and active participle stems they correspond to English object pronouns: *wiyyaana* 'with us', *šaafna* 'he saw us'. Further discussion of the pronoun suffixes is divided into two parts, the first dealing with the forms of the suffixes and the second with the forms of the stems to which they are attached.

9.1.2.1 Forms of suffixes

The forms of the pronoun suffixes are as follows:

	With consonant stems:	With all stems:	With vowel stems:	
3 M	*-a*		*-ø*	'his, its M, him, it M'
F		*-ha*		'her, its F, it F'
P		*-hum*		'their, them'
2 M	*-ak*		*-k*	'your M, you M'
F	*-ič*		*-č*	'your F, you F'
P		*-kum*		'your P, you P'
1 S	*-i*		*-ya*	'my, me'
		-ni		'me'
P		*-na*		'our, us'

For those speakers who use third-person and second-person feminine plural pronouns (see 9.1.1 above), the corresponding pronoun suffix forms are *-hin* 'their F, them F' and *-čan* 'your FP, you FP'.

A. In the case of the first person singular, the forms *-i* and *-ya* (see B below) are both used with noun and preposition stems; the form *-ni* with verb stems:

beet	'house'	*beeti*	'my house'
ʔil-	'to, for'	*ʔili*	'to, for me'
šaaf	'he saw'	*šaafni*	'he saw me'

In all the other cases, the same forms of the pronoun suffixes are used regardless of whether the stem is a noun, a preposition, or a verb:

beeta	'his house'
ʔila	'to, for him'
šaafa	'he saw him'

B. The suffixes *-ha*, *-hum*, *-kum*, *-ni*, and *-na* are invariable in form. The others have two alternant forms. In each case, one of the alternants is or begins with a vowel; this alternant is used with stems ending in a consonant:

beet (stem *beet-*)	'house'	*beeta̲*	'his house'
		beetak̲	'your M house'
		beetič̲	'your F house'
		beeti̲	'my house'

The other alternant in each case is used with stems ending in a vowel, which is always long. (If this vowel is *-ee-* or *-ii-*, it is changed to *-ay-* or *-iy-* respectively before the suffix *-ya* 'my, me'.) Except for the third person masculine, this alternant is, or begins with, a consonant:

ˀax (stem *ˀaxuu-*)	'brother'	*ˀaxuuk̲*	'your M brother'
		ˀaxuuč̲	'your F brother'
		ˀaxuuya	'my brother'
Ɛala (stem *Ɛalee-*)	'on'	*Ɛaleek̲*	'on you M'
		Ɛalayya	'on me'

In the case of the third person masculine, this alternant is zero (∅); that is, the absence of a suffix. Thus a word containing this alternant has the same form as the stem alone:

ˀaxuu   'his brother'

Since it has the same form as the suffixing stem alone, such a word always differs in some way from the basic word without a suffix, often by ending in a long instead of a short vowel and thus having stress on the final syllable, or in some other way. Additional examples (the suffixing stem is given in parentheses; see 9.1.2.2 below for the formation of these stems):

sira (*siraa-*)	'turn'	*siraa*	'his turn'
wara (*waraa-*)	'behind'	*waraa*	'behind him'
yinsa (*yinsaa-*)	'he forgets'	*yinsaa*	'he forgets him'
nsammi (*nsammii-*)	'we call'	*nsammii*	'we call him'
xallu (*xalluu-*)	'let P'	*xalluu*	'let P him'

šaafaw (*saafoo-*)	'they saw'	*šaafoo*	'they saw him'
yintaxbuun (*yintaxbuu-*)	'they elect'	*yintaxbuu*	'they elect him'
ɛala (*ɛalee-*)	'on'	*ɛalee*	'on him'

The facts set forth above are illustrated in the following paradigms:

Nouns

	Consonant stem		Vowel stem	
	beet (stem *beet-*)	'house'	*sira* (stem *siraa-*)	'turn'
3 M	*beeta*	'his house'	*siraa*	'his turn'
F	*beetha*	'her house'	*siraaha*	'her turn'
P	*beethum*	'their house'	*siraahum*	'their turn'
2 M	*beetak*	'your M house'	*siraak*	'your M turn'
F	*beetič*	'your F house'	*siraač*	'your F turn'
P	*beetkum*	'your P house'	*siraakum*	'your P turn'
1 S	*beeti*	'my house'	*siraaya*	'my turn'
P	*beetna*	'our house'	*siraana*	'our turn'

Prepositions

	Consonant stem		Vowel stem	
	giddaam (stem *giddaam-*)	'in front of'	*wara* (stem *waraa-*)	'behind'
3 M	*giddaama*	'in front of him'	*waraa*	'behind him'
F	*giddaamha*	'in front of her'	*waraaha*	'behind her'
P	*giddaamhum*	'in front of them'	*waraahum*	'behind them'
2 M	*giddaamak*	'in front of you M'	*waraak*	'behind you M'
F	*giddaamič*	'in front of you F'	*waraač*	'behind you F'
P	*giddaamkum*	'in front of you P'	*waraakum*	'behind you P'
1 S	*giddaami*	'in front of me'	*waraaya*	'behind me'
P	*giddaamna*	'in front of us'	*waraana*	'behind us'

Verbs

Consonant stem		Vowel stem	
šaaf (stem *šaaf-*)	'he saw'	*xalla* (stem *xallaa-*)	'he let'

3	M	*šaaf<u>a</u>*	'he saw <u>him</u>'	*xallaa*	'he let <u>him</u>'
	F	*šaaf<u>ha</u>*	'he saw <u>her</u>'	*xallaa<u>ha</u>*	'he let <u>her</u>'
	P	*šaaf<u>hum</u>*	'he saw <u>them</u>'	*xallaa<u>hum</u>*	'he let <u>them</u>'
2	M	*šaaf<u>ak</u>*	'he saw <u>you M</u>'	*xallaa<u>k</u>*	'he let <u>you M</u>'
	F	*šaaf<u>ič</u>*	'he saw <u>you F</u>'	*xallaa<u>č</u>*	'he let <u>you F</u>'
	P	*šaaf<u>kum</u>*	'he saw <u>you P</u>'	*xallaa<u>kum</u>*	'he let <u>you P</u>'
1	S	*šaaf<u>ni</u>*	'he saw <u>me</u>'	*xallaa<u>ni</u>*	'he let <u>me</u>'
	P	*šaaf<u>na</u>*	'he saw <u>us</u>'	*xallaa<u>na</u>*	'he let <u>us</u>'

9.1.2.2 Forms of stems

The form of a word as it occurs without a pronoun suffix is a <u>free form</u>, for example *beet* 'house', *ʔax* 'brother', *wara* 'behind'. The form to which a pronoun suffix is added is a <u>suffixing stem</u>, which in some cases is the same as the free form, for example *beet(na)* '(our) house', and in some cases differs from it, for example *ʔaxuu(na)* '(our) brother' and *waraa(na)* 'behind (us)'. Suffixing stems which end in a consonant are <u>consonant stems</u>; those which end in a vowel are <u>vowel stems</u>. As indicated in 9.1.2.1 above, certain pronoun suffixes have different forms depending upon whether they are attached to a consonant stem or a vowel stem. In discussing the forms of suffixing stems, two points must be considered. The first is the difference, if any, between the free form and the stem; the second is the variation, if any, in the form of the stem before different suffixes. Stems of nouns, prepositions, verbs, active participles, and others do not all behave alike in these respects; each of these categories is therefore treated separately below.

A. Nouns

Pronoun suffixes occur regularly and commonly with nouns which denote parts of the body or family relationships, and here and there with nouns in various other semantic categories, for example *raasi* 'my head' *ʔummha* 'her mother', *beetna* 'our house'. With a great many nouns, however, pronoun suffixes occur less commonly or not at all; in such cases the usual way of indicating the same relationships is the *maal-* phrase (13.8.1), for example *l-qaaṭ maali* 'my suit', *ṭ-ṭabiib maalkum* 'your P doctor'. It should therefore be borne in mind that some of the following examples may represent forms which are less common for those particular nouns than the corresponding *maal-* phrase.

(1) Nouns ending in a consonant, except those noted in (6), (7), and (8) below, have consonant stems. Before a suffix beginning with a consonant, the stem is the same as the free form. Before a suffix beginning with a vowel, the stem remains unchanged except for automatic loss of the stem vowel in certain cases, as follows: (1) In stems ending in *-iC* and *-uC*, the stem vowel is dropped if possible (see 4.1.3.1 A); (2) In stems of the pattern *FvMaL*, the stem vowel is usually dropped if the preceding consonant is *ʔ*, *z*, *x*, *ɛ*, *ġ*, or *q*. In the first group of examples below there is no change in the stem. (In these and subsequent examples, the suffix *-ha* 'her' is used to represent any pronoun suffix beginning with a consonant; *-a* 'his' to epresent any beginning with a vowel.)

beet	'house'	*bee<u>tha</u>*	'her house'	*bee<u>ta</u>*	'his house'
ṣadiiq	'friend'	*ṣadii<u>qha</u>*	'her friend'	*ṣadii<u>qa</u>*	'his friend'

ɛamm	'(paternal) uncle'	*ɛammha*	'her uncle'	*ɛamma*	'his uncle'
maẓall	'place'	*maẓallha*	'her place'	*maẓalla*	'his place'

In those that have a stem vowel *a* which is not dropped, there may be non-automatic stress on the stem vowel, but there is variation in these cases (see 3.2 B):

qalam	'pencil'	*qalamha*	'her pencil'	*qaláma*	'his pencil'
maṭɛam	'restaurant'	*maṭɛamha*	'her restaurant'	*maṭɛáma*	'his restaurant'

In the following group of examples, the stem vowel is dropped:

waɛad	'promise'	*waɛadha*	'her promise'	*waɛda*	'his promise'
ʔibin	'son'	*ʔibinha*	'her son'	*ʔibna*	'his son'
ʔuxut	'sister'	*ʔuxutha*	'her sister'	*ʔuxta*	'his sister'
malaabis	'clothes'	*malaabisha*	'her clothes'	*malaabsa*	'his clothes'
kutub	'books'	*kutubha*	'her books'	*kutba*	'his books'

(2) Feminine and plural nouns ending in *-a* have consonant stems ending in *-t-*. Before a suffix beginning with a consonant, the stem is the same as the free form, plus *-t-* (thus always ending in *-at-*). Before a suffix beginning with a vowel the following types of changes occur:

(a) In stems ending in the sequences *-(C)yat-*, *-iyat-*, or *-iyyat-* these are changed to *-(C)iit-*:

qarya	'village'	*qaryatha*	'her village'	*qariita*	'his village'
tarbiya	'upbringing'	*tarbiyatha*	'her upbringing'	*tarbiita*	'his upbringing'
kulliyya	'college'	*kulliyyatha*	'her college'	*kulliita*	'his college'

(b) In stems ending in the sequences *-(C)wat-*, *-uwat-* (rare), or *-uwwat-*, these are changed to *-(C)uut-*:

gahwa	'coffee (-shop)'	*gahwatha*	'her coffee'	*gahuuta*	'his coffee'
ʔuxwa	'brothers'	*ʔúxwatha*	'her brothers'	*ʔuxuuta*	'his brothers'
ɛaduwwa	'enemy F'	*ɛaduwwatha*	'her enemy F'	*ɛaduuta*	'his enemy F'

(c) In stems ending in a sequence *-CCat-*, the stem vowel *-a-* is shifted (4.1.3.1 C):

safra	'trip'	*safratha*	'her trip'	*safirta*	'his trip'
raġba	'wish'	*raġbatha*	'her wish'	*raġubta*	'his wish'
sitra	'jacket'	*sitratha*	'her jacket'	*sitirta*	'his jacket'
ġurfa	'room'	*ġurfatha*	'her room'	*ġurufta*	'his room'
haayša	'cow'	*haayšatha*	'her cow'	*haayišta*	'his cow'

(d) In other stems the stem vowel *-a-* is dropped:

ṣuura	'picture'	*ṣuuratha*	'her picture'	*ṣuurta*	'his picture'
waẓiifa	'job, position'	*waẓiifatha*	'her position'	*waẓiifta*	'his position'
ɛamma	'(paternal) aunt'	*ɛammatha*	'her aunt'	*ɛammta*	'his aunt'
muɛallima	'teacher F'	*muɛallimatha*	'her teacher F'	*muɛallimta*	'his teacher F'
ɛammaala	'workers'	*ɛammaalatha*	'her workers'	*ɛammaalta*	'his workers'

(3) Nouns ending in *-i* have vowel stems ending in *-ii-* before one of the invariable suffixes *-ha*, *-hum*, *-kum*, *-na*. With the other suffixes, there are three types of suffixing stem: (a) a consonant stem in which the final *-ii-* is changed to *-y-*; (b) a consonant stem in which the final *-ii-* is changed to *-iyy-*; and (c) a vowel stem in which the final *-ii-* remains unchanged. The facts must be learned for each noun; some may have more than one of the three types. Examples:

(a)	*raʔi*	'opinion'	*raʔiiha*	'her opinion'	*raʔya*	'his opinion'
(b)	*naadi*	'club'	*naadiiha*	'her club'	*naadiyya*	'his club'
(c)	*muzaami*	'lawyer'	*muzaamiiha*	'her lawyer'	*muzaamii*	'his lawyer'

With most such nouns, however, (though not *raʔi* 'opinion), *maal-* phrases are more common than pronoun suffixes.

(4) Nouns ending in *-u-* have vowel stems ending in *-uu-* before one of the invariable suffixes *-ha*, *-hum*, *-kum*, *-na*. With the other suffixes, there are two types of suffixing stem: (a) a consonant stem in which the final *-uu-* is changed to *-w-*, and (b) a consonant stem in which the final *-uu-* is changed to *-uww-*. The facts must be learned for each noun. Examples:

(a)	*zašu*	'filling, padding'	*zašuuha*	'its F padding'	*zašwa*	'its M padding'

(b) *Ɛadu* 'enemy' *Ɛaduuha* 'her enemy' *Ɛaduwwa* 'his enemy'

With most such nouns, however, *maal-* phrases are more common than pronoun suffixes.

(5) Masculine singular nouns ending in *-a* have vowel stems in *-aa-*:

Ɛaša	'supper'	*Ɛašaaha*	'her supper'	*Ɛašaa*	'his supper'
ġada	'lunch'	*ġadaaha*	'her lunch'	*ġadaa*	'his lunch'

With such nouns, however, *maal-* phrases are more common than pronoun suffixes.

(6) Dual nouns in *-een* have consonant stems identical with the free form. Except for a few referring to parts of the body, however, these nouns seldom take pronoun suffixes. Examples:

ʔiidteen	'two hands'	*ʔiidteenha*	'her two hands'	*ʔiidteena*	'his two hands'
Ɛeenteen	'two eyes'	*Ɛeenteenha*	'her two eyes'	*Ɛeenteena*	'his two eyes'

The two nouns *ʔiideen* 'hands, arms' and *rijleen* 'feet, legs', which have the dual ending *-een* but are also used as plurals (see 6.2.2.2 A (3)), have vowel stems ending in *-ee-* (except before the 1 S suffix *-ya* 'my', where the ending is *-ay-*), for example *ʔiideeha* 'her hands, arms', *ʔiidee* 'his hands, arms', and *ʔiidayya* 'my hands, arms'.

(7) Plural nouns in *-iin*. When pronoun suffixes occur with these nouns, there is considerable variation in the suffixing stem between a consonant stem in *-iin-* and a vowel stem in *-ii-* (*-iy-* before the 1 S suffix *-ya* 'my'). Below are shown full paradigms of the word *muƐallimiin* 'teachers', one with each type of stem. The less commonly used forms are enclosed in parentheses.

	Consonant stem (*muƐallimiin-*)		Vowel stem (*muƐallimii-*)
3 M	*muƐallimiina*	'his teachers'	*muƐallimii*
F	*muƐallimiinha*	'her " '	*muƐallimiiha*
P	*muƐallimiinhum*	'their " '	*muƐallimiihum*
2 M	*muƐallimiinak*	'your M teachers'	(*muƐallimiik*)
F	*muƐallimiinič*	' " F " '	(*muƐallimiič*)
P	*muƐallimiinkum*	' " P " '	*muƐallimiikum*
1 S	(*muƐallimiini*)	'my teachers'	*muƐallimiyya*
P	(*muƐallimiinna*)	'our " '	*muƐallimiina*

(8) Two common nouns, *ʔab* 'father' and *ʔax* 'brother' have vowel stems *ʔabuu-* and *ʔaxuu-* throughout, for example *ʔabuuha* 'her father', *ʔabuu-* 'his father', *ʔabuuk* 'your M father', *ʔabuuya* 'my father'.

B. Prepositions

For some prepositions the suffixing stem is not predictable and must be learned individually in each case; the most common of these are treated in (1) through (10) below. In others the suffixing stem is predictable from the free form in the same ways as that of a noun; these are illustrated in (11). See also 10.1.1.

(1) *ʔil-* 'to, for'. This form occurs only with a pronoun suffix; it is itself the suffixing stem. (See also 5.3.6.)

3 M	*ʔila*	'to, for him'
F	*ʔilha*	'to, for her'
P	*ʔilhum*	'to, for them'
2 M	*ʔilak*	'to, for you M'
F	*ʔilič*	'to, for you F'
P	*ʔilkum*	'to, for you P'
1 S	*ʔili*	'to, for me'
P	*ʔilna, ʔinna*[1]	'to, for us'

There are corresponding negative forms involving the negative prefix *ma-*, for example *ma-ʔila*, *ma-ʔilha*, and so on. These, however, are more commonly contracted to *maala*, *maalha*, and so on. The English equivalent is often 'there is/are not... for', as in *maali mukaan bis-sayyaara*. 'There isn't room for me in the car.' This contracted negative stem *maal-* is identical in form with one stem of *maal* 'of, belonging to' (see (9) below), but is quite different in meaning.

(2) *b-* 'in, with (by means of)'. This form is itself a prefix, always attached to the following word. The suffixing stem, used with pronoun suffixes, is a vowel stem *bii-* (*biy-* before the 1 S suffix *-ya* 'me').

3 M	*bii*	'in him'
F	*biiha*	'in her'
P	*biihum*	'in them'
2 M	*biik*	'in you M'
F	*biič*	'in you F'
P	*biikum*	'in you P'
1 S	*biyya*	'in me'
P	*biina*	'in us'

(3) *been* 'between, among'. There are two suffixing stems, *been-* and *beenaat-*. Only the former is used with singular pronoun suffixes, as in *beeni w-beenak* 'between me and you M' (note order). With plural pronoun suffixes only *been-* is used in a phrase with a preceding *been-*, for example *beeni w-beenhum* 'between me and them'; otherwise both occur but *beenaat-* more commonly.

---

[1]The form *ʔinna,* in which the *l* assimilates to the following *n*, is more common.

3 M	*beena*	'between him'
F	*beenha*	'between her'
P	*beenhum,* *beenaathum*	'between them'
2 M	*beenak*	'between you M'
F	*beenič*	'between you F'
P	*beenkum,* *beenaatkum*	'between you P'
1 S	*beeni*	'between me'
P	*beenna,* *beenaatna*	'between us'

(4) *ɛala* 'on, about, against'. The suffixing stem is a vowel stem *ɛalee-* (*ɛalay-* before the 1 S suffix *-ya* 'me').

3 M	*ɛalee*	'on him'
F	*ɛaleeha*	'on her'
P	*ɛaleehum*	'on them'
2 M	*ɛaleek*	'on you M'
F	*ɛaleeč*	'on you F'
P	*ɛaleekum*	'on you P'
1 S	*ɛalayya*	'on me'
P	*ɛaleena*	'on us'

(5) *ɛan* 'about, concerning'. The suffixing stem is *ɛan-* before a consonant; *ɛann-* before a vowel.

3 M	*ɛanna*	'about him'
F	*ɛanha*	'about her'
P	*ɛanhum*	'about them'
2 M	*ɛannak*	'about you M'
F	*ɛannič*	'about you F'
P	*ɛankum*	'about you P'
1 S	*ɛanni*	'about me'
P	*ɛanna* [1]	'about us'

(6) *ɛi(n)d* 'at the house of; in the possession of'. The suffixing stem is *ɛ* before a consonant; *ɛind-* before a vowel. One common English translation of this preposition plus a pronoun suffix is a phrase involving the verb <u>to have</u>: *ɛinda fluu* (literally 'in his possession is money') 'he has money'; this translation is used below.

3 M	*ɛinda*	'he has'
F	*ɛidha*	'she has'
P	*ɛidhum*	'they have'

[1] Rare; usually replaced by *ɛaleena* 'about us'.

2 M	*ʕindak*	'you M have'
F	*ʕindič*	'you F have'
P	*ʕidkum*	'you P have'
1 S	*ʕindi*	'I have'
P	*ʕidna*	'we have'

(7) *fii* 'in'. This is a Classical preposition which occurs only rarely in spoken Iraqi. The suffixing stem is *fii-*, and the forms are like those of *bii-* in (2) above.

(8) *foog* 'over, above, on top of'. There are two suffixing stems, *foog-* and *foogaa-*; both occur with all pronoun suffixes.

3 M	*fooga*	*foogaa*	'over him'
F	*foogha*	*foogaaha*	'over her'
P	*fooghum*	*foogaahum*	'over them'
2 M	*foogak*	*foogaak*	'over you M'
F	*foogič*	*foogaač*	'over you F'
P	*foogkum*	*foogaakum*	'over you P'
1 S	*foogi*	*foogaaya*	'over me'
P	*foogna*	*foogaana*	'over us'

(9) *maal* 'of, belonging to'. This word plays a major role in Iraqi grammar. It has three sets of stems used with pronoun suffixes: one is *maal-* before all suffixes; another is *maalat-* before consonants and *maalt-* before vowels; and the third is *maalaat-* before all suffixes. The use of one or another of these stems depends upon the antecedent noun (see 13.8). The usual English equivalent for *maal* with a pronoun suffix is a possessive adjective or pronoun such as 'my, mine'. The forms are shown below.

3 M	*maala*	*maalta*	*maalaata*	'his'
F	*maalha*	*maalatha*	*maalaatha*	'her, hers'
P	*maalhum*	*maalathum*	*maalaathum*	'their, theirs'
2 M	*maalak*	*maaltak*	*maalaatak*	'your M, yours M'
F	*maalič*	*maaltič*	*maalaatič*	'your F, yours F'
P	*maalkum*	*maalatkum*	*maalaatkum*	'your P, yours P'
1 S	*maali*	*maalti*	*maalaati*	'my, mine'
P	*maalna*, *maanna*[1]	*maalatna*	*maalaatna*	'our, ours'

(10) *min* 'from, of'. The suffixing stem is *min-* before a consonant; *minn-* before a vowel.

3 M	*minna*	'from him'
F	*minha*	'from her'
P	*minhum*	'from them'

[1] The form *maanna*, in which the *l* assimilates to the following *n*, is more common.

2 M	*minnak*	'from you M'
F	*minnič*	'from you F'
P	*minkum*	'from you P'
1 S	*minni*	'from me'
P	*minna*[1]	'from us'

(11) In the case of other prepositions, the forms of the suffixing stem are predictable in the same ways as those of nouns. The most common are shown below.

Consonant stem; no change before a vowel

	giddaam (stem *giddaam-*)	'in front of'
3 M	*giddaama*	'in front of him'
F	*giddaamha*	'in front of her'
P	*giddaamhum*	'in front of them'
2 M	*giddaamak*	'in front of you M'
F	*giddaamič*	'in front of you F'
P	*giddaamkum*	'in front of you P'
1 S	*giddaami*	'in front of me'
P	*giddaamna*	'in front of us'

Like *giddaam* are:

bdaal	'instead of, in place of'
bduun	'without'
ḍidd	'against'
ġeer	'other than, except'
yamm	'beside, by'

Consonant stem; stem vowel dropped before a vowel

	miθil (stem *miθil-*, *miθl-*)	'like'
3 M	*miθla*	'like him'
F	*miθilha*	'like her'
P	*miθilhum*	'like them'
2 M	*miθlak*	'like you M'
F	*miθlič*	'like you F'
P	*miθilkum*	'like you P'

[1] Rare; usually replaced by the phrase *min ʕidna* 'from us'.

1 S	*miθli*	'like me'
P	*miθilna*[1]	'like us'

Like *miθil* are:

baɛad	'after'
gabuḷ	'before' (in time)

Vowel stem:

	wiyya (stem *wiyyaa–*)	'with'
3 M	*wiyyaa*	'with him'
F	*wiyyaaha*	'with her'
P	*wiyyaahum*	'with them'
2 M	*wiyyaak*	'with you M'
F	*wiyyaač*	'with you F'
P	*wiyyaakum*	'with you P'
1 S	*wiyyaaya*	'with me'
P	*wiyyaana*	'with us'

Like *wiyya* are:

blayya	'without'
jawwa	'under, below'
ɛada, maaɛáda	'except'
wara	'behind, after'

C. Verbs

(1) Verb forms ending in a consonant, except for those noted in (2) and (3) below, have consonant stems. Before a suffix beginning with a consonant, the stem is the same as the free form. Before a suffix beginning with a vowel, the stem may undergo changes as follows:

(a) If the verb is a perfect-tense 3 M form (ending in *–aC*) or 3 F form (ending in *–at*), there is no change before a suffix beginning with a vowel, but the resultant verb forms have non-automatic stress (see 3.2 B) on the syllable preceding the suffix. (In these and subsequent examples, the suffix *–ha* 'her, it F' is used to represent any suffix beginning with a consonant, and *–a* 'him, it M' to represent any suffix beginning with a vowel.)

ðirab	'he hit'	<u>*ðirabha*</u>	'he hit her'	<u>*ðirába*</u>	'he hit him'
naððfat	'she cleaned'	<u>*naððfatha*</u>	'she cleaned it F'	<u>*naððfáta*</u>	'she cleaned it M'

[1] The *l* is usually assimilated to the *n*: *miθinna*.

(b) If the verb is an imperfect-tense Class I or IV verb form of the general pattern *CvCCvC,* the stem vowel is shifted (4.1.3.1 C) before a suffix beginning with a vowel:[1]

yilbas	'he wears'	*yilbasha*	'he wears it F'	*yilibsa*	'he wears it M'
tiɛjib	'it F pleases'	*tiɛjibha*	'it F pleases her'	*tiɛijba*	'it F pleases him'
nuɛruf	'we know'	*nuɛrufha*	'we know her'	*nuɛurfa*	'we know him'

(c) In other cases the stem remains unchanged before a suffix beginning with a vowel, except that in stems ending in *-iC* or *-uC* the stem vowel is dropped if possible (see 4.1.3.1 A), and except as noted below.

In the following there is no change:

nħibb	'we like'	*nħibbha*	'we like her'	*nħibba*	'we like him'
šaaf	'he saw'	*šaafha*	'he saw her'	*šaafa*	'he saw him'
yjaddid	'he renews'	*yjaddidha*	'he renews it F'	*yjaddida*	'he renews it M'
ytarjum	'he translates'	*ytarjumha*	'he translates it F'	*ytarjuma*	'he translates it M'
ʔatħammal	'I endure'	*ʔatħammalha*	'I endure her'	*ʔatħammala*	'I endure him'

In the following the stem vowel is dropped:

dirásit	'I studied'	*dirasitha*	'I studied it F'	*dirasta*	'I studied it M'
ɛayyǎnit	'you M appointed'	*ɛayyanitha*	'you M appointed her'	*ɛayyanta*	'you M appointed him'
ybaddil	'he changes'	*ybaddilha*	'he changes it F'	*ybaddla*	'he changes it M'
ʔaxaabur	'I phone'	*ʔaxaaburha*	'I phone her'	*ʔaxaabra*	'I phone him'

In Class VIII imperfect-tense 3 M, 3 F, 2 M, 1 S, and 1 P verb forms (including 2 M imperatives) ending in *-FtiMiL/-FtuMuL,* when the stem vowel is dropped

[1] Variant forms with unshifted stems, and non-automatic stress as in (a) above, also occur, for example *yilbása* 'he wears it M', but these are less common.

before a suffix beginning with a vowel, the preceding *-i-* or *-u-* is changed to *a*:[1]

yiqtiriẓ	'he suggests'	*yiqtiriẓha*	'he suggests it F'	*yiqtarẓa*	'he suggests it M'
nintiṣir	'we wait for'	*nintiṣirha*	'we wait for her'	*nintaṣra*	'we wait for him'

(2) Perfect-tense 3 P verb forms, which end in *-aw*, have vowel stems ending in *-oo-*:

šaafaw	'they saw'	*šaafooha*	'they saw her'	*šaafoo*	'they saw him'
ntixbaw	'they elected'	*ntixbooha*	'they elected her'	*ntixboo*	'they elected him'

(3) Imperfect-tense 3 P and 2 P verb forms, which end in *-uun*, have vowel stems ending in *-uu-*; imperfect-tense 2 F forms, which end in *-iin*, have vowel stems ending in *-ii-* :

yšuufuun	'they see'	*yšuufuuha*	'they see her'	*yšuufuu*	'they see him'
tšuufuun	'you P see'	*tšuufuuha*	'you P see her'	*tšuufuu*	'you P see him'
tšuufiin	'you F see'	*tšuufiiha*	'you F see her'	*tšuufii*	'you F see him'

(4) All verb forms ending in a vowel have vowel stems, ending in the corresponding long vowel:

nisa	'he forgot'	*nisaaha*	'he forgot her'	*nisaa*	'he forgot him'
štireena	'we bought'	*štireenaaha*	'we bought it F'	*štireenaa*	'we bought it M'
šifti	'you F saw'	*šiftiiha*	'you F saw her'	*šiftii*	'you F saw him'
nsammi	'we name, call'	*nsammiiha*	'we call her'	*nsammii*	'we call him'
jiibu	'bring P'	*jiibuuha*	'bring P her'	*jiibuu*	'bring P him'

[1] The same change occurs in these and Class VII verbs before the inflectional suffixes *-iin* and *-uun* ; see 5.2.2.2 A (4).

D. Active participles

Active participles (AP's) used as verbs (see 12.1.3) have suffixing stems which are in some respects like those of nouns, in others like those of verbs.

(1) Masculine singular AP's

(a) Those ending in a consonant have consonant stems. Before a suffix beginning with a consonant, the stem is the same as the free form. Before a suffix beginning with a vowel, the stem remains the same except that in stems ending in *-iC* or *-uC* the stem vowel is dropped if possible (see 4.1.3.1 A), and except as noted below. (In these and subsequent examples, the pronoun suffix *-ha* 'her, it F' is used to represent any suffix beginning with a consonant; *-a* 'him, it M' any suffix beginning with a vowel.) In the following there is no change:

daazz	'having sent'	*daazzha*	'having sent it F'	*daazza*	'having sent it M'
miʒtaaj	'having needed'	*miʒtaajha*	'having needed her'	*miʒtaaja*	'having needed him'
mjaddid	'having renewed'	*mjaddidha*	'having renewed it F'	*mjaddida*	'having renewed it M'
mtarjum	'having translated'	*mtarjumha*	'having translated it F'	*mtarjuma*	'having translated it M'

In the following the stem vowel is dropped:

laabis	'wearing'	*laabisha*	'wearing it F'	*laabsa*	'wearing it M'
ṭaabux	'having cooked'	*ṭaabuxha*	'having cooked it F'	*ṭaabxa*	'having cooked it M'
mbaddil	'having changed	*mbaddilha*	'having changed it F'	*mbaddla*	'having changed it M'

In Class VIII AP's of the pattern *miFtiMiL/miFtuMul*, when the stem vowel is dropped before a suffix beginning with a vowel, the preceding *-i-* or *-u-* is changed to *a*.

mintixib	'having elected'	*mintixibha*	'having elected her'	*mintaxba*	'having elected him'
mixtubur	'having tested'	*mixtuburha*	'having tested her'	*mixtabra*	'having tested him'

Note that in all these cases the form of the stem before a pronoun suffix beginning with a vowel is the same as before other suffixes beginning with a vowel, namely the feminine and plural suffixes *-a* and *-iin* (see 7.2.1 B (5)).

(b) Masculine singular AP's ending in a vowel (always *-i*) have vowel stems ending in *-ii-*:

baani	'having built'	*baaniiha*	'having built built it F'	*baanii*	'having built it M'
naasi	'having forgotten'	*naasiiha*	'having forgotten her'	*naasii*	'having forgotten him'
msawwi	'having done'	*msawwiiha*	'having done it F'	*msawwii*	'having done it M'
mištiri	'having bought'	*mištiriiha*	'having bought it F'	*mištirii*	'having bought it M'

(2) Feminine singular AP's end in *-a*, for example *kaatba* 'having written' and *naasya* 'having forgotten'. All have consonant stems ending in *-t-*. Before suffixes beginning with a consonant, the stem is formed by the addition of *-t-* to the free form and thus ends in *-at-*, for example *kaatbatha* 'having written it F'[1] and *naasyatha* 'having forgotten her/it F'. Before suffixes beginning with a vowel, there are two variant stems. One ends in *-at-* as above, but has non-automatic stress (3.2) on the syllable preceding the suffix, for example *kaatbáta* 'having written it M' and *naasyáta* 'having forgotten him/it M'. In the other, if the sequence *-at-* is preceded by a consonant other than *y*, the stem vowel *-a-* is shifted (or dropped, as appropriate; see 4.1.3.1), for example *kaatibta* 'having written it M'; if it is preceded by *-y-*, the sequence *-yat-* or *-iyat-* is changed to *-iit-*,[2] for example *naasiita* 'having forgotten him/it M'. However, although the two variant stems just described are both usually acceptable, they are not equally common in all cases; the illustrations below indicate only the more common variant for each group.

(a) If the stem before a consonant ends in *-at-* preceded by a doubled consonant or by a sequence *-vvc*, the stem before a vowel ends in *-at-* and has non-automatic stress:

daazza	'having sent'	*daazzatha*	'having sent it F'	*daazzáta*	'having sent it M'

---

[1] All AP's illustrated in paragraph (2) are feminine. The notations F and M in the English translations refer only to the gender of the pronoun suffix.

[2] Occasionally a sequence *-yat-* or *-iyat-* may be changed to *-iit-* also before a suffix beginning with a consonant.

mištamma	'having smelled'	*mištammatha*	'having smelled it F'	*mištammáta*	'having smelled it M'
mi ʒtaaja	'needing'	*mi ʒtaajatha*	'needing her'	*mi ʒtaajáta*	'needing him'

(b) If the stem before a consonant ends in *-at-* preceded by two consonants (or by a doubled and a single consonant) of which the second is not *y*, the stem vowel *-a-* is shifted (4.1.3.1 C) before a vowel. The resultant form of the stem is identical to the corresponding masculine AP (free form), plus *-t-:*

kaatba	'having written'	*kaatbatha*	'having written it F'	*kaatibta*	'having written it M'
šaayfa	'having seen'	*šaayfatha*	'having seen her'	*šaayifta*	'having seen him'
ṣaarba	'having hit'	*ṣaarbatha*	'having hit her'	*ṣaarubta*	'having hit him'
mbaddla	'having changed'	*mbaddlatha*	'having changed it F'	*mbaddilta*	'having changed it M'
mnaṣṣfa	'having cleaned'	*mnaṣṣfatha*	'having cleaned it F'	*mnaṣṣufta*	'having cleaned it M'

In Class VIII feminine AP's of the pattern *miFtaMLa* (masculine *miFtiMiL/miFtuMuL*), when the stem vowel *-a-* is shifted as above, the preceding *-a-* is changed to the same vowel (*i* or *u*) as in the masculine form:

mintaṣra	'having waited for'	*mintaṣratha*	'having waited for her'	*mintiṣirta*	'having waited for him'

(c) If the stem before a consonant ends in *-at-* preceded by a single consonant other than *y*, the stem vowel *-a-* is dropped before a vowel. The resultant form of the stem is identical to the corresponding masculine AP (free form), plus *-t-:*

mtarjuma	'having translated'	*mtarjumatha*	'having translated it F'	*mtarjumta*	'having translated it M'

(d) If the stem before a consonant ends in *-yat-* or *-iyat-*, these sequences are changed to *-iit-* before a vowel:

naasya	'having forgotten'	*naasyatha*	'having forgotten her'	*naasiita*	'having forgotten him'
mgaḷḷya	'having fried'	*mgaḷḷyatha*	'having fried it F'	*mgaḷḷiita*	'having fried it M'
miṣṭabṭiya	'having thought (s-o) overdue'	*miṣṭabṭiyatha*	'having thought her overdue'	*miṣṭabṭiita*	'having thought him overdue'

In Class VIII feminine APs of the pattern *miFtaMya* (masculine *miFtiMi*), when the final *-yat-* is changed to *-iit-* as above, the preceding *-a-* is changed to *-i-*. Thus the resultant stem form, as well as that of the others ending in *-iit-*, is like the corresponding masculine AP (free form), plus lengthening of the *-i-*, and *-t-*:

mištarya	'having bought'	*mištaryatha*	'having bought it F'	*mištiriita*	'having bought it M'

(3) Plural AP's, which end in *-iin*, usually have vowel stems ending in *-ii-* throughout:

	šaayfiin (stem *šaayfii-*)	'having seen'
3 M	*šaayfii*	'having seen him'
F	*šaayfiiha*	'having seen her'
P	*šaayfiihum*	'having seen them'
2 M	*šaayfiik*	'having seen you M'
F	*šaayfiič*	'having seen you F'
P	*šaayfiikum*	'having seen you P'
1 S	*šaayfiini*	'having seen me'
P	*šaayfiina*	'having seen us'

However, there is some variation between these forms and forms with a consonant stem in *-iin-* especially in the 3 M: *šaayfiina* 'having seen him'; and the 1 P: *šaayfiinna* 'having seen us'.

E. Others

Pronoun suffixes also occur with the stems of a few particles (10.1) functioning as conjunctions, as adverbs, or in various other ways. Some examples follow.

baʕad 'still, yet'. Stem before a consonant *baʕad-*; before a vowel *baʕd-*. Examples: *baʕadha da-taakul.* 'She's still eating.' *baʕda* 'he still . . .'. Takes the *-ni* form of the 1 S suffix: *baʕadni...* 'I still . . .'. Only in this last case is there a difference in form between this *baʕad* 'still, yet' plus pronoun suffix, and the preposition *baʕad* 'after' plus pronoun suffix: *baʕdi* 'after me'.

taww or *hastaww* 'just, just now'. Examples: *tawwha* (or *hastawwha*) *xaabratni bit-talafoon.* 'She just now called me on the phone.' *tawwa* (or *hastawwa*) ... 'he just now ...'. May take either the *-ni* or the *-i* form of the 1S suffix, but usually the former: *tawwni* (or *hastawwni*) ... 'I just now ...'.

doom 'always, constantly'. Examples: *doomha taʕbaana* 'She's always tired.' *dooma...* 'he always ...'. Takes the *-i* form of the 1S suffix: *doomi...* 'I always ...'.

šloon 'how'. Examples: *šloonha?* 'How is she?', *šloona?* 'How is he?'. May take either the *-ni* or the *-i* form of the 1S suffix, but is rarely used with these.

liʔann 'because'. Somewhat uncommon with pronoun suffixes. Examples: *liʔannha...* 'because she ...', *liʔanna...* 'because he ...'.

hiyyaat- 'here ... is/am/are'. This is a bound stem, occurring only with a pronoun suffix. Examples: *hiyyaatha* 'Here she/it F is.', *hiyyaata* 'Here he/it M is.' Takes the *-ni* form of the 1S suffix: *hiyyaatni* 'Here I am.'

ween 'where'. Examples: *weenha?* 'Where is she?', *weena?* 'Where is he?'. May take either the *-ni* or the *-i* form of the 1S suffix: *weenni, weeni?* 'Where am I?'

yaareet 'I wish ...'. Examples: *yaareetha hnaa.* Used in contrary-to-fact wishes. 'I wish she were here', *yaareeta...* 'I wish he ...'. Takes the *-ni* form of the 1S suffix: *yaareetni...* 'I wish I ...'.

9.2 Demonstrative Pronouns

There are two sets of demonstrative pronouns, each set containing masculine, feminine, and plural forms. (For agreement see 11.2.2.) Except for the masculine and feminine of the first set, these forms have four or more variants each; the most common are shown below.

M	*haaδa*	'this (one) M'
F	*haaδi, haay*	'this (one) F'
P	*δool, δoola,* *haδool, haδoola*[1]	'these'
M	*δaak, δaaka,* *haδaak, haδaaka*	'that (one) M'
F	*δiič, δiiča,* *haδiič, haδiiča*	'that (one) F'
P	*δoolaak, δoolaaka,* *haδoolaak, haδoolaaka*[2]	'those'

[1] Also occasionally *δooli, haδooli.*

[2] Also occasionally *δook, haδook.*

The pronouns of the first set correspond not only to English <u>this/these</u>, as shown above, but also in many cases to <u>that/those</u>. Those of the second set are used chiefly in referring to entities at some distance, either in space or in time, and, for contrast, in referring to a farther entity when a nearer is also mentioned. Moreover, in addition to their use as demonstratives, these pronouns (particularly those of the first set) are very frequently used as third-person personal pronouns instead of those described in 9.1, and are then best translated by English <u>he/him</u>, <u>she/her</u>, <u>it</u>, and <u>they/them</u>. Some examples:

triid haaδaʔ	'Do you want this one?'
haaδa xooš naadi.	'This (or that) is a good club.'
muu haaδa r-rijjaal ič-čaan gaaεid yammna bis-siinamaʔ	'Isn't that the man who was sitting next to us in the movie?'
čaan itwannasna hwaaya bis-safra loo ma-jaay haaδa.	'We would have enjoyed ourselves a lot on the trip if he hadn't come.'
minu yidri haaδi binit-manʔ	'Who knows whose daughter this is?'
haaδi nbaaεat, triid haayʔ	'This one is sold; do you want this?'
haay ʒilwa laakin δiiča ʔaʒla.	'This one (or she) is pretty, but that one's prettier.'
haaδi ma-da-tiqbal tiji.	'She refuses to come.'
δoola hwaaya xooš naas.	'Those (or they) are very nice people.'
ʔaani loo b-mukaanak ma-amši wiyya δoola.	'If I were in your place I wouldn't go around with them.'
loo muu δaak čaan mawwtooni.	'If it hadn't been for him, they would have killed me.'
ʔinta tgul-li ruuʒ w-δaak ygul-li laa.	'You tell me to go and he tells me not to.'
δiič ma-čaanat xooš dagga.	'That wasn't a nice thing to do.'
δiiča ʔaġla-ma εindi.	'That's the most expensive one I have.'
haδiiča tbayyin tuεurfak.	'That one over there seems to know you.'
ma-tgul-li δoolaak š-yriiduunʔ	'Would you tell me what those people want?'
δool š-aεleehum, δoolaak iδ-δabbaw l-iʒjaar.	'What do these (people) have to do with it – *Those* are the ones who threw the stones.'

9.3 INTERROGATIVE PRONOUNS

The four interrogative pronouns are *minu* 'who?', *šinu* 'what?', *yaahu* 'which (one)?', and *šgadd* 'how much?'. The first two have different forms, depending on the context.

9.3.1 *minu, -man, ʔil-man* 'who, whom, whose?'

A. *minu* 'who?'. This form is used (1) in a one-word question, (2) as one of the elements of an equational sentence (11.1.1), and (3) as the subject of a verbal sentence (11.1.2):

(1)	*minu?*	'Who?' 'Who is it?'
(2)	*minu haaδa?*	'Who is this?'
	minu r-raʔiis?	'Who's the boss?'
	minu lli gal-lak hiič?	'Who's the one who told you so?'
(3)	*minu raḥ-yiji?*	'Who's going to come?'
	minu nṭaak haay?	'Who gave you this?'

B. *-man* 'who(m), whose?'. This form, a suffix, is used (1) as the object of a preposition, (2) following a noun in an annexion (see 13.7.2), and (3) with *maal* 'of, belonging to'. In the last two cases the English equivalent is 'whose?'.

(1) The forms of prepositions used with *-man* are the suffixing stems appropriate for pronoun suffixes beginning with a consonant (9.1.2.2 B), except that prepositions ending in a vowel (e.g. *ʕala, wiyya, wara*) may also have stems identical to their free forms (e.g. *ʕalee-* or *ʕala-, wiyyaa-* or *wiyya-*):

ʔil-man dazzeet il-ifluus?	'Who did you send the money to?' ('To whom...')
bii-man nibdi?	'Who shall we start with?'
ʕala-man da-tiḥčuun?	'Who are you talking about?'
ʕid-man raḥ-tibqa l-leela?	'Who are you going to stay with tonight?' ('At whose house...')
min-man axaδt il-ifluus?	'Who did you get the money from?'
wiyya-man raḥ-itruuḥ?	'Who are you going with?'

(2) In an annexion with *-man*, a preceding noun is in its annexing form if it has one:

haaδa beet-man?	'Whose house is this?'
haay sayyaarat-man?	'Whose car is this?'
b-sayyaarat-man inruuḥ?	'Whose car shall we go in?'

(3) With the suffix *–man*, the form *maal* 'of, belonging to' may retain the masculine stem *maal–* after any noun or pronoun, or may have the feminine stem *maalat–* after a feminine noun or pronoun:

haaδa maal–man?	'Whose is this M?'
haay maal–man? *haay maalat–man?*	'Whose is this F?'
haθ–θoob maal–man?	'Whose is this shirt?'
has–sayyaara maal–man? *has–sayyaara maalat–man?*	'Whose is this car?'

C. *ʔil–man* 'whom?'. This form consists of the preposition *ʔil–* and the suffix *–man*, as in B above. It is used as the direct object of a verb:

ʔil–man šifit?	'Whom did you see?'
ʔil–man raḥ–tizzawwaj?	'Whom are you going to marry?'

9.3.2 *šinu, š–, (ʔ)eeš, –weeš* 'what?'

A. *šinu* 'what?'. This form is used (1) in a one-word question and (2) as one of the elements of an equational sentence:

(1) *šinu?*	'What?' 'What is it?'
(2) *šinu haaδa?*	'What's this?'
šinu raʔyak?	'What's your opinion?'
šinu s–sabab?	'What's the reason?'

B. *š–* 'what?'. This prefix form is used (1) as the subject of a verbal sentence, (2) as the direct object of a verb, (3) as the first element of an equational sentence, and (4) preceding *ʔaku* 'there is/are':

(1) *š–ṣaar?*	'What happened?'
(2) *š–itriid?*	'What do you want?'
š–da–taakul?	'What are you eating?'
š–sawwat?	'What did she do?'

(3) As the first element of an equational sentence, *š–* is in some cases interchangeable with *šinu* (A (2) above). It is always used when the second element is a preposition with a pronoun suffix, but never when the second element begins with the article prefix:

š–raʔyak?	'What is your opinion?'
š–ismak?	'What's your name?'

š-biik?	'What's wrong with you?'
š-aᶓlayya? [1]	'What's it to me?'
š-aku?	'What is there?' 'What's wrong?'
š-aku hnaak?	'What's going on there?'
š-aku b-iidak?	'What have you got in your hand?'

The element *š* is also found in a few other interrogative words, such as *šloon* 'how?' *šwakit* 'when?', and *šgadd* 'how much?' but in these it can be considered a part of the word rather than a prefix.

C. *-(ʔ)eeš*, *-weeš* 'what?'. These forms are used (1) as the objects of certain prepositions (2) following a noun in an annexion, and (3) with *maal* 'of, belonging to'. The combinations have the forms indicated below:

(1) *b-eeš it-tiffaaz?*	'How much are the apples?'
ʔinta ᶓala-weeš zaᶓlaan?	'What are you angry about?'
ᶓann-eeš da-tizčuun?	'What are you P talking about?'
hal-meez minn-eeš imsawwa?	'What is this table made of?'
guul šii bil-ingiliizi. miθl-eeš?	'Say something in English. Like what?'
hal-loon wiyya-ʔeeš yirham?	'What does this color go with?'

The element *(w)eeš* is also found in the forms *ʔilweeš*, *luweeš*, *leeš* 'why?'.

(2) Following a noun in an annexion, the form is *-eeš*; the noun is in its annexing form if it has one. The English equivalent of this kind of construction is generally 'what kind of ___?', 'a___ for what?', 'what ___?', or the like. There is often a derogatory implication, as in the last example:

haaδa ktaab-eeš?	'What kind of book is this?' (i.e., geography, history?)
ʔinta raayiz lil-zafla? zaflat-eeš?	'Are you going to the party?' What party?'
haay sayyaart-eeš?	'What kind of car is this!' (i.e., it's no good)

(3) Following *maal* 'of, belonging to', the form is *-eeš*. The *maal* may retain the masculine stem *maal-* when referring to any noun or pronoun, or it may have the feminine stem *maalt-* when referring to a feminine (or non-human plural) noun or pronoun. The English equivalent may be 'what kind of ___?' as above;

[1] Note that after *š-* the vowel *a* precedes the *ᶓ*.

where there is a distinction between *-eeš* and *maal(t)-eeš* the latter generally means 'used for what?' or 'belonging to, part of what?':

hal-burġi maal-eeš?	'What is this screw for?' 'What does this screw belong to?'
qmaaš maal-eeš itriid?	'What kind of cloth do you want?' (i.e., for a shirt, a suit?)
has-sayyaara maal-eeš? *has-sayyaara maalt-eeš?*	'What kind of car is this?' (i.e., used as a taxi, or what?)

9.3.3 *yaahu* 'which, which one?'. This form is used (1) as a one-word question, (2) as one of the elements of an equational sentence, (3) as the subject or direct object of a verb, and (4) as the object of a preposition:

(1) *yaahu?*	'Which one?'
(2) *yaahu ʔaxuuk?*	'Which is your brother?'
yaahu ʔuxtak?	'Which is your sister?'
yaahu ʔaqwa l-kull?	'Which one is the strongest of all?'
yaahu maalak? [1]	'Which is yours?'
yaahu l-gal-lak?	'Which is the one who told you?'
(3) *yaahu gal-lak?*	'Which one told you?'
yaahu triid?	'Which one do you want?'
(4) *b-yaahu ʔaku guṭin?*	'Which one has cotton in it?'
min yaahu štireeta?	'Which one did you buy it from?'

9.3.4 *šgadd* 'how much?'. This form is invariable. It is used (1) as a one-word question, (2) as one of the elements of an equational sentence, (3) as the subject or direct object of a verb, and (4) as the object of a preposition:

(1) *šgadd?*	'How much?' (quantity or price)
(2) *šgadd is-surʕa?*	'What's the speed?'
šgadd ʕumrak?	'How old are you?' (How much is your age?)
(3) *šgadd buqa?*	'How much remained?' (i.e., was left over)
šgadd itriid?	'How much do you want?'
(4) *ʕala šgadd ttifaqtu?*	'What amount did you P agree on?'

[1] This and *yaahu maaltak?* may mean: 'What business is it of yours?'

9.4 OTHERS

Other pronouns, and forms used as pronouns, are illustrated below.

A. *ʔaẓẓad* 'someone, anyone'

ma-...ʔaẓẓad }
la-...ʔaẓẓad } 'not...anyone, no one'

ʔaku ʔaẓẓad bil-baab? 'Is there someone at the door?'

ma-šifit ʔaẓẓad ihnaaka. 'I didn't see anyone there.'
'I saw no one there.'

Note also the common phrases *ʔay ʔaẓẓa* 'someone, anyone', *fadd ʔaẓẓad* 'someone', and *ma-...kull ʔaẓẓad* 'not...anyone'.

B. *maẓẓad* 'no one'

This is the negative equivalent of *ʔaẓẓad*. It is used only as a subject:

min yiji ṣ-ṣeef maẓẓad yibqa bil-wlaaya. 'When summer comes, no one stays in town.'

C. *laẓẓad* 'no one (is to), (don't) anyone'

This is a contraction of the negative prefix *la-* and *ʔaẓẓad*. It is used in negative third-person commands.

laẓẓad yitruk il-ġurfa 'no one is to leave the room.'

D. *šii* 'something, anything'

ma-...šii }
la-...šii } 'not...anything, nothing'

This form is also the noun *šii* 'thing'.

laazim agul-lak šii. 'I have to tell you something.'

ʔaku šii muhimm? 'Is there anything important?'

ma-štireet šii. 'I didn't buy anything.'

Note also the common phrases *ʔay šii* 'something, anything', *fadd šii* 'something', and *ġeer šii* 'something else'.

E. *kullši* 'everything'

la-...kullši 'not...anything, nothing'

kullši ẓaaḍir. 'Everything is ready.'

sawweet kullši miθil-ma triid.	'I did everything the way you want.'
la-taakul kullši l-yoom.	'Don't eat anything today.'

With *ma-* 'not', the meaning may be 'not...everything', for example *yuƐruf išwayya Ɛan il-mawḍuuƐ bass ma-yuƐruf kullši.* "He knows a little about the matter but he doesn't know everything.' More commonly, however, it means 'not...anything, nothing'; in such cases *kullši* often precedes the negative verb:

kullši ma-yuƐruf.	'He doesn't know anything.'
kullši ma-sawweet.	'I didn't do anything.'

F. *kull-man* 'everyone, each'

This form is more common as a conjunction (10.1.3.2 D), but occasionally occurs as here:

kull-man yidfaƐ izsaaba.	'Everyone pays his own bill.'
kull-man ʔila.	'Everyone for himself.'

G. *l-kull* 'all, the whole thing, everyone'

l-kull raz-yijuun s-saaƐa xamsa.	'They're all coming at five o'clock.'
ma-aqbal ib-nuṣṣ, ʔariid il-kull.	'I won't accept half; I want the whole thing.'

H. *waazid* , *wizda* 'one; someone'

These are the masculine and feminine forms of the numeral 'one'.

tigdar tinṭiini waazid?	'Can you give me one?'
waazid minhum zaraami.	'One of them is a thief.'
wizda mnil-banaat mariiḍa.	'One of the girls is sick.'

These forms are also used in the sense 'someone':

waazid zangiin	'someone M rich'
wizda zangiina	'someone F rich'
waazid miθla	'someone like him'
waazid ġeerak	'someone other than you'
šifit waazid naayim Ɛal-gaaƐ.	'I saw someone lying on the floor.'

Note also the common phrases *ʔay waazid* 'someone, anyone', *fadd waazid* 'someone', *kull waazid* 'each one, everyone', and *ġeer waazid* 'someone else'. The form *waazid* or *l-waazid* is also used in the sense 'one, you' (impersonal):

l-waaʒid ma-yuεruf š-ysawwi.	'One doesn't know what to do.'
waaʒid min yriid ysawwi šii laazim yiʒsib iʒsaab il-kullši.	'When you want to do something you have to take everything into account.'

I. *waaʒ(i)d (...) l-laax* 'each other'

This is the usual equivalent of English 'each other'. If the context requires a preposition it precedes *l-laax*.

bidaw yidifεuun waaʒd il-laax.	'They began to push each other.'
εaadatan yiddaaynuun waaʒid imnil-laax.	'They usually borrow from each other.'
giεadna waaʒid yamm il-laax.	'We sat next to each other.'

J. *baεaδ̣-...(l-)baεaδ̣* 'each other'

This phrase is less common than the preceding one in this meaning. The first *baεaδ̣-* has an attached pronoun suffix. The article prefix *l-* with the second *baεaδ̣* is optional. If the verb requires a preposition, it precedes the second *baεaδ̣*.

yikirhuun baεaδ̣hum (il-)baεaδ̣.	'They hate each other.'
zaεεal il-muwaδ̣δ̣afiin baεaδ̣hum εala baεaδ̣.	'He got the employees mad at each other.'

K. *kull-* 'all of, all'

The stem *kull-* with a pronoun suffix can be used as a pronoun, corresponding in meaning to English 'all of it, you, them, etc.' or 'it, you... all'.

kulla xalṣaan.	'It's all gone.'
kullha maalti.	'It F is all mine.'
kullna riʒna.	'We all went.'
kullhum ʒilwaat.	'All of them are pretty.'

L. *nafis-* '-self'

As a noun, *nafis* means 'spirit, soul; person'. With a pronoun suffix it corresponds in meaning to the English reflexive pronouns himself, herself, and so on.

ʔaδδa nafsa.	'He hurt himself.'
tšuuf nafisha ʔaʒla l-banaat.	'She considers herself the prettiest of girls.'
leeš tiʒčiin wiyya nafsič?	'Why do you F talk to yourself?'
sawweetha min nafsi.	'I did it on my own hook.'

These forms are also used as intensive pronouns after a noun or pronoun:

l-mudiir nafsa gal-li...	'The director himself told me...'

10. PARTICLES AND WORDS ENDING IN *-an*

This chapter deals with two types of forms which do not fall into any of the previously described categories.

10.1 PARTICLES

Particles are uninflected forms which in sentences generally function like English pronouns, prepositions, conjunctions, adverbs, or interjections. A few correspond to certain English adjectives, and some have functions peculiar to Iraqi. Particles are mostly rather short, but are not otherwise characterized by any particular form or ending. Some may take pronoun suffixes (see 9.1.2.2 B and E).

Particles which function as pronouns were included in the general discussion of pronouns in Chapter 9. Other major particle functions are illustrated below; interrogative particles are grouped together in 10.1.2.

10.1.1 Prepositions

The most common prepositions are listed below with sentences illustrating their use. (For forms of prepositions with pronoun suffixes, see 9.1.2.2 B.) Only one or two English equivalents are shown here for each Iraqi preposition, but it should be borne in mind that prepositions in one language seldom have exact equivalents in another, and that for some Iraqi prepositions there may be five or ten possible English translations, depending on the context.

ʔaθnaa(ʔ) — 'during'

la-txalliihum yjimᶜuun ifluus ʔaθnaaʔ il-ijtimaaᶜ. — 'Don't let them collect money during the meeting.'

ʔaθnaa wujuudi b-amriika tᶜarráfit b-ihwaaya naas. — 'During my stay in America I met a lot of people.'

ʔil- — 'to; for; until'

This form occurs with pronoun suffixes and *-man* 'whom' (9.1.2.2 B and 9.3.1). The form *l-*, or a form consisting of a duplication of the following consonant, occurs as a prefix with nouns (6.3.3 B). The form *-l-* plus a pronoun suffix occurs as a suffix with verbs and active participles (5.3.6).

ʔaku makaatiib ʔili? — 'Are there any letters for me?'

ʔil-man dazzeet l-ifluus? — 'To whom did you send the money?'

šwakit raḥ-tirjaᶜ il-baġdaad? — 'When are you returning to Baghdad?'

ntiḏarna lis-saaᶜa xamsa. — 'We waited until five o'clock.'

ʔilaa — 'until, up to'

Somewhat more formal than *ʔil-*.

| *jawaazak ṣaaliẓ ʔílaa* *xṃuṣṭaɛaš biš-šahar.* | 'Your passport is good until the fifteenth of the month.' |
| *ma-ɛindi fluus. tigdar tiṣṭubur-li ʔílaa baačir?* | 'I haven't got any money. Can you give me (wait for me) until tomorrow?' |

ʔilla   'except, but'; (with negative) 'only'

| *kullhum ʔijaw ʔilla l-mudiir.* | 'They all came but the director.' |
| *ma-ašuufa ʔilla marra bil-isbuuɛ.* | 'I only see him once a week.' |

b-   'in, on; with (by means of)'

This prefix form occurs with nouns and *-eeš* 'what'; with pronoun suffixes and *-man* 'whom' the stem is *bii-* (9.1.2.2 B).

ʔaxuuya hassa da-yiskun ib-baġdaad.	'My brother is living in Baghdad now.'
jeetu bis-sayyaara loo biṭ-ṭiyyaara?	'Did you P come in the car or on the plane?'
tigdar itguṣṣa b-muus.	'You M can cut it M with a razor blade.'

barra   'outside'

(More common as an adverb; see 10.1.4.)

| *ma-ariidak tiṭlaɛ barra l-ġurfa.* | 'I don't want you M to go outside the room.' |

baɛad   'after, in'

(Also an adverb; see 10.1.4.)

| *raẓ-ajiik il-yoom baɛad il-ġada.* | 'I'm coming to (see) you today after lunch.' |
| *ʔirjaɛ baɛad saaɛa.* | 'Come back in an hour.' |

been   'between, among'

With pronoun suffixes the stem is *been-* or *beenaat-* (9.1.2.2 B).

| *ma-aku xilaaf been il-uxwa.* | 'There's no quarrel between the brothers.' |
| *šifta been il-awraaq gabuḷ išwayya.* | 'I saw it M among the papers a little while ago.' |

bdaal   'instead of, in place of'

| *dazzooni bdaal axuuya.* | 'They sent me instead of my brother.' |

blayya[1]	'without'
ma-yigdar yšuuf ʔabadan blayya manaaḍra.	'He can't see at all without his glasses.'
jawwa	'under'
(Also an adverb; see 10.1.4)	
hiyyaata jawwa l-meez.	'There it M is under the table.'
ʒasab	'according to, in accordance with'
ʔuṣbuġ l-beet ʒasab ðawqak.	'Paint the house according to your taste.'
sawweetha ʒasab ṭalab il-mudiir.	'I did it in accordance with (at) the director's request.'
ʒawl	'around'
j-jihaal ltammaw ʒawl is-sayyaara.	'The children gathered around the car.'
(b-)xilaal	'within, in' (period of time)
haaði xooš šaġla bass l-ifluus laazim tiddabbar ib-xilaal yoomeen.	'This is a good deal, but the money has to be arranged for within two days.'
(b-)daaxil	'inside'
la-txalli j-junṭa hnaak, ʒuṭṭha daaxl il-ġurfa.	'Don't leave the suitcase there; put it inside the room.'
ḍidd	'against'
hal-ɛamal ḍidd il-qaanuun.	'This act is against the law.'
haaða daayman yištuġuḷ ḍiddi.	'He's always working against me.'
ɛala	'on; about (concerning); against'

With the article prefix this preposition usually has the prefix form *ɛa-;* with the pronoun suffix *-ya* 'me' the stem is *ɛalay-;* with the other pronoun suffixes the stem is *ɛalee-* (9.1.2.2 B).

xalleet il-maktuub ɛal-meez.	'I put the letter on the table.'
ma-ariid aʒči ɛala hal-qaḍiyya baɛad.	'I don't want to talk about this matter any more.'
raʒ-ysajjil šikiyya ɛala ṣadiiqa biš-šurṭa.	'He's going to register a complaint against his friend with the police.'
ɛan	'about (concerning); (away) from'

[1] Also, less commonly, *bala, bduun;* the latter is common with pronoun suffixes: *bduuni* 'without me'.

With pronoun suffixes, the stem is *ɛan-* before a consonant; *ɛann-* before a vowel (9.1.2.2 B). In the meaning 'about', less common than *ɛala*.

gul-li kull it-tuɛurfa ɛan haš-šaxiṣ.	'Tell me everything you know about this person.'
baɛɛid it-timman ɛan in-naar.	'Move the rice away from the fire.'

ɛi(n)d 'at the house or place of business of'; in the possession of'

The form is usually *ɛind* before a vowel, *ɛid* before a consonant (9.1.2.2 B). In the second sense above the English equivalent often involves the verb to have.

ṣaar-la tlat-tušhur da-yiskun ɛidna.	'He's been living at our house for three months.'
šifta ɛind il-ʒallaaq.	'I saw him at the barber's.'
ma-ɛindi fluus.	'I haven't any money.'
l-miftaaʒ ɛindak?	'Have you got the key?'

fii 'in'

Not common except in formal speech and in a few set expressions such as *fiimaanillaa* 'good-bye' (literally 'in the protection of God'); the usual word for 'in' is *b-* (see above). In combination with the article prefix (6.3.1) has forms *fil-*, *fit-*, *fid-*, and so on.

foog 'above, over; besides'

(Also an adverb; see 10.1.4.) With pronoun suffixes the stem is *foog-* or *foogaa-* (9.1.2.2 B).

ṭ-ṭiyyaara ṣaar-ilha saaɛa tṭiir foog baġdaad.	'The plane has been flying over Baghdad for an hour.'
foog il-nukta s-sawwaaha biyya, da-yiʒči ɛalayya.	'Besides the trick he played on me, he's saying things against me.'

ġeer 'other than, (nothing) but'

ma-čaan ʔaku šii zeen bil-ʒafla ġeer ič-čaay.	'There wasn't anything good at the party but the tea.'

lii 'to, up to'

Related to *ʔil-* (see above), but carries implication 'all the way to'. Common in phrases with adverbs of place and time: *lii giddaam* 'in advance; forward', *lii wara* 'backward', *lii foog* 'up(ward)'. Does not occur before nouns with the article prefix.

lii hassa ma-jaani maktuub minna.	'Up to now I haven't received a letter from him.'
xaššeena bil-maay lii hnaa.	'We went into the water up to here.'

maal 'belonging to, of'

See 9.1.2.2 B and 13.8.

maƐa 'with; in spite of'

Not common except in formal speech and in a few set phrases, for example *maƐa s-salaama* (literally 'with safety') 'good-bye'; *maƐa l-asaf* (literally 'with sorrow') 'unfortunately'; *maƐa kullin* 'in spite of everything'; *maƐa haaδa* 'in spite of this, nevertheless'.

miθil 'like, similar to'

ʔariid ṣanduug θaani miθil haaδa.	'I want another box like this one.'

min 'from, of; than'

(Also a conjunction; see 10.1.3.1.) With the article prefix the form is a prefix *mn-* (6.3.3 C); with pronoun suffixes the stem is *min-* before a consonant and *minn-* before a vowel (9.1.2.2 B). Used after comparatives in sense of 'than'.

stilämit maktuub min abuuya.	'I got a letter from my father.'
ʔay sana txarrajti mnil-kulliyya?	'What year did you F graduate from the college?'
bass waaẓid minkum yigdar yruuẓ.	'Only one of you can go.'
ʔaxuuya ʔakbar minni b-santeen.	'My brother is two years older than I.'

wara 'behind; after'

ʔaku ẓadiiqa ṣġayyra wara l-beet.	'There's a small garden behind the house.'
xaššaw waaẓid wara l-laax.	'They came in one after the other.'

wiyya 'with'

tirdiin itruuẓiin lis-siinama wiyya ʔuxti?	'Do you F want to go to the movies with my sister?'

yamm 'by, beside, next to'

taƐaal ugƐud yammi.	'Come sit by me.'
beetna yamm beethum.	'Our house is next to their house.'

gabuḷ 'before; ago'

(Also an adverb; see 10.1.4.)

l-muƐallim yriid yšuufak gabḷ id-daris. 'The teacher wants to see you before the class.'

šifta gabuḷ šahreen. 'I saw him two months ago.'

giddaam 'in front of'

xal-nitlaaga giddaam daaʔirt il-bariid. 'Let's meet in front of the post-office.'

gbaaḷ 'opposite, across from'

ʔaku xooš maṭƐam igbaaḷ il-uuteel. 'There's a good restaurant across from the hotel.'

10.1.2 Interrogatives

The principle interrogative particles are listed below. (For interrogative pronouns see also 9.3; for particles as modifiers, 13.3.)

ʔay, yaa 'which, what?'

These are noun modifiers, always preceding the noun (or pronoun *waaḥid* 'one') which they modify. Of the two, *yaa* is more common.

ʔay jariida triid tiqra? 'Which newspaper do you want to read?'

yaa waaḥid ʔaxuuk? 'Which one is your brother?'

šinu, š-, -(w)eeš 'what?'

Pronoun; see 9.3.

šloon 'how?, what kind of?'

May take pronoun suffixes (9.1.2.2 E). In the sense 'what kind of', *šloon* functions as a noun modifier. (It is also used in exclamations, with a meaning corresponding to English 'what (a)', for example *šloon ibnayya ḥilwa*! 'What a pretty girl!', *šloon yoom*! 'What a day!')

šloon il-ʔakil ib-hal-maṭƐam? 'How's the food in this restaurant?'

šloonak? 'How are you?'

šloon qanaadir Ɛindak? 'What kind of shoes do you have ?' (to salesman)

šwakit 'when?'

šwakit raḥ-yooṣal? 'When is he going to arrive?'

šgadd 'how much, how many, how far, how long (time)?'

May function as a pronoun (see 9.3), as a noun modifier preceding a noun, or as an adverb.

šgadd fluus ɛindak? 'How much money have you got?'

šgadd ṣaar-lak bil-ɛiraaq? 'How long have you been in Iraq?'

šgadd minnaa lil-baṣra? 'How far is it from here to Basra?'

leeš, luweeš, ʔilweeš 'why?'

leeš ma-waddaw ij-jihaal wiyyaahum? 'Why didn't they take the children with them?'

minu, ʔil-man, -man 'who, whom, whose?'

Pronoun; see 9.3.

ween 'where?'

May take pronoun suffixes (9.1.2.2 E). Note also the special combined form with the preposition *min* 'from': *mneen* 'from where?'.

ween is-sitra maalti? 'Where's my jacket?'

ween raayiz? 'Where are you going?'

weenhum? 'Where are they?'

mneen ištireeta? 'Where did you buy it?' (Literally: ('From where...')

yaahu 'which one?'

Pronoun; see 9.3.

čam 'how many?'

A noun modifier; precedes the noun (or pronoun *waazid* 'one') which it modifies, and the noun is always *singular*. In somewhat formal speech, the form *kam* is sometimes used instead.

čam iskamli triidni ʔajiib? 'How many chairs do you want me to bring?'

čam waazid ištireet? 'How many did you buy?'

10.1.3 Conjunctions

10.1.3.1 Simple

The main simple conjunctions are as follows:

ʔaw 'or'

Less common than *loo* (see below).

tiji hassa ʔaw baƐdeen? 'Are you coming now or later?'

ʔíδaa 'if'

(See 15 for use of this word and *loo* 'if'.)

zeen laƐad, ʔaani ʔagul-la ʔíδaa ma-Ɛindak maaniƐ. 'All right then, I'll tell him if you have no objection.'

ʔíδaa triid tištirik bin-naadi, gul-li ʒatta azakkiik. 'If you want to join the club, tell me so I can propose you.'

ʔimma... loo, ʔimma... ʔaw, ʔimma... w-imma 'either... or'

See also *loo... loo* below.

ʔariid ʔimma haaδa loo δaak. 'I want either this one or that one.'

bass 'but, only'

ʔaani aδδakkar saamiƐ hal-iʒčaaya bass ma-adri ween. 'I remember having heard this story but I don't know where.'

tara 'then; or, else'

Often used in conditional sentences (15) to introduce the result clause, and in sentences containing a negative command to introduce a clause indicating the result of failure to follow the command.

ʔíδaa ma-tinṭiini l-ifluus tara aštiki Ɛaleek. 'If you don't give me the money, then I'll bring suit against you.'

la-tilƐab wiyya č-čalib tara yƐaδ̣δ̣ak. 'Don't play with the dog or he'll bite you.'

ʒatta 'in order to, so (that)'

xal-niṭḷaƐ hassa ʒatta nooṣal gabuḷ-ma tumṭur. 'Let's leave now so we'll get there before it rains.'

laakin 'but'

šifta l-axuuk laakin ma-gitt-la Ɛaleeha. 'I saw your M brother but I didn't tell him about it.'

laa... wálaa 'neither... nor, (not) either... or'

(See also 11.3.)

laa ʒiča wálaa δ̣iʒak. 'He neither spoke nor laughed.'

ma-ariid laa haaδa wálaa δaak. 'I don't want either this one or that one.'

liʔann 'because'

May serve as stem for pronoun suffixes; see 9.1.2.2 E.

ḏṭarreena nibqa wara d-dawaam il-baarḥa li?ann čaan ʕidna šuġuḷ kulliš ihwaaya.	'We had to stay after hours yesterday because we had a very great deal of work.'

loo 'if; or'

(See 15 for use of this word and *?iḏaa* 'if'.)

loo raayiḥ wiyyaahum čaan itwannasit ihwaaya.	'If you had gone with them you would have enjoyed yourself a lot.'
š-tiṣṣawwar, raḥ-yḥaṣṣilha l-haš-šaġḷa loo laa?	'What do you think, is he going to get this job or not?'

loo...loo 'either...or'

loo tidfaʕ il-iijaar loo tiṭḷaʕ imnil-beet.	'Either you pay the rent or you get out of the house.'
štiri loo raggi loo tiffaaḥ.	'Buy either watermelon or apples.'

min 'when'

šifit hal-filim min čint ib-baġdaad.	'I saw this film when I was in Baghdad.'
min tištiri beetinjaan istangii wiḥda wiḥda w-xalli l-baggaaḷ yoozna giddaamak.	'When you buy eggplant select them one by one and have the grocer weigh them in front of you.'
raḥ-agul-la min yirjaʕ lil-beet.	'I'll tell him when he returns home.'

w- 'and'

Occurs only in prefix form: *ʕali w-aṣdiqaa?a* 'Ali and his friends', *štiraa w-baaʕa b-nafs il-yoom.* 'He bought it and sold it on the same day.' Combines with the article prefix as follows: *wil-meez* 'and the table', *wit-timman* 'and the rice'.

walaw 'although, even though'

ʕayynoo walaw huwwa muu min ḥizibhum.	'They appointed him even though he is not of their party.'

yaḷḷa 'until, before'

ḏṭarreet aḥči wiyyaa saaʕteen yaḷḷa qibal.	'I had to talk with him two hours before he agreed.'

čeef 'because, as'

ma-agdar aruuḥ lis-siinama čeef ma-ʕindi fluus.	'I can't go to the movies, as I don't have any money.'

10.1.3.2 Derived

Some conjunctions are derived from prepositions, interrogatives, and other forms, by the addition of the suffix *-ma*.[1] Some of the most common are illustrated below.

A. From prepositions

Prepositions		Conjunctions	
ʔaθnaa(ʔ)	'during'	*ʔaθnaa-ma*	'while'
ʔílaa	'to, up to'	*ʔílaa-ma*	'until'
baɛad	'after'	*baɛad-ma*	'after'
been	'between'	*been-ma*	'while'
bduun	'without'	*bduun-ma*	'without'
bdaal	'instead of'	*bdaal-ma*	'instead of'
ʒasab	'according to'	*ʒasab-ma*	'as, according to what'
ɛala	'on'	*ɛala-ma*	'as, according to'
miθil	'like, similar to'	*miθil-ma*	'as, the way that'
gabuḷ	'before'	*gabuḷ-ma*	'before'

Some examples:

Prepositions	Conjunctions
baɛad safirtak 'after your trip'	*baɛad-ma txaḷḷiṣ šuġḷak* 'after you finish your work'
bdaal haaδa 'instead of this one'	*bdaal-ma nruuʒ il-yoom* 'instead of (our) going today'
miθil ṣadiiqi 'like my friend'	*miθil-ma tuɛruf* 'as you know'
gabuḷ ziyaarta 'before his visit'	*gabuḷ-ma yooṣal* 'before he arrives'

B. From interrogatives

Conjunctions derived from interrogatives have various English equivalents, for example the phrase *ween-ma truuʒ* might be translated as 'wherever you go',

[1] In such forms, stress does not shift with the addition of *-ma*, but remains on the same syllable as in the underlying word.

'no matter where you go', 'everywhere you go', or 'anywhere you go', depending on the context. In the list which follows, only one or two English equivalents are given for each conjunction, though others may be possible.

Interrogatives		Conjunctions	
šloon	'how?'	*šloon-ma*	'however, any way that'
š-	'what?'	*š-ma*	'whatever'
ƹala-weeš[1]	'about what?'	*ƹala-weeš-ma*	'no matter about what, about anything that'
šwakit	'when?'	*šwakit-ma*	'whenever, any time that'
šgadd	'how much?'	*šgadd-ma*	'however much, no matter how much'
minu	'who?'	*minu-ma*	'whoever, anyone who'
ʔil-man	'whom? to whom?'	*ʔil-man-ma*	'who(m)ever, (to) anyone who'
wiyya-man[2]	'with whom?'	*wiyya-man-ma*	'with who(m)ever, with anyone who'
ween	'where?'	*ween-ma*	'wherever'
mneen	'from where?'	*mneen-ma*	'from wherever'
yaahu	'which one?'	*yaahu-ma*	'whichever one, any one that'

Some examples:

Interrogatives	Conjunctions
šloon sawweetha? 'How did you do it?'	*šloon-ma tsawwiiha* 'no matter how you do it, any way you do it'
š-itriid? 'What do you want?'	*š-ma-triid* 'whatever you want, anything you want'
šwakit tiji? 'When are you coming?'	*šwakit-ma triid tiji* 'whenever you want to come'

[1] Similarly, any preposition with *-(w)eeš* (9.3.2).

[2] Similarly, any preposition with *-man* (9.3.1).

šgadd triid? 'How much do you want?'	*šgadd-ma triid* 'however much you want, as much as you want'
	šgadd-ma ʒaawáalit 'no matter how much I tried'

C. From comparatives

A great many conjunctions are formed by the addition of the suffix *-ma* to comparatives. The English equivalent is generally 'the ---est (that)' or the like. Some examples:

ʔaʒla-ma šifit ib-ʒayaati	'the prettiest (one, thing, girl) I've seen in my life'
ʔarxaṣ-ma ʕindi	'the cheapest I have'
ʔashal-ma aku	'the easiest (one, thing) there is'

D. From other forms

Conjunctions are also formed by the addition of *-ma* (in one case also *-man*) to a few other forms, including a number of nouns denoting time. When *-ma* is suffixed to a feminine noun ending in *-a*, *-t-* is added to the stem of the noun, as in an annexion (13.7). Examples:

ʔawwal	'first'	*ʔawwal-ma*	'as soon as'
sana	'year'	*sanat-ma*	'the year that'
kull	'all, every'	*kull-ma*	'every time that' or 'everything that'
		kull-man	'everyone who'
wakit	'time'	*wakit-ma*	'the time when, when'
yoom	'day'	*yoom-ma*	'the day that'

ʔawwal-ma nooṣal ʔanṭii l-ifluus.	'As soon as we arrive I'll give him the money.'
kull-ma aʒči wiyyaa yizʕal.	'Every time I talk with him he gets mad.'
kull-man ʕinda sayyaara yigdar yruuʒ.	'Everyone who has a car can go.'
raʒ-agul-la kull-ma aʕruf.	'I'm going to tell him everything I know.'
wakit-ma ṣaarat il-ʒaadiθa činit bil-beet.	'When the incident occurred I was at home.'
yoom-ma dzawwájit tʒawwálit lil-beet ij-jidiid.	'The day I got married I moved to the new house.'

10.1.4 Others

Among the particles are also words of various other functions. Some of these are noun modifiers, and thus correspond to certain English adjectives; some serve as modifiers of verbs, adjectives, and other forms, and thus correspond to certain English adverbs, among them the adverbs of place and time; some are interjections and exclamations; a few fall into special categories without English equivalents. There are also some which may have more than one of these functions, and some which also may serve as nouns, pronouns, prepositions, or conjunctions. (See also 13.3.) Examples:

ʔaku	'there is, there are'
ʔay, yaa	'any'
ʔii, bali, naɛam[1]	'yes'
barra	'outside'
baɛad	'still, yet, more'
baɛdeen	'later, afterward'
balki	'maybe'
baḷḷa	'please'
jawwa	'below; downstairs'
xooš	'good'
suwa	'together'
šwayya	'a little'
fadd	'a; some; one'
foog	'above; upstairs'
kull	'all; every, each'
kulliš	'very'
laa	'no'
laɛad	'then, well then'
marra	'once, one time'
muu	'not'

[1] Of the three words for 'yes', *bali* is slightly more formal than *ʔii*, and *naɛam* more formal than *bali*.

hassa	'now'
halgadd	'so, so much'
hamm	'also, too; again'
hiič, hiiči	'such (a), this kind of; thus, this way'
hnaa, hnaana	'here'
hnaak, hnaaka	'there'
hwaaya	'much, a lot (of)'
waḷḷa	'really, certainly'
yaa	'any'
yaa	(vocative particle) [1]
yaḷḷa	'come on, let's go; just, just now'
yawaaš	'slowly'
yimkin	'maybe'
gabuḷ	'before(hand), previously'
gubaḷ	'straight ahead'
čam	'several, a few'

10.2 WORDS ENDING IN *-an*

A considerable number of words are derived from nouns and adjectives by the addition of the suffix *-an*, for example:

ʔaxiir	'last'	*ʔaxiiran*	'finally'

The major stem changes to be noted are the following: In stems of the pattern *CvCvC* if the stem vowel is *-i-* or *-u-* or if it is *-a-* preceded by any of the consonants *ʔ*, *q*, *x*, *ġ*, *ʒ*, or *ε*, it is dropped when *-an* is added:

ṭabuε	'nature'	*ṭabεan*	'naturally, of course'

In the case of feminine nouns ending in *-a-*, *-t-* is added to the stem (and the *-a* is not dropped):

ʒaqiiqa	'truth'	*ʒaqiiqatan*	'truly, really'

---

[1] Precedes names and some other nouns. Used in calling to or addressing someone: *yaa εali.* 'Ali!, Oh, Ali!' *yaa walad.* 'Hey, boy!, You, boy!' *taεaalu yaa šabaab.* 'Come on, you guys.'

In the case of nisba adjectives, which end in *-i*, *-yy-* is added to the stem:

šaxṣi	'personal'	*šaxṣiyyan*	'personally'

The majority of words ending in this suffix, including the four shown above, function as adverbs. Some other examples:

ʔabadan	'never; not at all'
ʔaḥyaanan	'sometimes'
ʔasaasan	'basically'
ʔawwalan	'firstly, in the first place'
baεḍan	'sometimes'
taqriiban	'nearly, approximately'
jabran	'forcibly, by force'
raʔsan	'directly'
salafan	'beforehand, already'
sanawiyyan	'annually'
εaadatan	'usually'
qariiban	'soon'
mubaašaratan	'directly'

Some occur exclusively or most commonly followed by a preposition and object. Such phrases have various English equivalents. Some examples:

badalan min	'instead of'
xawfan min	'for fear of'
raġman εan	'in spite of'
εtibaaran min	'with effect from, beginning as of'

A few words ending in *-an* occur in polite formulas used in various social situations. Examples:

ʔahlan (wa-sahlan).	'Welcome!'
rajaaʔan	'please'
šukran.	'Thank you.'

ɛafwan.	'Don't mention it.' (on being thanked) or 'Excuse me.'
naɛiiman.	(said to someone who has just had a haircut or a bath)
hanii?an.	(said to someone who has just had a drink of water)

PART THREE
SYNTAX

11. INTRODUCTION TO SYNTAX

The remaining chapters of this book contain a brief outline of the main features of Iraqi syntax. As an introduction, this chapter deals with the classification of simple sentences, and with the features of agreement, negation, the post-stated object, and the comparison of adjectives.

11.1 SENTENCE TYPES

Simple sentences in Iraqi fall into three main types, according to the structure of their major elements: equational, verbal, and topical sentences. The first two types are both composed of a subject and a predicate, and differ according to the nature of the predicate. Topical sentences are composed of a topic and a comment; the comment in turn consists of either an equational or a verbal sentence.

11.1.1 Equational sentences

Both equational and verbal sentences are composed of two major elements, a subject and a predicate. An equational sentence is one in which the predicate is a form (with or without modifiers) other than a finite verb. The English equivalent of such a sentence commonly contains a present-tense form of the verb to be (am, is, or are), for example *ʔaxuuya ṭabiib.* 'My brother is a doctor.' In the Iraqi sentence there is no word corresponding to any form of to be; the subject and predicate are directly juxtaposed without any verbal link. In equational sentences the subject is commonly a noun or pronoun (with or without modifiers), and the predicate may be a noun or pronoun, an adjective (including participles) an adverb of place, or a prepositional phrase. Additional examples:

haaδa beetna.	'This is our house.'
ʔaani šwayya mariiḍ il-yoom.	'I'm a little sick today.'
l-beeḍ ġaali hnaa.	'Eggs are expensive here.'
kull il-aθaaθ foog.	'All the furniture is upstairs.'
ʔabuuya bil-mustašfa.	'My father is in the hospital.'

The subject may also be expressed by a pronoun suffix attached to certain particle stems (9.1.2.2 E):

baʕadha ḍaʕiifa.	'She's still weak.'
yaareetni hnaak.	'I wish I were there.'

When the predicate is an interrogative it may precede the subject:

ween ij-jariida?	'Where's the newspaper?'
b-eeš har-raggiyya?	'How much is this watermelon?'

If the predicate is an active participle, the English equivalent may involve a present-tense form of to be plus an -ing form, or it may involve a verb phrase consisting of has or have plus a past participle:

ʔinta <u>raayiʒ</u> lil-ʒafla? — '<u>Are</u> you <u>going</u> to the party?'

ʔinta <u>qaari</u> l-maqall? — '<u>Have</u> you <u>read</u> the article?'

fadd waaʒid <u>maaxiδ</u> kull il-ġaraaδ̣. — 'Someone <u>has taken</u> all the things.'

11.1.2 Verbal sentences

A verbal sentence[1] is one in which the predicate is a finite verb form, with or without modifiers. The subject may be a noun or pronoun, with or without modifiers. Examples:

εali ṭilaε gabuḷ saaεa. — 'Ali went out an hour ago.'

kull il-εammaala raaʒaw lil-beet. — 'All the workers went home.'

ʔaani ma-aεruf šii εan il-mawδ̣uuε. — 'I don't know anything about the matter.'

l-ʒukuuma raʒ-itεayyin safiir jidiid. — 'The government is going to appoint a new ambassador.'

raasi da-yoojaεni. — 'My head hurts (me).' (i.e., I have a headache.)

The past-time equivalent of an equational sentence (11.1.1) is a verbal sentence, usually with some perfect-tense form of the verb *čaan* 'to be':

ʔabuu čaan ṭabiib. — 'His father was a doctor.'

The future-time equivalent of an equational sentence is a verbal sentence, usually with some imperfect-tense form of the verb *čaan* (imperfect *ykuun*) 'to be':

l-qaaṭ maalak ykuun ʒaaδ̣ir is-saaεa xamsa. — 'Your suit will be ready at five o'clock.'

The subject of a verbal sentence may be expressed by a pronoun suffix attached to a particle (9.1.2.2 E):

baεadha da-taakul. — 'She's still eating.'

The subject of a verbal sentence may be a personal pronoun reference expressed only by the inflectional form of the verb itself; it is then called an <u>included subject</u>. Most imperative sentences are of this type.

tʒibb gahwa? — 'Would you like coffee?'

ma-riʒit wiyyaa. — 'I didn't go with him.'

---

[1] The term "verbal sentence" has been used in grammars of Classical Arabic to mean "sentence beginning with a verb"; that is not its meaning in this book.

muṭrat ihwaaya.	'It rained a lot.'
jiib-li j-jariida.	'Bring me the newspaper.'

11.1.3 Topical sentences

A topical sentence consists of two major elements, a topic and a comment. The topic may be a noun or pronoun, with or without modifiers. The comment consists of an equational or a verbal sentence, and thus itself contains a subject and a predicate. Somewhere in the comment there is always a pronoun form (independent or suffix) which refers to the topic. In the following sentence, given here as a first example, the noun *ɛali* is the topic and the rest of the sentence is the comment:

ɛali šifta bil-gahwa.	'I saw Ali in the coffee-house.'

Within the comment, which here is a verbal sentence, the subject is a first-person singular pronoun reference 'I' expressed by the inflectional form of the verb (an included subject); the predicate is the whole sequence *šifta bil-gahwa*, with the verb form *šift-* as its nucleus. The object of the verb is the pronoun suffix *-a* 'him', which refers to the topic *ɛali*. The word-for-word translation of the sentence would be 'Ali I-saw-him in-the-coffee-shop.'

Topical sentences are extremely common in Iraqi, but there is no one particular equivalent construction in English. The difference between topical sentences and the other two types is primarily one of emphasis, or focus. When the pronoun referring to the topic is also the subject of the comment, and is thus an independent pronoun form, there is often an element of contrastive emphasis for which the usual English equivalent is extra-loud stress on a certain word or phrase. Some examples are given below. In these and subsequent examples, the topic and its pronoun reference in the comment are underlined; in the English translation the word or phrase corresponding to the topic is underlined. The parenthetical material given with the translations is intended to suggest contexts in which the sentences might be said.

l-mudiir huwwa l-mas?uul ihnaa.	'The director is the one in charge here.' (Not you)
?ummi hiyya triidni ?azzawwaj.	'My mother wants me to get married.' (I'm the one who doesn't want to)
l-ameerkaan humma ma-raadaw il-beet.	'The Americans didn't want the house.' (They are the ones who refused; it wasn't that the owner wouldn't rent it to them)

The pronoun reference in the comment may also be in the form of a pronoun suffix, attached to a verb, preposition, noun, or other form. In such sentences the element of contrastive emphasis mentioned above may be, but is not necessarily, present. The topic is the logical, rather than the grammatical, subject of the utterance: the speaker in effect announces in the topic that thing with respect to which the comment is interesting or significant. For example, in the sentence given at the beginning of this section, the point of interest is Ali and his whereabouts, and not so much the fact that it was the speaker ("I") who saw him. The context of this sentence might be: (You're asking about Ali?) 'I saw him in the coffee-house.' or 'Ali I saw in the coffee-house.' (but where his brother is I don't know.) The English equivalent may involve extra-loud stress or a word-order different from the usual one, but in the majority of cases the most natural English translation is the same as for an equational or verbal sentence and thus does not reflect the precise focus of the Iraqi topic. Examples:

l-εajuuza maʒʒad saεεadha b-šuġuḷha.	'No one helped the old lady in her work.'
bithum yirduun yzawwjuuha l-waaʒid zangiin.	'They want to marry their daughter to someone rich.'
wil-malaabis δ̣irabtiiha ʔuuti?	'And did you iron the clothes?'
ʔaani ma-yiεjibni j-jaww il-ʒaarr.	'I don't like hot weather.' (Literally: 'Hot weather does not please me.')
haaδa ma-agdar aštuġuḷ wiyyaa.	'I can't work with this guy.'
hal-ʒadiiqa taεbaaniin εaleeha hwaaya.	'They have cared for this garden very well.'
ʔinta š-biik?	'What's wrong with you?'
hal-fikra ma-biiha faayda.	'There's no advantage in this idea.'
hal-ġurfa ma-yinnaam biiha.	'One can't sleep in this room.'
l-banaat ma-εidhum ifluus.	'The girls haven't any money.'
w-abuuk šloona?	'And how's your father?'
l-ifluus ma-raʒ-tinṭiini-yyaaha?	'Aren't you going to give me the money?'
εali maat abuu w-rijaε il-baġdaad.	'Ali's father died and he went back to Baghdad.' (Literally: 'Ali his father died...')
ʔaxuuya nkisrat rijla w-dixal il-mustašfa.	'My brother broke his leg and went to the hospital.' (Literally: 'My brother his leg got broken...')

11.2 AGREEMENT

Adjectives, personal and demonstrative pronouns, and verbs have inflectional forms indicating distinctions of gender and number; in addition, adjectives may be definite or indefinite, and personal pronouns and verbs may be first, second, or third person. In a given context, the form of an adjective is determined by the noun or pronoun it modifies, that of a pronoun by its antecedent, and that of a verb by its subject. This relationship is agreement: an adjective is said to agree with what it modifies, a pronoun with its antecedent, and a verb with its subject. It should be noted, however, that the term "agreement" as used here does not mean that the agreeing form is necessarily of the same inflectional category as the determining form. (It is frequently the case, for example, that a masculine noun in the plural is modified by an adjective in its feminine singular form.) Rather, "agreement" designates a set of correlations in which not only the gender and number of the determining form but also several other factors play a role. These correlations are outlined below.

11.2.1 Adjectives

The forms of an adjective reflect two types of agreement, one of gender and number (see 11.2.1.2), and one - when the adjective is used attributively - of definiteness. The latter feature is discussed first below.

11.2.1.1 Definiteness

The term attributive is applied to an adjective when it occurs in a noun-adjective phrase (13.6). An attributive adjective follows (not necessarily immediately) the noun it modifies; if the noun is definite the adjective is also definite. A noun is definite when

(1) it has the article prefix:

l-beet 'the house'

(2) it has a pronoun suffix:

beetna 'our house'

(3) it is a proper name:

baġdaad 'Baghdad'

ɛali 'Ali'

(4) it is in an annexion (13.7) of which the last noun is definite by virtue of any of the three preceding features:

beet iṭ-ṭabiib 'the doctor's house'

beet axuuya 'my brother's house'

beet ɛali 'Ali's house'

An adjective is definite when it has the article prefix. Thus an attributive adjective has the article prefix when modifying a noun in any of the four categories above:

(1) *l-beet il-ɛatiig* 'the old house'

(2) *beetna l-ɛatiig* 'our old house'

(3) *baġdaad il-ɛatiiga* 'Old Baghdad' (the old section)

(4) *beet iṭ-ṭabiib il-ɛatiig* 'the doctor's old house'

beet axuuya l-ɛatiig 'my brother's old house'

beet ɛali l-ɛatiig 'Ali's old house'

Note that in the last examples the adjective does not immediately follow the noun it modifies: an adjective modifying a noun in an annexion normally follows the annexion as a whole. Occasionally there may be some ambiguity as to which noun is being modified (though not in the examples above, as the adjective *ɛatiig* is not applied to human beings).

A noun not in one of the four categories above is indefinite, and an attributive adjective modifying it is also indefinite; that is, it has no article prefix:

beet ɛatiig 'an old house'

beet dijaaj ɛatiig 'an old chicken coop'

When an adjective occurs in the predicate of a sentence (11.1) and refers to a noun or pronoun in the subject, it is called a predicate adjective. In this function the adjective has no article prefix, regardless of whether the noun to which it refers is definite or indefinite:

l-beet ɛatiig. 'The house is old.'

ɛali mariiḍ il-yoom. 'Ali is sick today.'

beetna čaan ɛatiig. 'Our house was old.'

However, an adjective functioning as a noun may have the article prefix, in which case the English translation is usually 'the ------ one', for example:

laa, ʔaani muu mariiḍ. ɛali l-mariiḍ. 'No, I'm not sick. Ali's the sick one.'

11.2.1.2 Gender and number

Whether attributive or predicate, an adjective agrees in gender and number with the noun or pronoun to which it refers, as follows:

A. If the noun is masculine singular (including collectives), the adjective is masculine singular:

beet ɛatiig 'an old house'

l-beet il-ɛatiig 'the old house'

ʔibni č-čibiir 'my old(est) son'

ʔaθaaθ jidiid 'new furniture'

tamur ɛiraaqi 'Iraqi dates'

In the case of collectives, however, the adjective in some contexts may be plural, as for example when the reference is to the individual items rather than to the collection as a whole:

hat-tiffaaζ iṣġaar.	'These apples are small.'

B. If the noun is feminine singular (including collectives), the adjective is feminine singular:

sayyaara ɛatiiga	'an old car'
s-sayyaara l-ɛatiiga	'the old car'
mudda ṭwiila	'a long time'
bnayya ṣġayyra	'a little girl'
ḅaaṃya ġaalya	'expensive okra'

In the case of collectives, the adjective is sometimes plural, as noted in A above.

C. If the noun is dual, the adjective may be masculine sound or broken plural, feminine sound plural, feminine singular, or dual. In general the form of the adjective depends on whether the noun refers to human beings or not, and to some extent on whether the adjective has a broken plural form or not; but there is some variation. The following statements reflect the most common usage.

(1) If the noun is masculine and refers to human beings, the adjective is masculine plural, sound or broken as the case may be (but see also (4) below):

muɛallimeen jiddad	'two new teachers'
ɛaamleen ʔaqwiyyaaʔ	'two strong workers'
waladeen zeeniin	'two good boys'
ṭayyaareen mumtaaziin	'two excellent pilots'

(2) If the noun is feminine and refers to human beings, the adjective is usually in the broken plural form if it has one (but see also (4) below):

bnayyteen iṣġaar	'two little girls'
muɛallimteen jiddad	'two new teachers F'
xiddaamteen inẓaaf	'two clean servants F'

If the adjective has no broken plural, and in some cases even if it does, the adjective is feminine sound plural:

bnayyteen ζilwaat	'two pretty girls'
raaqiṣteen mumtaazaat	'two excellent dancers F'

muɛallimteen laṭiifaat	'two nice teachers F'
bnayyteen ðakiyyaat	'two bright girls'

(3) If the noun is masculine or feminine, and does not refer to human beings, the adjective is usually in the broken plural form if it has one:

beeteen ɛittag	'two old houses'
ġurufteen ikbaar	'two big rooms'
ktaabeen zurug	'two blue books'
badilteen suud	'two black suits'

If the adjective has no broken plural, or as a less common alternative if it does, the adjective is feminine singular or feminine sound plural:

siččiinteen ḥaadda(at)	'two sharp knives'

(4) Dual forms of the adjective are less common. They occasionally occur attributively immediately following dual nouns, as alternatives to the forms shown above, and are usually restricted to adjectives which do not have broken plurals. Where they occur, dual adjectives are masculine after a masculine noun, feminine after a feminine noun.

jundiyyeen ɛiraaqiyyeen	'two Iraqi soldiers'
muɛallimteen ɛiraaqiyyteen	'two Iraqi teachers F'

D. If the noun is plural and refers to a group of human beings including at least one male, the adjective is masculine plural, sound or broken as the case may be:

suwwaaq mumtaaziin	'excellent drivers'
ṭullaab ʔaðkiyaaʔ	'bright students'
mumaθθiliin hazaliyyiin	'comic actors'
muwaẓẓafiin jiddad	'new employees'

E. If the noun is plural and refers to a group of human beings composed entirely of females, the adjective may be feminine sound plural:

banaat ðakiyyaat	'bright girls'
niswaan ɛiraaqiyyaat	'Iraqi women'
muɛallimaat zeenaat	'good teachers F'

However, some broken plural forms of adjectives (especially those of the patterns *FMaaL* and *FiMMaL/FuMMaL*) are also used with these nouns:

banaat iṣġaar	'little girls'
muεallimaat jiddad	'new teachers F'

In some cases the adjective may also be masculine sound plural or broken plural (any pattern) as the case may be. This kind of agreement is most commonly found when the adjective does not immediately follow the noun, as for example when it is used predicatively or refers to a noun mentioned in a previous utterance:

hal-banaat kulliš ʔaδkiyyaaʔ.	'These girls are very bright.'
w-muʔaddabiin hamm.	'And polite, too.'

When the adjective in question is an active participle functioning as a verb (12.1.3) it is always masculine sound plural. Thus the following question might be addressed to two or more males or two or more females:

leeš imbaddliin? ween raayḥiin?	'Why have you P changed (your clothes)? Where are you P going?'

F. If the noun is plural and does not refer to human beings, the adjective is in most cases feminine singular:

ʔašyaaʔ muhimma	'important things'
šiqaq imʔaθθiθa	'furnished apartments'
ġuraf naδ̣iifa	'clean rooms'
hawaayiš hooḷandiyya	'Dutch cows'
ʔaxbaarak ij-jidiida	'your new news'
l-imtiḥaanaat in-nihaaʔiyya	'the final examinations'

In some cases, however, the adjective may alternatively be broken plural, notably if it is a color with the singular pattern *ʔaFMaL* and plural *FuMuL*, *FuuL*, or *FiiL* (7.2.5), or if it has a broken plural of the patterns *FMaaL* or *FiMMaL/FuMMaL*:

booyinbaaġaat ḥumur	'red ties'
εyuun zurug	'blue eyes'
nafaaniif biiδ̣	'white dresses'
člaab suud	'black dogs'
ġuraf iṣġaar	'small rooms'
sayyaaraat jiddad	'new cars'
člaab ikbaar	'big dogs'

11.2.2 Pronouns and verbs

Pronouns and verbs show similar features of agreement and can be treated together.

11.2.2.1 First person

In first-person pronoun and verb forms there is no gender distinction; the forms are used by speakers of either sex:

ʔaani ma-ariid aruuʒ.	'I don't want to go.'
laazim abaddil ihduumi.	'I have to change my clothes.'
ʔiʒna raayʒiin lis-siinama.	'We're going to the movies.'
tigdar itruuʒ wiyyaana?	'Can you go with us?'

However, the forms of adjectives in the sentence may show gender distinctions:

ʔaani taʕbaan.	'I'm tired.' (man)
ʔaani taʕbaana.	'I'm tired.' (woman)

As to number, first-person singular forms are used by the speaker in referring to himself (or herself) alone; first-person plural forms, in referring to two or more persons including the speaker:

riʒit lis-siinama.	'I went to the movies.'
riʒna lis-siinama.	'We went to the movies.'
ʔaani w-axuuya riʒna lis-siinama.	'My brother and I went to the movies.'

Note that when *ʔaani* 'I' is part of a compound subject as in the last example, it precedes the other part, and the verb is first-person plural.

11.2.2.2 Second person

Second-person masculine singular pronoun and verb forms are used in addressing one male; feminine singular in addressing one female; plural in addressing two or more persons of either sex.[1]

The following sentences are addressed to one male:

ʔinta ma-triid taakul?	'Don't you M want to eat?'
haaδi sayyaartak?	'Is this your M car?'
jiib-li j-jariida.	'Bring M me the newspaper.'

[1] Some speakers use special feminine plural forms in addressing two or more females; see 9.1.

The following are addressed to one female:

ʔinti ma-tirdiin taakliin?	'Don't you F want to eat?'
haaδi sayyaartič?	'Is this your F car?'
jiibii-li j-jariida.	'Bring F me the newspaper.'

The following are addressed to two or more persons of either sex:

ʔintu ma-tirduun taaklun?	'Don't you P want to eat?'
haaδi sayyaaratkum?	'Is this your P car?'
jiibuu-li j-jariida.	'Bring P me the newspaper.'

Plural forms of pronouns and verbs are also used in addressing only one person, when the speaker means to include other persons not present, or as a mark of politeness (for example, in speaking to a stranger on the telephone, and in certain polite formulas):

ʔintu šwakt issafruun?	'When are you P leaving?' (i.e., you and your family)
ʔil-man tirduun?	'Whom do you wish?' (i.e., to speak to)
s-salaamu ʕalaykum.	'Peace be upon you.' (a greeting)

When a singular personal pronoun is part of a compound subject it precedes the other part, and the verb is plural:

ʔinta w-axuuk ween issuknuun?	'Where do you M and your brother live?'

11.2.2.3 Third person

Third-person agreement, including the agreement of a verb with its noun subject,[1] and of personal pronouns, demonstratives, and other forms which have gender distinctions with the noun to which they refer, is as follows:

A. If the noun is masculine singular (including collectives), the verb or pronoun is masculine singular:

ʔaxuuya raẓ-yooṣal baačir.	'My brother will arrive tomorrow.'
ṣaar-inna santeen ma-šifnaa.	'We haven't seen him for two years.'
saaʕa b-eeš yibtidi l-filim?	'What time does the movie begin?'

[1] If the subject of a verb is an expressed pronoun, the verb has the same gender-number inflection as the pronoun, whatever the ultimate noun antecedent of the latter may have been.

xal-da-nruuẓ inšuufa l-leela.	'Let's go see it M tonight.'
t-tiin ma-yinbaaɛ ihnaa.	'Figs aren't sold here.'
tẓibb it-tiin? ma-aẓibba hwaaya.	'Do you like figs? I don't like them very much.'

In the case of collectives, however, the verb or pronoun may also be plural. This kind of agreement occurs most commonly when the verb or pronoun does not follow the noun closely, or refers to a noun in a previous utterance, and when the collective might be viewed as a collection of entities, rather than as a species as in the last example above. Note the shift from singular to plural in the following exchange:

ɛali wugaɛ mnil-ṗaaysiḳil wil-beeẓ itkassar.	'Ali fell off the bicycle and the eggs got broken.'
laa, ma-tkassraw kullhum.	'No, they didn't all get broken.'

B. If the noun is feminine singular (including collectives), the verb or pronoun is feminine singular:

šloonha ʔumṃak? zeena. hiyya hamm siʔlat ɛaleek.	'How's your mother? Fine. She asked about you too.'
hal-beeẓa tbayyin muu zeena. ẓibbha.	'This egg seems bad. Throw it away.'
haṭ-ṭamaaṭa mneen ištireetha?	'These tomatoes - where did you buy them?'

In the case of collectives, the verb or pronoun may also be plural, as noted in A above.

C. If the noun is dual or plural and refers to human beings, the verb or pronoun is plural:

niẓtaaj muwaẓẓafeen yištaǧḷuun ib-šuɛbat iẓ-ẓaatiyya. ʔagdar astaɛiirhum min šuɛubtak?	'We need two employees to work in the personnel section. Can I borrow them from your section?'
jiiraanna j-jiddad raẓ-yijuun yzuuruuna l-leela.	'Our new neighbors are coming to visit us tonight.'
garaaybi kullhum yištaǧḷuun bil-ẓukuuma.	'My relatives all work in the government.'
l-muwaẓẓafiin raaẓaw ywaajhuun il-mudiir w-ma-qibal yšuufhum.	'The employees went to see the director and he refused (did not agree) to see them.'
xawaati kullhum izzawwjaw gabḷi.	'My sisters all married before me.'

D. If the noun is dual and does not refer to human beings, the verb or pronoun is usually plural:

ween xalleeti θ-θoobeen ij-jiddad l-ištireethum il-baarza? ma-ʕijbooni, ʔariid arajjiʕhum.	'Where did you F put the two new shirts I bought yesterday? I don't like them (they didn't please me) and I want to return them.'
haj-junutteen zaaδraat. zutthum bis-sayyaara.	'These two suitcases are ready. Put them in the car.'

However, feminine singular agreement also sometimes occurs:

ʕidna junutteen laakin raz-indizzha bil-qitaar.	'We have two suitcases but we're going to send them by train.'

E. If the noun is plural and does not refer to human beings, the verb or pronoun may be feminine singular:

člaab hal-mazalla kullha tʕaδδ, diir baalak minha mn-itfuut.	'The dogs in this neighborhood all bite; watch out for them when you go by.'
tilʕat nataayij l-imtizaanaat?	'Have the results of the examinations come out?'
ween xalleet ij-junat maalatna? xalleetha kullha bis-sirdaab.	'Where did you put our suitcases? I put them all in the basement.'

The verb or pronoun may also be plural, however. This type of agreement is particularly common when the subject or antecedent does not closely precede or follow, or when it refers to animals:

la-tzutt il-kutub ʕar-raff, yoogʕuun tara.	'Don't put the books on the shelf, they'll fall.'
zeen, ween axalliihum laʕad?	'Well, where shall I put (leave) them then?'
da-tšuuf hal-ičlaab? la-truuz yammhum tara yʕaδδuuk.	'See those dogs? Don't go near them or they'll bite you.'

11.3 NEGATION

The chief forms and processes of negation are as follows.

11.3.1 *laa* 'no, not'

This particle is the equivalent of English 'no', the opposite of *ʔii*, *bali*, or (more formal) *naʕam* 'yes'.

triid gahwa? laa, šukran.	'Want some coffee? No, thanks.'

As the final element in a few phrases, it may also correspond to English 'not', for example:

ma-adri íδaa raz-yiji lil-zafla loo laa.	'I don't know whether he's coming to the party or not.'

11.3.2 *la-* 'not'

This prefix is used with second-person imperfect *indicative* verb forms to make negative commands. Such constructions are the negative equivalents of second-person imperative forms. Examples of the latter are shown on the left below, with their negative equivalents on the right.

ruuz	'go M'	*la-truuz*	'don't go M'
ruuzi	'go F'	*la-truuziin*	'don't go F'
ruuzu	'go P'	*la-truuzuun*	'don't go P'
ʔiktib	'write M'	*la-tiktib*	'don't write M'
(ʔi)kitbi	'write F'	*la-tkitbiin*	'don't write F'
ʔukul	'eat M'	*la-taakul*	'don't eat M'
taɛaal	'come M'	*la-tiji*	'don't come M'

The prefix *la-* is also used with third-person imperfect indicative verb forms to make negative indirect commands, for example *gul-la la-yruuz gabuḷ-ma ašuufa.* 'Tell him not to go before I see him.' (See also 5.3.4.)

11.3.3 *ma-* 'not'

This particle is used to form the negative of verbs (except for negative commands; see 11.3.2 above), of active participles functioning as verbs (see 12.1.3), and of *ʔaku* 'there is/are'. In some contexts it may have the independent form *maa*, but occurs more commonly as a prefix *ma-*. (See also 5.3.4.)

ma-yxaalif.	'It doesn't matter.'
ma-agdar aji s-saaɛa xamsa.	'I can't come at five o'clock.'
haay safra ma-titfawwat.	'This is a trip that can't be passed up.'
ɛali ma-yizči wiyyaahum.	'Ali doesn't speak to them.'
ma-raz-itxaḷḷiṣ šuġḷak.	'You're not going to finish your work.'
ṣaar nuṣṣ saaɛa da-adawwir ɛalee w-ma-da-algii.	'I've been looking for it for half an hour and I can't (don't) find it.'
ma-rizna lis-suug il-yoom.	'We didn't go to the market today.'

ʔaani ma-baayit ihnaa gabuḷ.	'I haven't stayed (spent the night) here before.'
δoola baƐadhum kullši ma-msawwiin.	'Those people still haven't done anything.'
ma-aku ʒaaja txaabra.	'There's no need for you to phone him.'
ma-aku ʔaʒʒad yigdar yqanniƐhum yijuun wiyyaana?	'Isn't there someone who can persuade them to come with us?'

This particle is also used with several prepositions when pronoun suffixes are attached and when the meaning is 'there is/are not... in, there is/are not...for', and the like. These include *ʔil-* 'to, for' (see 9.1.2.2 B (1)), *bii-* 'in', *Ɛalee-* 'on, about', *Ɛan(n)-* 'about, concerning', *Ɛi(n)d-* 'in the possession of', and *min(n)-* 'from'.

hal-fikra ma-biiha faayda.	'There's no advantage in this plan.'
hal-iqmaaš ma-Ɛalee ṭalab ihwaaya.	'There isn't much demand for this cloth.'
ma-Ɛindi fluus.	'I haven't any money.'
ma-minna natiija.	'There won't be any result from it.'

The particle *ma-* is commonly used with adjectives of active and passive participle pattern and those of the pattern *FaMLaan*, and occasionally with some other forms, for example the particles *hwaaya* 'much, a lot' and *halgadd* 'so much, so'. With these, however, *muu* (see 11.3.4 below) is also used.

ʔibni l-iṣġayyir ma-mizzawwij.	'My youngest son isn't married.'
laazim ašuuf-li šiqqa ma-mʔaθθiθa.	'I have to find an unfurnished apartment.'
maƐa l-asaf, id-diktoor ma-mawjuud.	'Sorry, the doctor is not in.'
laa, ʔaani ma-taƐbaan.	'No, I'm not tired.'

11.3.4 *muu* 'not'

In general *muu* serves as the negating particle for all forms other than those mentioned in the preceding paragraph.

haaδa muu šuġḷi.	'That's not my affair.'
haaδa muu l-iktaab il-gitt-lak Ɛalee.	'This isn't the book I told you about.'
hal-quṣṣa muu ṣaʒiiʒa, la-ṣṣaddig biiha.	'This story is not true. Don't believe it.'

huwwa lli sawwaaha, muu ʔaani.	'He's the one that did it, not I.'
hal-maktuub muu ʔilak.	'This letter is not for you.'
nṭii fluus, bass muu ʔakθar min ƐašR-idnaaniir.	'Give him some money, but not more than ten dinars.'
ʔariidak issawwiiha l-yoom, muu baačir.	'I want you to do it today, not tomorrow.'
ʔaxuuya muu bil-beet, baƐda biš-šuġuḷ.	'My brother's not at home; he's still at work.'

Although *muu* is not used to negate verbs, it may sometimes occur immediately before a verb in sentences such as the one shown below, in which it serves to negate not the verb but a whole sentence.

ʔaani muu zzawwajit ḥatta aṣiir murḍiƐa maal ʔaṭfaal.	'I didn't get married in order to become a nursemaid for children.' (i.e., the reason I got married was not . . .)

In addition, *muu* is frequently used in exclamatory or rhetorical questions; in these too it sometimes precedes a verb.

laakin muu ʔaani taƐbaan!	'But I'm tired!'
muu l-ġada θallaj!	'Lunch has got cold!'
ðaak l-isbuuƐ muu riḥna tlaθ-marraat lis-siinama?	'Didn't we go to the movies three times last week?'
ʔaani muu gitt-lak la-truuḥ?	'I told you not to go, didn't I?'

11.3.5 *wala* 'and not, nor, or'

When two or more items in a series are negated, the second (and any subsequent one) may be negated by a preceding particle *wala* (sometimes also *wálaa*). The first item is negated by one of the negative forms described in the preceding paragraphs, as indicated below. The English equivalent of a construction involving one of these negatives followed by *wala* may be variously 'neither . . . nor', 'not either . . . or', 'not . . . and not', or 'not . . . or'.

If the first item is a form ordinarily negated by *la-* (11.3.2), it is here also negated by *la-*:

la-tinṭiihum fluus wala tiḥči wiyyaahum.	'Don't give them money or (and don't) talk with them.'
la-taakul wala tišrab il-yoomeen.	'Don't eat or drink for two days.'

If the first item is a form ordinarily negated by *ma-* (11.3.3), it may here be negated by *ma-*, but also occasionally by *la-*:

wuld ij-jiiraan ma-ydirsuun
(or *la-ydirsuun*) *wala yištaġluun.*

'The neighbors' children don't
study or work.'

ma-yitɛaamal (or *la-yitɛaamal*)
wala ybiiɛ bid-deen.

'He neither bargains (about prices)
nor sells on credit.'

*ma-yiẓči wiyyaaya wala ysallim
ɛalayya.*

'He doesn't talk with me or
greet me.'

If the first item is a form ordinarily negated by *muu* (11.3.4), it may here be negated by *muu*, but also commonly by *laa* or *la-*:

ɛali muu bil-beet (or *la-bil-beet*)
wala bil-ẓadiiqa. ma-adri weena.

'Ali's not in the house and not in
the garden. I don't know where
he is.'

haaδi muu madrasa (or *la-madrasa*)
*wala bang. haaδi daaʔira
ẓukuumiyya.*

'This is neither a school nor a
bank. This is a government
office.'

*laa ʔinta wala waaẓid ġeerak
yigdar yijburni asawwiiha.*

'Neither you nor anyone else can
force me to do it.'

If a form negated by *la-* or *ma-* is followed by two (or more) coordinate forms
(that is, both related in the same way to the preceding negated form, for example
two direct objects of a verb, or two verbs dependent on the same auxiliary), the
first of these may for greater emphasis (but need not) be preceded by *laa* or *la-*;
the second is preceded, as above, by *wala*:

ma-ariid laa fluus wala musaaɛada.

'I don't want either money
or help.'

ma-yuɛruf la-yiqra wala yiktib.

'He doesn't know how either to
read or write.'

ma-ɛinda laa ʔakil wala fluus.

'He has neither food nor money.'

After a form negated by *la-* or *ma-*, a single form may be preceded by *wala*.
The English equivalent of such a construction is generally 'not...a single', 'not
...even a' or the like, for example:

la-tinṭii wala filis

'Don't give him a single penny.'

ma-ẓiča wala čilma.

'He didn't say a (single) word.'

ma-sawweet wala šii l-yoom.

'I haven't done a (single) thing
today.'

ma-nijaẓ wala b-daris.

'He didn't pass (succeed in) even
one course.'

11.4 POST-STATED OBJECT

11.4.1 Object of verb

A noun or demonstrative pronoun serving as the object of a verb or active participle may follow it directly, as in English, for example:

fallšaw il-madrasa l-ε̄atiiga. 'They tore down the old school.'

There is,however, a very common alternative construction in which an appropriate pronoun suffix is attached to the verb, and the noun to which it refers follows thereafter, always preceded by the preposition prefix *l-* 'to' (in either its *l-* form or its doubled form, as the case may be; see 6.3.3 B), for example:

fallšooha lil-madrasa l-ε̄atiiga. 'They tore down the old school.'

In such a construction the pronoun suffix is the object; the noun with the preposition prefix *l-* is a post-stated object. The construction occurs only when the noun in question is definite; that is, when it has the article prefix (as above), or has a pronoun suffix, or is followed by a definite noun in annexion, or is a proper noun. With that restriction, the two kinds of constructions - verb followed by noun object, and verb plus pronoun suffix followed by post-stated object - can be used interchangeably in most contexts. The English translation is usually the same for both. Some additional examples:

čaan iṣdamta lil-ε̄amuud.	'I would have hit the pole.'
faṣṣáxa lir-raadyo.	'He took the radio apart.'
ʔaani šaayfa lil-matḥaf.	'I've seen the museum.'
š-šurṭa maššṭooha lil-wlaaya kullha.	'The police combed the whole city.'
bil-ε̄ajal iftihmatha lil-fikra.	'She immediately grasped the idea.'
ma-aḥibba l-haaδa.	'I don't like him.'
jibitha lid-dijaaja loo baε̄ad?	'Have you brought the chicken yet?'
da-yṣallḥuuha lil-madxana.	'They're repairing the chimney.'
ṭirdoohum lil-ε̄ummaal kullhum.	'They fired all the workers.'
šaggaghum lil-iθyaab.	'He wore out the shirts.'
xaabroo l-axuuya.	'They phoned my brother.'
raḥ-axaabra l-mudiir il-bang.	'I'm going to phone the director of the bank.'
laazim itxaabra s-saami.	'You have to phone Saami.'

Not only a noun or demonstrative pronoun, as in the examples above, but also a pronoun suffix may be a post-stated object, in which case it is attached to the preposition stem *ʔil-*. A pronoun suffix as a post-stated object implies a greater degree of emphasis than does a noun, and the usual English equivalent involves extra-loud stress on the corresponding pronoun. Compare *laazim ašuufa.*

'I have to see him' (simple statement of fact) with the post-stated object construction *laazim ašuufa ʔila.* 'I have to see *him*' (no one else will do). Other examples:

ʔaani aƐurfa ʔila.	'I know him.' (not the others)
raadooha ʔilha.	'They wanted her.' (not you)
dawwroohum ʔilhum hamm.	'They searched them too.' (as well as the others)
Ɛayynooni ʔili.	'They appointed me.' (not him)

The pronoun suffix as a post-stated object is also used when there is a compound object of which the first is a pronoun and the second a noun:

waqqfoo ʔila w-aṣdiqaaʔa.	'They arrested him and his friends.'

11.4.2 Object of preposition

In the case of a preposition and its object there are also two possible constructions parallel to those described above. The object may follow the preposition directly, as in English:

šgadd mistaƐmil imnid-duwa?	'How much have you used of the medicine?'

Or there may be a post-stated object construction, with a pronoun suffix attached to the preposition, and the noun to which it refers following thereafter, preceded by the preposition prefix *l-* :

šgadd mistaƐmil minna lid-duwa?	'How much have you used of the medicine?'

The latter construction, however, is not always substitutable for the former, and is somewhat less common than the cases described in 11.4.1. Additional examples:

ʔaani ma-aṣaddig biihum il-han-naas.	'I don't believe these people.'
š-ʒaaṭṭ bii j-jeebak?	'What have you got (put) in your pocket?'
leeš ma-salldmit Ɛalee ṣ-ṣadiiqak?	'Why didn't you greet your friend?'
š-maaxiδ minha l-ʔuxtak?	'What did you take from your sister?'
šgadd ddaaydnit minna l-axuuk?	'How much did you borrow from your brother?'
raʒ-aʒčii-lak wiyyaa lil-mudiir.	'I'm going to speak with the director for you.'
leeš ziƐdlit wiyyaa l-Ɛali?	'Why did you get mad at Ali?'

When the preposition in question is itself *l-*, as in *ṣoofárit lit-taksi* 'I whistled to the taxi', it becomes the suffix *-l-* attached to the preceding verb, as in *ṣoofarit-la lit-taksi* (here the prefix *l-* with *t-taksi* is the *l-* of the post-stated object). Other examples:

š-gal-la l-abuu?	'What did he say to his father?'
š-sawweet-ilha lis-sayyaara, ma-da-tištuğuḷ?	'What did you do to the car? It doesn't run.'
la-ṭabṭub-la lič-čalib.	'Don't pet the dog.'

11.5 COMPARISON OF ADJECTIVES

The Iraqi equivalent of an English comparative construction such as 'bigger than____' or 'more important than____' is a construction consisting of a comparative (7.1.4) followed by the preposition *min* and its object. If the Iraqi adjective is one which does not have a comparative form (see also 13.4.2), the construction consists of the simple adjective and one of the comparatives *ʔakθar* or *ʔazyad* (or *ʔázeed*) 'more' followed by *min* and its object. If a clause follows instead of a noun or pronoun object, 'than' is expressed by the conjunction *mim-ma* (10.1.3.2). Examples:

ɛali ʔaṭwal min abuu.	'Ali is taller than his father.'
dzawwaj ibnayya ʔakbar minna b-xams-isniin.	'He married a girl five years older than he.'
j-jaww il-yoom ʔabrad imnil-baarẓa.	'The weather today is cooler than yesterday.'
j-jaahil juuɛaan ʔázeed minnak.	'The child is hungrier than you.'
haš-šuğuḷ ʔaṣɛab mim-ma ẓanneet.	'This work is harder than I thought.'
jibit ʔázeed mim-ma niẓtaaj.	'You brought more than we need.'

The equivalent of an English construction such as 'the bigger/biggest' or 'the more/most important' — there is no distinction in Iraqi between 'the bigger' (of two) and 'the biggest' (of three or more), as in English — is a comparative with the article prefix or, more commonly, with a following form in annexion (see also 13.4.1). Examples:

ɛali l-ʔaṭwal.	'Ali is the tallest.'
yaahu ʔarxaṣ il-kull?	'Which is the cheapest (of all)?'
haaδi ʔakbar wlaaya bid-dinya.	'This is the biggest city in the world.'

12. VERB PHRASES

This chapter deals with verbs and verbal auxiliaries from the point of view of their meanings and functions in sentences. Included here are not only the finite perfect and imperfect verb forms described in Chapter 5, but also active participles (7.1.1), which often have a verb-like function, and a few similarly functioning particles. The first section below outlines the main uses of simple perfect, imperfect, and active participle forms; subsequent sections describe auxiliary-plus-verb combinations and other verb phrases.

12.1 USE OF TENSE AND ACTIVE PARTICIPLE FORMS

12.1.1 Perfect tense

Except in conditional sentences (15), the perfect tense refers in general to an action which took place in the past and was completed in the past. It generally corresponds to the English simple past tense, as in talked, didn't talk, or took, didn't take. Some examples:

kitab-la maktuub.	'He wrote him a letter.'
maatat gabuḷ santeen.	'She died two years ago.'
baddlaw ihduumhum.	'They changed their clothes.'
minu dagg il-baab?	'Who knocked on the door?'
siman ihwaaya b-baġdaad.	'He got very fat in Baghdad.'
ɛabbas min simaɛ il-xabar.	'He frowned when he heard the news.'
baat leelteen ib-beet axuu.	'He stayed two nights at his brother's house.'
ʔaxað ʔaẓsan daraja biṣ-ṣaff.	'He got the best grade in the class.'
l-filim bida gabḷ iš-šwayya.	'The film began a little while ago.'
šifta bis-suug il-baarẓa laakin ma-ẓčeet wiyyaa.	'I saw him at the market yesterday but I didn't talk with him.'

12.1.2 Imperfect tense

The simple imperfect tense (without the prefix *da-*) refers in general to an action which has not been completed, and thus particularly to a recurrent, habitual, or characteristic action, or to an action which is yet to take place. It sometimes corresponds to the English simple present tense, as in talks, doesn't talk, or eats, doesn't eat; and sometimes to a phrase involving shall or will, as in will eat, won't eat. Some examples:

tumṭur ihwaaya hnaa.	'It rains a lot here.'
yaakul kullši.	'He eats everything.'
ʔamši miil kull yoom.	'I walk a mile every day.'

tuɛurfa l-axuuya?	'Do you know my brother?'
haaδa ma-ydaayin ifluus il-aẓẓad.	'He doesn't lend money to anyone.'
raasi yoojaɛni minaqra.	'My head hurts me (i.e., I get a headache) when I read.'
baġdaad tiɛjibni hwaaya.	'Baghdad pleases me a lot.' (i.e., I like ...)
ʔiδaa tẓuṭṭa hnaa yoogaɛ.	'If you put it here it will fall.'
ʔarjaɛ ɛalee saaɛa xamsa.	'I'll come back to him (to see him) at five o'clock.'
ʔantaδrak jawwa.	'I'll wait for you downstairs.'
raẓ-aruuẓ lis-suug baɛad išwayya. ʔaštirii-lak šii?	'I'm going to go to the market after a while. Shall I buy something for you?'

The simple imperfect is also used in dependent clauses after certain conjunctions, for example *gabuḷ-ma* 'before' and *ẓatta* 'so that, in order (to)', regardless of the tense of the verb in the main clause. In such cases it is sometimes translated by an English past tense, an infinitive, or an -ing form. Examples:

ʔaani ẓaδδartak gabuḷ-ma truuẓ.	'I warned you before you went.'
ṭilaɛ mnil-beet gabuḷ-ma nugɛud imnin-noom.	'He left the house before we woke up.'
čaan yẓuurna ʔaẓyaanan baɛad-ma yiṭlaɛ imniš-šuġuḷ.	'He used to visit us occasionally after he left (after leaving) work.'
riẓna lil-maṭaar ẓatta nšuuf iṭ-ṭiyyaaraat.	'We went to the airport to see (so that we could see) the planes.'

The imperfect tense of the verb *čaan* 'to be' is a special case. It is used, not to describe a situation existing at the moment of speech (for this see equational sentences, 11.1.1), but to express a recurrent or habitual situation. Compare the two sentences below. The first, which is an equational sentence and has no verb, describes a situation existing at that moment. The second, a verbal sentence in which the verb is an imperfect form of *čaan*, describes a habitual situation; the speaker may or may not be at the office at that moment.

ʔaani bid-daaʔira.	'I'm at the office.'
ʔaani ʔakuun bid-daaʔira kull yoom mnis-saaɛa θmaanya lis-saaɛa tlaaθa.	'I'm at the office every day from eight to three.'

The imperfect tense of *čaan*, with or without the future prefix *raẓ-*, may also refer to a future situation:

ʔaani ʔakuun ihnaa baačir is-saaɛa xamsa.	'I'll be here tomorrow at five o'clock.'

With the prefix *da-*, the imperfect tense may refer to an action which is in progress at the moment; the English equivalent may then be a present-tense form

of to be plus an -ing form, such as is eating or are talking, or, in the case of those English verbs which in these constructions do not normally take -ing forms, it may be a simple present such as hurts or see. Examples:

da-tumṭur.	'It's raining.'
baᶓadha da-taakul.	'She's still eating.'
š-da-ssawwi?	'What are you doing?'
baṭni da-toojaᶓni.	'My stomach hurts.'
ʔiskut! ma-da-ššuuf ij-jaahil naayim?	'Be quiet! Don't you see the child is asleep?'

Such constructions may also refer to an action which, though not in progress at the moment, is recurrent or habitual. In some contexts, either an imperfect without *-da* or an imperfect with *da-* can be used in this sense without distinction; in others, the form with *da-* may imply that the action has recently become recurrent or habitual, or will be so only for a certain period of time. Here also the English equivalent is usually to be plus an -ing form.

da-tumṭur hwaaya has-sana.	'It's raining a lot this year.'
da-yuṣruf ihwaaya fluus ᶓala beeta j-jidiid.	'He's spending a lot of money on his new house.'
baᶓda da-yaaxuð idruus.	'He's still taking lessons.'

Certain verbs have both a punctual and a durative aspect, and their English translations may differ accordingly. For example, the verb *libas*, may mean either 'to put on' (punctual, a single act) or 'to wear' (durative, an action continuing over a period of time). Others are *šaal* 'to pick up' or 'to carry'; *rikab* 'to get on, board' or 'to ride'; and *wugaf* 'to stop, come to a halt' or 'to stand (still)'. In the case of such verbs *da-* plus the imperfect may have either the progressive or the habitual meaning, as above; if the former, the reference is generally to the punctual aspect and the English translation is to be plus an -ing form: *da-albas ihduumi* 'I'm putting on my clothes'; if the latter, the reference is generally to the durative aspect, and the English translation may be to be plus an -ing form or a simple present: *da-tilbas ihduum ġaalya* 'she wears (or is wearing) expensive clothes' (i.e., not necessarily at the moment, but 'lately', or 'these days').

For further examples of the imperfect, with *da-* and other prefixes, see 5.3. For imperatives and their negative equivalents, see 11.3.2.

12.1.3 Active participle

The active participle form frequently has a function in sentences like that of a verb. It may, for example, take a direct object (noun, pronoun, or pronoun suffix), or be negated by the prefix *ma-*; and it expresses a tense or time aspect contrasting with that of the perfect or imperfect. Even when functioning as a verb, however, its position in the sentence is that of a predicate adjective (and the sentence itself is an equational sentence; see 11.1.1); and it agrees with the noun or pronoun it modifies (the subject) as does any predicate adjective (11.2.1.2), with the restriction that its plural form is always the sound masculine plural with the ending *-iin* (i.e., never the sound feminine ending *-aat* or a broken plural).

In its verbal function, the active participle usually refers to a present situation which has come about as a result of some previous action, or, to put it another way, it refers to a past action of which the results are still apparent or of interest. It differs from the perfect tense in that the latter refers to a past action with no necessary implication as to its effect on the present situation. Compare the two sentences *ʔakálit* 'I ate.' and *ʔaani maakil.* 'I have eaten.' The first, which is perfect tense, makes a simple statement about a completed action in the past with no implication about the speaker's present condition. The second, which is an active participle, states both that the speaker has eaten and that his present state, as a result, is one of not yet being ready for the next meal. The active participle, however, need not refer to an action only recently completed, as in the example just given: it may also refer to an experience long past, as long as that experience still has relevance to the present. In this sense the active participle is frequently found in sentences involving the equivalents of such phrases as 'Have you ever (in your life) . . . ', 'I've never . . . ', 'I still haven't . . . ', and the like. In the examples below, the material in parentheses is intended to suggest ways in which the active participle might imply relevance to a present situation.

saamiε il-ʔaxbaar?	'Have you heard the news?' (Are you aware . . . ?)
šaayif ij-jaamiέa?	'Have you seen the university?' (Is it now part of your experience?)
minu šaayil il-ʔadawaat?	'Who took away the tools?' (They're gone.)
ʔaxuuk maaxiδ iktaabi.	'Your brother has taken my book.' (He has it.)
j-jaahil maakil kull ʔakla.	'The child has eaten all his food.' (His plate is clean.)
ween ʒaaṭṭ ir-raadyo?	'Where did you put the radio?' (Where is it?)
š-ṭaabxa lil-ġada?	'What have you F cooked for lunch?' (What's ready?)
ʔaani baεadni ma-qaari kullši.	'I haven't read anything yet.' (I'm unprepared.)
maʒʒad imʒaδ̣δ̣ir ʔay šii.	'No one has prepared anything.' (Nothing is ready.)
minu mʒayyin-lak šaεrak haš-šikil?	'Who cut your hair (for you) that way?' (It looks funny.)
mnaδ̣δ̣fa l-beet?	'Have you F cleaned the house?' (Is it now clean?)

δoola baʕadhum kullši ma-msawwiin lii hassa.	'They haven't done anything up to now.' (No results are to be seen.)
hal-ʕaa?ila mištağla b-haṣ-ṣanʕa ṣaar-ilha sniin.	'This family has worked at this trade for years.' (And still does.)

In the case of verbs with both a punctual and a durative aspect (12.1.2), the active participle may refer to past action, as above, for example *minu laabis ihduumi?* 'Who's been wearing my clothes?', but more commonly refers to action now in progress, for example *laabis qundara jdiida* 'I'm wearing new shoes.'. Note that this is only an extension of the active participle meaning described in the preceding paragraph: present-time situation resulting from past action. That is, I am now wearing (durative aspect) the shoes as a result of having put them on (punctual aspect). Other examples:

diir baalak minna, šaayil musaddas.	'Watch out for him; he's carrying a revolver.'
š-laazim b-iidak?	'What are you holding in your hand?'
s-sayyaara waagfa giddaam il-beet.	'The car is standing in front of the house.'
δoola kullhum gaaʕdiin bil-gahwa.	'They're all sitting in the coffee-house.'

In the case also of a few other verbs, generally those referring to change of location, such as going, coming, going in, out, up, down, or on a trip, the active participle may refer to action now in progress; in some instances it may also refer to future action. Examples:

ween raayiz?	'Where are you going?'
?inta jaay lil-zafla hal-leela?	'Are you coming to the party tonight?'
ma-msaafriin lil-xaarij has-sana.	'We're not travelling abroad this year.'

12.2 AUXILIARY *čaan*

Further tense distinctions in the Iraqi verb system are expressed by phrases consisting of a perfect or imperfect form of the verb *čaan* 'to be', here serving as an auxiliary, and one of the forms described in the preceding section. The various possible combinations are shown below.

12.2.1 Perfect of *čaan* with perfect of verb

Phrases in which both the auxiliary *čaan* and the main verb are in the perfect tense occur primarily in the result clause of conditional sentences (15.1), where they correspond to English phrases consisting of would have and a past participle, such as would have talked or would have given. In such phrases the auxiliary is invariably in the third-person masculine form *čaan*; the main verb agrees with the subject in the usual way (11.2.2.3). Two examples follow; for others see 15.1.

loo daarsa čaan ʔaxδat daraja zeena.	'If she had studied she would have got a good grade.'
loo gaayil-li kullši ma-čaan dazzeet il-maktuub.	'If you had told me everything I wouldn't have sent the letter.'

Such phrases may also occur in sentences with an implied, rather than a stated, condition:

leeš ma-gitt-li? čaan dazzeet-lak ifluus.	'Why didn't you tell me? I would have sent you some money.'
čaan δ̣aag il-ʔakil, bass maẓẓad ṭilab minna.	'He would have tasted the food, but no one asked him.'

By extension, these phrases may also indicate something which might have happened or almost happened, often in conjunction with an adverbial phrase such as *ʔilla šwayya* 'almost' or *baεad išwayya* 'in a moment, (was) about (to)':

čaan sadd iš-šaariε w-ma-xalla l-ẓaraami yinhizim bis-sayyaara.	'He could have blocked the street and not let the thief escape in the car.' (Why didn't he ... ?)
čaan wugεat ʔilla šwayya.	'She almost fell.'
baεad išwayya čaan šaal ʔawraaqa w-raaẓ.	'He was about to pick up his papers and go.'

12.2.2 Perfect of *čaan* with imperfect of verb

In phrases consisting of the perfect tense of the auxiliary *čaan* and a verb in the imperfect, both the auxiliary and the main verb agree with the subject (11.2.2.3). If the main verb has no prefix *da-*, these phrases usually refer to habitual or recurrent action in the past, and often correspond to English phrases such as used to go.

čaan yẓuṭṭ ihwaaya filfil bil-akil.	'He used to put a lot of pepper on the food.'
čaanat tirsim zeen.	'She used to draw well.'
čaanaw yaaxδuun ġaraaδ̣i.	'They used to take my things.'
ma-čaan ysidd iθ-θillaaja baεad-ma yṭalliε minha šii.	'He never would close the refrigerator after he took something out.'
čint adugg kamanja min čint iṣġayyir.	'I used to play the violin when I was small.'
čaan ydalġum kull-ma yšuufni ʔaṭlaε.	'He would scowl every time he saw me go out.'
čaanat itgaššir kull il-fawaakih gabuḷ-ma taakulha.	'She used to peel all the fruit before eating it.'

If the main verb has a prefix *da-*, the phrase usually refers to action in progress at some time in the past. The usual English equivalent is a past-tense form of <u>to be</u> plus an *-ing* form:

čaan da-yaakul min wuṣalna.	'He was eating when we arrived.'
čaanat da-tsidd iš-šibbaak min šaafat waaẓid bil-ẓadiiqa.	'She was closing the window when she saw someone in the garden.'
ṭ-ṭayyaariin čaanaw da-yɛalluun ẓatta yitfaaduun il-ɛaaṣifa.	'The pilots were going higher in order to avoid the storm.'
l-quuri wugaɛ min ʔiidi min činit da-aẓuṭṭa ɛan-naar.	'The pot fell from my hand when I was putting it on the fire.'
manaaẟra l-ɛatiiga čaanat da-tsabbib-la wujaɛ raas.	'His old glasses were causing him headaches.'

In the case of those verbs with both a punctual and a durative aspect (12.1.2), these phrases refer to action of the punctual type in progress at the moment in question:

činit da-albas qundarti min dagg it-talafoon.	'I was putting on my shoes when the phone rang.'
wugɛat min čaanat da-tirkab il-paaṣ.	'She fell when she was getting on the bus.'

12.2.3 Perfect of *čaan* with active participle

In a phrase consisting of the perfect tense of *čaan* and an active participle, the former agrees with the subject like a verb (11.2.2.3) and the latter like a (predicate) adjective (12.1.3). Such a phrase is the equivalent, for past time, of the active participle alone (12.1.3): it refers to a situation in the past which resulted from some previous action. English translations vary with the context; the usual ones are <u>had</u> with a past participle, and <u>had been</u> with an *-ing* form.

čaan raasim nuṣṣ ir-rasim.	'He had drawn half the drawing.'
ma-čaan ẟaayig il-mašruub gabuḷ leelat zawaaja.	'He had not tasted (strong) drink before the night of his wedding.'
čaan ẓaaṭṭ il-ifluus ib-jeeba.	'He had put the money in his pocket.'
čaan maakil min xaabarta.	'He had eaten when I phoned him.'
min wuṣálit lil-maṭbax čaanat mgaššra kullši.	'When I got to the kitchen she had peeled everything.'
čaanaw mqašmuriini mudda ṭwiila.	'They had been making fun of me for a long time.'
smaɛit čaanat daagga bsaamiir bil-ẓaayiṭ.	'I heard she had been driving nails into the wall.'

l-ɣafla čaanat baadya min wuṣalna.	'The party had begun when we arrived.'
ð-ðaahir haaða čaan mhaddidhum bil-qatil.	'It seems this man had threatened them with murder.'
minu čaan imfakkir haaða raɣ-yiṭlaᶜ haš-šikil?	'Who would have thought he was going to turn out this way?'
niqálit l-iɣčaaya miθil-ma činit saamiᶜha bið-ðabuṭ.	'I passed on the story exactly the way I had heard it.'
čaanaw ṭaabxiin ʔakil kulliš ihwaaya.	'They had cooked a great deal of food.'

In the case of verbs with both a punctual and a durative aspect (12.1.2), *čaan* with the active participle generally refers to action of the durative type in progress at some time in the past, and the English equivalent is generally was/were with an -ing form:

min šifnaa čaan šaayil musaddas.	'When we saw him he was carrying a revolver.'
čaanat laabsa qundaratha j-jidiida.	'She was wearing her new shoes.'

12.2.4 Perfect of *čaan* with particles

The auxiliary *čaan* occurs in phrases with *ʔaku* 'there is/are', and with several preposition-plus-pronoun-suffix combinations which have a similar meaning, e.g. 'there is/are ... in', 'there is/are ... in the possession of', and the like (see also 11.3.3). In such phrases the form *čaan* is invariable. The English equivalent is generally 'there was/were' or 'there used to be'; where the preposition *ᶜind-* is involved the English equivalent is usually 'had'. Examples:

čaan ʔaku hwaaya naas bil-ɣafla.	'There were a lot of people at the party.'
čaan ʔaku jisir hnaa laakin fallšoo.	'There used to be a bridge here but they tore it down.'
sayyaarti čaan biiha galin banziin.	'There was a gallon of gas in my car.'
min čint ib-baġdaad čaan ᶜindi ʔaṣdiqaaʔ ihwaaya.	'When I was in Baghdad I had a lot of friends.'

12.2.5 Imperfect of *čaan* with imperfect of verb

In phrases consisting of the imperfect tense of *čaan* and a verb in the imperfect with *da-*[1], both auxiliary and verb agree with the subject (11.2.2.3). These

---

[1] See 12.2.7 for *ykuun* with simple imperfect.

phrases have two general meanings, corresponding to the two meanings of the imperfect tense of the verb *čaan* itself (12.1.2). They may refer to action which is habitually in progress during each of certain recurrent periods of time, for example:

haaδa laazim ʔabu l-bariid. ma-yiji ʔilla min inkuun da-naakul.	'That must be the postman. He never comes except when we are eating.'

They may also refer to action which will be in progress at some future point of time, for example:

la-txaaburhum is-saaƐa sabƐa. ykuunuun da-yaakluun.	'Don't call them at seven. They'll be eating.'

12.2.6 Imperfect of *čaan* with active participle.

In phrases consisting of the imperfect of *čaan* and an active participle, the former agrees with the subject like a verb (11.2.2.3) and the latter like a (predicate) adjective (12.1.3). These phrases have two general meanings, corresponding to the two meanings of the imperfect tense of the verb *čaan* itself (see 12.1.2). They may refer to a recurrent situation in the present which results each time from some previous action, for example:

kull yoom min arjaƐ lil-beet marti tkuun ṭaabxa l-akil.	'Every day when I return home my wife has cooked the food.'

They may also refer to a situation in the future which will result from some previous action. The usual English equivalent here is will have plus a past participle. Examples:

min tooṣal lil-beet ʔakuun mxaḷḷiṣ kull šuġḷi.	'When you get home I will have finished all my work.'
ʔirjaƐ baƐad ṣaaƐa. nkuun mzaδδriin il-qaaṭ maalak.	'Come back in an hour. We will have prepared your suit.' (i.e., will have it ready)

12.2.7 The form *ykuun* as auxiliary

The imperfect third-person masculine form of *čaan*, that is *ykuun*, also occurs preceding the forms listed in 12.1 (and elsewhere as well), with meanings different from those described in the preceding two sections. The form *ykuun* is then usually[1] invariable, regardless of the person and gender of the subject. It may indicate that the following statement is hearsay; English equivalents are he (she) says that, I understand that, they tell me, it seems that, and the like. Examples:

[1] Occasionally *tkuun* is also used, if the subject is third-person feminine or second-person masculine.

ykuun raajƐa lil-baṣra.	'They say she's gone back to Basra.'
(leeš ma-štira s-sayyaara?) ykuun biiha Ɛeeb.	'(Why didn't he buy the car?) It seems there's something wrong with it.'

It may also indicate hope, sometimes a somewhat doubtful hope, on the part of the speaker. In this case there is usually an extra stress on the word *ykuun* which is not present in the first meaning above. The English equivalent is usually I hope (that). Examples:

ykúun itzaṣṣil il-waḍiifa.	'I hope she gets the job.'
ykúun ?aku ?azzad bil-beet min nooṣal.	'I hope there's someone at home when we arrive.'
ykúun Ɛidhum fraašaat kaafya.	'I hope they have enough beds.'

The negative *la-ykuun* followed by a second-person or third-person imperfect indicative form expresses a strong negative command:

la-ykuun tinsiin!	'Don't you F forget!' 'You'd better not forget!'
la-ykuun yizčuun wiyyaaha.	'They are not to talk to her.'

12.3 OTHER VERB PHRASES

Other common verb phrases consist of a string of two (sometimes three or more) verbs with the same subject. In such phrases the first verb may be in the perfect tense, the imperfect tense with or without *da-* (or other verbal prefixes), or the active participle form, and may be further modified by a form of the auxiliary *čaan*; while the second and any subsequent verbs are in the imperfect. The phrase as a whole takes its tense from the first verb. Both, or all, verb or active participle forms agree with the subject. These sequences often correspond to English phrases involving an auxiliary verb and an infinitive (with or without to) or an -ing form, such as can go, had to see, want to take, began to cry, and kept on eating. Among the verbs which commonly occur as the first verb in such strings are the following:

bida, btida 'to begin'

btidaw yištaġluun bil-maƐmal il-baarza.	'They began to work in the factory yesterday.'

buqa 'to go on, continue' (doing something) [1]

bqeena nisbaz lis-saaƐa xamsa.	'We went on swimming until five o'clock.'

[1] When not followed by another verb, *buqa* means 'to remain, stay'.

ʒaawal 'to try'

ʒaawal ybaddil fikri.	'He tried to change my mind.'
da-aʒaawil axaḷḷiṣ l-iktaab hal-leela.	'I'm trying to finish the book tonight.'

raad 'to want'

ma-raad yiji lil-ʒafla.	'He didn't want to come to the party.'
čaan raad yiji loo saamiƐ biiha ʔakil.	'He would have wanted to come if he had heard there was food.'
ʔaani ma-da-ariid aʒči wiyyaa.	'I don't want to talk with him.'

ḍall 'to go on, continue' (doing something)

šgadd raʒ-iḍḍalluun itfakkruun bii?	'How long are you P going to go on thinking about it?'

ḍṭarr 'to have to, be forced to'

ḍṭarreet addaayan ifluus imnil-ḅang.	'I had to borrow money from the bank.'

gaam 'to begin'[1]

min šaafáta gaamat tibči.	'When she saw him she began to cry.'
haaḍa min yxaḷḷiṣ šuġḷa yguum yiktib makaatiib.	'When he finishes his work he begins to write letters.'

gidar 'can, to be able'

ma-gidraw ydifƐuun il-iijaar.	'They couldn't (weren't able to) pay the rent.'
tigdar tiji tšuufna baačir?	'Can you come to see us tomorrow?'
loo bass gaadriin niʒči wiyyaa!	'If only we had been able to talk with him!'

The two verbs *raaʒ* 'to go' and *jaa* 'to come' (and some others) also may be followed in verb phrases by a verb in the imperfect tense. Such constructions indicate the purpose of the coming or going, but with no implication as to whether the purpose was achieved, for example:

---

1 When not followed by another verb, *gaam* means 'to get up, stand up'.

yirduun yijuun yšuufuuna baačir.	'They want to come to see us tomorrow.'
raaz yis?al il-mudiir.	'He went to ask the director.'

The verb *jaa*, followed by a verb in the imperfect, may also indicate intended action, usually not carried out, as in the English phrase was about to, for example:

jaa ygul-la laakin ?aani ma-xalleeta.	'He was about to tell him but I didn't let him.'

These verbs may also be followed in verb phrases by a verb in the perfect tense; this indicates the achievement of the purpose, for example:

jaa ziča wiyyaana.	'He came and talked with us.'

In each of the phrases illustrated thus far, all the verbs have the same subject. In another kind of verb phrase the first verb has an object (often a pronoun suffix), which becomes the subject of the following verb. Such constructions correspond exactly to English verb-object-infinitive constructions, for example:

?ariid Eali yiji wiyyaaya.	'I want Ali to come with me.'
?ariidak tšuuf-li fadd šii aguṣṣ bii l-ixyaar.	'I want you to find me something to cut the cucumbers with.'
leeš ma-txalliini ašuufha?	'Why won't you let me see her?'

12.4 AUXILIARY *laazim*

The word *laazim* 'necessary' may occur as part of a verb phrase; it is then invariable in form. A *laazim* phrase has two general meanings:

(1) Followed by a verb in the imperfect, it implies necessity or obligation, moral or otherwise. The usual English equivalents are have to, must, should, and ought to:

laazim insawwi kullši baEad-ma yiji.	'We have to do everything after he comes.'
b-xilaal šahar waazid laazim aqra Eašir-kutub.	'Within one month I have to read ten books.'
hal-iḍbaara kulliš muhimma w-laazim titsallam bil-yadd.	'This file is very important and must be delivered personally.'
haay laazim iṭṣiir ib-?aqrab furṣa mumkina.	'This must be done at the first possible opportunity.'
?íδaa baEadha mariiḍa ma-laazim itruuz lid-daa?ira.	'If she's still sick she shouldn't go to the office.'

haaδa ktaab laazim kull waaζid minkum yiqraa.	'This is a book that every one of you ought to read.'
laazim itruuζ itšuuf ʔaxuuk ʔawwal-ma tooṣal.	'You have to go see your brother as soon as you arrive.'

The auxiliary *čaan*, invariable in form, is used in forming the past-tense equivalents of phrases like those above. The negative *ma-* 'not' is usually prefixed to the auxiliary. The usual English equivalents are <u>should have</u> plus a past participle and, less commonly, <u>had to</u>[1]:

čaan laazim tiζjiz bil-uuteel gabuḷ-ma tiji.	'You should have made a reservation at the hotel before you came.'
čaan laazim itζaδδruun il-beet gabuḷ raas iš-šahar.	'You P should have got the house ready before the first of the month.'
čaan laazim itζaδδirni gabuḷ-ma aruuζ.	'You should have warned me before I went.'
ma-čaan laazim niṭlaʕ.	'We shouldn't have come out.'
minu čaan laazim yilzam xafaara l-baarζa bil-leel?	'Who was supposed to keep watch last night?'
riζna liʔann čaan laazim inruuζ.	'We went because we had to go.'

(2) Followed by a verb or verb phrase of any tense, *laazim* is equivalent to English <u>must</u> in the sense 'it can be assumed that' or 'the facts indicate that':

laazim da-yidrus kulliš ihwaaya hal-ayyaam.	'He must be studying a very great deal these days.'
laazim čaan imζaawil min zimaan.	'He must have been trying for a long time.'
laazim qibal biš-šuruuṭ.	'He must have accepted the terms.'
laazim naayim.	'He must be sleeping.'
laazim čaan naayim min dagg it-talafoon.	'He must have been sleeping when the telephone rang.'

[1] The perfect of *δtarr* 'to have to, be forced to', is used with a following imperfect verb in the sense <u>had to</u>. See 12.3 above.

13. NOUN, PRONOUN, AND ADJECTIVE PHRASES

A noun, pronoun, or adjective phrase is a phrase consisting of a noun, a pronoun, or an adjective, and one or more modifiers. This chapter deals with the major categories of words or constructions which function as modifiers in such phrases, the ways in which these modifiers are used, and the kinds of phrases which result.

13.1 NUMERALS AS MODIFIERS

A cardinal numeral or numeral phrase (8.1) may modify a noun.[1] A phrase consisting of a noun modified by a preceding numeral is a numeral-noun phrase, for example:

ʔarbaƐ-makaayin	'four motors'
xams-isniin	'five years'
ʔarbaƐ w-Ɛišriin saaƐa	'twenty-four hours'
tlaθ-miyya w-xamsa w-sittiin yoom	'three hundred and sixty-five days'
ʔalif diinaar	'a thousand dinars'

Numeral-noun phrases are closely-knit constructions. With rare exceptions, no form other than another numeral occurs between the numeral and the noun; noun prefixes (6.3) such as the article prefix and the demonstrative prefix apply to the phrase as a whole and are attached to the first word rather than to the noun; and the phrase as a whole may be preceded by certain words which in other types of phrases normally precede the noun directly, such as the (independent) demonstrative, a comparative, or *fadd* 'a, some'. Examples:

l-xams-isniin	'the five years'
hal-xams-isniin	'these five years'
haaδi l-xams-isniin	'these five years'
ʔaʒsan xams-isniin	'the best five years'
fadd xams-isniin	'some five years, about five years'

In certain cases a noun is modified by a following numeral; such phrases are in several respects like noun-adjective phrases (13.6). The numeral *waaʒid* 'one', which is an adjective, follows the noun it modifies and agrees with it in gender; the numeral *θneen* 'two' may do so (see 8.1). Numerals between three and ten (rarely those higher) may follow the noun they modify if it is definite. A following numeral, like an adjective, agrees in definiteness with the noun it modifies; that is, if the noun is definite, the numeral has the article prefix. A following

---

[1]A numeral from eleven up may also modify the pronoun *waaʒid* 'one': *Ɛišriin waaʒid* 'twenty (of a certain thing), twenty people'.

numeral between <u>three</u> and <u>ten</u> has its independent form; these and higher numerals do not vary with the gender of the noun. Examples:

banaat θinteen	'two girls'
hal-banaat iθ-θinteen	'these two girls'
l-kutub il-arbaƐa	'the four books'
wulda s-sitta	'his six sons'

13.2 DEMONSTRATIVES AS MODIFIERS

A noun may be modified by one of the demonstrative pronoun forms listed in 9.2; this combination constitutes a <u>demonstrative phrase</u>, for example *haaδa l-beet* 'this house'. The demonstrative forms most frequently used as modifiers are the following:

M	*haaδa*	'this M'
F	*haaδi, haay*	'this F'
P	*δool*	'these'
M	*δaak*	'that M'
F	*δiič*	'that F'
P	*δoolaak*	'those'

A phrase consisting of a noun preceded by one of the demonstratives in the first set above (or one of their variants shown in 9.2) is generally equivalent in meaning to the same noun with the demonstrative prefix (6.3.2), for example *haaδa l-beet* or *hal-beet* 'this house'. Either of these two types of constructions may, depending on the context, correspond to English <u>that</u> or <u>those</u> with a noun as well as to <u>this</u> or <u>these</u>; whereas a phrase consisting of a noun preceded by one of the demonstratives in the second set usually corresponds to <u>that</u> or <u>those</u>. (See 9.2 for general comments on the range of meaning of the two sets of demonstratives.)

The demonstrative agrees in gender and number with the noun it modifies, as described in 11.2.2.3. The demonstrative more commonly precedes, but may also follow the noun; the noun is always definite. When the demonstrative precedes, the noun bears the article prefix. In such phrases, no form except a numeral (13.1) or the particle *xooš* 'good' (13.3.3) normally comes between the demonstrative and the noun. Some examples:

haaδa l-walad	'this boy'
haaδa š-šaariƐ	'this street'
haaδa t-tiffaaz	'these apples'
haaδi l-mara / *haay il-mara*	'this woman'

haaδi l-muškila *haay il-muškila* }	'this problem'
haaδi l-ġuraf *haay il-ġuraf* }	'these rooms'
δool iṭ-ṭullaab	'these students'
δool in-niswaan	'these women'
δool in-naas	'these people'
δaak ir-rijjaal	'that man'
δaak il-beet	'that house'
δiiĉ il-muġanniya	'that singer'
δiiĉ il-qaḍiyya	'that matter'
δiiĉ il-manaaṭiq	'those regions'
δoolaak ir-riyaajiil	'those men'

In some contexts the demonstratives of the second set have a specialized meaning 'the other, the previous', particularly with a few nouns referring to periods of time:

δaak iš-šaariƐ	'the other street' (the one we were on before)
δaak il-yoom	'the other day' (a few days ago)
δaak il-isbuuƐ	'last week; a week or two ago'
δaak iš-šahar	'last month; a month or two ago'
δiiĉ is-sana	'last year; a year or two ago'

The demonstrative may also follow the noun it modifies, in which case the noun may have the article prefix or a pronoun suffix, or be followed by a definite noun in an annexion:

θ-θoob haaδa	'this shirt'
s-sayyaara haay	'this car'
qaaṭi haaδa	'this suit of mine'
saaƐt il-iid haay	'this wrist-watch'

When the demonstrative follows, other forms may occur between the noun and the demonstrative, such as a following noun in an annexion, as in the last example above, or a modifying adjective, for example:

l-ġurfa l-iṣġayyra haay 'this little room'

Occasionally the noun may have the demonstrative prefix and also be followed by a demonstrative:

has-sayyaara l-Ɛatiiga haay 'this old car, this old car here'

13.3 PARTICLES AS MODIFIERS

A few particles may serve as the modifiers of nouns, certain pronouns, adjectives, and other particles. (Some of them may have other functions as well; see 10.1.) Although the particles which function in this way are relatively few in number, they are frequently used, and phrases containing them are common. The major ones are shown below. [1] Except where otherwise noted, the particle precedes the word it modifies.

13.3.1 Particle *ʔay* (1) 'any' (2) 'which?, what?'

In the meaning 'any', this particle is followed by a singular noun, a numeral-noun phrase, or the pronoun *waaẓid* 'one, someone'; in the meaning 'which?, what?' it may also be followed by a plural noun; in either meaning the particle *yaa* (13.3.15) may be used, and in the second meaning more commonly is used, instead.

(tigdar taaxuδ) ʔay ktaab (itriida.)	'(You can take) any book (you want.)'
(Ɛayyin) ʔay tlaθ-mawaaḏiiƐ (b-hal-iktaab.)	'(Assign) any three subjects (in this book.)'
(ma-raẓ agul-la) ʔay šii.	'(I'm not going to tell him) anything.'
ʔay waaẓid (yigdar ysawwiiha.)	'Anyone (can do it.)'
ʔay ktaab?	'which book?'
ʔay mawaaḏiiƐ?	'what subjects?'
ʔay waaẓid?	'which one?'

13.3.2 Particle *baƐaḏ* 'some'

This particle modifies a noun, usually a collective or a plural. The noun may be indefinite, in which case the English equivalent is <u>some</u>; more commonly it is definite, in which case the English equivalent is <u>some</u> or <u>some of the</u>, depending on the context.

---

[1] The forms *baƐaḏ, ġeer, kull,* and *nafis* are included here as particles, but in some contexts they function differently from the others.

baʕaḍ ašyaaʔ	'some things'
baʕḍ il-ašyaaʔ	'some things, some of the things'
baʕḍ il-azyaan	'sometimes'
baʕḍ il-banaat	'some girls, some of the girls'
baʕḍ iš-šuğuḷ	'some of the work'

13.3.3 Particle *xooš* 'good, fine, nice'

This particle is a noun-modifier. The noun may be of any number or gender; the particle itself is invariable in form. A phrase consisting of *xooš* and a noun is a very closely-knit construction: no form occurs between these two; and forms which elsewhere precede a noun immediately, such as the article and demonstrative prefixes, and numerals, here precede the phrase as a whole.

xooš walad	'good boy, fine man, nice guy'
xooš ṭabiib	'good doctor'
xooš beet	'nice house'
xooš ibnayya	'good girl, nice girl'
xooš fikra	'good idea'
xooš suwwaaq	'good drivers'
xooš naas	'nice people'
xooš wulid	'nice boys'
hal-xooš wulid	'these nice boys'
tlaθ-xooš wulid	'three nice boys'

13.3.4 Particle *šloon* (1) 'what kind of?' (2) 'what (a), how!'

This particle may modify a singular or plural noun or the pronoun *waazid* 'one'. In the exclamatory meaning it often modifies a noun followed by an adjective, and may also modify an adjective alone.

šloon meez?	'what kind of table?'
šloon waraq?	'what kind of paper?'
šloon baraamij?	'what kind of programs?'
šloon waazid?	'what kind of one, what kind?'

šloon ibnayya zilwa. — 'What a pretty girl!'

šloon zilwa. — 'What a pretty one F!' or 'How pretty F!'

13.3.5 Particle *šwayya* 'a little'

This particle refers not to size but to quantity or degree. It may modify a noun, a comparative, or an adjective. When modifying a noun, *šwayya* generally precedes, and may occur either in that form or in an annexing form *šwayyat*. When modifying a comparative it generally precedes. When modifying an adjective it may precede or follow.

šwayya(t) gahwa — 'a little coffee'

šwayya(t) fluus — 'a little money'

šwayya ʔazsan — 'a little better'

šwayya mariiṣ — 'a little sick'

taɛbaan išwayya — 'a little tired'

13.3.6 Particle *šgadd* (1) 'how much, how many?' (2) 'what a lot of, how!'

In the interrogative meaning this particle usually modifies a noun. It refers not to the number of individual units but to bulk quantity.

šgadd ifluus? — 'how much money?'

šgadd maay? — 'how much water?'

šgadd tiin? — 'how many figs?'[1]

In the exclamatory meaning it may modify a noun or an adjective.

šgadd naas. — 'What a lot of people!'

šgadd zilwa. — 'How pretty F!'

13.3.7 Particle *ġeer*

(1) '(an)other, different'
(2) 'someone other than, something other than'
(3) 'what (a)!, really (a)'
(4) 'not, non-'

In the first meaning above, this particle may modify a noun or a pronoun. When the noun or pronoun is indefinite, the English equivalent is usually as illustrated below.

---

[1] That is, 'what quantity of figs?'. In asking about the number of individual figs, the question would be *čam tiina?* (13.3.16).

ġeer maṭƐam	'another (a different) restaurant'
ġeer ġurfa	'another (a different) room'
ġeer madaaris	'other schools'
ġeer šii	'another thing, something else'
ġeer yoom	'another day, some other day'
ġeer mukaan	'another place, somewhere else'
ġeer waaẓid / *ġeer aẓẓad* }	'someone else'

The English equivalent may also be a pronoun phrase such as those shown in (2) above, or, with a negative, '(not) . . . anyone/anything other than' or 'no one/ nothing other than'. The noun is usually definite.

ʔagdar aruuẓ ib-ġeer il-qiṭaar?	'Can I go on something other than the train?'
ma-Ɛidkum ġeer is-simač?	'Haven't you got anything besides fish?'
ġeer il-aṭibbaaʔ ma-yfiiduuk.	'No one but doctors can do you any good.'
ma-ariid ġeer Ɛali b-hal-waḍiifa.	'I don't want anyone but Ali in this job.'

The particle *ġeer* may be used to modify a noun or an adjective in an exclamatory or intensifying sense. English equivalents vary; the following examples will illustrate.

haaδa ġeer maṭƐam.	'What a restaurant that is!' (i.e., superb or terrible, depending on tone or gesture)
haaδa ġeer čaδδaab.	'What a liar he is.' 'He's really a liar.'
haj-jaahil ġeer muškila.	'This child's a real problem.'
Ɛinda ġeer afkaar.	'He has some strange ideas.'
δiič l-ibnayya ġeer ẓilwa.	'That girl's really pretty.'
kitab fadd maqaal ġeer laṭiif.	'He wrote a really fine article.'

Finally, *ġeer* before a noun or an adjective may correspond to English not or non-, but in this meaning it is less common, occurring mostly in a few set phrases or official terminology.

ġeer qaanuuni	'not legal, illegal'
ġeer maqbuul	'not accepted'
ʕiraaqiyyiin w-ġeer ʕiraaqiyyiin	'Iraqis and non-Iraqis'

13.3.8 Particle *fadd*

(1) 'a, an'
(2) 'some'
(3) 'one, the same'

Phrases consisting of the particle *fadd* and a noun are extremely common. In most contexts, *fadd* corresponds in meaning to the English indefinite article a or an. However, it may also correspond to other English words, such as some, one, or the same; and a few specific combinations involving *fadd* have other translations as well. The illustrative sentences below are grouped according to the English translation.

A. Corresponding to English 'a/an'.

ʕindak fadd qalam zaayid?	'Have you got an extra pencil?'
tigdar tiji yammi fadd daqiiqa?	'Can you come here a minute?'
haaða čaan fadd suʔaal baṣiiṭ.	'That was an easy question.'
čaan ʔaku fadd ħiss bis-sayyaara.	'There was a noise in the car.'
xal-da-rruuħ nišrab-inna fadd peek.	'Let's go have a drink.'
hal-laħam bii fadd ṭaʕam kulliš ġariib.	'This meat has a very strange taste.'
haay čaanat fadd fikra mumtaaza.	'That was an excellent idea.'
šifna fadd ibnayya kulliš ħilwa.	'We saw a very pretty girl.'
ṣadiiqi ʕali fadd ṭabiib ma-aku miθla.	'My friend Ali is a doctor without equal.'

B. Corresponding to English 'some'. There are three uses of this English word to which *fadd* may correspond. When a plural noun follows, it corresponds to some in its function as the plural of the indefinite article.

siʔal fadd ʔasʔila kulliš ṣaʕba.	'He asked some very hard questions.'
jaabaw fadd muʕallimiin kullši ma-yiftahmuun.	'They brought in some teachers who don't know anything.'

nṭaani fadd asbaab saxiifa.	'He gave me some silly reasons.'
ʔaku Ɛindak fadd kutub zeena ʔaqra biiha bil-Ɛuṭḷa?	'Have you got some good books I can read in the vacation?'

When a singular noun follows, *fadd* may correspond to some in the sense 'some ... (or other)' or '(any) one ... (of a number)'. In this sense some is close to the meaning of the indefinite article a/an, and in many contexts either of the English forms may serve as the translation of *fadd*.

kull-ma aṭḷub minna ysaaƐidni yṭalliƐ-la fadd ʒijja.	'Every time I ask him to help me he brings out some excuse.'
ma-yṣiir haš-šikil. laazim tilgii-lak fadd ʒall.	'It won't do (can't go on) this way. You'll have to find some solution.'
ʔawwal-ma yṣiir iṣ-ṣeef laazim irruuʒ il-fadd maṣiif.	'As soon as it gets to be summer we have to go to some summer resort.'

When a numeral follows, *fadd* may correspond to some in the sense 'about, approximately'.

fadd Ɛašir-daqaayiq	'some ten minutes, about ten minutes'
fadd xamsiin diinaar	'some fifty dinars, about fifty dinars'

C. Corresponding to English 'one' or 'the same'. In this case the word *fadd* generally has slightly louder stress than the following noun. The noun is singular.

b-xilaal fadd šahar nizal muṭar ʔazeed imnis-sana kullha.	'During one month more rain fell than (during) the whole year.
qreet l-iktaab mnil-bidaaya lin-nihaaya b-fadd yoom.	'I read the book from beginning to end in one day.'
šloon dabbárit itxaššiš kull il-ašyaaʔ b-fadd ġurfa?	'How did you manage to get all the things in one room?'
rummaanteen ib-fadd ʔiid ma-tinlizim.	'Two pomegranates can't be held in one hand.' (Proverb: You can't do two things at once.)
š-aku fariq? l-ġuraf kullha fadd šikil.	'What's the difference? The rooms are all the same (kind).'
l-ʒaala hassa w-gabuḷ fadd šii tamaaman.	'The situation now and before is exactly the same (thing).'

D. Other translations. Several common combinations of *fadd* with certain nouns and a few other forms have various English equivalents. Some examples:

fadd šii	'something, anything'
jiib-li fadd šii ʔaktib ɛalee.	'Bring me something to write on.'
ma-ɛindak fadd šii ʔazsan min haaδa?	'Haven't you got something better than this?'
l-kutub ij-jidiida ɛan hal-mawδuuɛ ma-biiha fadd šii yiswa.	'The new books on this subject don't have anything worthwhile in them.'
fadd marra	'once, one time' (i.e., on a certain occasion in the past)
fadd marra sʔalta ɛan waδiifta w-gal-li raz-yinniqil.	'Once I asked him about his job and he said he was going to be transferred.'
fadd mukaan	'somewhere, some place'
kull-ma nriid nruuz l-fadd mukaan tguum tumṭur.	'Every time we want to go somewhere it begins to rain.'
fadd yoom	'one day, sometime'
fadd yoom raz-awaddiik wiyyaaya lis-sibiz.	'One day I'll take you swimming with me.'
fadd ʔazzad } *fadd waazid* }	'someone, anyone' (only *waazid* is used when the reference is to some specific person; otherwise the two are generally interchangeable.)
leeš ma-tšuuf-lak fadd ʔazzad (waazid) yɛallmak siyaaqa?	'Why don't you find yourself someone to teach you to drive?'
gabuḷ-ma ṭiṭbaɛ il-baziθ maalak xalli fadd ʔazzad (waazid) ydaqqiq-lak-iyyaa min naazyat il-luġa.	'Before you type your paper let someone polish it up for you from the point of view of language.'
ʔaku fadd ʔazzad (waazid) ihnaa yuɛruf ydugg ɛuud?	'Is there anyone here who knows how to play the *ɛuud?*' (a lute-like instrument)
fadd waazid xaabar gabuḷ išwayya w-siʔal ɛaleek.	'Someone called a little while ago and asked for you.'
ʔaɛruf fadd waazid yigdar yɛallmak ʔingiliizi.	'I know someone who can teach you English.'

fadd čam	'a few, several' (Here, as elsewhere, *čam* is followed by a *singular* noun.)
kull-ma čaan ʔaku hnaak fadd čam iskamli w-fadd zuuliyya ɛatiiga.	'All that was there were a few chairs and an old rug.'
fadd išwayya	'a little, a little bit'
baḷḷa ma-tiḥčii-li fadd išwayya ɛan il-mawḍuuɛ?	'Would you mind telling me a little bit about the subject?'

13.3.9 Particle *kull*

(1) 'each, every'
(2) '(the) whole, all'
(3) '(not) a, (not) any'

This particle may modify nouns and certain pronouns. Followed by a singular indefinite form, it corresponds to English each or every.

kull muwaḍḍaf	'every employee'
kull yoom	'every day'
kull marra	'each time'
kull waaḥid	'each one, everyone'

Followed by a definite form, it corresponds to (the) whole, all (the), or all of (the).

kull il-beet	'the whole house'
kull il-wlaaya	'the whole city'
kull baġdaad	'all Baghdad'
kull haaḏa	'all this'
kull il-muwaḍḍafiin	'all the employees'
kull in-naas	'all the people'
kull il-kutub	'all the books'
kull il-beeḍ	'all the eggs'

In another kind of construction, with similar English equivalents, *kull* follows the definite form and bears a pronoun suffix referring to it.

l-beet kulla	'the whole house'
l-wlaaya kullha	'the whole city'
l-muwaḍḍafiin kullhum	'all the employees'

The combination of a negative and a phrase beginning with *kull* may correspond to English not a, not any, no, or none of.

kull filis ma-ʕindi.	'I haven't got a fils.' (i.e., not even a penny)
kull maaniʕ ma-aku.	'There isn't any objection.'
kull muqaawama ma-bayyan.	'He showed no resistance.'
kull aζζad ma-xaabar.	'No one called.'
ma-aku kull ζubb beenaathum.	'There's no love between them.'
ma-aʕruf kull nukta.	'I don't know any joke(s).'
kull il-muwaδδafiin ma-da-yištaġluun.	'None of the employees are working.'
kull ihduumi ma-tinlibis.	'None of my clothes can be worn.'

13.3.10 Particle *kulliš* 'very'

This particle may modify an adjective, either preceding or following it, or one of the other particles *xooš* 'good' and *hwaaya* 'much', usually preceding these. When modifying the adjective in a noun-adjective phrase, *kulliš* may precede an adjective without the article prefix, but usually follows one with it.

ζaarra kulliš / *kulliš ζaarra*	'very hot'
kulliš zeen	'very good'
filim kulliš zeen	'a very good film'
kulliš ṭuwiil	'very long'
mudda kulliš ṭuwiila	'a very long time'
kulliš muhimm	'very important'
l-ʔašyaaʔ il-muhimma kulliš	'the very important things'
kulliš xooš šaġḷa	'a very good job'
kulliš xooš ζalawiyyaat	'very good sweets' (dessert)
šuġuḷ kulliš ihwaaya	'a very great deal of work'
mašġuuḷ kulliš ihwaaya	'very, very busy'

13.3.11 Particle *nafis* 'same'

This particle may modify a definite noun. It corresponds most commonly to English (the) same.

nafs il-yoom	'the same day'
nafs is-sana	'the same year'
nafs il-mašaakil	'the same problems'
nafis nooɛ il-gahwa	'the same kind of coffee'

It may also correspond to English (the) very, (the) . . . -self, then usually following the noun and bearing a pronoun suffix referring to the noun.

l-mudiir nafsa	'the director himself'
ʔummak nafisha	'your mother herself'
l-wuzaraaʔ nafishum[1]	'the ministers themselves'

13.3.12 Particle *halgadd* (1) 'so much, so many' (2) 'so, such (a)'

This particle may modify a noun or an adjective. In the first case it refers to numbers or quantity, and corresponds to English so much or so many. In the second case it refers to degree, and corresponds to so or, when modifying the adjective in a noun-adjective phrase, to such (a).

halgadd sayyaaraat	'so many cars'
halgadd ifluus	'so much money'
halgadd muhimm	'so important'
waḍiifa halgadd muhimma	'such an important position'

13.3.13 Particle *hiič(i)* (1) 'this/that kind of (a), such (a)' (2) 'so, such (a)'

This particle may modify a noun, the pronoun *waaḥid,* or an adjective. In the first two cases it corresponds to the first meaning shown above; in the third case, to the second meaning. The forms *hiič* and *hiiči* both occur, the latter more commonly.

hiiči šaxiṣ	'such a person, a person like that'
hiiči ḥači	'such talk, that kind of talk'
hiiči furṣa	'such an opportunity'
hiiči šii	'such a thing, a thing like that'

[1] The form *nafis* may also function as an independent noun meaning 'soul', plural *ʔanfus*. When following a plural noun referring to human beings, as here, the plural form may also occur: *l-wuzaraaʔ ʔanfushum* 'the ministers themselves'.

hiiči šii muhimm	'such an important thing'
hiiči byuut	'such houses'
hiiči naas	'such people'
hiiči ġaali	'so expensive, this expensive'
hiiči muhimm	'so important, that important'

13.3.14 Particle *hwaaya*

(1) 'much, many, a lot of'
(2) 'very'

This particle may modify a noun or a comparative. It may also modify a (non-comparative) adjective, with the translation 'very', but is not as common in that function as is *kulliš*. It may itself be modified by *kulliš*. It may either precede or follow the word it modifies.

hwaaya fluus *fluus ihwaaya*	'a lot of money'
(ma-. . .) hwaaya fariq	'(not . . .) much difference'
hwaaya naas	'a lot of people'
hwaaya ašyaaʔ	'a lot of things'
kulliš ihwaaya muwaḍḍafiin	'a great many employees'
ʔakil kulliš ihwaaya	'a great deal of food'
hwaaya ʔaḥsan	'much better'
hwaaya ʔaḷṭaf	'much more pleasant'
hwaaya waṣix	'very dirty'
mamnuun ihwaaya	'very grateful'
mašġuuḷ kulliš ihwaaya	'very, very busy; extremely busy'

13.3.15 Particle *yaa*

(1) 'any'
(2) 'which?, what?'
(3) vocative

In the first two meanings above, this particle may be used instead of *ʔay* (see 13.3.1); in the interrogative meaning it is much more common. As a vocative particle it may be followed by a proper name or a noun, and is used in calling to or addressing someone. The common English equivalent of *yaa* in such phrases may be an attention-getting interjection such as oh or hey, or there may be no English equivalent at all.

yaa ktaab	'any book'
yaa madrasa	'any school'
yaa beet?	'which house?'
yaa ġurfa?	'which room?'
yaa jaraayid?	'what newspapers?'
yaa waaʒid?	'which one?'
yaa ɛali	'oh, Ali!; hey, Ali!'
(taɛaalu) yaa šabaab.	'(Come on,) boys.'

13.3.16 Particle *čam* (1) 'several, a few' (2) 'how many?'

This particle may modify a noun or the pronoun *waaʒid* 'one'; the noun is always singular. In the first meaning above, it may be preceded by *fadd* (13.3.8). In its interrogative meaning, *čam* refers to numbers of individual units, not to quantity as in the case of *šgadd* (13.3.6).

čam yoom	'several days'
čam daqiiqa	'a few minutes'
fadd čam diinaar	'a few dinars'
čam waaʒid	'several, a few'
čam meez?	'how many tables?'
čam saaɛa?	'how many hours?'
čam waaʒid?	'how many?'

13.4 COMPARATIVES AS MODIFIERS

A comparative (7.1.4) may modify a noun, certain pronouns, or, in a few cases, an adjective.

13.4.1 Modifying a noun

A comparative modifying a noun may follow or precede it, and English equivalents differ accordingly. Phrases in which a comparative modifies a pronoun are similar in structure.

A. Following the noun. In a phrase consisting of a noun followed by a comparative, the comparative is like the adjective in a noun-adjective phrase (13.6) in that it lacks the article prefix if the noun is indefinite and bears it if the noun is definite. (Unlike such an adjective, however, a comparative is invariable as to gender and number.) If the noun is indefinite, which is the more common case, the comparative corresponds to an English comparative form such as bigger or comparative phrase such as more important.

beet ʔakbar	'a bigger house'
waaẓid ʔakbar	'a bigger one, someone bigger'
byuut ʔakbar	'bigger houses'
ġurfa ʔakbar	'a bigger room'
ġuraf ʔakbar	'bigger rooms'
laẓam ʔaẓsan	'better meat'
ʔuuteel ʔarxaṣ	'a cheaper hotel'
šii ʔarxaṣ	'a cheaper thing, something cheaper'
ʔakil ʔaṭyab	'tastier food'
mudda ʔaṭwal	'a longer period'
qaṣ̌iyya ʔahamm	'a more important matter'
niswaan ʔajmal	'more beautiful women'

The comparative in such phrases may itself be modified by a phrase beginning with *min* 'than':

beet ʔakbar min haaδa	'a bigger house than this, a house bigger than this'
mudda ʔaṭwəl min šahreen	'a period longer than two months'

In certain restricted contexts a definite noun may be followed by a comparative, which then bears the article prefix. In such a phrase, the comparative corresponds to an English superlative such as (the) biggest or (the) most important,[1] for example *l-beet il-ʔəkbar* 'the biggest house', but the same meaning is more commonly expressed by a phrase like those described in B below.

B. Preceding the noun. In a phrase in which the comparative precedes the noun, the comparative never has the article prefix, and in this respect is like the first term in most annexions (13.7). If the noun is indefinite, the comparative corresponds to an English superlative form or phrase such as (the) biggest or (the) most important.[1] (It should be noted that, despite the definiteness of the English translation, the noun in the Iraqi phrase is grammatically indefinite: if it is further modified by an adjective, for example, the latter has no article prefix.)

ʔakbar beet	'the biggest house'
ʔakbar waaẓid	'the biggest one'

---

[1] Or, in the case of two entities, to (the) bigger, (the) more important. There is no distinction in Iraqi between the bigger (of two) and the biggest (of more than two).

ʔakbar ġurfa	'the biggest room'
ʔahamm šii	'the most important thing'
ʔaṣʕab imtiḥaanaat	'the most difficult examinations'

If the noun is definite, the comparative may refer either to one or to more than one entity, and the English translation may differ accordingly:

ʔaḥla l-banaat	'the prettiest (one) of the girls' 'the prettiest (several) of the girls' 'the prettiest girls'

13.4.2 Modifying an adjective

The two comparatives *ʔakθar* and *ʔazyad* (or *ʔázeed*), both meaning 'more', may modify certain adjectives which do not themselves have comparative forms. The comparative follows the adjective. A phrase consisting of one of these adjectives and *ʔakθar* or *ʔazyad* is equivalent in meaning to the simple comparative form of other adjectives.

mdallal ʔakθar	'more pampered'
mistaʕjil ʔazyad	'more urgent, more in a hurry'

An adjective thus modified may occur following and modifying a noun, and agreeing with it in gender and number.

bnayya mdallila ʔakθar	'a more pampered girl'

13.5 ORDINALS AS MODIFIERS

An ordinal (8.2) may modify a noun or the pronoun *waaḥid* 'one'. The ordinal may follow or precede.

A. Following the noun. When the ordinal follows the noun (or pronoun), it agrees in gender and definiteness, as in any noun-adjective phrase (13.6). If the noun is indefinite, the equivalent English phrase generally begins with the indefinite article a/an. Such constructions are not as common in Iraqi as in English except in the case of *θaani* 'second', which is frequently used in the meaning 'another'.

paaṣ θaani	'a second bus, another bus'
waaḥid θaani	'a second one, another one'
marra θaanya	'a second time, another time'
šaxiṣ θaaliθ	'a third person'

If the noun is definite, the equivalent English phrase generally begins with the or an appropriate possessive form.

l-yoom il-ʔawwal	'the first day'
s-sana l-ʔuula	'the first year'
ṣ-ṣaẓiifa θ-θaalθa	'the third page'
l-qaaṭ ir-raabiƐ	'the fourth floor'
ẓaflat iz-zawaaj iθ-θaalθa	'the third wedding-party'
ʔibinhum iθ-θaani	'their second son'
marta r-raabƐa	'his fourth wife'

In the case of a few specific nouns, most of them referring to time, the phrase may have a structure in some respects like that of an annexion (13.7): the noun has no article prefix, and it occurs in its annexing form if it has one. The ordinal follows the noun, agrees with it in gender, and has the article prefix. The English equivalent begins with the.

yoom il-ʔawwal	'the first day'
sant il-ʔuula	'the first year'
marrt iθ-θaanya	'the second time, the next time'
šahr iθ-θaaliθ	'the third month'

B. Preceding the noun. When the ordinal precedes the noun (or pronoun), the ordinal never has the article prefix, and in this respect is like the first term in most annexions (13.7). The ordinal occurs in its masculine form regardless of the gender of the noun. The noun is indefinite,[1] bearing neither the article prefix nor a pronoun suffix; the phrase is nevertheless equivalent in meaning to an English phrase beginning with the. (Note the similarity of structure and meaning to the comparative phrases described in 13.4.1 B.)

ʔawwal yoom	'the first day'
ʔawwal waaẓid	'the first one'
ʔawwal sana	'the first year'
θaani beet	'the second house, the next house'
θaani marra	'the second time, the next time'

[1] In a few expressions with specialized meaning, *ʔawwal* 'first' and *ʔaaxir* 'last' are followed by a definite noun: *ʔawwal is-sana* 'the first part of the year', *ʔaaxr iš-šahar* 'the end of the month, the last part of the month'.

θaaliθ šahar	'the third month'
θaaliθ ṣaẓiifa	'the third page'

The adjective *ʔaaxir* 'last' functions like an ordinal in phrases of this kind:

ʔaaxir yoom	'the last day'
ʔaaxir marra	'the last time'

13.6 ADJECTIVES AS MODIFIERS: NOUN-ADJECTIVE PHRASES

An adjective may modify a noun or a pronoun.[1] A noun-adjective phrase is a noun phrase consisting of a noun modified by one or more adjectives. The adjective follows the noun and agrees with it in definiteness, gender, and number, as described in 11.2.1.1 and 11.2.1.2. Phrases in which a pronoun is modified by an adjective are similar in structure. If the noun is indefinite, the adjective has no article prefix:

beet ɛatiig	'an old house'
waaẓid čibiir	'a big one, someone big'
šii muhimm	'an important thing, something important'
madrasa zeena	'a good school'
šuɛaraaʔ mašhuuriin	'famous poets'
kaatib ɛarabi mašhuur	'a famous Arab writer'

If the noun is definite, the adjective has the article prefix:

l-beet il-ɛatiig	'the old house'
l-madrasa z-zeena	'the good school'
š-šuɛaraaʔ il-mašhuuriin	'the famous poets'
l-kaatib il-ɛarabi l-mašhuur	'the famous Arab writer'
θoobi j-jidiid	'my new shirt'

The adjective follows the noun it modifies immediately, with one exception: if the noun is the first term of an annexion (13.7), the adjective follows the complete annexion. Since that is also the position for an adjective modifying the last term of an annexion, some ambiguity of reference may result unless the two nouns are of different gender-number categories, in which case the form of the adjective indicates which noun it modifies:

---

[1] Occasionally also another adjective, as in *ʔaxḍar faatiẓ* 'light green'.

ġurfat noom čibiira	'a big bedroom'
beet ʔuxti j-jidiid	'my sister's new house'
beet ir-raʔiis ij-jidiid	'the president's new house' 'the new president's house'

Such ambiguity may be avoided by the use of a *maal* phrase (13.8):

l-beet ij-jidiid maal ir-raʔiis	'the president's new house'

Certain nouns and adjectives, mostly referring to time or color, may occur together either in noun-adjective phrases like those just described, or in phrases which in some respects resemble annexions (13.7): the noun, which precedes, has no article prefix, and occurs in the annexing form if it has one. The adjective has the article prefix, and agrees with the noun in gender and number. (Note the similarity of structure between these phrases and those described at the end of 13.5 A.)

sbuuʕ il-maaḍi	'the past week, last week'
sant il-maaḍya	'the past year, last year'
šahr ij-jaay	'the coming month, next month'
sant ij-jaaya	'the coming year, next year'
ḥṣaan l-abyaḍ	'the white horse' (or 'white horses' in general)
ʕeen iz-zarga	'the blue eye(s)' (or 'blue eyes' in general)
bnayyt is-samra	'the brunette girl' (or 'brunette girls' in general)

The adjective *laax* (feminine *lux*) may also occur either in regular noun-adjective phrases or in annexion-like phrases of the type just illustrated. In the latter case, the meaning may be definite or indefinite:

šii l-laax	'the other thing' 'another thing, something else'
qaaṭ il-laax	'the other suit' 'another suit'
marrt il-lux	'the other time, the next time' 'another time'

13.7 ANNEXIONS

There are several different kinds of annexions, classified according to the number and type of their constituent elements. In its most typical form, an annexion is a noun phrase consisting of a noun modified by a following noun, for example *beet Ɛali* 'Ali's house'. Most annexions, like this one, are composed of two elements; these are called the first term and the last term respectively. Those composed of three or (less commonly) more elements are multiple annexions; in these, any element between the first and the last is a middle term. A middle term modifies the preceding term and is in turn modified by the following term, for example *beet ʔibin Ɛali* 'Ali's son's house'. For further comments on multiple annexions see 13.7.4.

When a feminine singular or a plural noun or adjective ending in *-a* occurs as the first term or a middle term in an annexion, it has (except as noted in 13.7.1.2) a special annexing form ending in *-t*, for example *sayyaara* 'car', *sayyaarat Ɛali* 'Ali's car'. (If, as in this example, the following word begins with a consonant, the ending is *-at*, and the annexing form is thus identical to the (pre-consonant) suffixing stem described for such words in 9.1.2.2 A (2). If the following word begins with a (helping) vowel, the annexing form may or may not be identical to the pre-vowel suffixing stem: the stem vowel *-a-* is generally dropped where possible (see 4.1.3.1 A), for example *sayyaart il-waziir* 'the minister's car'; but words of the types described in 9.1.2.2 A (2) (a), (b), and (c) may retain the pre-consonant form in *-at* instead of changing to *-iit* and *-uut* or undergoing shift.) When one of the two nouns *ʔab* 'father' and *ʔax* 'brother' occurs as the first term or a middle term in an annexion, it has an annexing form ending in *-u*, as in *ʔabu Ɛali* 'Ali's father' and *ʔaxu Ɛali* 'Ali's brother'.

Besides annexions in which the last term is a noun, there are also those in which the last term is a pronoun, and those in which the first term is an adjective.

13.7.1 Annexions in which the last term is a noun

The most common type of annexion is one in which both the first term and the last term are nouns, the first modified by the last. The last term may bear the article prefix or the demonstrative prefix, or it may be preceded by a demonstrative, a numeral, a modifying particle, or a comparative; no other kind of form normally occurs between any two successive terms of an annexion. (See 13.6 for the position of an adjective modifying the first term.) The first term does not bear the article prefix (with exceptions in certain cases noted below) or a pronoun suffix; the first term, or the annexion as a whole, is definite if the last term bears the article prefix, the demonstrative prefix, or a pronoun suffix, or if it is a proper noun; otherwise it is indefinite.

13.7.1.1 English equivalents

An annexion of this kind can express a number of different kinds of relationship between two nouns. It is, along with *maal* phrases (13.8) and possessive *l-* phrases (13.9), one of the chief mechanisms for expressing possession: the first term is possessed by the last. It also expresses relationships in which the first term is part of, full of, used for, or made of the last, and various others as well. In most cases the English equivalent of this kind of an annexion is one of the constructions shown in A, B, and C below; some other equivalents for special cases are shown in D, E, and F.

A. The English equivalent is a construction consisting of two nouns connected by a preposition, usually of but sometimes another such as in or on. The first noun corresponds to the first term of the annexion.

maaƐuun timman	'a plate of rice'
buṭul duwa	'a bottle of medicine'
masaafat miileen	'a distance of two miles'
wuṣḷat iqmaaš	'a piece of cloth'
wuṣḷat l-iqmaaš	'the piece of cloth'
ɀukuumt il-Ɛiraaq	'the government of Iraq'
raˀiis ij-jumhuuriyya	'the president of the republic'
muɀarrir ij-jariida	'the editor of the newspaper'
muˀallif hal-iktaab	'the author of this book'
čruux is-sayyaara	'the wheels of the car'
siƐr il-beet	'the price of the house'
siƐir beetna	'the price of our house'
loon il-qaaṭ	'the color of the suit'
loon Ɛeenha	'the color of her eye(s)'
ˀuuteelaat baġdaad	'the hotels of Baghdad'
ˀawraaq l-ašjaar	'the leaves on the trees'
jaam iš-šibbaač	'the glass in the window, the pane'
yaddat ij-jidir	'the handle on the pot, the pot-handle'
ˀakil tlat-tiyyaam	'food for three days'

B. The English equivalent is a construction consisting of a noun bearing the possessive suffix (<u>-'s</u> or <u>-s'</u>) followed by another noun. The second noun corresponds to the first term of the annexion.

Ɛuṭḷat šahar	'a month's vacation'
šuġuḷ santeen	'two years' work'
ɀallaaq niswaan	'a women's barber, hairdresser'
ˀibin xabbaaz	'a baker's son'
ˀibn il-xabbaaz	'the baker's son'
bint ij-jiiraan	'the neighbors' daughter'

ɛiyaadt iṭ-ṭabiib	'the doctor's office'
ġuraf iṭ-ṭullaab	'the students' rooms'
bint axuuya	'my brother's daughter' (i.e., my niece)
beet ɛammak	'your (paternal) uncle's house'
ʔuxut ɛali	'Ali's sister'
ṃarat jaasim	'Jaasim's wife'

C. The English equivalent is a construction consisting of two elements directly juxtaposed in a compound noun or in a phrase. The second element corresponds to the first term of the annexion. The first element of the English construction is normally in the singular form, whereas the corresponding (last) term in the annexion is often plural.

wujaɛ sinn	'a toothache'
maɛjuun asnaan	'toothpaste'
junṭat ʔiid	'a handbag, a purse'
ġurfat noom	'a bedroom'
baayiɛ biṭaaqaat	'a ticket-seller'
muẓarrir jariida	'a newspaper editor'
rṣaaṣat musaddas	'a revolver bullet'
makiinat ṭiyyaara	'an airplane engine'
makiint iṭ-ṭiyyaara	'the airplane engine'
dihn il-makaayin	'the machine oil'
ṭabiib l-iɛyuun	'the eye doctor'
jayš il-ɛadu	'the enemy army'

D. When the first term of the annexion is a verbal noun and the last term refers to the object of the action, the English equivalent may be one of the constructions noted above: *beeɛ il-beet* 'the sale of the house, the selling of the house'; *tanẓiif il-beet* 'house-cleaning, the cleaning of the house'. It may also be a construction consisting of an <u>-ing</u> form followed directly by the noun referring to the object: 'cleaning the house', for example:

taṣliiẓ is-saaɛa	'repairing the watch'
taɛyiin waziir	'appointing a minister'
ʔaxiδ ṣuwar / *ʔaxδ iṣ-ṣuwar*	'taking pictures'

E. A very common kind of annexion has as the first term one of the nouns *ʔabu* 'father', or *ʔumm* 'mother'. There are several possible English equivalents.

(1) When a noun referring to a person is the last term, the annexion has the expected meaning:

ʔabu ƹali	'Ali's father'
ʔumm jaasim	'Jaasim's mother'

Phrases like these are commonly used as forms of address: a man is addressed or referred to by a phrase consisting of *ʔabu* followed by the name of his eldest son (or, if he has only daughters, that of his eldest daughter); and similarly, with the substitution of *ʔumm,* for a woman. If the man is unmarried, or has no children, there are certain conventions according to which, for example, a man whose own name is *ƹali* is called *ʔabu ʒseen,* a man whose own name is *mʒammad* is called *ʔabu jaasim,* and so on.

(2) An *ʔabu* or *ʔumm* phrase may also refer to a person who sells a certain product, or is engaged in a certain trade, or owns a certain kind of property. For the plural, *ʔummahaat* 'mothers' is used if only females are involved, otherwise *ʔahal* 'people' or *ʔaṣʒaab* 'owners':

ʔabu jaraayid	'a newspaper vendor'
ʔabu beet	'head of a household'
ʔabu sayyaara	'a car-owner'
ʔabu j-jaraayid	'the newspaper vendor'
ʔabu t-tamur	'the date vendor'
ʔabu l-ibwaari	'the plumber' (*bwaari* 'pipes')
ʔumm il-ʒaliib	'the (female) milk vendor, the milk woman'
ʔumm il-xubuz	'the (female) bread vendor, the bread woman'
ʔahl ij-jaraayid	'the newspaper vendors'
ʔahl is-sayyaaraat	'the car-owners'
ʔaṣʒaab id-dukaakiin	'the shop-owners'
ʔummahaat il-xubuz	'the bread women'

(3) An *ʔabu* or *ʔumm* phrase may have the general meaning '(the) one with (a certain attribute or characteristic)':

ʔabu l-liʒya	'the one with the beard'
ʔumm in-nafnuuf il-axʃar	'the one in the green dress'

ʔahl ij-junaṭ	'the ones carrying the briefcases'
ʔummahaat il-ɛibi	'the ones in the abayas' (long black garments worn by women)

Such phrases may be used as noun modifiers, following the noun like the adjective in a noun-adjective phrase:

ṭaabiɛ ʔabu xamsiin filis	'a fifty-fils stamp'
ṭiyyaara ʔumm ʔarbaɛ-makaayin	' a four-motored plane'

(4) Some *ʔabu* phrases have specialized noun meanings:

ʔabu flees	'a miser'
ʔabu jinneeb	'a crab'
ʔabu breeṣ	'a lizard'

F. Finally, there are annexions in which the first term refers to a portion or a quantity, and the last term refers to the thing thus quantified. Fractions (8.3.1) and a small number of other nouns may function as the first term in such annexions; here also may be included those comparatives and particles which may be followed by a noun in annexion-like constructions (see 13.3 and 13.4.1 B). English equivalents are varied. Examples:

nuṣṣ saaɛa	'a half-hour, half an hour'
nuṣṣ il-leel(a)	'half the night'
(b-)nuṣṣ il-leel	'(in) the middle of the night'
rubuɛ diinaar	'a quarter-dinar, a fourth of a dinar'
šwayyat čaay	'a little tea'
ɛiddat marraat	'a number of times, several times'
baqiyyat il-luwaaɛiib	'the rest of the players'
ʔakθariyyat in-naas / *ʔakθar in-naas*	'the majority of the people, most of the people'
baɛḍ il-akil	'some of the food'
kull il-binaayaat	'all of the buildings'

Constructions of this sort differ syntactically in some ways from other annexions; for example, when the phrase is functioning as the subject of a verb, it is the last term, rather than the first, which generally determines the inflectional form of the verb:

nuṣṣ saaɛa ma-tkaffi.	'Half an hour is not enough.'
baqiyyat il-luwaaɛiib š-ysawwuun?	'What do the rest of the players do?'

13.7.1.2 Structure of annexions: special cases

There are certain categories of noun-plus-noun annexions to which previous remarks on the annexing form (13.7, second paragraph) and general structure (13.7.1) do not, or may not, apply.

A. Annexions in which the last term refers to the material or substance of which the preceding term is composed are in two respects like noun-adjective phrases rather than annexions:

(1) Except as noted in (2) below, the first term occurs in the independent, not the annexing, form:

badla ʒariir	'a silk suit' (woman's)
saaɛa δahab	'a gold watch'

(2) The first term may bear the article prefix, the demonstrative prefix, or a pronoun suffix; the last term then, like an adjective, agrees in definiteness by having the article prefix:

l-badla l-ʒariir	'the silk suit'
haš-šiiš il-ʒadiid	'this iron bar'
θoobi ṣ-ṣuuf	'my wool shirt'

Alternatively, however, the first term may lack the article prefix and occur in the annexing form if it has one, as in any annexion:

badlat il-ʒariir	'the silk suit'

The first term may be modified by an immediately following definite noun. It is then in annexion with that noun rather than with the last term, and occurs in the annexing form if it has one. The last term has the article prefix:

badlat naziiha l-ʒariir	'Naziiha's silk suit'

B. Annexions in which the first term refers to a container or a measure, and the last term to the substance measured or contained, may also differ in certain respects from other annexions.

(1) Except as noted in (2) below, the first term occurs in either the independent or the annexing form:

quuṭiyya(t) simač	'a can of fish'
ʒafna(t) timman	'a handful of rice'
kooma(t) traab	'a pile of dirt'

(2). In the definite forms of such annexions, the first term may bear the article prefix or the demonstrative prefix. If it does, it occurs in either the independent or the annexing form; if it does not, it occurs in the annexing form. The last term normally bears the article prefix in all cases:

l-quuṭiyya(t) is-simač	'the can of fish'
hal-quuṭiyya(t) is-simač	'this can of fish'
quuṭiyyat is-simač	'the can of fish'

Some annexions of this sort are occasionally treated as single units, the article prefix being attached to the first term only:

l-finjaan gahwa	'the cup of coffee'

13.7.2 Annexions in which the last term is a pronoun

Some annexions consist of a noun modified by a following pronoun, generally one of the demonstratives or *waaḥid* 'one, someone'.

kalaam haaδa	'that man's words, his words'
sayyarat waaḥid (zangiin)	'the car of someone (rich), a (rich) person's car'
ʕeen il-waaḥid	'one's eye(s), a person's eye(s)'
wulid δoola	'those people's boys, their boys'

13.7.3 Annexions in which the first term is an adjective

There is a type of annexion which consists of an adjective modified by a following noun. If the adjective is a feminine or plural ending in *-a*, it occurs in the annexing form. The following noun always has the article prefix. In this kind of annexion, which is limited to a relatively few stereotyped combinations, the noun refers to that feature to which the quality expressed by the adjective applies. Typical English equivalents are illustrated by the examples which follow. Both masculine and feminine forms of the Iraqi adjectives are shown.

M	*baʕiid in-naδ̣ar*	'far-sighted'
F	*baʕiidt in-naδ̣ar*	(usually in abstract sense)
M	*xafiif id-damm*	'charming, pleasant'
F	*xafiift id-damm*	(literally 'light of blood')
M	*θigiil id-damm*	'dull, boring'
F	*θigiilt id-damm*	(literally 'heavy of blood')
M	*δ̣aʕiif il-bunya*	'having a delicate
F	*δ̣aʕiift il-bunya*	constitution'
M	*qaṣiir il-qaama*	'short of stature'
F	*qaṣiirt il-qaama*	

M	*ɛaḍiim il-ʔahammiyya*	'of great importance'
F	*ɛaḍiimt il-ʔahammiyya*	

An annexion of this type is an adjective phrase, and functions in a sentence like a single adjective. It may occur as a predicate:

hal-ibnayya kulliš xafiift id-damm.	'That girl is very charming.'

Or it may occur in attributive position following the noun it modifies. If that noun is definite, the adjective in the annexion has the article prefix:

bnayya xafiift id-damm	'a charming girl'
l-ibnayya l-xafiift id-damm	'the charming girl'

13.7.4 Multiple annexions

In annexions of more than two terms, any middle term modifies the preceding term and is in turn modified by the following term. With the exceptions noted in 13.7.1.2 above, each term except the last occurs in the annexing form if it has one, and only the last term may have the article prefix or a pronoun suffix. Three-term annexions are fairly common; four-term annexions occasionally occur; longer ones are rare. Some examples:

mart ibn axuuya	'my brother's son's wife' (i.e., my nephew's wife)
beet ibin xaaḷa	'his (maternal) uncle's son's house' (i.e., his cousin's house)
saayiq sayyaaraat sibaaq	'a driver of racing cars'
xayyaaṭ nafaaniif niswaan	'a tailor of women's dresses' (i.e., a (male) dressmaker)
mudiir maɛmal ṭaabuug	'a brick-factory director'
mulaaḥiḍ šuɛbat iḍ-ḍaatiyya	'the supervisor of the personnel section'
ṣaaḥib dukkaan doondirma	'an ice-cream shop proprietor'
ġurfat muɛallim il-kiimya	'the chemistry teacher's room'
saaɛat ʔiid il-ɛaruus	'the bride's wristwatch'
masʔalat dafiɛ ḍariibt id-daxal	'the matter of paying the income tax'

13.8 PHRASES CONTAINING *maal*

The particle *maal* 'of, belonging to' (see 9.1.2.2 B (9)) is extensively used in Iraqi phrase construction. There are two major types of *maal* phrases, one involving a form of the stem *maal–* with an attached pronoun suffix, and the other involving the independent form *maal*[1] followed by a noun or noun phrase.

13.8.1 Suffix *maal* phrases

A suffix *maal* phrase is a noun phrase consisting of a definite noun followed by one of the stems *maal–, maal(a)t–,* or *maalaat–* with an attached pronoun suffix (see 9.1.2.2 B (9) for forms), for example *r–raadyo maali* 'my radio'. The use of one or the other of these three stems depends upon the gender and number of the preceding noun: the first is used after a masculine singular noun, the second after a feminine singular noun, or a dual or plural noun not referring to human beings, and the third after a feminine dual or plural noun referring to human beings. In the case of a masculine dual or plural noun referring to human beings, the first stem is sometimes used, but generally the *maal* construction is avoided. The noun in such a phrase is most commonly definite by virtue of having the article prefix, but may also be definite by virtue of having the demonstrative prefix or of being the first term in a definite annexion.

In meaning, a suffix *maal* phrase is equivalent to that of a noun with an attached pronoun suffix, and both are commonly translated by an English phrase consisting of a noun preceded by one of the possessives my, your, his, and so on: *θ–θoob maali* or *θoobi* 'my shirt'. Both constructions are in common use, and with many nouns the two are interchangeable. With certain kinds of nouns however, notably those referring to close or permanent possessions or relationships, such as parts of the body, articles of clothing, or members of a family, the noun with pronoun suffix is more common. The suffix *maal* phrase, on the other hand, is more commonly used with—but is not restricted to—nouns borrowed from other languages, dual nouns, and nouns in an annexion. Examples:

t–talafoon maalak	'your M telephone'
t–taktiik maala	'his tactics'
l–ʒači maala	'his talk' (i.e., the things he says)
ṭ–ṭabiib maalkum	'your P doctor'
l–liʕba maalta	'his game'
l–xiṭṭa maalatha	'her plan'
l–ʒadiiqa maalatna	'our garden'
l–qaaṭeen maalti	'my two suits'
l–booyinbaaǵaat maalta	'his neckties'
ẓ–ẓaraayib maaltič	'your F taxes'
l–xaddaamteen maalaathum	'their two maids'
l–mumarriẓaat maalaata	'his nurses'

[1] The same form is also a noun (plural *ʔamwaal*) meaning 'property, possessions'

If the noun is further modified by an adjective, or a following noun in an annexion, or both, *maal-* follows these:

š-šiqqa j-jidiida maalta	'his new apartment'
makiint iz-ziyaan maalti	'my razor'
makiint iz-ziyaan il-kahrabaaʔiyya maalti	'my electric razor'

13.8.2 Independent *maal* phrases

An independent *maal* phrase is a noun phrase consisting of (1) a noun or noun phrase followed by (2) *maal* and another noun or noun phrase, for example *r-raadyo maal* *ɛali* 'Ali's radio' and *ṣaabuun maal ʒilaaqa* 'shaving-soap'. In such phrases, *maal* sometimes occurs in the form *maal(a)t* if the preceding noun is feminine, but more commonly remains invariable in all cases.

Independent *maal* phrases cover approximately the same range of meaning as do annexions (13.7), and have the same English equivalents. The two types of construction are in many cases interchangeable. The annexion, however, is more commonly used in expressing close or permanent possession, family relationships, or the association between measure and substance or container and contained; and it is exclusively used when the first term is a quantifier of the type illustrated in 13.7.1.1 F. The *maal* phrase, on the other hand, is commonly used in—but is not restricted to—situations where the first noun is one borrowed from another language, where the first noun is modified by an adjective, and where one or both nouns are already part of an annexion. Some examples:

l-ʒadiiqa maal il-beet	'the garden of the house'
l-mazriib maal beetna	'the gutter on our house'
l-ʒašwa maal sinni	'the filling in my tooth'
s-saguf maal il-ġurfa	'the ceiling of the room'
l-ʔiṭaar maal manaaḍri	'the frame of my glasses'
s-sayyaara maal il-mudiir	'the director's car'
t-talafoon maal jiiraanna	'our neighbors' telephone'
hduum maal riyaajiil	'men's clothes'
madrasa maal banaat	'a girls' school'
l-iʒsaab maal il-yoom	'today's account'
r-rasim maal il-walad	'the boy's photograph'
dihin maal šaɛar	'hair oil'
saaɛa maal ʒaayiṭ	'a wall clock'

čiswa maal sibiz	'a pair of swimming trunks'
l-muɛallim maal il-ɛarabi	'the Arabic teacher' (teacher of Arabic)
l-makiina maal is-sayyaara	'the car engine'
ktaab it-taariix maal ɛali	'Ali's history book'
l-pardaat maal ġurfat in-noom	'the curtains in the bedroom, the bedroom curtains'

13.9 POSSESSIVE PHRASES WITH PREPOSITION *l-*

There is, in addition to annexion and the *maal* phrase (13.7 and 13.8), a third method of expressing possession: a phrase consisting of (1) a noun with an attached pronoun suffix, followed by (2) a prepositional phrase consisting of the preposition prefix *l-* 'to' and its object, for example *ṣadiiqa l-ɛali* (literally 'his-friend to-Ali) 'Ali's friend'. The first noun in such a phrase refers to the possessed entity; the attached pronoun suffix and the noun following *l-* both refer to the possessor. The preposition prefix *l-* occurs in either its *l-* form or its doubled form, as appropriate (see 6.3.3 B). The noun following the preposition is always definite: it has the article prefix or a pronoun suffix, or it is a proper noun, or it is followed by a definite noun in an annexion. (Note the precise parallel between this kind of phrase and the post-stated object construction described in 11.4.) Some other examples:

ṣadiiqatha l-uxti	'my sister's friend'
xaaḷa s-saami	'Saami's (maternal) uncle'
ġurufta lil-mudiir	'the director's room'

A pronoun suffix may occur as the object of the preposition instead of a noun, in which case the preposition has its independent-stem form *ʔil-*. A phrase of this kind expresses greater emphasis on the identity of the possessor than those described above, and the English equivalent generally involves extra-loud stress on the possessive:

ṣadiiqi ʔili	'<u>my</u> friend' (not yours)

14. RELATIVE CLAUSES

Relative clauses fall into two major categories, adjectival and nominal. These are discussed below in 14.1 and 14.2 respectively.

Certain relative clauses are introduced by the relative particle, which may correspond to any of a number of English words or phrases, as illustrated below. This particle has two sets of forms: (1) the independent form *ʔilli,* which generally occurs at the beginning of a sentence or after a slight pause, with the variants *illi*, which occurs after a word ending in a consonant, and *lli,* which occurs after a word ending in a vowel; and (2) a set of prefix forms identical with those of the article prefix; that is, before certain consonants the prefix *l-,* and before other consonants a prefix consisting of the same consonant as the following one (see 6.3.1). The two sets are interchangeable in most contexts, the difference between them being primarily one of style: the independent forms occur more frequently in somewhat precise or formal speech; the prefix forms more frequently in fast or informal speech. The former are also perhaps more commonly found in nominal relative clauses; the latter in adjectival relative clauses.

14.1 ADJECTIVAL

An adjectival relative clause functions like an attributive adjective in a noun-adjective phrase (13.6), following and modifying a noun or a pronoun. The noun or pronoun modified by such a clause is the antecedent. The structure of the clause is determined by the antecedent in two respects, as shown in 14.1.1 and 14.1.2 below.

14.1.1 Indefinite and definite antecedents

In a noun-adjective phrase, when the noun is indefinite the adjective does not have the article prefix; when the noun is definite, it does (see 11.2.1.1); for example *beet ɛatiig* 'an old house', *l-beet il-ɛatiig* 'the old house'. In the case of an adjectival relative clause the structure is analogous: when the antecedent is indefinite the clause is not introduced by the relative particle; when the antecedent is definite, it is. In either case, the corresponding English clause may be introduced by who(m), which, or that.[1] (In the following examples, the antecedent in the Iraqi sentence and the corresponding word or phrase in the English translation are underlined.)

Indefinite antecedents

da-yriid ɛaamil yiqbal ib-ʔaqall min diinaar bil-yoom.	'He wants a worker who will accept less than a dinar a day.'
šuuf-li waaḥid yiṭbaɛ zeen.	'Find me someone who types well.'

[1] It should be noted, however, that the Iraqi relative particle *ʔilli* does not itself precisely correspond to these words. In an English relative clause, the relative pronoun participates in the grammatical structure of the clause, functioning for example as the subject of the clause or the object of a verb or preposition. In an Iraqi relative clause these functions are served by other forms (see 14.1.2), and the relative particle acts only as a connector between the antecedent and the clause.

tuεruf fadd waaḥid yinṭiini hal-maεluumaat? — 'Do you know someone who will give me this information?'

ma-aku qiṭaar yooṣal lil-baṣra gabḷ il-fajir? — 'Isn't there a train that gets to Basra before dawn?'

tzawwaj ibnayya tiḥči xamis-luġaat. — 'He married a girl who speaks five languages.'

ḥiča nukta ḍaḥḥkat il-kull. — 'He told a joke that made everyone laugh.'

ʔilgii-li sayyaara ma-tkallif ʔazyad min miit-diinaar. — 'Find me a car that doesn't cost more than a hundred dinars.'

da-ysawwi fadd šii ma-yraḍḍi ʔaḥḥad. — 'He's doing something that doesn't please anyone.'

kull waaḥid raaḥ itwannas. — 'Everyone who went had a good time.'

Definite antecedents

minu l-mara lli xaabrátak? — 'Who's the woman who phoned you?'

ween iṣ-ṣanduug illi čaan εal-meez? — 'Where's the box that was on the table?'

š-šaxṣ il-xaabar ma-gaal isma. — 'The person who phoned didn't say his name.'

ʔisʔal iš-šurṭi lli da-ynaḍḍum il-muruur. — 'Ask the policeman who is directing traffic.'

l-ibnayya d-da-tibči taayha. — 'The girl who is crying is lost.'

tuεruf kull ir-riyaajiil ič-čaanaw bil-ijtimaaε? — 'Do you know all the men who were at the meeting?'

l-iḥṣaan illi ġiḷab haš-šooṭ εawwar rijla. — 'The horse that won this race hurt his leg.'

ṭ-ṭiyyaara l-haajmat l-wlaaya wugεat. — 'The plane which attacked the city crashed.'

When the antecedent is definite and the relative clause is introduced by the relative particle, as in the last set of examples above, another kind of construction, resembling in some respects an annexion (13.7), may also occur: the antecedent noun lacks the article prefix, and occurs in the annexing form if it has one, for example *sant il-faatat* 'the year that has passed' (i.e., 'last year'). This kind of construction is never obligatory, but is fairly common in some cases. Examples (for underlined pronoun suffixes see 14.1.2 below):

ṭabxat iṭ-ṭubaxha falla. — 'The meal (that) he cooked is excellent.'

čilimt id-da-tguulha maalha maεna.	'The word (that) you're saying has no meaning.'
diinaar iṣ-ṣirafta εalee raaζ ζaraamaat.	'The dinar (that) I spent on him was wasted.'
noom in-nimta hal-isbuuε maal šahar.	'The sleep (that) I've had (slept) this week is enough for a month.'

14.1.2 Reference to antecedent

With the exception noted in 14.1.2.1 B (1) below, an adjectival relative clause contains a verb or pronoun form which refers to and agrees with the antecedent, and thus serves the function of tying the clause grammatically to that particular antecedent. This may be a verb form alone, an independent personal pronoun or a pronoun suffix, or a combination.

14.1.2.1 When antecedent and subject are the same

A. When the clause consists of a verbal sentence (11.1.2), and is the same as the subject of the verb (that is, when the antecedent and the subject both refer to the same entity), there are three possibilities:

(1) The referential function may be served solely by the inflectional form of the verb itself, which agrees with the antecedent in person, gender, and number. This is by far the most common case, and it is illustrated by all the examples in 14.1.1 above except the last four.

(2) Reference to the antecedent may be expressed both by a verb form, as above, and by a pronoun suffix attached to a particle (9.1.2.2 E) and agreeing with the antecedent in person, gender and number. (In the Iraqi examples given below and in the remainder of this chapter, the antecedent and the pronoun form referring to it in the relative clause are underlined. In the English translations the word or phrase corresponding to the antecedent is underlined; there is no word corresponding to the pronoun form.)

ma-aku hwaaya niswaan baεadhum ylibsuun puuši.	'There aren't many women who still wear a veil.'
minu l-walad il-hastawwa gaam yaakul?	'Who's the boy who just now began to eat?'

(3) Reference to the antecedent may be expressed by a verb form, as in (1) above, and by an independent pronoun functioning as the subject of the verb, and agreeing with the antecedent in person, gender, and number. This construction is rather rare, and the independent pronoun may always be omitted.

la-tisʔalni, ʔisʔal il-laaεuub illi huwwa ḍirabha hiiči.	'Don't ask me; ask the player who hit it (e.g., the ball) that way.'

B. When the clause consists of an equational sentence (11.1.1) or of a word or phrase of a type which may function as the predicate of an equational sentence, and the antecedent is the same as the subject of the equation, there are three possibilities:

(1) There is no pronoun reference to the antecedent. This kind of construction is not very common when the predicate is a noun; but it occurs freely when the predicate is an active particle functioning as a verb (12.1.3), in which case the active participle agrees in gender and number with the antecedent, and when the predicate is a particle or prepositional phrase.

ʔaεruf waaʒid mudiir ḅang w-agdar asʔal-ilk-iyyaa. — 'I know someone who is a bank director and I can ask him for you.'

tεarráfit εala walad laaεuub ib-firqat ij-jeeš. — 'I met a fellow who's a player on the army team.'

tuεruf aʒʒad šaayif hal-filim gabuḷ? — 'Do you know anyone who's already seen that film?'

ʔaku mwaδ̣δ̣afiin ma-maaxδiin ʔijaaza has-sana. — 'There are some employees who haven't taken leave this year.'

l-muʒaami lli kaatib hal-maqaal ma-yuεruf il-qaanuun. — 'The lawyer who wrote this article doesn't know the law.'

r-riyaajiil il-mitzawwjiin ʔajnabiyyaat ysiknuun b-fadd maʒalla. — 'The men who have married foreign women live in the same neighborhood.'

ʔisʔal ir-rijjaal illi bil-baab. — 'Ask the man (who is) at the door.'

s-sayyaara l-waraana da-titgarrab εaleena b-surεa. — 'The car (which is) behind us is coming up to us fast.'

minu saakin bil-beet l-igbaaḷ beetkum? — 'Who lives in the house (which is) across from yours?'

Note from the last three examples that in English a noun may be modified by an immediately following prepositional phrase, as in the man at the door, whereas in Iraqi, if the noun is definite, the corresponding phrase is preceded by the relative particle.

(2) Reference to the antecedent may be expressed by a pronoun suffix attached to a particle (9.1.2.2 E) and agreeing with the antecedent in person, gender, and number. (Compare A (2) above.)

la-tišlaε il-meewa lli baεadha ma-laaʒga. — 'Don't pick the fruit that's still not ripe.'

(3) Reference to the antecedent may be expressed by an independent pronoun functioning as the subject of the equational sentence, and agreeing with the antecedent in person, gender, and number. This construction is rather rare, and the independent pronoun may always be omitted. (Compare A (3) above.)

ʔiḥči wiyya l-muεallimiin illi huṃṃa b-madrastak.	'Talk to the teachers (who are) in your school.'
ʔibni lli huwwa bij-jeeš itraffaε.	'My son (who's) in the army (i.e., not the one in the air force) was promoted.'

14.1.2.2 When antecedent and subject are different

When the antecedent does not refer to the same entity as the subject of the relative clause, reference to the antecedent is expressed by a pronoun suffix attached to a verb, preposition, or noun within the clause, and agreeing with the antecedent in person, gender, and number. In certain less common cases (see C below) an independent pronoun may occur in addition to the pronoun suffix.

A. The pronoun suffix may be attached to a verb or preposition in the relative clause. The English equivalent is generally a clause containing whom, which, or that as the object of the corresponding verb or preposition; in English clauses of this type, however, the relative may be omitted.

d-diinaar l-iddaayanta minna ma-kaffa.	'The dinar (that) I borrowed from him wasn't enough.'
l-mara l-itzawwajha ʔajnabiyya.	'The woman (whom) he married is a foreigner.'
l-ifluus illi nṭeetni-yyaaha maalta.	'The money (which) you gave me is his.'
ʔaku ʔaḥḥad minhum tuεurfa?	'Is there someone among them (that) you know?'
ma-aku šii yguula ma-nṣaddig bii.	'There isn't anything (that) he says (that) we don't believe.'
š-šaxiṣ illi ḥčeet εalee simaεak.	'The person (that) you talked about heard you.'
minu l-wulid id-da-tilεab wiyyaahum?	'Who are the boys (that) you are playing with?'
da-adawwur-li beet bii xamis-ġuraf.	'I'm looking for a house with five rooms.' (literally: '...in which there are...')
yaahu d-dawla lli biiha xams-anhaar?	'Which is the country that has five rivers?' (literally: '...in which there are...')
n-naas il-εidhum akθar min sitt-ijhaal maεfiyyiin imni ð̣-ð̣araayib.	'People who have more than six children are exempt from taxes.'

B. The pronoun suffix may be attached to a noun in the relative clause. In such a case the English equivalent is sometimes a clause containing whose or of which, sometimes another construction as illustrated below.

εindi ṣadiiq ʔaxuu ytarjim kutub ajnabiyya.	'I have a friend whose brother translates foreign books.'
tzawwaj ibnayya ʔabuuha yištuġuḷ ib-daaʔirt il-bariid.	'He married a girl whose father works in the post-office.'
tzawwaj ibnayya ʔabuuha zangiin.	'He married a girl whose father is rich.'
tzawwaj ibnayya εyuunha zurug.	'He married a girl whose eyes are blue.' 'He married a girl who has blue eyes.' 'He married a girl with blue eyes.'
šuuf-lak fadd maṭεam ʔakla naḍiif.	'Look for a restaurant that has clean food.'
štireena haayša ʒaliibha dihiin.	'We bought a cow that has rich milk.'
ʔajjárit beet ʒammaama ġarbi.	'I rented a house with a western-style bathroom.'
ṭaabiεa ʒruufha naaεma ma-tfiidna.	'A typewriter with small characters is of no use to us.'
kull in-niswaan lli wulidhum wiyyaahum ma-xaššaw lis-siinama.	'All the women whose children were with them didn't get into the movie.'
minu r-rijjaal illi ʔiida maksuura?	'Who's the man whose arm is broken?' 'Who's the man with the broken arm?'
l-qappuuṭ id-dugumta magṭuuεa εind il-xayyaaṭ.	'The overcoat with the button off is at the tailor's.'
l-meez illi ṣubġa raayiʒ maalak.	'The table with the paint gone is yours.'

Within the relative clause, the predicate sometimes precedes the subject:

ʔuxuḏ l-iktaab ij-jilda mašguug. *ʔuxuḏ l-iktaab il-mašguug jilda.*	'Take the book with the torn binding.'

C. In addition to a pronoun suffix, the corresponding independent pronoun may also occur, usually immediately after *ʔilli*. This is a less common construction than the two preceding ones. The independent pronoun may be omitted.

haay il-mazraεa lli hiyya εaleeha l-εarka.	'This is the farm that the dispute is about.'

14.2 NOMINAL CLAUSES INTRODUCED BY *ʔilli*

A nominal clause is one which in a sentence has the function of a noun; for example, it may serve as the subject of the sentence or as the object of a verb or preposition. This section deals with nominal clauses introduced by the relative particle *ʔilli,* which may occur in either its independent or its prefix form (see first paragraph of this chapter). In internal structure, a clause of this type is similar to a construction consisting of a (definite) noun modified by an adjectival relative clause, with *ʔilli* functioning simultaneously as (1) a pronoun, which is the antecedent of the relative clause, and (2) the relative particle which introduces the clause; and the remarks made in 14.1.2 concerning reference to the antecedent also apply here. However, there are two ways in which the verb or pronoun form expressing that reference may agree with the antecedent *ʔilli*. First, *ʔilli* may have an indefinite meaning, not referring to any specific noun, and generally corresponding to such English phrases as he who, whoever, anyone who, what (that which), whatever, and anything that. In this case the verb or pronoun is third-person masculine singular, for example:

ʔilli gal-lak hiiči čaδδaab.	'Whoever told you so is a liar.'
ʔilli faat faat.	'That which has passed has passed.' (i.e., 'What's done is done.')
la-tiḥči wiyya l-ma-tɛurfa.	'Don't talk with anyone (whom) you don't know.'

Second, *ʔilli* may refer to some specific noun or pronoun which someone has previously mentioned or which the speaker has in mind; in this case the verb or pronoun agrees in person, gender, and number with the noun or pronoun which *ʔilli* represents. The English equivalent may then be a phrase such as the one(s) who, those who, or the one(s) which, for example:

saami w-ɛali lli xaabrook.	'Saami and Ali are the ones who phoned you.'
ʔinti lli ḥčeeti ɛalayya.	'You F are the one who talked against me.'
l-ma-yirḥuun biṭ-ṭiyyaara yirḥuun bil-qiṭaar.	'Those who don't go by plane will go by train.'
δibb illi ma-triidhum.	'Throw away those that you don't want.'

In some cases *ʔilli* might have either kind of meaning, depending on the context.

As in adjectival relative clauses, the reference to the antecedent may be expressed by a verb form, a pronoun suffix, or an independent pronoun, and in certain cases may not be expressed at all. Additional examples:

ʔilli yḥibb ma-yfakkir.	'He who loves doesn't think.'
minu lli siʔálak?	'Who's the one who asked you?'

hiyya lli ddaaynat ifluus minni.	'She's the one who borrowed money from me.'
stangi lli yεijbak.	'Pick out the one that pleases you.'
baεd illi ṣaar ma-agdar ašuufa.	'After what happened I can't face him.'
ʔaani ma-atεaamal wiyya lli yġušš aṣdiqaaʔa.	'I don't deal with someone who cheats his friends.'
ʔilli yguula yijri.	'What he says goes.'
mn-illi tguula ʔastantij inta ma-tzibba.	'From what you say I gather you don't like him.'
xallii yamm illi ma-bii qapaġ.	'Put it next to the one with no top.'
l-ma-εinda tikit ma-yirkab.	'Whoever doesn't have a ticket doesn't ride.'
nṭiini lli ʔarxaṣ.	'Give me the one that's cheapest.'
nṭiini lli b-jeebak.	'Give me the one that (or what) is in your pocket.'
ʔuxuδ illi mawjuud.	'Take what's available.'
haaδa lli zaεlaan. *haaδa lli huwwa zaεlaan.*	'He's the one who's angry.'
εabaali haaδa lli ridta minni. *εabaali haaδa lli huwwa ridta minni.*	'I thought this was what you wanted from me.'
haaδa lli εeena εal-beet. *haaδa lli huwwa εeena εal-beet.*	'He's the one whose eye is (who has his eye) on the house.'

15. CONDITIONAL SENTENCES

A conditional sentence in Iraqi typically consists of two major elements, an if-clause and a result clause, occurring in either order. The if-clause is introduced by one of the particles *loo* or *ʔiδaa,* both corresponding to English if. This chapter describes the use of these particles and the structure of the conditional sentences in which they occur.

15.1 IF-CLAUSE INTRODUCED BY *loo*

In unreal conditions (15.1.1), and sometimes in conditions referring to a future possibility (15.1.2), the if-clause is introduced by *loo*. In some instances (15.1.3), *loo* in these clauses may be translated by English forms other than if.

15.1.1 Unreal conditions

An unreal condition is one which expresses an assumption contrary to the actual facts of the matter, for example if I had seen him (but I didn't) or if they were here (but they're not). The Iraqi particle corresponding to if in clauses of this type is *loo*.

In English unreal conditions, the form of the verb or verb phrase in the if-clause generally indicates whether the reference is to past time (first example above) or present time (second example). In Iraqi the situation is somewhat different. An active participle form in the if-clause usually refers to past time (15.1.1.1). A form other than an active participle, however, does not necessarily express any time distinction; thus the same if-clause may refer to the past in one context and to the present in another, with correspondingly different English translations (15.1.1.2).

15.1.1.1 Past unreal conditions

An if-clause introduced by *loo* and containing an active participle usually refers to past time, for example *loo šaayfa* 'if I had seen him'.[1] The active participle may be preceded (not necessarily immediately) by the auxiliary verb *čaan* 'to be', either in the invariable form *čaan* or in a perfect-tense form agreeing with the subject of the clause, but commonly occurs without it. The result clause usually contains the invariable form *čaan* followed by a perfect-tense verb, for example *čaan gitt-la;*[2] but may also contain the invariable form *čaan* followed by an imperfect-tense verb, for example *čaan agul-la,* or a perfect-tense form of *čaan* agreeing with the subject of the clause and followed by an imperfect-tense verb, for example *čint agul-la.* These various forms all correspond (in the context of an if-clause containing an active participle) to an English result clause containing would have with a past participle: 'I would have told him'. If a negative prefix occurs, it may be attached to the main verb or the auxiliary. Examples:

loo šaayfa čaan inṭeeta l-ifluus.	'If I had seen him I would have given him the money.'

[1] Or any masculine singular subject: 'if you M had seen him', 'if he had seen him'.

[2] A clause of this type may occur as a complete utterance: *čaan gitt-la* 'you might have told him' (i.e., why didn't you?).

loo ʒaaṭṭa kifaaya dihin bij-jidir ma-čaan iʒtirag it-timman.	'If you F had put enough oil in the pot, the rice wouldn't have burned.'
čaan ʔijaw naas ʔdzeed loo msawwiin l-istiƐraaδ bil-leel.	'More people would have come if they had held the parade at night.'
loo mʒaδδirni ma-čaan hiiči šii ṣaar.	'If you had warned me, such a thing wouldn't have happened.'
loo ma-mnabbihni bil-wakit čaan iṣdamta lil-Ɛamuud.	'If you hadn't alerted me in time, I would have hit the pole.'
loo raayʒiin wiyyaahum čaan itwannasna hwaaya.	'If we had gone with them we would have enjoyed ourselves a lot.'
loo gaaylii-li raʒ-tijuun čaan ʒaδδart-ilkum mukaanaat tibqquun biiha.	'If you P had told me you were coming I'd have got you some places to stay.'
loo gaayil-li š-raʒ-ysawwi čaan ma-xalleeta.	'If he had told me what he was going to do, I wouldn't have let him.'

An active participle form of *čaan* 'to be', rare in other contexts, sometimes occurs in if-clauses of this type:

loo abuuha čaayin ihnaaka, ma-čaan gaalat hiiči šii.	'If her father had been there, she wouldn't have said such a thing.'

15.1.1.2 General unreal conditions

An if-clause introduced by *loo* and containing forms other than an active participle expresses an unreal condition but does not necessarily indicate a distinction of time. (It may also express another kind of condition; see 15.1.2.) For example, *loo ʔadri* might correspond to either 'if I had known' (in the past) or 'if I knew' (now). Although if-clauses containing some form of *čaan* (see next paragraph) more commonly refer to past time and those without more commonly refer to the present, they do not invariably do so. It is the total context of the sentence, rather than the forms it contains, which provides the clue to time reference in conditions of this kind.

The if-clause of a general unreal condition may contain various kinds of forms, most commonly one of the following: (1) an imperfect-tense verb, sometimes preceded (not necessarily immediately) by a perfect-tense form of the auxiliary *čaan* (2) the particle *ʔaku* 'there is/are', sometimes preceded by the invariable form *čaan*; (3) an equational sentence, or a form which can function as the predicate of an equational sentence, sometimes preceded by the invariable form *čaan*; (4) a perfect-tense form of *čaan* as the main verb of the clause. The result clause may have the same structure as that illustrated in 15.1.1.1; in any case it generally, though not invariably, contains some form of the auxiliary *čaan*. It may correspond to an English result clause containing either would have with a past participle or would with an infinitive. Examples:

loo ˀadri ɛidkum hiiči ˀaxbaar čaan jeet min wakit.	'If I had known you had such news I would have come early.'
ˀaani loo ˀadri l-mawḏuuɛ halgadd muhimm čaan axáδit raˀyak gabuḷ-ma asawwi šii.	'If I had known the matter was so important I would have asked your opinion before doing anything.'
loo ˀadri leeš da-yriid l-ifluus čaan inṭeeth-iyyaa.	'If I knew why he wants the money, I'd give it to him.'
loo yuɛruf ingiliizi čaan ɛayynoo.	'If he knew English they would appoint him.'
loo ˀaku hiiči šii čaan ismaɛnaa bir-raadyo.	'If there were anything like that we would hear it (would have heard it) on the radio.'
loo ˀaku ɛindi wakit čaan ˀaani darrastak.	'If I had time I'd teach you.'
loo ˀaani l-mudiir čaan aṭarrda.	'If I were the boss I would fire him.'
loo ġeer waaẓid, čaan tirak iš-šuġuḷ baɛad-ma ṣaarat haay.	'If it had been anybody else he'd have quit the job after that happened.'
ˀaani loo b-mukaanak ma-asawwiiha.	'If I were in your place I wouldn't do it.'
loo kull in-naas haš-šikil maẓẓad čaan gidar yištuġuḷ.	'If everybody were that way no one could work.'
loo čaan ɛindi šamsiyya čaan iṭḷdɛit.	'If I had had an umbrella I would have gone out.'
loo čaan b-iidi fluus čaan ištireet is-sayyaara.	'If there had been money in my hand (i.e., available to me), I would have bought the car.'
loo ˀabuuya hnaa čaan gitt-la.	'If my father were here I'd tell him.'
loo činit mawjuud čaan siˀalta b-nafsi.	'If I had been there I would have asked him myself.'

15.1.2 Conditions referring to the future

In certain conditions referring to a future possibility, not necessarily contrary to present facts, the if-clause may be introduced by *loo*. When the if-clause contains a verb, it is generally in the imperfect but may also be in the perfect; the structure of the result clause is varied. Examples:

loo bass ˀanjaẓ ib-hal-imtiẓaan kullši baɛdeen sahil.	'If I just pass this examination everything will be easy afterward.'

loo ysidd ʒalga hwaaya ʔašraf-la.	'If he'd close his mouth (i.e., not talk so much), it would be better for him.'
loo tištiri beet tiqtiṣid.	'If you buy a house you'll save money.'
loo tiji saaƐa θmaanya lid-daaʔira ma-tilgi kull aʒʒad jaay.	'If you came to the office at eight o'clock you wouldn't find anyone there.'
loo tiktib-la maktuub čaan yjaawbak.	'If you wrote him a letter he would answer you.'
loo šifta ma-tƐurfa.	'If you saw him you wouldn't know him.'
loo tiji waʒdak ʔaʒsan.	'If you come alone it'll be better.'
yimkin ʔaʒsan loo niskun qariib min beet axuuya.	'Maybe it'll be better if we live near my brother's house.'
š-tugliin loo nibnii-nna beet?	'What do you say we build us a house?'

In many such cases *ʔiδaa* (15.2) and *loo* are interchangeable. Where there is a distinction, it is that the former is neutral, while the latter may imply 'if only' or 'I wish'. When that implication is present, the if-clause may occur as a complete utterance:

loo tʔajjliiha lii baačir.	'I wish you F would put it off until tomorrow.' 'How about putting it off until tomorrow?'

15.1.3 Special contexts

The following English equivalents of *loo* when it occurs in certain specific contexts may be noted: The phrase *Ɛabaalak loo* may be translated by as though, you'd think that, or the like. Here the pronoun suffix *-ak* is impersonal and does not vary with the sex or number of the person(s) addressed:

yiʒči Ɛabaalak loo huwwa čaan ihnaak min ṣaar il-ʒaadiθ.	'He talks as though he had been there when the accident happened.' 'The way he talks you'd think he had been there when the accident happened.'

The phrase *loo maa* followed by a noun or pronoun may be translated if it weren't for:

loo maa ʔinta čaan abuṣṭa.	'If it weren't for you I'd beat him up.'

The phrase *ɛatta loo* generally corresponds to <u>although</u> or <u>even though</u>:

laazim yiktib fadd maktuub il-marta yoomiyya ɛatta loo mašġuul kulliš ihwaaya. — 'He has to write a letter to his wife every day even though he's extremely busy.'

In statements of emphatic determination *loo* alone may correspond to <u>even if</u>:

loo yinṭuuni miit-diinaar ma-aqbal! — 'Even if they gave me a hundred dinars I wouldn't accept!'

A phrase consisting of *loo* followed by a conjunction ending in *-ma* (10.1.3.2 B) may be translated <u>no matter...</u>:

ma-yisman loo šgadd-ma yaakul. — 'He doesn't get fat no matter how much he eats.'

loo šgadd-ma yṣiir ɛinda fluus hamm yriid baɛad. — 'No matter how much money he gets he still wants more.'

loo š-ma timši ɛeel ma-tlaɛɛig bii. — 'No matter how fast you walk, you won't catch up with him.'

15.2 IF-CLAUSES INTRODUCED BY *ʔíδaa*

A <u>real condition</u> is one which expresses an assumption in accordance with actual facts or an assumption about a future possibility. Except in the cases noted in 15.1.2, when *loo* may also occur, the if-clause in conditions of this kind is introduced by *ʔíδaa*.

Various constructions occur in both the if-clause and the result clause of real conditions. In those which refer to a future possibility, a verb in the if-clause may be either perfect or imperfect, for example *ʔíδaa šifta* (or *tšuufa*) *gul-la yxaaburni.* 'If you see him, tell him to phone me.' Further examples:

ʔíδaa triid tiji ʔadabbur-lak fadd ʔaɛɛad ywaṣṣlak ib-sayyaarta. — 'If you want to come I'll get someone for you to take you in his car.'

ʔíδaa tištiri ɛašir-purtaqaalaat ib-nuṣṣ diinaar b-eeš tištiri xmuṣṭaɛaš purtaqaala? — 'If you buy ten oranges for half a dinar, what would you pay for fifteen oranges?'

haaδi kulliš xooš šaġla ʔíδaa waaɛid ɛinda fluus. — 'This is a very good deal if one has money.'

zeen laɛad ʔaani ʔagul-la ʔíδaa ma-ɛindak maaniɛ. — 'All right then, I'll tell him, if you have no objection.'

ʔíδaa da-yiɛči bit-talafoon la-tziɛja. — 'If he's talking on the phone don't disturb him.'

ʔuxuδ waaɛid ʔíδaa triid. — 'Take one if you want.'

xalli rruuz lis-siinama ʔíδaa aku filim zeen hal-leela.	'Let's go to the movies if there's a good film this evening.'
laʕad leeš ma-rizit ʔíδaa halgadd čaan zeen il-filim?	'Well, why didn't you go, if the film was so good?'
ʔíδaa had-daʕwa ʔaxδat xamis-tušhur daʕwatna šgadd raz-taaxuδ?	'If that case took five months, how long will our case take?'
ʔíδaa mariiδ leeš ma-truuz lil-beet?	'If you're sick why don't you go home?'
hassa ʔíδaa ktabit ʕalee tawṣiya zeena raz-itfiid ihwaaya.	'If you write a good (letter of) recommendation for him now, it will do a lot of good.'
haaδa xooš naadi. ʔaʕtiqid tirtaaz ʔíδaa štirákit bii.	'This is a good club. I think you'll be satisfied if you join it.'
ʔadizzak ween-ma triid ʔíδaa tzaṣṣil ʕala darajaat ʕaalya.	'I'll send you anywhere you want if you get high grades.'
ʔíδaa l-zaala haš-šikil laʕad ihwaaya raz-nigdar ništuġul.	'If the situation is like this, we'll be able to work a lot!' (i.e., we won't be able to work much at all)
ʔíδaa tumṭur ʔakiid yibrad ij-jaww.	'If it rains the weather will surely get cooler.'

The phrase *zatta ʔíδaa* corresponds to English <u>even if</u>; *ʔilla ʔíδaa* to <u>unless</u>:

ma-yiqbal ybiiʕa zatta ʔíδaa dfaʕit-la miit-diinaar.	'He wouldn't agree to sell it even if you paid him a hundred dinars.'
ʔaji azuurkum hal-leela ʔilla ʔíδaa muṭrat.	'I'll come to visit you P tonight unless it rains.'